THE ARDEN SHAKESPEARE

THIRD SERIES
General Editors: Richard Proudfoot, Ann Thompson,
David Scott Kastan and H.R. Woudhuysen

DOUBLE FALSEHOOD
OR
THE DISTRESSED LOVERS

THE ARDEN SHAKESPEARE

ALL'S WELL THAT ENDS WELL	edited by G.K. Hunter*
ANTONY AND CLEOPATRA	edited by John Wilders
AS YOU LIKE IT	edited by Juliet Dusinberre
THE COMEDY OF ERRORS	edited by R.A. Foakes*
CORIOLANUS	edited by Philip Brockbank*
CYMBELINE	edited by J.M. Nosworthy*
DOUBLE FALSEHOOD	edited by Brean Hammond
HAMLET	edited by Ann Thompson and Neil Taylor
JULIUS CAESAR	edited by David Daniell
KING HENRY IV Part 1	edited by David Scott Kastan
KING HENRY IV Part 2	edited by A.R. Humphreys*
KING HENRY V	edited by T.W. Craik
KING HENRY VI Part 1	edited by Edward Burns
KING HENRY VI Part 2	edited by Ronald Knowles
KING HENRY VI Part 3	edited by John D. Cox and Eric Rasmussen
KING HENRY VIII	edited by Gordon McMullan
KING JOHN	edited by E.A.J. Honigmann*
KING LEAR	edited by R.A. Foakes
KING RICHARD II	edited by Charles Forker
KING RICHARD III	edited by James R. Siemon
LOVE'S LABOUR'S LOST	edited by H.R. Woudhuysen
MACBETH	edited by Kenneth Muir*
MEASURE FOR MEASURE	edited by J.W. Lever*
THE MERCHANT OF VENICE	edited by John Russell Brown*
THE MERRY WIVES OF WINDSOR	edited by Giorgio Melchiori
A MIDSUMMER NIGHT'S DREAM	edited by Harold F. Brooks*
MUCH ADO ABOUT NOTHING	edited by Claire McEachern
OTHELLO	edited by E.A.J. Honigmann
PERICLES	edited by Suzanne Gossett
SHAKESPEARE'S POEMS	edited by Katherine Duncan-Jones and H.R. Woudhuysen
ROMEO AND JULIET	edited by Brian Gibbons*
SHAKESPEARE'S SONNETS	edited by Katherine Duncan-Jones
THE TAMING OF THE SHREW	edited by Barbara Hodgdon
THE TEMPEST	edited by Virginia Mason Vaughan and Alden T. Vaughan
TIMON OF ATHENS	edited by Anthony B. Dawson and Gretchen E. Minton
TITUS ANDRONICUS	edited by Jonathan Bate
TROILUS AND CRESSIDA	edited by David Bevington
TWELFTH NIGHT	edited by Keir Elam
THE TWO GENTLEMEN OF VERONA	edited by William C. Carroll
THE TWO NOBLE KINSMEN	edited by Lois Potter
THE WINTER'S TALE	edited by J.H.P. Pafford*

* Second series

THE ARDEN SHAKESPEARE

DOUBLE FALSEHOOD
OR
THE DISTRESSED LOVERS

Edited by
BREAN HAMMOND

Arden Shakespeare

1 3 5 7 9 10 8 6 4 2

This edition of *Double Falsehood* edited by Brean Hammond, first published 2010 by Methuen Drama

Editorial matter copyright © 2010 Brean Hammond

Arden Shakespeare is an imprint of Methuen Drama

Methuen Drama
A & C Black Publishers Ltd
36 Soho Square
London W1D 3QY
www.methuendrama.com
www.ardenshakespeare.com

A CIP catalogue record for this book is available from the British Library
Hardback ISBN: 978 1 9034 3676 9
Paperback ISBN: 978 1 9034 3677 6

The general editors of the Arden Shakespeare have been
W.J. Craig and R.H. Case (first series 1899-1944)
Una Ellis-Fermor, Harold F. Brooks, Harold Jenkins and
Brian Morris (second series 1946-82)

Present general editors (third series)
Richard Proudfoot, Ann Thompson, David Scott Kastan and H.R. Woudhuysen

Printed by Zrinski, Croatia

This book is produced using paper made from wood grown in managed, sustainable forests. It is natural, renewable and recyclable. The logging and manufacturing processes conform to the environmental regulations of the country of origin.

The Editor

Brean Hammond is Professor of Modern English Literature at the University of Nottingham. Most of his work relates to the eighteenth-century period. Amongst his recent publications are *Jonathan Swift* in the Irish Writers in Their Time series (2009) and (with Shaun Regan), *Making the Novel* (2006).

For Janette

CONTENTS

Contents

LIST OF
ILLUSTRATIONS

GENERAL EDITORS' PREFACE

The earliest volume in the first Arden series, Edward Dowden's *Hamlet*, was published in 1899. Since then the Arden Shakespeare has been widely acknowledged as the pre-eminent Shakespeare edition, valued by scholars, students, actors and 'the great variety of readers' alike for its clearly presented and reliable texts, its full annotation and its richly informative introductions.

In the third Arden series we seek to maintain these well-established qualities and general characteristics, preserving our predecessors' commitment to presenting the play as it has been shaped in history. Each volume necessarily has its own particular emphasis which reflects the unique possibilities and problems posed by the work in question, and the series as a whole seeks to maintain the highest standards of scholarship, combined with attractive and accessible presentation.

Newly edited from the original Quarto and Folio editions, texts are presented in fully modernized form, with a textual apparatus that records all substantial divergences from those early printings. The notes and introductions focus on the conditions and possibilities of meaning that editors, critics and performers (on stage and screen) have discovered in the play. While building upon the rich history of scholarly activity that has long shaped our understanding of Shakespeare's works, this third series of the Arden Shakespeare is enlivened by a new generation's encounter with Shakespeare.

THE TEXT

On each page of the play itself, readers will find a passage of text supported by commentary and textual notes. Act and scene divisions (seldom present in the early editions and often the product of eighteenth-century or later scholarship) have been retained for ease of reference, but have been given less prominence than in previous series.

In the text itself, unfamiliar typographic conventions have been avoided in order to minimize obstacles to the reader. Elided forms in the early texts are spelt out in full in verse lines wherever they indicate a usual late twentieth-century pronunciation that requires no special indication and wherever they occur in prose (except where they indicate non-standard pronunciation). In verse speeches, marks of elision are retained where they are necessary guides to the scansion and pronunciation of the line; wherever the required pronunciation diverges from modern usage a note in the commentary draws attention to the fact. Where the final -ed should be given syllabic value contrary to modern usage, e.g.

Doth Silvia know that I am banished?
(*TGV* 3.1.214)

the note will take the form

214 **banished** banishèd

Conventional lineation of divided verse lines shared by two or more speakers has been reconsidered and sometimes rearranged. Except for the familiar *Exit* and *Exeunt*, Latin forms in stage directions and speech prefixes have been translated into English and the original Latin forms recorded in the textual notes.

COMMENTARY AND TEXTUAL NOTES

Notes in the commentary, for which a major source will be the *Oxford English Dictionary*, offer glossarial and other explication of verbal difficulties; they may also include discussion of points of interpretation and, in relevant cases, substantial extracts from Shakespeare's source material. Editors will not usually offer glossarial notes for words adequately defined in the latest edition of *The Concise Oxford Dictionary* or *Merriam-Webster's Collegiate Dictionary*, but in cases of doubt they will include notes. Attention, however, will be drawn to places where more than one likely interpretation can be proposed and to significant verbal and syntactic complexity. Notes preceded by * discuss editorial emendations or variant readings from the early edition(s) on which the text is based.

Headnotes to acts or scenes discuss, where appropriate, questions of scene location, Shakespeare's handling of his source materials, and major difficulties of staging. The list of roles (so headed to emphasize the play's status as a text for performance) is also considered in the commentary notes. These may include comment on plausible patterns of casting with the resources of an Elizabethan or Jacobean acting company and also on any variation in the description of roles in their speech prefixes in the early editions.

The textual notes are designed to let readers know when the edited text diverges from the early edition(s) or manuscript sources on which it is based. Wherever this happens the note will record the rejected reading of the early edition(s), in original spelling, and the source of the reading adopted in this edition. Other forms from the early edition(s) recorded in these notes will include some spellings of particular interest or significance and original forms of translated stage directions. Where two or more early editions are involved, for instance with *Othello*, the notes also record all important differences between them. The textual notes take a form that has been in use since the nineteenth century. This comprises, first: line reference, reading adopted in the text and closing square bracket; then: abbreviated reference, in italic, to the earliest edition to adopt the accepted reading, italic semicolon and noteworthy alternative reading(s), each with abbreviated italic reference to its source.

Conventions used in these textual notes include the following. The solidus / is used, in notes quoting verse or discussing verse lining, to indicate line endings. Distinctive spellings of the basic text follow the square bracket without indication of source and are enclosed in italic brackets. Names enclosed in italic brackets indicate originators of conjectural emendations when these did not originate in an edition of the text, or when the named edition records a conjecture not accepted into its text. Stage directions (SDs) are referred to by the number of the line within or immediately after which they are placed. Line numbers with a decimal point relate to centred entry SDs not falling within a verse line and to SDs more than one line long, with the number after the point indicating the line within the SD: e.g. 78.4 refers to the fourth line of the SD following line 78. Lines of SDs at the start of a scene are numbered 0.1, 0.2, etc., with the exception of indications of location in the basic text, which are numbered 0 SD. Where only a line number precedes a square bracket, e.g. 128], the note relates to the whole line; where SD is added to the number, it relates to the whole of a SD within or immediately following the line. Speech prefixes (SPs) follow similar conventions, 203 SP] referring to the speaker's name for line 203. Where a SP reference takes the form e.g. 38+ SP, it relates to all subsequent speeches assigned to that speaker in the scene in question.

Where, as with *King Henry V*, one of the early editions is a so-called 'bad quarto' (that is, a text either heavily adapted, or reconstructed from memory, or both), the divergences from the present edition are too great to be recorded in full in the notes. In these cases, with the exception of *Hamlet*, which prints an edited text of the quarto of 1603, the editions will include a reduced photographic facsimile of the 'bad quarto' in an appendix.

INTRODUCTION

Both the introduction and the commentary are designed to present the plays as texts for performance, and make appropriate reference to stage, film and television versions, as well as introducing the reader to the range of critical approaches to the plays. They discuss the history of the reception of the texts within the theatre and scholarship and beyond, investigating the interdependency of the literary text and the surrounding 'cultural text' both at the time of the original production of Shakespeare's works and during their long and rich afterlife.

A NOTE ON THIS EDITION

The inclusion, for the first time, of Lewis Theobald's *Double Falsehood, or the Distressed Lovers* (1728) in the Arden Shakespeare (or indeed in any other edition of the plays and poems) reflects the unique interest of this avowedly thorough eighteenth-century adaptation as containing what may be the sole surviving textual evidence for a lost Shakespeare–Fletcher collaboration. The lost play was performed at court in 1613, when it was referred to as 'Cardenno' or 'Cardenna'. In 1653 the stationer Humphrey Moseley entered in the Stationers' Register: *'The History of Cardenio. By Mr Fletcher. & Shakespeare'*. This edition makes its own cautious case for Shakespeare's participation in the genesis of the play – a case that could be substantiated beyond all doubt only by the discovery of an authenticable manuscript or altogether disproved by other equally convincing forms of external evidence. This Arden edition offers readers, students and performers the first modernized annotated edition of the play, as well as a full account of its history and the controversy it has provoked.

ACKNOWLEDGEMENTS

My major debt is to Richard Proudfoot, Arden general editor, whose knowledge, thoroughness and eye for detail are astonishing and whose intellectual generosity is unstinting. To Henry Woudhuysen, similar honours should be extended. Margaret Bartley of A & C Black has been a very steady hand at the tiller, ably assisted by Charlotte Loveridge. Of my copy-editor, Hannah Hyam, I cannot speak sufficiently highly. On so many occasions when I felt that my brain was not configured for this task, Hannah reassured me that all would be well because hers is. Ann Thompson read early drafts of the introduction and to her I am also greatly indebted. I owe a debt of gratitude to Michael Dobson, who began this project in collaboration with me. His schedule and commitments made it impossible for him to continue beyond a certain point, but he got us started and was unqualified in his generosity thereafter. Anna Brewer and Matthew Lane have been diligent and effective picture researchers. Very many people have helped me along the way. They include: Jonathan Bate, Maureen Bell, David Carnegie, Gregory Doran, Stephen Greenblatt, Robert Hume, John W. Kennedy, Edmund King, Lori Leigh, Keith Maslen, Tom Mason, Judith Milhous, Neil Pattison, Bernard Richards, Fiona Ritchie, Shef Rogers, Valerie Rumbold, Peter Sabor, Alexander Samson, Sara Selim, Helene Solheim, Gary Taylor, Richard Wilson, Michael Wood and Georgianna Ziegler. My most intense debt is to Janette Dillon, not only because she is a Shakespearean scholar who often gave me direct assistance, but because she supplied the motivation to do this at all. The edition is dedicated to her.

INTRODUCTION

THE *DOUBLE FALSEHOOD* ENIGMA

The date 13 December 1727 saw the premiere of an intriguing play called *Double Falshood; Or, The Distrest Lovers*.[1] It was prepared and presented for production by Lewis Theobald, who had it published in January 1728 after a successful run in the Theatre Royal, Drury Lane, London. The title-page to the published version claims that the play was 'Written Originally by *W.SHAKESPEARE*'. *Double Falsehood*'s plot is a version of the story of Cardenio found in Miguel de Cervantes' *Don Quixote* (1605) as translated by Thomas Shelton, published in 1612 though in circulation earlier (see Fig. 1). Documentary records testify to the existence of a play, certainly performed in 1613, by William Shakespeare and John Fletcher, probably entitled *The History of Cardenio* and presumed to have been lost. What relationship, if any, exists between these two sets of independent historical facts? One answer, advocated by some, is 'none at all'. The view that Theobald's play is an out-and-out forgery, despite his claims to the contrary made in the Preface to the published version, has been espoused by some, both in his own time and in more recent times. Others, then and now, have considered that *something* of an earlier date lies behind *Double Falsehood* but that this is not simply a lost play by Shakespeare. It is a play by James Shirley, or by Philip Massinger, or by Fletcher. At very best, it is a collaborative play by Shakespeare and Fletcher. Whatever they consider it to be, all students of the play have recognized that

---

1 Henceforth this edition adopts the modern spelling of the title, *Double Falsehood*, except in quotations from texts which retain the eighteenth-century spelling.

1

1   Title-page of Thomas Shelton's *The History of the Valorous and Witty Knight Errant, Don Quixote of the Mancha. Translated out of the Spanish. The first part* (1612)

Theobald must himself be responsible for at least some aspects of the final product.

This introduction posits some relationship between the lost play performed in 1613 and the play printed in 1728. Later sections will discuss fully the issues raised by the *Double Falsehood* enigma; this opening section will summarize and clarify what is at stake with minimal detail.

Lewis Theobald was a lawyer by training who was making a difficult living in the 1720s as a professional writer for the theatre. He was a pioneer in the devising of pantomime – a lucrative entertainment very different from the form it now takes. He had a long-standing interest in Shakespeare, whose *Richard II* he had adapted for the stage and whose narrative poetry was influential on his (Theobald's) early original verse. After the appearance of Alexander Pope's Shakespeare edition in 1723–5, he turned his attention to editing Shakespeare. In *Shakespeare Restored* (1726), Theobald savaged Pope's work on the text of *Hamlet*. The following year, the *London Journal* (10 May 1727) gives the earliest notice in print that Theobald was working on an addition to the Shakespeare canon: 'through his [Theobald's] Hands [our readers] may expect to receive an undoubted original Play written by *Shakespeare*, some Time between his Retirement and Death'. In the Preface to the published version of *Double Falsehood*, Theobald claimed to possess no fewer than three manuscript copies, in differing states of legibility and preservation, of an original play by Shakespeare. One of those copies is quite specifically described as being in the handwriting of the prompter to Sir William Davenant's Duke's company in the 1660s, John Downes, who retired in 1706 and published his memoirs in 1708 – a date not wholly remote from that of Theobald's claims. There is little information about the other copies, and none about their provenance. Neither is there any clear evidence that anyone other than Theobald himself was ever shown them. Based on the Cardenio story as told in Cervantes' *Don Quixote*, the play had already run into opposition, as the Preface makes

3

clear, from those who thought, wrongly, that Shakespeare could not have known *Don Quixote*; and from those who claimed that the style owed more to Fletcher than to Shakespeare. Theobald deals with this scepticism in his preface, though in his extensive revision of it for a second issue of the play published a couple of months later, he is somewhat less assured in denying Fletcher's possible contribution.

Almost at once, the play was appropriated by the cultural politics of the period. Through its patriotic prologue and epilogue and the surrounding newspaper promotion, *Double Falsehood* laid claim to be reviving English theatre and by extension Englishness itself, rescuing it from the debasement to which bastardized continental art forms such as opera had subjected it, by bringing England's genius, the mighty Shakespeare, back to the stage in an as yet undiscovered form. In the process, Theobald was asserting his credentials to succeed Pope as the next editor of Shakespeare. What could achieve that end more successfully than the addition to the received canon of a lost play? Still smarting from *Shakespeare Restored*, Pope and those of an anti-government persuasion who supported him spared no opportunity to ridicule the play and Theobald's claims for its authorship. Pope went so far as to enthrone Theobald as King Dunce in the early versions of his mock-epic *The Dunciad* (1728–9). Lampooning *Double Falsehood* is a leitmotif of the poem. Such rhetoric as Theobald adopted in the prefatory matter to the play, emanating from a writer who had himself, in Pope's eyes, made a signal contribution to the effeminization and traduction of native English theatre through the confections of pantomime, was not to be borne. After its initial performance and publication, Theobald went relatively quiet about the play. He sold the rights to it to his publisher John Watts at a point when he could still get a decent price (he was probably considerably in need of money) and he did not include it in his 1733 edition of Shakespeare.

4

Scholars who examined the play in the half-century following Theobald's death were not much inclined to uphold its authenticity. Edmond Malone's annotations made on a copy of the second issue survive in the Bodleian Library (Malone, *DF*). They document his belief that Theobald was a fraudster trying to pass off a play by Massinger as Shakespeare's work, injecting additional Shakespeare into the text to render his forgery more plausible. A similar view is sustained by one modern student of the play, Harriet C. Frazier, who worked on the conundrum in the 1960s and 1970s, and was convinced by the forgery hypothesis because of what she saw as epidemic borrowing from *Hamlet*. Malone's opinion may have changed, however, at a later date, because it is he who is credited with discovering documentary evidence for the existence of a Shakespeare–Fletcher play called *The History of Cardenio*. As Malone first published this evidence in 1782 (Malone, '*Cardenio*'), it has naturally been assumed that Theobald, who died in 1744, must have been ignorant of it. Certainly, there is no reference to the seventeenth-century documents in anything Theobald wrote. Malone surely appreciated the implausible degree of coincidence required to sustain the hypothesis that Theobald forged a play having exactly the same plot-source as one that, unbeknown to him, actually had existed.

Relatively little notice was taken of *Double Falsehood* in the nineteenth century, one spectacular flop of a revival merely endorsing the play's absence of interest. Resurgence of scholarly attention can be dated to the early twentieth century, and in the course of the last hundred years some of the greatest Shakespearean scholars have contributed to a growing conviction that Theobald's adaptation is indeed what remains to us of an otherwise lost Shakespeare–Fletcher collaboration once called *Cardenio* or *The History of Cardenio*. John Freehafer's landmark *PMLA* essay of 1969 provided a highly speculative but inspiring account of how a Cardenio play might have been transmitted from Shakespeare's day down to Theobald's, starting from Theobald's preface and setting out to explicate its unclarities and vindicate its authenticity. Freehafer postulates that between the original and Theobald's version was an intermediate version prepared in the Restoration. With Theobald's own further alterations engrafted upon it, what we now have is a palimpsest or pentimento – at all events, nothing that is *straightforwardly* Shakespeare–Fletcher. Nevertheless, sophisticated recent analysis of authorship based on linguistic and stylistic analysis lends support to the view that Shakespeare's hand, and even more plainly Fletcher's, can be detected in the eighteenth-century redaction.

This edition complicates the story by suggesting that Theobald *could* have known, and probably *did* know, that there was a Cardenio play, and that in 1718 it may have been acquired by the publishing firm claiming to own the sole right to publishing the works of Shakespeare: that of Jacob Tonson. Though this inconveniently removes the main pillar from the anti-forgery hypothesis (the unlikely coincidence of Theobald faking a play on a theme that he did not know to have been used by Shakespeare and Fletcher), it also destroys the forgery hypothesis since it argues that in 1718 a Cardenio (or Cardeino/Cardenna/Cardenno) play was a still-surviving literary property. Previously published work of mine has established that manuscripts relating to *Cardenio/Double Falsehood* were said to be 'treasured up' in the Covent Garden Theatre Museum in 1770, and so probably perished in the fire which destroyed that theatre in 1808 (Hammond, 'Cheat'). There is no information, though, about exactly *what* was treasured up and subsequently perished in the conflagration. Neither is it clear why the working papers for a Drury Lane play should be in Covent Garden, though we may speculate that they were acquired for the 1767 Covent Garden revival and perhaps put on display.

Part of the argument surrounding the issue of possible forgery depends, of course, on internal rather than external evidence: in particular, on the status of allusions to other works by Shakespeare to be found in *Double Falsehood*. The commentary for this edition establishes that, *pace* Frazier, *Hamlet* is not nearly as significant an influence on the play as are Shakespeare's later plays, especially *All's Well That Ends Well*, *The Two Noble Kinsmen*, *Pericles* and *Cymbeline*. If Theobald was a forger, he knew which plays to concentrate on to make the forgery as plausible as possible. His view, that is, of the chronology of Shakespearean composition accords with that of modern scholarship. Long prior to Malone's groundbreaking work in establishing the order of Shakespeare's plays,[1] he knew which ones were the 'last plays'. It is more likely that he was *not* a forger.

Intriguingly, however, one of Shakespeare's earliest plays – *The Two Gentlemen of Verona* – is also very significant, as are the poems *Venus and Adonis* (1593) and *The Rape of Lucrece* (1594). Indebtedness to *Two Gentlemen* is particularly tantalizing in view of Theobald's expressed opinion of that play, in his 1733 edition:

> Mr. Pope has observ'd, that the Stile of this Comedy is less figurative, and more natural and unaffected, than the greater Part of our Author's Plays, tho' supposed to be one of the First he wrote. I must observe, too, that as I take it to be One of his very worst, it happens to be freest from accidental Corruptions of the Editors.
>
> *(Shakespeare*, 1.153)

The dating of *Two Gentlemen* is in itself an enigma. Clifford Leech, the editor of the second Arden edition, suggested that it was put together in phases, with Proteus's soliloquy in 2.6 being perhaps the final component (see Carroll, 126). This soliloquy is very close in dramatic content and function to that of Henriquez in 2.1 of *Double Falsehood*. No one suggests that Proteus's soliloquy could have been a very late addition to the play; no

---

1 On Malone's work (Malone, *Order*) see Peter Martin, *Edmond Malone, Shakespearean Scholar: A Literary Biography* (Cambridge, 1995), 31–5.

one dates the play after 1598, when a reference to it in Francis Meres' *Palladis Tamia* occurs. On the other hand, no record of performance exists for *Two Gentlemen*, and general similarities between it and *The Two Noble Kinsmen* are frequently observed. Is it possible that the two plays form some kind of a triptych with the lost *Cardenio*? Did Shakespeare, and/or Fletcher, have all three closely in mind in 1612–13? As for the poems, this ingredient in the mix is more likely to be a contribution made by Theobald. He had imitated *Venus and Adonis* in his poem *The Cave of Poverty* (1715). Given the theme of rape in *Double Falsehood*, *The Rape of Lucrece* would have been a natural poem for him to re-read. Moving further into the realm of speculation, the commentary to this edition suggests that some lexical items in *Double Falsehood* find parallels in Theobald's writings of around 1715, which is the point at which he was imitating *Venus and Adonis*. Might he have begun work on *Double Falsehood* then, possibly learning about *Cardenio*, even getting sight of it, from Tonson in 1718 when Tonson himself was thinking of acquiring the copy? It is time to stop, or I will be in the terrain of *The Shakespeare Secret* (2007), J.L. Carrell's murder-mystery thriller – of which more later (pp. 133–4).

Finding a manuscript of the lost *Cardenio* would be the only way of proving beyond all doubt that Theobald did not forge it. I cannot claim to have achieved that, but I hope that this edition reinforces the accumulating consensus that the lost play has a continuing presence in its eighteenth-century great-grandchild.

DOUBLE FALSEHOOD: PREMIERE AND PUBLICATION

The long-traditional view that Shakespeare's career as a playwright ended with *The Tempest* (1610–11) is no longer shared by most scholars working in the field. In 1612 and 1613, it is now generally agreed, Shakespeare collaborated on three plays with the writer who was by now replacing him as the

King's Men's leading dramatist, John Fletcher. One of these, *Henry VIII*, would be printed in the First Folio in 1623; another, *The Two Noble Kinsmen*, would appear in quarto in 1634. The third much less known play is listed as having been performed at court in 1613 in a document which refers to it as 'Cardenno' or 'Cardenna': two records of a play variously called *Cardenna* and *Cardenno* have come down to us from the King's Treasurer's accounts for 20 May and 8 June 1613, recording payments to the actor John Heminges (see Fig. 2).[1] From existing records we know that 'the prince', Lady Elizabeth and the Elector Palatine were in the audience for the earlier performance and that the later one took place at Greenwich in front of the Savoyard Ambassador, Giovanni Batista Gabaleoni.[2] There may be a very direct 'fossil' of the lost play to be found in two surviving song settings by the lutenist to the King's Men, Robert Johnson (who composed music for the two other Shakespeare–Fletcher collaborations referred to above) as Michael Wood has argued in an unpublished essay discussed more fully on p. 105 and in Appendix 5.

Not much doubt exists amongst modern scholars, then, that a play based on the Cardenio story in *Don Quixote* existed and was performed. Reference to this play resurfaces in 1653. On 9 September of that year, the bookseller Humphrey Moseley, publisher of the Beaumont and Fletcher Folio of 1647 and often considered to be the chief publisher of fine literature in his era, entered in the Stationers' Register an arresting item: 'The History of Cardenio. By Mr Fletcher. & Shakespeare' (see Greg, 1.61). Moseley's career as bookseller began in 1627 when he was made free of the Stationers' Company. He had his own shop, the Princes Arms in St Paul's Churchyard, by 1637. As the Stationers' Register for the 1640s and 1650s shows, he became a

---

1 They are in Bodleian MS Rawl. A.239, fol. 47^{r-v}, and are sometimes referred to as the 'Lord Stanhope of Harrington' item. Transcripts, not reliable in every detail of spelling, are printed in Chambers, *Shakespeare*, 2.343. The full text is given in the 'Stage history' section of the Introduction.

2 See Gurr, *Playing Companies*, 389; and Orrell.

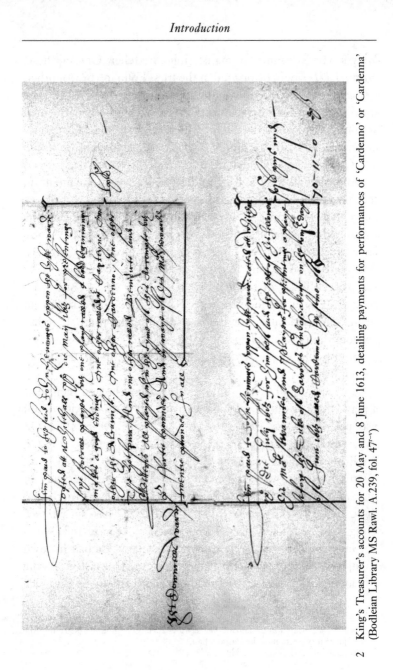

2 King's Treasurer's accounts for 20 May and 8 June 1613, detailing payments for performances of 'Cardenno' or 'Cardenna' (Bodleian Library MS Rawl. A.239, fol. 47ʳ⁻ᵛ)

specialist publisher of playtexts. In 1646, Moseley and his then partner Humphrey Robinson claimed possession through the Register of thirty-eight King's Men plays that had appeared on a list made in 1641 by the Lord Chamberlain of plays not to be printed without consent.[1] In 1653, a further large entry (this time in his sole name) added an additional thirteen from the 1641 list. The play would have to wait until 1727, however, before reappearing in print and on the stage. It would do so then only in adapted form, and under a new title: *Double Falsehood*.

The 1727/8 theatrical season was for that reason one of the most remarkable in British theatre history, giving rise as it did to two premieres of spectacularly successful plays. John Gay's *The Beggar's Opera* began its amazing run at Lincoln's Inn Fields on 29 January 1728 and was to become the century's biggest box-office success. Colley Cibber's reworking of an older play by Sir John Vanbrugh, *The Provoked Husband*, had its first performance on 10 January 1728 at Drury Lane and provided real competition for Gay's triumph, with twenty-eight nights in its initial run. These two titans have helped to occlude one of the most curious and surprising theatrical events of that, and perhaps of any other, season: the premiere of what was advertised as a newly discovered play by William Shakespeare. The first published indication that Theobald was working on such a project appeared in the *London Journal* for 10 May 1727. The newspaper's rhetoric in presenting Theobald's theatrical coup gives some idea of what is at stake and helps to explain the later antipathy of Theobald's opponents:

> How long and ardently have the Sons of Verse desired
> that some other *Shakespeare* might arise, blest with the
> Force and Master-Genius of the first; who might be able
> to deliver the Stage from the little Follies that now usurp
> it, and restore the old manly *English* taste . . . At length

1 The list is transcribed by Chambers ('Plays'). Unfortunately, it makes no mention of *The History of Cardenio*.

our Wishes are more than accomplish'd. The good old Master of the *English* Drama is by a kind of Miracle recall'd from his Grave, and given to us once again.

The confection of Shakespeare, elevated taste and Englishness in this is powerful, and it made enemies. Even before the first performance on Wednesday 13 December 1727 at the Theatre Royal, Drury Lane, then, *Double Falsehood* had been causing a stir. On 4 December 1727, the *Daily Post* and the *Evening Journal* both reported its author/adapter/impresario Theobald's unusual step of obtaining a royal licence for his play because, as the licensing document states, he had 'at a considerable Expence, Purchased the Manuscript Copy of an Original Play of WILLIAM SHAKESPEARE, called, *Double Falshood; Or, the Distrest Lovers*; and, with great Labour and Pains, Revised, and Adapted the same to the Stage' (1728a, sig. A1ᵛ; ll. 6–10).[1] Both papers continued to express interest in the production, the *Daily Post* advertising it on Tuesday 12th and supplying the cast list for the first performance on Wednesday 13th, while the *Evening Journal* pushed quickly into print with a review of the performance on Thursday 14 December:

Last Night was acted an original play of William Shakespear's in Drury-Lane, where the Audience was very numerous and [gave] the most remarkable attention through the whole. Mr. Williams supplied, not unsuccessfully, Mr. Booth's part; Mrs. Booth and Mrs. Porter most amiably distinguish'd themselves; Mr. Wilks shone with his usual Spirit in the Prologue; and Mrs. Oldfield even exceeded herself, with the highest Gracefulness in the Epilogue. We are pleased that we can oblige our Readers, by giving them the following Song, sung by the Lady who plays the part of *Violante* in the Fourth Act.

1   See pp. 162–71 for the full (modernized) text of the Royal Licence, together with the Dedication and Preface referred to on pp. 20–2. Line nos are to the modernized text.

The paper goes on to print Violante's song, 'Fond Echo, forego thy light Strain' (4.2.16–23), which in its attractive setting by Gouge had clearly captured the hearts of the audience (see Fig. 3).[1] One of the many sources of interest in this production was the doubt as to whether the great veteran actor Barton Booth would appear in the leading role of Julio, suffering as he was from what his doctors diagnosed as 'an inveterate Jaundice'.[2] In the event, his understudy Charles Williams took the stage, but Theobald persuaded Booth to take the part on Tuesday 19 December; and he gave his last performance on any stage in the role of Julio on 9 January 1728.

Double Falsehood, or The Distressed Lovers is a romantic tragicomedy, indebted for its plot to the story of Cardenio as originally told in Cervantes' *Don Quixote*, from Part 3 chapter 9 to Part 4 chapter 9, in the version translated by Thomas Shelton and published in 1612.[3] Set in Andalucia, the action shows the notorious libertine Henriquez ravishing the virtuous Violante and at the same time attempting to marry Leonora, the fiancée of his friend Julio. Henriquez's worthy elder brother Roderick is instrumental in exposing this double perfidy, reconciling Henriquez with Violante and with his father the Duke, and reuniting Leonora with Julio. The respective fathers of Leonora and Julio, Don Bernard and Camillo, play important roles in the plot. Don Bernard is at first happy to breach his understanding with Camillo and Julio in view of a better offer from the noble-man Henriquez. He comes to regret that profoundly, and in the play's final resolution both fathers are relieved and delighted when their children prove to be alive, readily blessing their union.

1 Gouge's first name is not known.
2 *Memoirs of the Life of Barton Booth* (1733), 14.
3 The relevant passages of Shelton are reproduced in Metz, *Sources*. He has, however, used a nineteenth-century edition for his copy-text, which differs in accidentals and some substantives from the first edition of Shelton. Appendix 6 contains excerpts from the first edition.

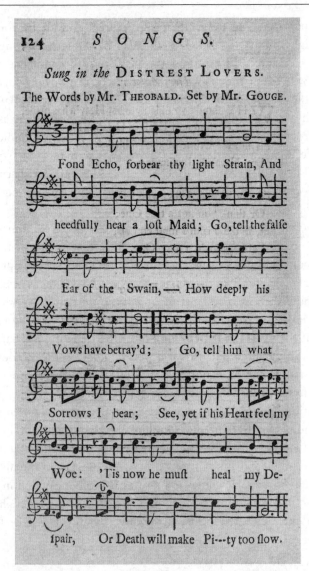

3   Setting of 'Fond Echo, forego thy light strain' (4.2.16–23), by the composer Gouge, as reprinted in the *Musical Miscellany*, vol. 2 (1729). The word 'forbear' replaces the text's 'forego' in all early printings of the song, and is possibly what was performed onstage (British Library G.307, fol. 184)

An initial run of ten successive performances (with a further three at different times before the end of the season) was a considerable success at a time when audiences demanded a constantly changing repertoire. As was usual in the period, performance was followed, early in 1728, by publication. The bookseller-publisher John Watts brought out the first edition of the play, at a cost of 1s 6d, in an octavo volume that boasts some unusual features.[1] The royal arms are prominently displayed above the licensing document (Fig. 4), which granted

> Our Royal Licence, for the sole Printing and Publishing the said Play, in such Size and Manner, as He and They shall think fit, for the Term of Fourteen Years, to be computed from the Date hereof; strictly forbidding all our Subjects within our Kingdoms and Dominions, to Reprint the same, either in the like, or in any other Size, or Manner whatsoever; or to Import, Buy, Vend, Utter or Distribute any Copies thereof, Reprinted beyond the Seas, during the aforesaid Term of Fourteen Years, without the Consent, or Approbation of the said *Lewis Theobald*, his Heirs, Executors, and Assigns, under his, or their Hands and Seals first had, and obtained; as they will answer the contrary at their Peril.
>
> (sig. A1ᵛ; 18–29)

Theobald had taken the precaution of gaining this licence from the Duke of Newcastle on 5 December, before the play's run began, as an extra precaution against piracy. Although the 1710 Act of 8 Anne, for the 'Encouragement of Learning, by Vesting the Copies of Printed Books in the Authors or Purchasers of such Copies during the Times therein mentioned', was not initially interpreted to mean that authors retained rights to their own copy, Theobald was clearly taking advantage of the legislation to do just this. His obtaining and printing of this licence makes

1   The price of the volume is recorded on sig. A1ʳ of 1728a.

G E O R G E R.

EORGE the Second, by the Grace of God, King of *Great-Britain, France* and *Ireland*; Defender of the Faith, *&c.* To all to whom thefe Prefents fhall come, Greeting. Whereas our Trufty, and Well-beloved *Lewis Theobald,* of our City of *London,* Gent. hath, by his Petition, humbly reprefented to Us, That He having, at a confiderable Expence, Purchafed the Manufcript Copy of an Original Play of WILLIAM SHAKESPEARE, called, *Double Falfhood*; Or, *the Diftreft Lovers*; and, with great Labour and Pains, Revifed, and Adapted the fame to the Stage; has humbly befought Us, to grant him Our Royal Privilege, and Licence, for the fole Printing and Publifhing thereof, for the Term of Fourteen Years; We, being willing to give all due Encouragement to this his Undertaking, are gracioufly pleafed to condefcend to his Requeft: and do therefore, by thefe Prefents, fo far as may be agreeable to the Statute in that Behalf made and provided, for Us, Our Heirs, and Succeffors, grant unto Him, the faid *Lewis Theobald,* his Executors, Adminiftrators, and Affigns, Our Royal Licence, for the fole Printing and Publifhing the faid Play, in fuch Size and Manner, as He and They fhall think fit, for the Term of Fourteen Years, to be computed from the Date hereof; ftrictly forbidding all our Subjects within our Kingdoms and Dominions, to Reprint the fame, either in the like, or in any other Size, or Manner whatfoever; or to Import, Buy, Vend, Utter or Diftribute any Copies thereof, Reprinted beyond the Seas, during the aforefaid Term of Fourteen Years, without the Confent, or Approbation of the faid *Lewis Theobald,* his Heirs, Executors, and Affigns, under his, or their Hands and Seals firft had, and obtained; as they will anfwer the contrary at their Peril: —— Whereof the Commiffioners, and other Officers of our Cuftoms, the Mafter, Warden, and Company of Stationers, are to take Notice, that the fame may be entred in the Regifter of the faid Company, and that due Obedience be rendred thereunto. Given at Our Court at St. *James*'s, the Fifth Day of *December*, 1727; in the Firft Year of Our Reign.

By His Majefty's Command,

HOLLES NEWCASTLE.

4   The royal licence gained by Lewis Theobald to protect the copyright of *Double Falsehood*, printed before the play's title-page (British Library 841.d.32)

clear that he wanted to avoid alienating his literary property to a bookseller-publisher for a lump-sum payment. Theobald considered, then, that this was an unusually valuable piece of literary real-estate – a view echoed by the book trade, since on 31 July 1728 he sold the copyright on to Watts for the unusually high sum of 100 guineas.[1] The document of sale is reproduced in Fig. 5.[2] In respect of the price paid for the copyright, Thomas Southerne's £150 for *The Spartan Dame* and Colley Cibber's £105 for *Caesar in Egypt* and *The Provoked Husband* provide comparators. Theobald's remuneration was not unprecedented, but was at the very high end of the spectrum. Peter Seary has argued that 'when Theobald sold the copyright of *Double Falshood* to John Watts, he also relinquished the original manuscripts'.[3] The document of sale, extant but as yet uncatalogued in the Folger Shakespeare Library, still maintains that the play was written originally by Shakespeare and only adapted by Theobald. This has some bearing on the question, to be discussed, of authorship. Would Theobald have knowingly sold a forgery by means of a signed and witnessed legal instrument?

In the 1728 edition, the royal licence is followed by a title-page (Fig. 6) claiming that the play was 'Written Originally by *W.SHAKESPEARE*; And now Revised and Adapted to the Stage / By Mr. THEOBALD, the Author of *Shakespeare Restor'd*.'[4] This bold claim is bolstered by a well-known motto from Virgil's *Aeneid*, stressing the extreme felicity of Theobald's discovery:

> *Quod optanti Divum promittere nemo*
> *Auderet, volvenda Dies, en! attulit ultro.*

1   This is reported by Eu. [Joseph] Hood in the *Gentleman's Magazine*, 94 (March 1824), 223. Hood comments that after its run, it was 'most properly consigned by the managers to the tomb of the Capulets'.
2   I acknowledge the kind assistance of Georgianna Ziegler in finding the document of sale.
3   Seary, *Theobald*, 219; see his Appendix C (219–20) for further discussion. Seary reports the information concerning the sale of Theobald's copyright to Watts, comparing it with the six guineas obtained for his adaptation of *The Duchess of Malfi* as *The Fatal Secret* (26).
4   The title capitalizes on the fame of Theobald's *Shakespeare Restored*, the work in which he demolished Pope's edition of *Hamlet*.

81

Know all men by these Presents, That Lewis Theobald, Gent: of the Parish of St Giless in the fields in the County of Middlesex, For and in Consideration of the Sum of One Hundred Guineas of Lawfull Mony of Great Britain to him in Hand paid by John Watts of London, Stationer, He the said Lewis Theobald, Gent: hath Bargain'd, Sold and assigned and Set over, and by these Presents doth Bargain, Sell, assign and Sett Over all that the full and sole Right and Title, of, in and to the Copy of a Play, Intitled, Double Falshood, or the Distrest Lovers, Written Originally by W. Shakespeare; and now Revised and Adapted to the Stage by the said Lewis Theobald, Gent: the author of Shakespeare Restor'd, To have and to hold the said Copy of the said Play unto the said John Watts, his Heirs and assigns for Ever, notwithstanding any Act or Law to the Contrary. In Witness whereof the said Lewis Theobald, Gent: hath hereunto sett his hand and seal this Thirty First Day of July 1728

Lew: Theobald

Witnesses,

Tho: Smith Cowell.
Mary Wade

5   Document of sale drawn up between Lewis Theobald and John Watts for
the copyright sale of *Double Falsehood*, 31 July 1728

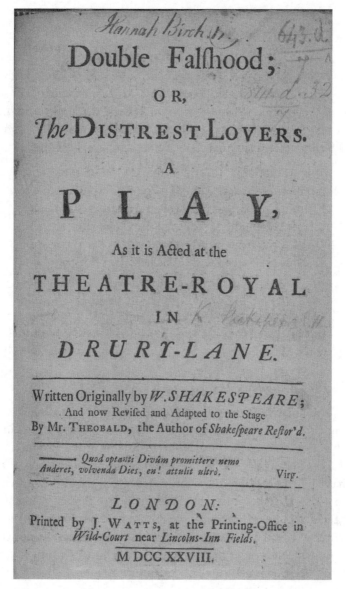

6 Title-page of the first edition of *Double Falsehood*, January 1728 (British Library 841.d.32)

(What none of the Gods would have dared promise to
your prayers, see! rolling time has brought unasked.)

(9.6–7)

Following this with a dedication to the powerful Whig patron
George Bubb Dodington, Theobald takes the opportunity not so
much for egregious flattery as to underwrite the authenticity of
the text.[1] Suggesting that Dodington could become a major patron
of Shakespeare, a latterday Earl of Southampton, he writes:

> You are not only a distinguish'd *Friend* of the *Muses*,
> but most intimately *allied* to them: And from hence it is
> I flatter Myself, that if You shall think fit to pronounce
> this Piece genuine, it will silence the Censures of those
> *Unbelievers*, who think it impossible a Manuscript
> of *Shakespeare* could so long have lain dormant; and
> who are blindly paying Me a greater Compliment
> than either They design, or I can merit, while they
> cannot but confess Themselves *pleased*, yet would fain
> insinuate that they are *imposed upon*. I should esteem it
> some Sort of *Virtue*, were I able to commit so *agreeable*
> a *Cheat*.

(sig. A3ᵛ–4ʳ; 16–26).

The final item in Theobald's introductory machinery is
a preface, in which he proposes rather to 'wipe out a flying
Objection or two, than to labour at proving it the Production
of *Shakespeare*' (sig. A5ʳ; 6–7). Insouciantly, Theobald suggests
that while there is not the slightest doubt that this is the authentic work of Shakespeare, there are one or two infidels who have
difficulty in believing that it would not have surfaced in over a
century. To silence such scepticism as has come to his notice,
he informs the reader that there are 'Great Judges' (3) to whom
it has been communicated in manuscript. John Cadwalader's

---

1 See the fuller description of Dodington's life and career in the commentary,
Dedication 1n.

location of a letter from Theobald to the Countess of Oxford dated 10 December 1727 in which he offers her the chance 'to read the play in manuscript' (Cadwalader, 109) suggests that she was one of the 'Great Judges'. The Countess of Oxford was Henrietta Cavendish Harley, née Holles (1694–1755), only daughter of John Holles, Duke of Newcastle (1662–1711). She was married to Edward Harley, first earl of Oxford and Mortimer, son of Robert Harley, the first minister and the greatest bibliophile in the eighteenth century, whose collection is one of the foundational collections of the British Library. Her cousin was the Lord Chamberlain who granted Theobald his licence, so she was an appropriate choice of person to look at the manuscripts.

Theobald then makes the more documentary assertion that

> one of the Manuscript Copies, which I have, is of above Sixty Years Standing, in the Handwriting of Mr. *Downes*, the famous Old Prompter; and, as I am credibly inform'd, was early in the Possession of the celebrated Mr. *Betterton*, and by Him design'd to have been usher'd into the World.

(sig. A5^r; 11–16)

Further information ensues, deepening the enigma. According to 'a Tradition' handed down to Theobald by a 'Noble Person' from whom he obtained one of his three copies, the play was written during Shakespeare's retirement from the stage as a present for his 'Natural Daughter' (18–22). (Although Sir William Davenant was rumoured to be a natural son of Shakespeare's, there is no known tradition of Shakespeare having had a natural daughter. It is perhaps of relevance in this connection that in 1720 Theobald, dedicating his adaptation of *Richard II* to the Earl of Orrery, had made a comparable claim, albeit metaphorically, referring to the play as 'an Orphan Child of *Shakespear*; who throws her Self at

21

your Lordship's Feet'.[1]) The two other copies of the manuscript that have come into his possession, one of which he purchased at a 'very good Rate' (24) (though the licence claimed that it had been acquired 'at a considerable Expence' (6), but this may not be the same manuscript: see Preface, 23n.), are more recent, but one at least is much more readable, with 'fewer Flaws and Interruptions in the Sense' (26).

In addition to the question of provenance, the Preface confronts two further issues: chronology and authorship. Challenging those who say that the plot's basis in Cervantes rules it out as being by Shakespeare, Theobald states, erroneously, that '*Don Quixot* was publish'd in the Year 1611, and *Shakespeare* did not dye till *April* 1616, a sufficient Interval of Time for All that We want granted' (sig. A5ᵛ; 31–3). Theobald scarcely dignifies those who detect the hand of Fletcher in the play with a reply, relying instead on the *bon mot* that 'my Partiality for *Shakespeare* makes me wish, that Every Thing which is good, or pleasing, in our Tongue, had been owing to his Pen' (sig. A5ᵛ; 40–2). His final remarks are an even-handed vindication of the theatre managers from the charge that they do not promote new work. Stressing once again that he himself is an editor, rather than author, on this occasion (and so has no vested interest), he refers to the 'damned if you do, damned if you don't' predicament of the managers who may offend both by promoting and by rejecting new plays.

Two months later, a second issue of the first edition of the play was published (more evidence of demand for it amongst readers of playtexts), in which the Preface is altered and augmented. The changes are designed first of all to correct the error in his earlier Cervantic chronology. He now writes that

> the *First* Part of *Don Quixot*, which contains the Novel
> upon which the Tale of this Play seems to be built, was

---

1 Theobald, *Richard II*, sig. A2ʳ. Cf. the identification of *Double Falsehood* as Shakespeare's 'last child . . . Lost to the world' in Frowde's prologue (see p. 65).

publish'd in the Year 1605, and our *Shakespeare* did not dye till *April* 1616; an Interval of no less than Eleven Years . . .

(sig. A5ᵛ)

The second alteration makes reference to the question of authorship, and obliquely sets out Theobald's stall as a future editor of Shakespeare's complete works. The *bon mot* cited above is subtly altered from 'Every Thing which is good, or pleasing, in our Tongue' to 'Every Thing which is good, or pleasing, in that other great Poet'. Theobald now heartily wishes, not that everything in the English language deemed good or pleasing should be Shakespeare's, but that everything *by Fletcher* deemed good or pleasing should be Shakespeare's. Does this, or does it not, make a concession to the possibility of Fletcher's having a hand in the play? His continuation is truculent, however:

I had once design'd a *Dissertation* to prove this Play to be of *Shakespeare*'s Writing, from some of its remarkable Peculiarities in the *Language*, and Nature of the *Thoughts*: but as I could not be sure but that the Play might be attack'd, I found it adviseable, upon second Consideration, to reserve *that* Part to my *Defence*. That Danger, I think, is now over; so I must look out for a better Occasion. I am honour'd with so many powerful Sollicitations, pressing Me to the Prosecution of an Attempt, which I have begun with some little Success, of *restoring* SHAKESPEARE from the numerous Corruptions of his Text: that I can neither in Gratitude, nor good Manners, longer resist them. I therefore think it not amiss here to promise, that tho' *private Property* should so far stand in my Way, as to prevent me from putting out an *Edition* of *Shakespeare*, yet, some Way or other, if I live, the Publick shall receive from my Hand his *whole* WORKS corrected,

23

with my best Care and Ability. This may furnish an
Occasion for speaking more at large concerning the
present *Play*: For which Reason I shall now drop it for
another Subject.

(sig. A5ᵛ)

The arch typographic reference to '*restoring* SHAKESPEARE'
here is a snide reminder of his aggressive *Shakespeare Restored*
(1726), the work in which Theobald massacred Pope's edition
of *Hamlet*, and which did more than anything else to ensure that
Double Falsehood would attract vengeful attention for some time
to come.

DOUBLE FALSEHOOD: THE PLAY

So what was the play like that Theobald, possibly following in
the footsteps of an earlier adapter, presented to an eighteenth-
century audience as *Double Falsehood*? Elaborating on my
earlier bald summary, the action is as follows. Duke Angelo's
younger son Henriquez, a notorious libertine, is in love with
Leonora, his friend Julio's intended. With the collusion of
Don Bernard, Leonora's status-seeking father, he forces her
to the altar, having first lured Julio to court on a false errand.
She manages to convey a letter to Julio, who arrives at Don
Bernard's house in disguise just as the nuptials are taking
place. With a dagger concealed in the folds of her dress,
Leonora assures Julio that she would rather be dead than
wed to Henriquez, and Julio consents to be concealed behind
an arras, only to burst out of hiding in time to prevent the
nuptial knot being tied. He is forcibly ejected from the house.
Earlier in the action, Henriquez has ravished the humble but
worthy Violante and sent her a heartless letter, abandoning
her to her fate.

In the play's second half, the maddened and grief-stricken
Julio is living in a mountainous plateau. Violante, in shepherd's

attire, has joined a group of shepherds in this terrain, Leonora has taken refuge in a nunnery in the same region, Henriquez is in pursuit of her, and Roderick (the Duke's virtuous elder son) is on everyone's track, arriving in time to save Violante from further infamy at the hands of the Master of the Flocks, who has seen through her transvestite disguise. Julio and Violante are discovered to one another and go off to languish in their mutual sense of Henriquez's baseness (the 'double falsehood' of the title).

In Act 5, the Duke, Don Bernard (now penitent) and Julio's much-maligned father Camillo have been requested by Roderick to wait at a lodge. Roderick and Henriquez arrive with Leonora, whom they have recovered from the convent, and with Violante, still disguised, who by pre-arrangement with Roderick claims to be a page cruelly abandoned by Henriquez. He denies the story, but in proof of it she presents him with the same heartless letter that he had earlier employed to her ruin. She exits, returning as Violante, and with Julio in train. Henriquez seems to fall in love with her anew and perhaps for real, Leonora is overjoyed to be reunited with Julio, Don Bernard is mightily relieved, Camillo ecstatic to find his son alive, and all ends happily.

The play has much to offer its audience. Scenically, it alternates interiors and exteriors using the stock resources of the painted back shutters (see further Appendix 4) – a village in distant perspective and in closer view, an apartment interior – until the dramatic discovery scene 3.2, considered more fully below. The balcony scene 1.3 provides variety by shifting the axis of playing from the horizontal to the vertical, as Violante looks down on the serenading Henriquez. In the later action, the play opens out into the country, with the back shutter depicting '*A wide plain, with a prospect of mountains at a distance*' (4.1.0 SD) providing the atmosphere for the entire fourth act and 5.1, before the final scene again moves indoors, but into a rustic interior.

There is a clean single line of action, without what the period would have considered the 'clutter' of a subplot – though the Master of the Flocks's design upon Violante offers something in terms of diversification of the action and the titillation of virtue in distress. The near-Manichaean extreme of good and evil in the two brothers was, as commentators on Samuel Richardson's *Pamela* (1740) and the early novel have shown, a more satisfying ethical structure in early modern society than it may be in our own.[1] The fathers provide a comic texture that the overall earnestness of the play otherwise excludes. In particular, the passage of action in which Don Bernard barefacedly snubs Camillo's suit (2.3.152–215) might appeal to the audience's sense of social realism. The rest of 2.3 is a scene structured round the contrasting intensity of the actor Robert Wilks's palpable insincerity as Henriquez; and Leonora's love-versus-duty predicament, so popular in Dryden's heroic dramas of an earlier era, which provided rich opportunities for Mary Porter, playing opposite him, to exercise her striking trademark postures of injured propriety. Meanwhile the punctuation of the scene in a lower, or one might say more 'realistic', idiom by Don Bernard operating in the role of pander, provides a satisfying contrast with the higher dramatic registers. Leonora is, throughout the action, a gratifyingly spirited heroine. It is she, not Julio, who in 1.2 is prepared to urge disobedience to their respective fathers in the interests of their love. And whereas in the source her equivalent Luscinda actually says 'I will' to Fernando (Shelton, 3.13.275)[2], Leonora does not explicitly comply with the forced marriage to Henriquez in 3.2.

Structured around moments of climax, 3.2 makes for a powerfully theatrical effect. Wedding ceremonies have their own inbuilt drama, particularly during the moment when 'just impediments' are called for, and the entire edifice could collapse into farce and tawdriness if any voice is heard. The presence of Julio, who appears at the beginning of the scene in disguise,

---

1 See J. Paul Hunter, *Before Novels: The Cultural Contexts of Eighteenth-Century English Fiction* (New York, 1990), ch. 9.

2 Abbreviated references to Shelton's translation of *Don Quixote* are to Parts, chapters, and pages where applicable, i.e. 3.13.275 = Part 3 chapter 13, page 275.

provides rich foreboding of such disaster. Music, wedding bells, lights, the opening out of the scenery into an atmospherically lit great hall: the scene calls for as much as the period's non-operatic stage can offer in terms of 'special effects'. The handling of the action between Julio and Leonora demands some subtlety. When she tells him that she has 'forethought the means / To disappoint these nuptials' (63–4), the audience intuits a possible suicide or murder attempt, and the bells that then knoll ambiguously betoken a wedding or a funeral. Suspense builds. Julio is to 'rest a silent statue' (72) and is sworn not to interfere in the action whatever may happen, even though Leonora shows him her dagger. A particularly Shakespearean resonance is constructed by the secreting of Julio 'behind yon arras' (66), operating subliminally in tandem with the language to create for the audience some parallel intuition of the killing of Polonius in *Hamlet*. Does he, or does he not, hear Leonora's lines 75–7 ('I dare not tell thee of my purpose, Julio . . .') when he is concealed behind the arras?

Leonora's rhetoric in the face of Henriquez's and her father's attempts to coerce her affections is impressive. Her spiritedness, and the unclarity of her motives, persists in her shrewd question to Henriquez at 87–8: 'Why would you make a wife of such a one, / That is so apt to change?' Henriquez is forced to deny his own rationality: 'No shot of reason can come near the place / Where my love's fortified' (108–9). At the point of the joining of hands – with clear indications that Leonora is 'dragging back' (120) – Julio appears from behind the arras (one assumes that he can see what has been going on through convenient apertures), confronts a shocked and embarrassed Henriquez, and the action erupts into physicality, as Julio is seized and Leonora swoons, somewhat melodramatically dropping '*a paper*' (153 SD) that contains her suicide note.

By the scene's close, the audience is ready for the less claustrophobic set that features in 3.3, returning to the '*Prospect of a village at a distance*' (0 SD) that is the standard non-court setting. In 3.3 there are repeated intimations, from the characters, of a possible happy ending (99–105 and 128). This somewhat trite trust in Providential interference is a note absent from Shakespeare's last plays but more commonly discovered in Fletcher. It is somewhat offset by the fact that Violante's distrust of men as a result of the rape is at its height (138–40).

In Act 4, Violante and Julio are to assume a more powerful stage presence. For the audience, there is the frisson of knowing that offstage, they were the real-life married couple Hester and Barton Booth. Hester in particular needs to give a performance of limpid innocence and virtue, intensifying the pathos attaching to her actually ruined state; while Barton has to exploit the possibilities that stage madness always presents to the actor. Violante's vulnerably transvestite situation, at the mercy of the Master of the Flocks and perhaps even of the vagaries of Julio's insanity, will again set up Shakespearean and Fletcherian resonances for sufficiently experienced members of the audience. The situation here, of a disguised vulnerable female wandering in an unknown terrain, is similar to that of Imogen in the Welsh scenes in *Cymbeline*, except that the latter has found herself fortunately amongst virtuous rather than vicious denizens. There is a general resemblance to Act 4 of Beaumont and Fletcher's *Philaster* (1609), in which Philaster, his beloved Arathusa, and their page Bellario (actually the disguised Euphrasia) are all in flight in a forest. In 4.5, Philaster begs death at Arathusa's hands, but she requires it even more ardently of him. He wounds her, but is interrupted by a 'Countrey Fellow', who fights with Philaster to prevent him doing more injury. Fletcher had previous, if not entirely happy, experience of writing pastoral tragicomedy set amongst the Thessalian, rather than Andalucian, plains; his *The Faithful Shepherdess* (1608), although it has no scene closely resembling this one, revolves entirely around sexual predation, incorporating would-be rapists and seducers of both sexes.

Viola, Portia, Rosalind, Imogen – a series of Shakespearean heroines partially liberated and partially inhibited by assuming male clothes and aspects of maleness itself while their female attractions shine transparently through – will form a frame or an intertext for the spectator of this act. Roderick's nick-of-time rescue of Violante has obvious theatrical effect, while the audience might enjoy the carnivalesque impropriety of the Master's brutal rudeness to the aristocratic heroic brother during his exceptionally blunt and shameless defence of his action with respect to his 'boy' (4.1.196–204). In 4.2, a passage of supreme aesthetic appeal is achieved in the *Tempest*-like 'sweet airs' of the song that Violante renders offstage: 'Fond Echo, forego thy light strain' (16–23). In Gouge's lovely setting (see Fig. 3), the music is permitted to begin the pacification of Julio and effect his return to sanity. Indeed, the song changes the play's mood as much as the transitional scene in *The Winter's Tale*, when the Shepherd announces to the Clown that 'thou met'st with things dying, I with things new-born' (3.3.111–12). When Violante enters, her own mood is one of celebration of the simplicities of nature as against the vile corruptions of the Court, and the touching speech in which she represents herself and her experience as the stuff of future moral tales (4.2.61–71) has, as has been noticed, cadences of speeches given by 'ruined maids' in other plays by Fletcher. This address, directly made to the audience, has the charm of earlier dramatic forms: the prefatory verse to *Godly Queen Hester*, say, written in 1529–30, or a passage such as that in *A Warning for Fair Women* (1596–1600), where an adulterous wife implores her children to learn from her fall (ll. 2474–11) (see Dillon, 174–5).

Act 5 is mainly devoted to retrospective exposition and denouement, but in being so, it is again powerfully reminiscent of the endings of Shakespeare's, and Shakespeare–Fletcher's, late romantic tragicomedies. The audience would have undergone a similar set of theatrical manipulations in the endings of *Cymbeline*, *The Two Noble Kinsmen*, *Measure for Measure* and *All's Well That Ends Well*. Reconciliation between the two destined couples (Julio/Leonora and Henriquez/Violante) has to be effected, but based on true confession, in such a way as to *perform* penitence and forgiveness. Fathers need to come together with their children, and with each other, but they have to face up to the wrongs they have perpetrated upon their children by acting in too absolute a fashion: both between and across generations, difficult truths need to be confronted. The audience needs to experience some possibility of things not working out, both of Leonora's capitulation to her father's desire that she marry Henriquez, and of lies and deceit prevailing, before they can be permitted to revel in the happiness of the final chaconne. The pacing of the scene (5.2) is vital here, the accreting instalments of the denouement: the seeming movement towards union between Henriquez and Leonora arrested, it appears, only by her sense that some time needs to elapse; Violante's interruption of that process in male disguise and Henriquez's Angelo-like adherence to falsehood; his exposure effected, in a moment of satisfying poetic justice, by exactly the heartless letter that he wrote to give Violante the brush-off; the staged return to light of Violante as a beautiful woman, and, slightly delayed by disguise, Julio's 'resurrection'.

Although Roderick seems firmly in control of the denouement (at 65–6, and earlier, at 3.3.99ff.), the audience never knows whether he is in control of Julio's safe return, not effected until 5.2.197 SD and with Julio still in disguise. Here it seems that the dramatist is making a distinction between what human beings can effect and what Providence alone can achieve. This is a distinction typical enough of Shakespeare's last plays, but on the other hand in plays such as *Measure for Measure*, *All's Well* and *Cymbeline,* the wronged woman seeking restitution is not likely to conceive the plot by means of which she will gain justice entirely on her own initiative. It is not clear why Violante should continue her transvestite disguise and invent a name for herself. Both Rosalind and Imogen provide similar fictional histories for their disguises as Ganymede and Fidele, however, and such a question about Violante's disguise may be the wrong question to ask. Certainly, the heavy emphasis on parental authority that comes through in the Duke's speech at 73–84 seems un-Shakespearean, its didacticism misplaced as part of closing sentiments that, in Shakespeare, usually require the older generation to learn from, not preach at, their children. One might hazard the guess that this heavy-handed moralism is Theobald's addition.

When Leonora is restored to her father at 5.2.58, Camillo remains as the only object of pathos. Camillo is placed here in a similar position to Alonso in *The Tempest*, who has to wait longest for the knowledge that his son Ferdinand still lives, and experiences it like a resurrection. Throughout the ending, Camillo seems to stand slightly apart, like Lafeu in *All's Well* or Lucio in *Measure for Measure* or Jaques in *As You Like It*. Typical of Shakespeare is a device through which the happy final resolution is at least compromised. It has to be earned, and is not offered to the audience without expecting them to work for its enjoyment.

What gave the audience in 1727 any reason to think, even for a second, that Shakespeare could have had a hand in what they were watching? For those less convinced that an entire play by Shakespeare was behind it, how could they believe that *something* Jacobean lurked in the background: that it was, say, a later adaptation of a 1612–13 Shakespeare–Fletcher dramatization of the Cardenio story from *Don Quixote*? Some answers have been suggested above, in the resonances that the play sets up with Shakespearean and Fletcherian situations and 'structures of feeling'. The most immediate answer, however, is that from the very outset, the language, whatever it *is*, is certainly not entirely eighteenth-century English. Audiences who hear this:

RODERICK

 My gracious father, this unwonted strain
 Visits my heart with sadness.

DUKE   Why, my son?
 Making my death familiar to my tongue
 Digs not my grave one jot before the date.

I've worn the garland of my honours long   5
And would not leave it wither'd to thy brow
But flourishing and green; worthy the man
Who with my dukedoms heirs my better glories.

RODERICK

This praise, which is my pride, spreads me with blushes.

DUKE

Think not that I can flatter thee, my Roderick,   10
Or let the scale of love o'erpoize my judgement.
Like a fair glass of retrospection, thou
Reflect'st the virtues of my early youth,
Making my old blood mend its pace with transport;
While fond Henriquez, thy irregular brother,   15
Sets the large credit of his name at stake,
A truant to my wishes and his birth.
His taints of wildness hurt our nicer honour
And call for swift reclaim.

                                        (1.1.1–19)

or this:

JULIO

I do not see that fervour in the maid
Which youth and love should kindle. She consents,
As 'twere, to feed without an appetite;   65
Tells me she is content and plays the coy one,
Like those that subtly make their words their ward,
Keeping address at distance. This affection
Is such a feign'd one as will break untouch'd;
Die frosty ere it can be thaw'd; while mine,   70
Like to a clime beneath Hyperion's eye,
Burns with one constant heat. I'll straight go to her,
Pray her to regard my honour – but she greets me –

                                        (1.2.63–73)

or this:

VIOLANTE

> What you can say is most unseasonable; what sing,
> Most absonant and harsh.

(1.3.53–4)

are assuredly hearing something other than the contemporary idiom of the day, however heightened for the stage. Theobald's audience were seeing and hearing a play that had many Shakespearean echoes (extensively documented in the commentary), and before they had leisure to consider whether the reason for this was that Shakespeare had put them there, or that someone else had, they were being convinced subliminally that they were in Shakespeare's presence. As I have said, those in the audience who knew their Shakespeare very well – and Pope had published a new edition of Shakespeare as recently as 1725 – would recognize stage situations and dramatic structures and patterns reminiscent of those in canonical plays. The following two sections of the introduction will consider what the original version of *Cardenio* might have looked like, and will retrace the steps from that to the play as described above – as the audience in 1727 experienced it.

FROM *DON QUIXOTE* TO *CARDENIO*

When James VI of Scotland ascended the English throne in 1603, a speedy end to Elizabeth's Spanish wars was a strong expectation placed upon him, duly delivered by the Treaty of London ratified in Valladolid in June 1605. Richard Wilson writes: 'This was the occasion (the Cervantes scholar Astrana Marín speculated) when the creators of *Hamlet* and *Don Quixote* met face-to-face, Shakespeare having come to Spain in the train of Charles Howard, Earl of Nottingham' (Wilson, 'Shakespeare's Spain', 28). Such a meeting is a consummation devoutly to be wished, more in the realm of fantasy than fact. What is less speculative is that when the diplomatic mission returned to London, a wave of Cervantic enthusiasm began, embodied in the interest of Shakespeare and Fletcher. Shakespeare and Cervantes met, certainly, but only between the covers of the lost *Cardenio*.

Recent work by Roger Chartier alerts us to the extraordinarily widespread awareness of *Don Quixote* in the years immediately following its first Castilian edition. In the Seagram Lecture delivered at McGill University on 4 September 2008, Chartier points out that there were seven editions in Castilian between 1605 and 1608 (five in 1605 alone), and that incidents from the book had already become popular in festival entertainments as early as 1607 and 1608, in locations as far flung as Peru. More important still is Chartier's adumbration of a Spanish play written between 1605 and 1608 by Guillén de Castro, a '*comedia*' entitled *Don Quixote de la Mancha*. This is a dramatization of the Cardenio story, with some additional elements (including the incidental onstage presence of the Don). Chartier's description of the play's plot has great resonance for readers of *Double Falsehood*. Whereas in Cervantes Cardenio is of noble birth, in de Castro he is a peasant – valiant where de Castro's Marquess (Cervantes' Fernando) is a coward. This reversal of social and genetic origins is a notable feature of characterization in *Double Falsehood*. De Castro does not stage the seduction of Dorotea, preferring to have it reported by the Marquess with the radical alteration of his sentiments, providing a precedent for the non-staging of Henriquez's seduction of Violante in *Double Falsehood*. Chartier's description of how the marriage between Luscinda and the Marquess was adapted by de Castro for the stage shows how the playwright took account of the context of the Catholic reformation. The promises made between the couple are deprived of any sacramental character; ceremonial words are kept to a minimum and the role of the priest is subsumed to that of the father. In all of these respects, this play's marriage scene resembles that of *Double Falsehood* and may indeed be a precedent for it via Shakespeare and Fletcher. The existence of de Castro's *Don Quixote de la Mancha* assists the imaginative reconstruction of a 1612–13 Shakespeare–Fletcher dramatization of the Cardenio story from *Don Quixote.* Indeed, it may form a 'missing link' between Cervantes' prose work and the lost *History of Cardenio.*

Detective work on the lost play can approach it from at least two angles, one conjecturing backwards from its extant derivative and one forwards from before it was composed, since we possess not only Theobald's adaptation but the original play's major source. In this respect we are in much the position we would occupy in relation to *The Two Noble Kinsmen* had the 1634 Quarto never been published but had Davenant's 1664 adaptation *The Rivals* nonetheless existed and survived: we would be forced to reconstruct the Shakespeare–Fletcher play as a missing intermediary stage between Chaucer's 'Knight's Tale' and Davenant's abbreviated revision. However, the very survival of *The Two Noble Kinsmen* means that we can attempt to reconstruct *Cardenio* with slightly more confidence than would in that instance be the case, since we have not only *Don Quixote* and *Double Falsehood* but also an example of how Shakespeare and Fletcher worked together on a closely analogous project at just this stage in their careers.

The first point to make about *Cardenio* is what a remarkable and telling decision it was to single out this particular element from Cervantes' novel for dramatization in the first place. Responsibility for that inspiration may lie with Fletcher as much as it did with Shakespeare. Assuredly, Shakespeare's familiarity with Spanish material went back a long way. He had exploited Bartholomew Yong's manuscript translation of Jorge de Montemayor's Portuguese-language *Diana* (1582–3) for the plot of *The Two Gentlemen of Verona* in the early days of his career. In so doing, he was taking advantage of Anglo-Spanish connections forged by the Sidney family (Sir Philip Sidney's *Arcadia* is also indebted to Yong) since the 1580s. By the early years of the seventeenth century, however, as Alexander

Samson has shown, those 'culturally Hispanophile' connections were more ardently pursued by Fletcher than by Shakespeare. Through his collaborator Francis Beaumont, who was a cousin of Henry Hastings, fifth Earl of Huntingdon, Fletcher gained the patronage of a kinship group – Hastings and the Sidneys – who had long been interested in Spanish romance and culture more broadly.[1] Samson offers convincing evidence that Fletcher could read Spanish well and that at least three of his plays depend on material only available in the Spanish language. The year 1607 defined a Cervantic 'moment' in English literary culture as evidenced by Beaumont's *The Knight of the Burning Pestle*, George Wilkins's *The Miseries of Enforced Marriage* and Thomas Middleton's *Your Five Gallants*, all published or performed in that year.[2] The translators Leonard Digges and James Mabbe, who both contributed commendatory verses to the Shakespeare First Folio, were in Spain during the period 1611–14. All these developments consolidated an Anglo-Spanish connection that created a context for the possible success of a stage adaptation at this time.

The passages from *Don Quixote* lying behind those parts of *Cardenio* that survive in *Double Falsehood* (reproduced in Appendix 6) cannot alone give a full sense of what work this story does within Cervantes' novel, where it is continually being used to highlight the nature of Don Quixote's literature-induced insanity and the extent to which the people around him are equally though differently imprisoned within cultural clichés. To understand the missing Jacobean dramatization of the Cardenio plot, then, it is necessary to know a little more about how that plot was originally fitted by Cervantes into the latter two-thirds of the first volume of *Don Quixote*.

1   Trudi Darby's essay (in the same volume as Samson's) has further discussion of Fletcher's familiarity with the Spanish language.
2   Middleton's *Your Five Gallants*, for example, shows awareness of Cervantes in the character Piamont's line: ''Sfoot, I could fight with a windmill now' (4.6.7–8) (Middleton, *Works*, 626).

Obsessed with the imaginary world of chivalry which has been his reading matter for years, Don Quixote, assisted by his pragmatic but credulous squire Sancho Panza, leaves his native La Mancha in quest of adventures in Part 1 chapter 2. He has already suffered a great deal from various collisions between the real fallen world he encounters and his sense of himself as the quest-hero of a chivalric romance before he ever meets Cardenio in Part 3 chapter 9. In 3.5, for example, he has become convinced that a nocturnal procession of mourners carrying a coffin are malefactors abducting the body of a slain knight, whom he seeks to avenge by attacking them all, and in 3.8 he has gallantly freed a number of convicted criminals being marched to the galleys from their ecclesiastical police escort. Beaten up by some of the ungrateful fugitives, and realizing that he is now wanted urgently by the Church authorities (the Holy Brotherhood), Don Quixote takes refuge in the barren mountains of the Sierra Morena, and it is here that Cervantes begins one of his most elaborate and dazzling exercises in the combination and mutual interruption of narrative modes. In the Sierra Morena, Don Quixote and Sancho discover a dead mule and, nearby, an abandoned port-manteau fixed to its saddle, which turns out to contain not just money but an accomplished sonnet lamenting the fatal pains of love and a letter accusing a woman of betrayal, among many other letters and verses. Soon they catch a glimpse of a wild man leaping among the rocks, whom Don Quixote immediately surmises to be the owner of the portmanteau. This hypothesis is confirmed by some goatherds, who recount how this courtly young man arrived in great melancholy some six months earlier, asking directions to the most remote part of the mountain, and has since lived there in a state of intermittent madness, some-times courteously accepting gifts of food, but dangerously prone to suddenly attacking goatherds while ranting against someone called Fernando.

In a manner which must immediately have struck a chord with the author of *Hamlet* and *King Lear*, Cervantes sets about drawing repeated parallels and contrasts between the genuine madness of this young man, who turns out to be called Cardenio (though Don Quixote calls him 'The Knight of the Rock', just as the Don calls himself 'The Knight of the Ill-favoured Face'), and the monomania, originally bred of affectation, displayed by Don Quixote. When the two meet during one of Cardenio's lucid intervals, in 3.10, Cardenio begins to recount the events which brought him to the Sierra Morena – the results of a fatal friendship with Duke Ricardo's younger son Don Fernando, who, after seducing a farmer's daughter by means of a sham marriage, began to take a marked interest in Cardenio's beloved Luscinda. Unfortunately, he is interrupted by Don Quixote when he chances to mention the chivalric romance *Amadis de Gaula*,[1] and, drawn briefly into a pointless argument about the chastity of one of its characters, Cardenio runs mad again prior to reaching his tale's conclusion. (He beats Don Quixote, Sancho Panza and a goatherd before disappearing into a wood.) Two chapters intervene before Cardenio's story is resumed, during which Don Quixote, as if inspired to emulation both by Cardenio's specimen of love-induced madness and by the recollection of the literary example provided by Amadis de Gaul, sets about performing his own display of love-madness in honour of his imaginary lady-love Dulcinea del Toboso. Insisting that Sancho should witness him stripping himself naked and running mad among the rocks, in a manner explicitly based on the behaviour of both Amadis and another love-maddened chivalric hero, Orlando,[2] Don Quixote sends his squire away to La Mancha to deliver a ridiculous love-letter to Dulcinea.

1 *Amadis de Gaula*, or in English *Amadis of Gaul*, is a neo-Arthurian romance published in Spanish around 1495, well known in Elizabethan England long before Anthony Munday published the first volume of his translation in 1590. A soubriquet derived from the fiction – Oriana – was being applied to Queen Elizabeth in the 1560s.
2 Ludovico Ariosto's *Orlando Furioso* first appeared in 1516. Sir John Harington's translation into 'English heroical verse' was published in 1591. *Orlando Furioso* had as much influence on English imaginative writing as did *Don Quixote* itself. Robert Greene's dramatization as *The History of Orlando Furioso* was first printed seven years after his death in 1599.

In a comparable manner to Shakespeare's own affectionate debunking of the story of Orlando's love-madness – in
As You Like It, where the young man to whom Shakespeare
lends Orlando's name merely pins love poems on trees, rather
than tearing trees up with his bare hands – Cervantes at once
ridicules and perpetuates the literary conventions of courtly
love: the more the plot of love-madness in the wilderness is
burlesqued by the willed and absurd antics of Don Quixote,
the more it can be straight-facedly recycled in the inset story of
Cardenio. That story is resumed in 3.13, when the curate who
hopes to take Don Quixote home and cure him, accompanied by
his friend the barber and by Sancho Panza, overhears Cardenio
singing melancholy love songs and begs him to continue the
narrative the curate has already heard from Sancho Panza.
Cardenio now recounts how Don Fernando promised to help
him gain his unwilling father's permission to marry Luscinda
but then, sending Cardenio away on a pretext, obtained permission to marry her himself. Alerted by a letter from a desperate
Luscinda, Cardenio rushed home just in time to conceal himself
behind a curtain and witness, aghast, their wedding ceremony.
Instead of stabbing herself, as Cardenio had believed Luscinda
would rather than marry Don Fernando, she breathed 'I will'
but then fainted, and, though Cardenio saw Don Fernando
discontentedly read a document which fell from her clothing as
she swooned, he became convinced that Luscinda's will must
finally have been swayed in his absence by pressure from her
family. Creeping away in horror and despair, he took refuge in
the Sierra Morena, and has since, when not enduring his mad
fits, been trying and failing to forget false friend and apparently
faithless fiancée alike.

The eventual resolution of this narrative remains deeply
entwined with the continuing story of Don Quixote, and offers
even more material of kinds which Anglophone readers are
nowadays inclined to associate with Shakespearean comedy and
romance. In 4.1, immediately after the curate has heard the

end of Cardenio's narration, the party overhear the laments of what seems to be a young shepherd, but who on closer observation turns out to be a beautiful young woman disguised in male clothing. Questioned, she reluctantly and with shame consents to narrate her story, and turns out to be Dorotea, the farmer's daughter seduced into a fraudulent clandestine marriage and then abandoned by Don Fernando just before his pursuit of Luscinda. Leaving her parents' house in quest of her truant bridegroom, she had learned more than had Cardenio of what happened at the forced wedding ceremony: the document which fell from the unwilling bride's clothes declared that she could never marry Don Fernando because she was already betrothed to Cardenio, and asserted that she would indeed kill herself sooner than wed the duke's son in his place. Luscinda, Dorotea had learned, had since been reported missing, but, sought herself by her own anxious parents, Dorotea had not stayed to await further developments but had fled into the mountains and obtained sheep-herding work in male disguise – successfully defending herself en route against a rape attempt by her formerly trusty servant, and subsequently having to defend herself against a similar assault by her new employer. In the next chapter, Cardenio reveals his identity to her, and, comforted to learn of Luscinda's resolve, points out that both he and Dorotea can perhaps hope to be reunited in due course with their respective partners.

Another seven whole chapters intervene, however, before this occurs. Meanwhile Dorotea becomes instrumental to the curate's plans for decoying Don Quixote home in order to get him some therapy: as well read in chivalric romance as anyone else in the novel and just as adept at literary pastiche, she agrees to claim to be the Princess Micomicona, a damsel in distress who needs Don Quixote to abandon his self-inflicted penance among the rocks and accompany her and her attendants (the curate and the barber, disguised) to save the kingdom of Micomicon from an ogre. The denouement of her own plot finally occurs during a long and eventful night at an inn on the way back towards La Mancha, the very inn which Don Quixote had decided was a castle during a major comic set-piece back in 2.3 and 2.4. After an argument with the innkeeper about the truth or otherwise of the tales of chivalry in his library, the curate reads aloud to the assembled company from a manuscript, the choice of which is approved by Cardenio, called 'The Tale of the Curious Impertinent', a story which seems in this context to exorcise the tragic possibilities of the Cardenio story itself. (It recounts how a husband decides to test his wife's fidelity by persuading his best friend to attempt to seduce her, with fatal consequences.) This long inset narrative, occupying two and a half chapters, is inter-rupted by Don Quixote, who, left asleep in the cellar, has awoken and destroyed a number of wineskins in the belief that they are ogres; but after the tale is finally concluded the Cardenio plot is likewise brought to its resolution, in chapter 9, when a group of horsemen arrive at the inn with a sobbing masked woman under their guard. This turns out to be Don Fernando and some hired servants, who have abducted Luscinda from the monastery in which she had taken refuge. Implored by Dorotea to honour his earlier promises to her and relinquish Luscinda to her own beloved Cardenio, Don Fernando relents, and the two couples are properly reunited amidst tears of repentance, joy and for-giveness. The novel has plenty more in store for the characters introduced by the Cardenio plot – who witness the next story to interpolate itself into the inn, that of the Moorish convert known simply as the Captive, and who continue to participate in the story of the curate's attempts to cure Don Quixote, with Dorotea required to impersonate the Princess Micomicona for some time to come. But for the purposes of Shakespeare and Fletcher, Cardenio's story ends here.

As this account should make clear, the Cardenio plot retailed by Cervantes is equally important for how it is told as for its contents, because the reader, along with certain characters in the novel, for example the curate, retrospectively deduces and assembles its events from the testimonies of a number of different participants and witnesses, ranging from goatherds to aristocrats, met by chance at different junctures of Don Quixote's own story. Its traces include, too, a range of different kinds of literary and other evidence – found poems, undelivered letters, overheard songs and soliloquies, even a dead mule. Cardenio's story is, moreover, intricately juxtaposed with other elements of the novel: as Cervantes, or his narrator, puts it with ironic self-congratulation at the start of Part 4, his readers can enjoy 'not only the sweetnesse of [Don Quixote's] true Historie, but also of the other tales, and digressions contained therein, which are in some respects [no] lesse pleasing, artificiall and true, than the very Historie it selfe' (4.1.281). But of this long, rich and elaborately self-conscious piece of fiction, described by Cervantes as a 'carded, spun, and selftwined threde' (281), Shakespeare and Fletcher seem to have made an almost insouciantly straightforward piece of drama, to judge by the fourteen short scenes of *Double Falsehood* as it stands. The first English dramatization of *Don Quixote*, co-written by the most talented of all English playwrights, appears to have omitted Don Quixote entirely, though it did possibly retain, to judge by its original title, the unaltered names of such Cervantic characters as it included. *Double Falsehood* confines itself strictly to the Cardenio story, concentrating primarily on its two central couples and recounting their adventures in strict chronological sequence, with little entrusted to retrospective narration.

The action begins just as Fernando (renamed Henriquez in *Double Falsehood*) has devised his pretext for sending Cardenio (Julio) out of the way. This occasions in the second scene a declaration of love reluctantly made by Luscinda (Leonora) at his departure reminiscent of Julia's to Proteus early in *The Two Gentlemen of Verona*. The play proceeds in a linear fashion from there to its denouement. There is no subplot, although dialogue is provided for some characters who do not directly appear in *Don Quixote*: the second rape attempt on Dorotea (Violante), for example, is not merely reported but is carried out onstage by the Shepherd who employs her in the wilderness when he realizes her true sex. Most strikingly, *Double Falsehood* opens with a discussion between two high-ranking men whom we never actually meet in *Don Quixote*, Fernando's father and elder brother (respectively Duke Angelo and Roderick in the play), both of them already concerned about Fernando's behaviour. At the story's conclusion – which is partly stage-managed by this virtuous elder brother at a lodge in the mountains, rather than happening by chance at an inn – not only is the Duke present as a witness but so are the fathers of Cardenio and Luscinda, whose respective views on the unfolding events of the play have been aired at intervals throughout.

It would be rash to make too many judgements about *Cardenio* on the evidence of *Double Falsehood*, given the adaptation the script certainly underwent at Theobald's hands and had probably already suffered before Theobald ever saw it (see p. 50), but what is most interesting from the point of view of deducing what Shakespeare and Fletcher may have done to Cervantes' material is what *Double Falsehood* omits from the Cardenio plot. The disappearance of Don Quixote – although it is always possible that the original *Cardenio* retained at least some of his antics as a subplot – is the most obvious alteration, for which one could speculatively attribute a number of motives. In general terms, attention paid to Jacobean collaborative authorship does not suggest many examples of multiple plots being drawn from a single source: purely on the pragmatic level, this would have entailed authors sharing that source, an awkward arrangement. In the case of *King Lear*, for example, when Shakespeare derived the Gloucester subplot from Sidney's *Arcadia* (1590) he saw no reason to involve the major characters Pyrocles and Musidorus simply because they were around when the story he wanted (the Prince of Paphlagonia talking with his son Leonatus) presented itself.[1] Bringing in Don Quixote would inevitably have made *Cardenio* an *hommage* or a satire: neither would necessarily have suited Shakespeare's purpose. The one previous English attempt at a *Don Quixote*-like stage comedy in which fantasies of chivalry combined with present-day social realism to mutually satirical effect, namely Beaumont's *The Knight of the Burning Pestle*, had had conspicuous lack of success. The printer Walter Burre commented on the failure of the play on stage owing to its audience's inability to read 'the pr[i]vie marke of irony about it' (McMullan, *Fletcher*, 261). The Prologue to its 1613 printed edition admits as much,[2] and in 1614 Richard Brathwaite could still write disparagingly of 'the phantasticke writings of some supposed Knights, (*Don Quixotte* transformed into a Knight with the *Golden Pestle*) with many other fruitlesse inuentions, moulded onely for delight without profite.'[3] Satire at the expense of chivalry seems to have been particularly unwelcome in the early Jacobean period, at a time when Henry, Prince of Wales (whose death in 1612, according to one commentator at least, provided a major context for *Cardenio*[4]), was determined to revive the ideal of the Protestant crusader.

One other possible reason for the omission of Don Quixote from *Cardenio*, if omitted he was, is provided by Cervantes himself, who devotes a good deal of space, before Cardenio and the other characters of his story have even left the inn where it is resolved, to an earnest discussion about dramatic theory and practice between the curate, another guest, a canon, and, later, Don Quixote (4.20–3). The canon espouses an orthodox,

1 On Shakespeare's use of Sidney in the subplot of *King Lear*, see the Arden Third Series edition, ed. R.A. Foakes (1997; reprinted 2004), 100–2.
2 'Where the bee can suck no honey, she leaves her sting behind; and where the bear cannot find origanum to heal his grief, he blasteth all other leaves with his breath. We fear it is like to fare so with us, that seeing you cannot draw from our labours sweet content, you leave behind you a sour mislike and with open reproach blame our good meaning because you cannot reap the wonted mirth' (Prologue to Beaumont, *Knight*, in Hattaway, 6).
3 Richard Brathwaite, *The scholar's medley* (1614), 99.
4 See Wilson, '*Cardenio*'. The argument is further elaborated, with more reference to the text of Theobald's play, in his *Shakespeare*, ch. 10.

44

neo-classical view to the effect that the public stage should be regulated to ensure that the players in future mount dramas that are either more purely tragic or more purely comic. It is just imaginable, then, that in transforming the Cardenio material into a play, Fletcher and Shakespeare, with whatever degree of irony, decided to take Cervantes at his apparent word.

Double Falsehood does, however, suggest that *Cardenio* also added material to Cervantes' plot: the increased participation of the fathers is one such element, implying the development of a motif much more prevalent in other Shakespeare plays of this period than in *Don Quixote*, the reunion of fathers with daughters. More teasingly, the adaptation includes what looks like the truncated remains, in 5.1, of a more thoroughly developed series of incidents involving the smuggling of Don Fernando, concealed in a hearse, into Luscinda's monastery – perhaps the remnant of a Shakespeare–Fletcher elaboration inspired by Don Quixote's attack on the funeral procession a little earlier in *Don Quixote*. Walter Graham points out that there are places in Shelton where incidents that could have suggested the plot occur: 'the hearse trick (invading the convent by means of a fake funeral procession, and abducting Leonora) probably needs no other sources than the suggestions furnished by two incidents in other parts of *Don Quixote*' (Graham, 'Problem', 279). He points to a funeral procession in 1.5 featuring a hearse; and to two separate incidents in 4.24–5, one in which a girl is confined in a convent and a second in which a procession of clerics and laity surround a statue of the Virgin shrouded in black, on their way to a mountain hermitage to pray for rain. Those are not sufficiently convincing to rule out other possibilities. Iachimo's concealment in a trunk in *Cymbeline* resembles this action in intent. In Beaumont's *Knight of the Burning Pestle* Jasper gains access to the Merchant's daughter Luce, his beloved, by pretending to be dead and in a coffin. They use the coffin to carry Luce out of the house. There is a hilarious moment of burlesque

45

tragicomedy when Luce, convinced that Jasper is dead, salutes the shroud:

> *Luce:* Thou sable cloth, sad cover of my joies
> I lift thee up, and thus I meete with death.
> *Jasper:* And thus you meete the living.
>   (4.4.269–71)

In *The Maid's Tragedy* the forlorn Aspatia sings the song 'Lay a garland on my hearse / Of the dismall Yew' (2.1.72–3), and in the lament following she imagines her own coffin and funeral in great detail. Act 5 also includes a much-elaborated reconciliation sequence, in which Dorotea/Violante is at first presented to Fernando/Henriquez still in male disguise, before returning in her own clothes to confront him with the heartless letter by which he jilted her in Act 2.

Recent critics who have dared to take the view that *Double Falsehood* does provide reliable clues about *Cardenio* may be divided into those who privilege the last acts of the play, stressing its depiction of reconciliation and marriage (and the addition to Cervantes' story of the reunions of parents with lost children), and those who instead focus on the play's violence, its broken nuptials and its rough juxtapositions of comedy and tragedy. Richard Wilson straddles both camps. He makes the most ambitious claims for the significance of *Cardenio* as part of the broader position that Shakespeare was a recusant writer. Working back from *Double Falsehood*, Wilson infers that *Cardenio* must have been a highly topical tragicomedy purpose-made, at the instigation of Catholic patrons, for the special circumstances and mood surrounding the funeral of James I's older son Henry, Prince of Wales, on 7 December 1612 and the near-synchronous wedding of the King's daughter Princess Elizabeth to Prince Frederick of the Rhine. Wilson makes the ingenious but speculative argument that *Cardenio* would have had in the background Frances Howard's arranged marriage with the Earl of Essex and intrigue with Robert Carr, Viscount Rochester. Since Shelton dedicated his translation of Cervantes to Theophilus, Lord Howard de Walden, and the Howard family were in a sense sponsors of it, they would have seen themselves in the play. The play is to Wilson a virtual *pièce à clef*, where the Duke represents King James; Henriquez, Prince Henry; Leonora, Frances Howard; and Cardenio/Julio, Robert Carr.[1] Julia Briggs, less inclined to view the play as a direct commentary on contemporaneous events almost in the mode of Middleton's *A Game at Chess*, stresses its discords, treating *Henry VIII*, *Cardenio* and *The Two Noble Kinsmen* as a coherent group of plays all equally interested in depicting a bleak world, presided over neither by the pagan deities of *Pericles*, *Cymbeline* and *The Winter's Tale* nor by Prospero, in which one person's happiness (be it that of Anne Boleyn, Henriquez, or Palamon) can only ever be achieved at someone else's expense. She sees *The Two Noble Kinsmen* as a play which followed *Cardenio* and perfected some of what she discerns as its structure, conceiving Violante as a precursor of the Jailer's Daughter and the role of the (added) Duke Angelo as paralleled by that of Theseus (Briggs, 'Tears'). Charles Frey, although more inclined to detect similarities with the earlier romances, similarly draws close parallels between *Cardenio* and *The Two Noble Kinsmen*, considering Julio as comparable to Palamon and Henriquez to Arcite: the former are 'relatively passive', worshippers of women rather than enjoyers, while their counterparts, 'more lusty-active', 'have less right and [are] presented with less sympathetic interiority of love' (Frey, 311). Frey assumes that Don Quixote did appear in *Cardenio*, and regards

---

1   Wilson, *Shakespeare*. As Richard Proudfoot points out, however, Wilson's argument depends to an extent on retaining the Cervantic name Cardenio (so that it can refer to Robert Carr), while deploying Theobald's name Henriquez (rather than the Cervantic Fernando) so that it can refer to Prince Henry (Proudfoot, *Shakespeare*, 80–1). Would audiences really recognize the puritanically inclined Prince Henry Stuart in the libertine character of Henriquez? From what is known of him, he more closely resembled Roderick. See for example J.W. Williamson, *The Myth of the Conqueror. Prince Henry Stuart: A Study of 17th Century Personation* (New York, 1978), 129. Nothing is done, in Wilson's reading, with the character of Violante.

him rather than Dorotea/Violante as the play's precursor of the Jailer's Daughter.

FROM *CARDENIO* TO *DOUBLE FALSEHOOD*

Let us now turn from these conjectural reconstructions of Shakespeare and Fletcher's *Cardenio* to the text we actually have in *Double Falsehood*. In the form in which Theobald published it, the play is a simple enough exercise in early eighteenth-century love-and-honour intrigue, though with enough interesting discrepancies of style and structure both to vindicate most of Theobald's claims for its provenance and to suggest that another adapter too may have been involved in rewriting *Cardenio* before Theobald himself set about his own redactions.

Compared with the single-authored late romantic tragicomedies of Shakespeare, *Double Falsehood* is lacking in complexity. It has a linear structure, the only complication being that there are two victims of Henriquez's baseness. He is false both to Julio and Leonora and to Violante. The initial anti-comic drive, Don Bernard's demand that Leonora give her hand where her heart cannot follow, is presented only in domestic terms. In most of the plays in which Fletcher collaborated from around 1610, including his collaborations with Shakespeare, politics is an issue. Powerful, independent protagonists will have their loyalty to a corrupt and absolute leader tested to the full, sometimes by that leader's attempts to seduce the protagonist's loved one. *Double Falsehood* does not raise the question of leadership or the proper exercise of power. The ending of the play is more comic than tragicomic. There is no punishment and very little mortification for Henriquez; no figure who remains wholly outside the harmonious social arrangements of the ending (though Camillo is made to wait); no persisting melancholic sense of the fallen world remaining; nothing of the supernatural or the miraculous; no sense of the cyclical in human life, the young atoning for the sins of an older generation; nothing that lends itself to any form of quasi-religious or allegorizing interpretation; and the ending is the celebratory one in which existing social arrangements are strengthened by love and marriage. Despite the various echoes of situations that occur in other Shakespearean romantic tragi-comedies or 'problem' plays – the recognitions that remind us of *Pericles*, and Violante's managing of Henriquez's exposure that is very like the endings of *Two Gentlemen of Verona*, *Measure for Measure* and *All's Well* – our sense of the ending is not similar to our sense of the endings of Shakespeare's last plays.

Supplementing some of the stylometric evidence given below, however (see pp. 99ff.), experienced readers of Shakespeare certainly have intuited the presence of *echt* Shakespeare in the text on the linguistic level. Kenneth Muir, for example, points to the use of 'heirs' as a verb in the opening scene:

> worthy the man
> Who with my dukedoms heirs my better glories
> (1.1.7–8)

He singles out the Duke's line 'But I, by fears weighing his unweigh'd course' (1.1.24), Julio's soliloquy 'I do not see that fervour in the maid' (1.2.63–77), and the Julio–Leonora exchange beginning 'Urge not suspicions of what cannot be' (1.2.106–16) (Muir, *Shakespeare*, 156–9). To this might be added the prose exchange that opens 5.2 between the Duke, Don Bernard and Camillo, which, in its bawdy, is not a typical feature of tragicomedies written in Theobald's period. Fletcher is more easily camouflaged by Restoration and later language, but the entirety of Act 4 has a Fletcherian atmosphere, as has Don Bernard's near-miraculous penitence at the close of Act 3. In 4.1, there is precisely the dramatization of surprising incident and shifting emotion that one associates with Fletcher. The scene most resembles the Welsh portions of *Cymbeline*: the transvestite Violante lives amongst the shepherds as Imogen lives with Belarius and his sons, while the virtuous Roderick saves her from the Master just as Guiderius saves Imogen from Cloten. Within this framework, the way in which our emotions are manipulated by Julio's whirling words, his violence towards the Second Shepherd, the soothing beauty of Violante's song, the Master's attempted rape, Roderick's nick-of-time appearance and the return to the stage of the villain Henriquez with Roderick's seeming subscription to his plan to abduct Leonora, is typical of Fletcherian manipulation of the audience's emotions.

The relative unsubtlety and lack of sophistication of *Double Falsehood* (when judged against the standards of Shakespeare's and Shakespeare–Fletcher's plays) can be attributed to its status as an adaptation, and indeed some of its imperfections as eighteenth-century drama serve to confirm Theobald's claims for it as a Jacobean play. An eighteenth-century redaction of a Shakespeare–Fletcher collaboration would certainly be shorter than the original, and the play as we have it bears all the signs of having been cut down from a longer piece. As both Eduard Castle and John Freehafer have observed, the gaps, incoherences, inadequacies of motivation and awkwardnesses of pace militate strongly against the view that Theobald composed it from scratch, since he would have had to build in the imperfections (Castle, 196–7; Freehafer). It is far more likely that there was an *ur*-text that he wanted to compress. In the first scene, an opening that groans somewhat under the weight of its own exposition, the Duke declares his misgivings about his louche younger son. This father–son relationship is never further developed. Roderick declares that he is awaiting Julio's arrival; yet in scene 2, Julio is summoned to court by letter. Scene 2 begins a 'reluctant mistress' theme, as Leonora capriciously tantalizes Julio with the refusal of her hand, but this interest is abandoned at once. Scene 3 introduces the collateral action of Henriquez's making love to Violante, but it is not explained here or elsewhere what Violante's relationship is to the other characters in the Dramatis Personae. When Act 4 closes on the 'curtain' of Violante's recognition of Julio, the audience does not know how those characters came to be acquainted. Although Act 1 ends with Violante sending Henriquez firmly about his business, at the opening of Act 2 he has clearly done that business. This lacuna is in itself unsatisfactory, but the stagecraft makes it worse. His post-coital confession is overheard by two characters, Fabian and Lopez, who never appear again. They may possibly be the remains of a low-life comic element to the play that came under Theobald's excising pencil. At the end of 2.3 Leonora's father, Don Bernard, rejects Camillo's offer of Julio's hand. The sequence is very compressed; and instead of Camillo's gradually realizing that Don Bernard is playing him false, he catches on with implausible rapidity. Earlier in the same scene, Leonora has been appealing to Henriquez's conscience by asking him to recall Julio's 'services, his well-tried faith' (91), but there is no scene between Henriquez and Julio that establishes their friendship's sacred bond. (There is such a scene between Amintor and Melantius in Fletcher's *The Maid's Tragedy* (1610), which is a useful comparator.) Possibly a scene is omitted between the end of Act 2 and the opening of Act 3, in which Julio would receive Leonora's letter and set out for the country.

There are fewer obvious difficulties with the latter half of the play, though it too has some sticky patches of stagecraft, for instance in 4.1 when Roderick, searching for his brother Henriquez, is at the same time receiving letters from him informing him of Leonora's whereabouts. Andalucia has a remarkably efficient postal system. At the close of 4.1, the brothers decide to dress as friars transporting a corpse in order to gain entrance to the nunnery, but this stratagem, with its apparent comic/spectacular possibilities, is not staged and is a wasted opportunity. Finally, in addition to these lesions that suggest revision, there are a number of 'verse fossils', as Pope called them, in the text, especially Henriquez's speech in 2.1 ('Now then to recollection', 20–31), which, as noted in the commentary, Pope observed was printed as prose but was actually verse.

From what kind of longer Restoration pre-text might *Double Falsehood* have been an abridgement? Various elements may strike the reader as belonging to the Restoration or later. There is much business with letters being handed down from windows. The stagecraft here is closer to Restoration than Jacobean. Also, many of the play's predicaments nod in the direction of the classic dilemmas of Restoration heroic drama. Thus, Leonora experiences her plight in terms of the conflict between love and duty:

> I conjure you,
> By all the tender interests of nature,
> By the chaste love 'twixt you and my dear mother
> (O holy heav'n, that she were living now!)
> Forgive and pity me. O sir, remember,
> I've heard my mother say a thousand times
> Her father would have forc'd her virgin choice,
> But when the conflict was 'twixt love and duty,
> Which should be first obey'd, my mother quickly
> Paid up her vows to love and married you.
>
> (2.3.104–13)

Later, in the passage that includes the line 'None but itself can be its parallel' so celebrated by Pope for its utter banality (see pp. 68–9 and Appendix 3), Julio apostrophizes the importance of friendship in typical Restoration fashion:

> Is there a treachery like this in baseness
> Recorded anywhere? It is the deepest.
> None but itself can be its parallel –
> And from a friend profess'd! Friendship? Why, 'tis
> A word forever maim'd. In human nature
> It was a thing the noblest
>
> (3.1.15–20)

Sentiments like these, and what Robert D. Hume would call 'honour-mongering', are typical of the play that began the fashion for Spanish romances in the Restoration, Sir Samuel Tuke's and the Earl of Bristol's *The Adventures of Five Hours*

(1663).[1] This play, an adaptation of *Los empeños de seis horas* by Antonio Coello, although long thought to be by Calderón, is a tragicomedy incorporating love/honour dilemmas that move towards heroic drama but also involve mistaken identity, darkness and disguise. This very successful trendsetting play may have served as a model for a notional Davenant/Betterton Restoration version of *Cardenio*. Tuke's protagonist, the choleric and jealous Henrique, is not unlike Henriquez. Both plays demand rapid scenery changes and both have eight principal characters, so that, since Tuke's play was presented by the Duke's company at Lincoln's Inn Fields – as the notional Bettertonian *Cardenio* would have been – both could have been similarly cast. In passing, it might be noted that there is in *Five Hours* a line every bit as self-reflexive as the infamous 'None but itself . . .'; Antonio says to Porcia in Act 4, 'Your own clear mind's the Glass, which to your self / Reflects your self'.[2] Perhaps the fatuous line that gave Theobald so much trouble is a Restoration carry-over.

If a version of the Cardenio story did exist in the Restoration, in the form of a play by Shakespeare and Fletcher, it seems likely that Davenant's company would have found it an attractive proposition to modify. The resultant text would satisfy the demand for Shakespearean adaptations as well as for Spanish plays, especially if the original were modified in the direction of Tuke – if the sentiments were exalted, some extravagant action such as abduction from a nunnery inserted, and a suitable low-life comic character supplied. The other essential would be to prune away a great deal of the Shakespeare. As I have already remarked, there is an analogue to the textual situation I propose for *Double Falsehood* in the relationship between Shakespeare and Fletcher's *The Two Noble Kinsmen* and Davenant's Restoration

1 Hume, *Drama*, 73–8. His account suggests other parallels that would enable us to read *Double Falsehood* as a latter-day Restoration Spanish play.
2 Tuke, *Five Hours*, p. 79. B. Van Thal's edition takes as copy-text the third impression of 1671, revised by the author, in which the lines appear. This printing introduces some 330 new lines not present in the first printed edition.

adaptation published in 1668, though performed in 1664, called *The Rivals*.

Davenant's main objective as an adapter was domestication. He removed all the elements of ritual, mythology and medievalism from *The Two Noble Kinsmen*. This amounted to amputating virtually all of the first and last acts of the existing play. Modern editors give the entire first act of *Kinsmen*, and the first scene of Act 5, to Shakespeare (Vickers, 402ff.). In *The Rivals*, the three Queens are excised completely, the mythological pair Theseus and Hippolyta are reduced to a single duke (Arcon) with workaday anxieties about his lack of an heir; and the magnificent ending in which Palemon, Arcite and Emilia pray to their respective divinities is replaced by a banal test of virtue written in heroic couplets. The Jailer and his Daughter are raised in social status, becoming a Provost and Celania, so that there is a qualified candidate to marry the disappointed rival at the end. This is, of course, the major difference. Shakespeare's tragicomic ending, in which Arcite wins Emilia's hand, only to die accidentally and, in dying, bless her union with Palemon (thus satisfying both legal and natural justice), is altered to a comic ending in which Philander weds Celania because she is constant, and Theocles wins Heraclia by a crude process of elimination. Like *Double Falsehood*, *The Rivals* does not make the demands on the audience required by late Shakespearean tragicomedy. Instead of the comic interlude that the Schoolmaster and his country dancers afford in *Kinsmen*, Davenant offers a more seemly hunting masque (Celania too bears her madness in a more seemly fashion than the Jailer's Daughter); and to provide the comedy, Davenant invents a low-life turnkey called Cunopes, ludicrously in love with Celania. Like *Double Falsehood*, the moral terrain is the familiar love/honour dilemma, as expressed in this speech by Philander:

> My heart did first Heraclia's captive prove,
> To her, I am oblig'd in bonds of love.

Celania gave my person liberty.
To her by honour I shou'd grateful be.
I owe my self to both, what shall I doe
To be in Love, and yet to honour true.
(Davenant, *Rivals*, 5.1, pp. 55–6)

Songs are added and the list of principals reduced to the Restoration norm of nine. In short, we are well on the way towards the kind of play that Theobald would have sanctioned sixty years later.

It is noteworthy also that Davenant here changes the names of his principal characters, just as the names of the characters in *Double Falsehood* were changed. In the original *Cardenio* the characters may well have retained, like the eponymous hero, names provided in *Don Quixote*. This, however, might conceivably have been one of Theobald's own contributions to the play, motivated by the continuing presence in the early eighteenth-century theatrical repertory of Thomas D'Urfey's three-part *The Comical History of Don Quixote*, which tells the Cardenio story in part 1 and retains Cardenio and Luscinda as characters in part 2. D'Urfey's part 2 was actually revived at Lincoln's Inn Fields in the same season that saw the premiere of *Double Falsehood*, and Theobald may have been reluctant to have his own version of what he thought of as Shakespeare's Cardenio play look like a direct competitor with an established low-comedy musical that dealt with the same material, albeit in an entirely different style.[1]

Consideration of the characters' names strengthens the view developing here that *Double Falsehood* is a palimpsest that contains elements dating back to *c.* 1611–12, elements dating to the mid-1660s, and elements first introduced in the mid-to-late 1720s. The original play presumably used the Cervantic names

1   There is no similarity between D'Urfey's burlesque treatment of the Cardenio story in *Don Quixote* and the version of it presented in *Double Falsehood*. D'Urfey has Fernando rescue Luscinda from her convent and bring her to an inn, where Dorothea (*sic*) is already present. In the course of that single scene (3.1) Fernando is reconciled to Dorothea, and the rest of the action concerning this trio takes the form of recovering Cardenio and reuniting him with Luscinda.

for the main characters. Assuming that Thomas Betterton decided to alter them for his post-Restoration adaptation, perhaps to dilute somewhat the indebtedness to *Don Quixote*, he might have selected names that occur in later plays. The names Angelo, Henrique(z), Leonora and Violante could have derived from Fletcher and Massinger's *The Spanish Curate* (1622) and Shirley's *The Gamester* (1633).[1] Roderick might have been borrowed from Dryden's *The Rival Ladies* (1664), which features a character called Rodorick; and from Theobald's point of view the names (H)enriquez and Violante would both have been given more recent repertory currency by Dryden's *Don Sebastian* (1689), Violante also being used by John Crowne in the popular *Sir Courtly Nice* (1685) and by Susanna Centlivre in her very successful *The Wonder! A Woman Keeps a Secret* (1714).[2]

What further adjustments might Theobald himself have made to an inherited text that subjected Shakespeare and Fletcher's *Cardenio* to a treatment similar to that which Davenant had accorded *The Two Noble Kinsmen* in creating *The Rivals*? The text's extensive borrowings from *Hamlet* and other plays in the Shakespeare canon are noted in the commentary. This has raised the suspicion that Theobald might have been writing, as Muir said, 'with a copy of Shakespeare's works open in front of him' (Muir, *Shakespeare*, 154). Other possibilities exist, however. As Richard Proudfoot and David Frost, among others, have pointed out, the Beaumont and Fletcher canon is replete with borrowings from and echoes of Shakespeare, both of individual lines and of dramatic situations (Proudfoot, 'Dramatists'; Frost, *passim*). *Philaster* and *The Maid's Tragedy*, for example, are steeped in *Hamlet*. Even in those parts of *The Two Noble Kinsmen* that Fletcher is supposed to have written, 4.1 for example, the debt to Shakespeare is very strong. This scene is fashioned on Ophelia's

1 See Kahan, '*Spanish Curate*', for comment on the overlap in naming between the two plays.
2 See further the notes on the List of Roles.

56

mad scene in *Hamlet* and alludes to the willow song from *Othello* 4.3 (*TNK* 4.1.80).

It is overwhelmingly likely that Theobald's degree of immersion in Shakespeare would have resulted in a subconscious importation of even more echoes and allusions. We would expect Shakespeare's last and Beaumont and Fletcher's early plays to be reflected in *Double Falsehood*, but, as evidenced in the commentary, the dramatic structures of particular well-known scenes from earlier Shakespeare are also visibly reflected in the text as we have it. Amongst the most prominent are the 'closet' scene from *Hamlet* (3.4), the 'trial' scene from *King Lear* (3.6), the 'Patience on a monument' encounter between Viola and Orsino in *Twelfth Night* (2.4), three scenes in *The Two Gentlemen of Verona* (1.2, 1.3 and 4.2), the encounter between Prince Hal and his father from *1 Henry IV* (3.2), the betrayal of Hero in *Much Ado About Nothing* (4.1), the paired soliloquies of Angelo and Isabella that conclude *Measure for Measure* 2.2 and 2.4 – and somewhat less predictably, echoes of *Troilus and Cressida* and *The Rape of Lucrece*.[1] Theobald was particularly knowledgeable about Shakespeare's poetry, and given the thematic overlap between *Lucrece* and *Double Falsehood*, there is perhaps no real surprise here.

Another of Theobald's innovations was certainly the song in 4.2, Violante's 'Fond Echo, forego thy light strain'. Julio experiences the song in the mysterious way that Caliban experiences music on the island and Ferdinand hears Ariel's song in *The Tempest*. In context there is a Shakespearean texture to this passage of action. The lyrics, however, are probably Theobald's – though there may have been a song at this point in his source. The song is further discussed in Appendix 5.

Sooner or later, all scholars putting their minds to the *Cardenio/Double Falsehood* question will be forced upon speculation. Picking

---

1 See the following commentary notes: 3.2.66n. (*Ham*); 4.1.28–36, 40–8nn. (*KL*); 2.3.109–18n. (*TN*); 1.2.1–11, 3.1–27, 30, 40–6nn. (*TGV*); 1.1.16n. (*1H4*); 3.2.77.1–3n. (*MA*); 2.3.1–23n. (*MM*); 1.2.143–5n. (*TC*); 2.1.29, 2.3.104–6, 4.2.24nn. (*Luc*).

up from my opening summary of the issues involved, let me at this point, before turning to the eighteenth-century context, attempt to place *Double Falsehood* within an intelligible account of Shakespeare's later career. There are three other plays in which Shakespeare deals very directly with the theme of a man torn between two women: *The Two Gentlemen of Verona* (?1594–8), *Measure for Measure* (late 1604) and *All's Well That Ends Well* (1604/5). *The Two Noble Kinsmen* (1613/14) has some material in common, but it seems somewhat distanced from the others by its classical setting and Chaucerian origin, the different make-up of the love triangle and the tone of high-minded seriousness. Provoked, perhaps, by Fletcher's interest in Spanish material and knowledge of Cervantes, Shakespeare could see that there was remaining mileage in the situation of a man who betrays himself and his own better nature, forcing a woman to sexual relations perhaps with a promise of marriage. The potential rape in *Two Gentlemen* is here realized in a play that must manage the subsequent relations between a rapist and his victim. How will the play enable the marriage of Henriquez and Leonora with less unease than accompanies the endings of *Measure* and *All's Well*, despite the even greater extent of the mismatch? *Double Falsehood* is an imperfect record of one of Shakespeare's latest explorations of a recurrent theme in his work from *The Rape of Lucrece* onwards: the ways in which men and women deal differently with sexual guilt. Henriquez credits himself with unacted finer feelings while Violante is ready to debit herself with some complicity in her fall. Violante cannot be thought, in the play as we have it, to approach the level of perception and subtlety evidenced by Mariana or by Helena, as they consider just what happened in Angelo's garden-house or in Diana's bedroom. Julio's extreme reaction to his friend's sexual perfidy is less internalized and easier to manage through (mainly) Fletcher's adroitness in harnessing Cervantes' story for dramatic plot.

PARTY POLITICS AND CULTURAL POLITICS: *DOUBLE FALSEHOOD* IN CONTEXT

That Theobald never did speak 'more at large' about the play, as his revised preface promised (see p. 24), is the result, perhaps, of the quality of attention that it continued to solicit. His judgement that the danger of its being attacked was over by the publication of the second issue was premature. Press interest in the play persisted beyond what would usually have been accorded. *Double Falsehood* became a talking-point. It furnished, for example, the theme of one of the celebrated Orator Henley's tub-thumping orations. The *Weekly Journal, or British Gazetteer* for 23 December 1727 reports that 'the new play of Shakespear's affords [the eccentric Henley] a new theme, and from an Ecclesiastical Censor he is going to set up for a Theatrical Critique'. Henley's *Oratory Transactions* for 20 December 1727 records an entry 'On *Shakespear*, and the Tragick Muse, with a Critique on a present Dramatick Piece restor'd'. Along with other pro-government papers, the *British Journal* reprinted the Prologue to the play.

Newspapers were in the habit of advertising what was on at the theatre, but coverage beyond this was relatively unusual unless, like *The Beggar's Opera*, a play was sucked into the wider vortex of politics. All the signs are that Theobald's play became embroiled in the nascent war between Sir Robert Walpole's government and Henry St John, Lord Bolingbroke's opposition, to which the arts were often a second front in this period.[1] With and without the assistance of Theobald, Shakespeare himself was by the 1720s already caught up in a struggle to represent the true heart of the British nation, both his works and his authorial image subjected to rival claims by different political factions (see Dobson). The practice of rewriting his plays to make them

1 On the politicization of imaginative writing from the mid-1720s, there is an extensive literature. See Maynard Mack, *The Garden and the City* (Toronto and Oxford, 1969); Bertrand A. Goldgar, *Walpole and the Wits* (Lincoln, Neb., 1976); Brean S. Hammond, *Pope and Bolingbroke* (Columbia, Miss., 1984); and Gerrard.

support particular present-day agendas, commonplace since the Restoration, was still alive and well. In the wake of the Jacobite rebellion of 1715, for example, Shakespeare had been invoked on both sides of the quarrel between exiled Stuarts and arriviste Hanoverians: in *The Invader of His Country, or The Fatal Resentment* (1719), John Dennis made Caius Martius Coriolanus into a warning from history which the Stuarts ought to have heeded, while in 1716 both Christopher Bullock and Charles Johnson based farces attacking lower-class Jacobite supporters on the Induction to *The Taming of the Shrew* (both, confusingly, called *The Cobler of Preston*). The Jacobite statesman John Sheffield, Duke of Buckingham, by contrast, rewrote *Julius Caesar* (at this time usually understood as a proto-Whiggish vindication of constitutional liberty) to make it more supportive of Caesar's absolute royal power (in two parts, *The Tragedy of Julius Caesar, Altered* and *The Tragedy of Marcus Brutus*, written around 1716 but published only posthumously in 1723).[1] Theobald himself hedged his bets, producing in his 1720 version of *Richard II* a play which wallowed safely in the pathos of 'a Prince . . . Forc'd by his Subjects to Renounce his Throne' (Prologue, ll. 12–13), when the danger of any actual restoration of the Stuarts appeared to be safely over.

But more pervasive than such continuing bids to make particular plays speak locally to early eighteenth-century politics was a general sense that Shakespeare, rapidly coming to be seen as the greatest voice of his country's Elizabethan golden age, was himself worth co-opting as a spokesman of supposedly timeless and national virtues – which some saw as in the ascendant and some under threat, whether (depending on one's viewpoint) from a servile dependence on Continental art forms such as Italian opera, or from the corruptions of modern commerce and

---

1 See Michael Dobson, '"Accents yet unknown": canonization and the claiming of *Julius Caesar*', in Jean Marsden (ed.), *The Appropriation of Shakespeare* (Hemel Hempstead, England, 1991), 11–28. For the general background to the highly politicized aftermath of 1715, see Pat Rogers, *Pope and the Destiny of the Stuarts* (Oxford, 2005).

liberalism, or from the unchecked exertion of aristocratic power. In 1701, for example, Bevill Higgons had brought Shakespeare's ghost on to the stage of Lincoln's Inn Fields theatre to lament the unprecedented sexual perversity of modern London (in the Prologue to George Granville's adaptation of *The Merchant of Venice*, entitled *The Jew of Venice*). John Dennis, following suit in more epic mode, had deployed this authoritative spectre at Drury Lane to speak a prologue to *Julius Caesar* in which he (Shakespeare's ghost) claimed that it was his own Roman tragedy which had inspired Elizabeth I and her subjects to defeat the Spanish Armada. Theobald, as an adapter and as an editor, inevitably participated in this custody dispute over who could best speak for Shakespeare, or best put words into his mouth. It is one of the ironies of the *Double Falsehood* affair that, thanks to Theobald's labours, Shakespeare and Fletcher's reworking of part of the masterpiece of Spanish literature should have reappeared in a cultural climate which mandated its being provided with an epilogue celebrating Shakespeare for having helped '[humble] to the dust the pride of Spain' (36) – even if the irony is somewhat diminished by the observation that Fletcher's own respect for Spanish cultural achievement must be understood against a context of membership of an anti-court faction, all deeply interested in Spanish writing and all powerfully opposed to Spanish politics (see Darby & Samson).

Given this increasing participation of Shakespeare (or perhaps we should say the emerging Shakespeare 'brand') in public affairs, it is not surprising that *Double Falsehood* should have attracted the attention of the most influential government-sponsored newspaper of the day, the *London Journal*. Despite not normally carrying theatre news, it printed Philip Frowde's Prologue to *Double Falsehood* on the front page on 23 December and the Epilogue a week later. Another government organ, the *Weekly Journal, or British Gazetteer*, gave the play its most substantial contemporary notice on 10 February 1728. The *Gazetteer*'s critic, 'Dramaticus', was Sir William Yonge, who might aptly be described as Premier Minister Walpole's liaison officer with the press. Yonge (1693–1755) was Member of Parliament for Honiton from 1715 to 1754, and a very staunch Walpolean Whig. Although in 1727 he temporarily lost office as a Treasury lord on the accession of George II (who loathed him and referred to him as 'stinking Yonge'), he was restored to high office in the Admiralty in 1728. He was interested in the theatre, being responsible for an adaptation of a play by Richard Brome, *The Jovial Crew*, into operatic form in 1731. Given his concern for foreign policy and hatred of Jacobitism, he would have welcomed the patriotic and Whiggish aspects of *Double Falsehood*. Yonge/Dramaticus gave the play a 'rave' review:

> The Town found themselves rous'd from their Effeminacy and Infatuation; and summoned, upon the Peril of forfeiting all their Pretensions to common Understanding for the future, to pay their Obedience to the *celebrated Name*, that call'd them to the Theatre. By the unanimous Applause, with which this Play was receiv'd by considerable Audiences, for *Ten* Nights, the true Friends of the *Drama* had the Satisfaction of seeing that *Author* restor'd to his rightful Possession of the Stage, *whose* Works had been such an Ornament and Income to it, in his Life-time, and such an invaluable Legacy to it, after his Death.

Dramaticus's review is clearly partisan and is set in the context of a postulated corruption of public taste caused by the ascendancy over theatre programming of culturally valueless forms such as the Harlequinade pantomimes. The management of Drury Lane are given the credit for revitalizing the spirit of patriotism and restoring the true greatness of the English stage:

> They have bravely shewn a Resolution of redeeming, together with their own Credit, the common Sense and Dignity of their Audiences, by inviting them to a

Return of their old noble and rational Taste, by such
Performances, as are only able to reflect an Honour on
the Attention and Encouragement of a *British* People.
They have made the most handsome Attonement for,
and Acknowledgement of, their past Indiscretion, for
descending to enter into a scandalous Competitorship
with those, who were never judg'd capable of being in
the least Degree their Rivals, in aught, but the low and
despicable Absurdities, to which they prostituted their
Stage, in Opposition to them.

Dramaticus is relieved to find that Theobald had turned his
attention to serious work, abandoning the extravagance of his
operatic pantomimes such as *The Rape of Proserpine*, premiered
at Lincoln's Inn Fields in the previous season, with John Rich
(under his stage name Lun) playing the part of Harlequin, and
with spectacular effects designed by George Lambert.[1] Yonge
was trying to annexe the play for the government, reinforcing
through it Walpole's desired press image as the creator of a new
era of British prosperity, liberty and greatness.

As the party politics of the period went, there is a 'Whiggish'
cast to the *Double Falsehood* project. In so far as any party
allegiance can be detected in Theobald's work prior to *Double
Falsehood*, that allegiance is Whig. Theobald was seduced by
the Whig triumph represented by the production of Joseph
Addison's *Cato* in 1713 into writing *The Life and Character of
Marcus Portius Cato Uticensis ... Design'd for the Readers of
Cato, a Tragedy* (1713). Addison's play tells the story of Cato the
Stoic's opposition to the dictatorial ambitions of Caesar, com-
mitting suicide in the encircled town of Utica rather than submit

---

1   A typical stage direction reads: '*The Nymphs renew their Dance, and erect a Trophy,
    in honour to* Jupiter, *that is form'd of the Spoils of the Giants whom* Jupiter *overcame.
    An Earthquake is felt, and part of the Building falls; and through the Ruins of the fall'n
    Palace Mount Aetna appears, and emits Flames. Beneath, a Giant is seen to rise, but is
    dash'd to pieces by a Thunder-bolt hurld from* Jupiter' (6).

to the tyrannical Romans. As Theobald's brief biographical account of Cato emphasizes, he

> seem'd indeed design'd by Fate a Pattern of Integrity, in Opposition to the general Corruption of the Times; for he thought the only Way to be honest, was to run counter to the Age, and not be ashamed of his own Singularities, but his Contemporaries Vices.
>
> (*Cato*, 4)

Memorably, the play dramatizes Cato's reading of Plato's *Phaedo*, a treatise on the immortality of the soul, on his last night alive, and this Theobald translated into English, also in 1713, as *Plato's Dialogue of the Immortality of the Soul. Translated from the Greek, By Mr. Theobald, Author of the Life of Cato Uticensis*,

> *It being the very Treatise, which* Cato *read no less than twice before he kill'd himself: The Treatise which shew'd him all the Calamities of Life magnified and redoubled, which made him justly weary of so frail a Being, while it pointed out to him a bright Dependance of Futurity.*
>
> (*Plato*, sig. A2$^{\text{r-v}}$)

Theobald's classical and English heroes were those whom Christine Gerrard has shown to be typical of the early eighteenth-century Whigs, such as Sir Walter Ralegh (Gerrard, *passim*), about whom Theobald wrote his hagiographic and anti-Spanish 1719 *Memoirs*, a celebration of a great Elizabethan free spirit.

Before *Double Falsehood*, then, Theobald would have already been identified as a writer in the Whig interest. His alliance with Philip Frowde in that play would have cemented this identification. Frowde's Whig associations were of long standing. Addison had been his tutor at Oxford, and verses in Latin, purportedly his early work, were published in Addison's *Musarum Anglicanarum Analecta* collection of 1699.[1] His prologue to *Double Falsehood* is

---

1 See Peter Smithers, *The Life of Joseph Addison* (Oxford, 1954), 39–41.

an unctuous piece of government propaganda, going as far as to make the comparison between George II and Augustus that was frequently ironized by opposition writers:

> O, could the Bard, revisiting our light,
> Receive these honours done his shade tonight,
> How would he bless the scene this age displays,
> Transcending his Eliza's golden days!
> When great AUGUSTUS fills the British throne,
> And his lov'd consort makes the muse her own,
> How would he joy to see fair merit's claim
> Thus answer'd in his own reviving fame!
> How cry with pride – 'Oblivion I forgive;
> This my last child to latest times shall live:
> Lost to the world, well for the birth it stay'd;
> To this auspicious era well delay'd.'
>
> (29–40)[1]

Frowde, a writer strongly associated with the government, was squaring a debt to Theobald in contributing this prologue. In the previous season, Theobald had done him the same favour, writing a prologue for Frowde's *The Fall of Saguntum* premiered on 16 January 1727, which compares British virtues to those of the Saguntines, whose heroic resistance to the besieging army of Hannibal in 219 BCE is celebrated in the play. The Roman–Carthaginian treaty guaranteeing the independence of Saguntum was breached: and Theobald's prologue obscurely cautions the audience to avoid parallel malfeasances in contemporary European politics, perhaps referring to Russia's desertion of England and France in joining the interests of the Empire in August 1726:

> The brave Example pictur'd to your Eyes,
> Be just, and your own Virtues recognize:
> Applaud the Bard, whose artful Muse has known

---

1   See commentary (Prologue, 33n.) for Pope's later satirical comparison of George II and Augustus.

> To trace the Springs of Worth, so much your own.
> Our *British* Arms this gen'rous Pride avow,
> To guard Allies, – and Empires to bestow.
> (Frowde, *Saguntum*, ll. 21–6)

Frowde nailed his colours to the mast by dedicating the play to Walpole in fulsome terms:

> Yet so far, without any divining Gift, I can take upon me to pronounce, from my early knowledge of that first Dawn, and Promise of Genius in You at *Eton*, that while You bring the *Learning* and the *Arts* of Greece and Rome into the Cabinet; either *that* to instruct in the Depths of Reasoning; or these in the Rules of *Governing*; no Impression can ever be made to our Prejudice, from the *Intrigues* or *Menaces* of a *Foreign Power*.

Composed by a writer who would in the following year provide 'Verses on Her Majesty's Birthday' for Queen Caroline, *The Fall of Saguntum* is an obviously pro-government production, and in allying himself with it, Theobald was consciously identifying himself with the court Whig power bloc. Just as Theobald's prologue obscurely credits the Whig faction with restoring British greatness to the high seas, so Frowde would credit Theobald with restoring British greatness to the theatre. Theobald's own allegiance was made clear when he dedicated the published 1735 edition of his adaptation of John Webster's *The Duchess of Malfi* (called *The Fatal Secret*) to Walpole. The play was performed in 1733 at the height of the Excise Crisis, when Walpole's political future was at its most uncertain, and the dedication was a post-facto endorsement of Sir Robert's handling of that affair.

LEWIS THEOBALD AND ALEXANDER POPE

Inevitably, a play presented in this political context would become party fodder and its success would be contested. The extent to which artistic culture in general, and Shakespeare in particular, became politicized in the period is manifest in Theobald's struggle with Pope over possession of Shakespeare. To document this in detail would be to distract the reader from the main purpose of introducing *Double Falsehood*, so at this point only those details that have a direct bearing on the play will be included. Interested readers are referred to the fuller account in Appendix 1.

In 1725, Jacob Tonson the Younger published Pope's six-volume edition of Shakespeare, the first to appear since Nicholas Rowe's of 1714, also published by the firm of Tonson. In the following year, Theobald put out a study of Pope's edition of *Hamlet*, aggressively entitled *Shakespeare Restored: or a specimen of the many errors, as well committed, as unamended, by Mr Pope in his late edition of this poet. Designed not only to correct the said edition, but to restore the true reading of Shakespeare in all the editions ever yet published.* His comments have a thinly veiled ironic tone that quietly subverts the achievement of Pope's edition and his premises as an editor. Throughout this work, Pope is sneered at and mocked as an inadequate editor who failed to collate his text with the early Quartos. The analysis of Pope's *Hamlet* edition that follows, and the smaller-fount Appendix giving a sample of what Theobald could do to the rest of Pope's edition – the whole running to close on 200 pages – left readers in no doubt that Pope had met a powerful cultural adversary. Hard on the heels of *Shakespeare Restored*, *Double Falsehood* can clearly be seen as a bid for cultural ownership of the supremely valuable literary property that Shakespeare had become. As noted, the revised version of the Preface to *Double Falsehood* is an unmistakeable self-puff, probably directed to Tonson's attention: the stationer who had published Pope's edition of Shakespeare and who, as holder of the copyright, would certainly commission its successor. The booksellers, not the editors and scholars involved, held the copyright to Shakespeare's works.

By 1727, Pope was actively involved in the Opposition cell organized by his friend Henry St John, Lord Bolingbroke, based at the latter's residence at Dawley Farm, Middlesex. To Pope and his associates, *Double Falsehood* was an especially timely target – a point at which Theobald and hence his government sponsors were clearly vulnerable. Pope's first direct attack on the play was published in *Peri Bathous, or The Art of Sinking in Poetry*, in the third volume of *Miscellanies in Prose and Verse* by Pope and Jonathan Swift, on 8 March 1728, in the month in which John Watts published the second issue of the play itself. In chapter 7, Pope singled out and misquoted the line 'None but Itself can be its Parallel' from the play (3.1.17) as an unrivalled instance of bathos: Pope prints '*None but* himself *can be his* parallel'; and two further lines from a play that Pope wilfully mistitled *Double Distress* are also mocked.[1] Theobald replied to Pope in an article in *Mist's Weekly Journal* for 27 April 1728, in which he accused Pope of personal malice towards him brought about by his being 'right, in the Main, in my Corrections' of his Shakespeare. He defends the line 'None but Itself' by reference to what was doubtless intended to be an impressive series of parallel examples of similarly self-reflexive lines in the *Amphitryo* of Plautus and in various of Shakespeare's other plays.[2] Theobald's learning here, however, simply made him seem to conform more closely to the stereotype of the pedantic trifler whose obscure knowledge blinded him to beauty and truth alike, exactly the role in which Pope's mighty *Dunciad* would cast him later in the year.

The Dunciad, Pope's most important poem, was published in its first version in May 1728 with Theobald as the hero of the mock-epic, the individual who instantiates its central values as the hero does in classical epic. By April 1729, when *The Dunciad Variorum* appeared with its endless critical apparatus, the by-now notorious line 'None but Itself' had gained a lengthy explication

---

1 Pope, *Peri Bathous*, 31. See p. 310, n. 1, for Pope's other selections from *Double Falsehood*.
2 'Reply to Pope', 40–8. The letter is discussed further in Appendix 1.

which not only ridiculed Theobald's heavy-handedness as a textual editor, but also implied that the play was a forgery. (This accusation was particularly hurtful in that Theobald was due a benefit night of *Double Falsehood* on 21 April, a performance of which he would receive the profits: the more people stayed away on the grounds that the play wasn't really by Shakespeare, the less would Theobald earn.) Theobald had his defenders in the pamphlet war that followed the publication of *The Dunciad*,[1] but despite his attempts to prevent it, Pope's insinuation that he had forged a play and passed it off as Shakespeare's stuck.

Summarizing Pope's literary quarrel with Theobald (discussed in more detail in Appendix 1), it might be said that on the broad intellectual front it represented a late episode in the long-running quarrel between the ancients and the moderns that had begun in the seventeenth century. Theobald's method of textual criticism and passion for conjectural emendation were an inheritance from the eminent classical scholar Richard Bentley, who had been attacked for a generation by Swift, Pope, and others who considered themselves in the polite tradition of wit. Although Theobald actually thought of himself as an 'ancient' and several times excoriated 'modern' innovations, from Pope's perspective he was a scholar of the new methodical stamp, not of the older humane tradition. More narrowly considered, *Shakespeare Restored* and *Double Falsehood* represented an attempt to wrest from Pope the cultural capital of Shakespeare. Taking Shakespeare away from an editor in the laureate tradition – one great poet paying homage to another – and making him the property of an erudite critic seemed to Pope to be an unacceptable cultural shift, but it was exactly what the publisher

---

1 James Ralph, for example, defended Theobald in *Sawney, an Heroic Poem*, published in the *Monthly Chronicle* for 26 June 1728. For further information on the pamphlet wars following the publication of *Shakespeare Restored*, see J.V. Guerinot, *Pamphlet Attacks on Alexander Pope: A Descriptive Bibliography* (1969), indexed under 'Theobald'. The fuller context of Pope's quarrel with Theobald is described in Jones, ch. 4. The concern here is only with those aspects of it that affected *Double Falsehood*.

Tonson would do next after bringing out a second, corrected edition of Pope's Shakespeare in eight volumes at the height of the controversy in 1728. Further, as this introduction has already made clear, possession of Shakespeare also had party political implications having to do with the fierce identification that political leaders and their propaganda machines wished to make between the emerging 'Bard of Avon' and particular brands of patriotic Englishness.

THE AUTHORSHIP, PROVENANCE AND NATURE OF *DOUBLE FALSEHOOD*

The question of the authenticity or otherwise of *Double Falsehood* has been so intertwined with the question of Theobald's personality and whether he would have been capable of out-and-out forgery (as Pope and some of his contemporaries appeared to suspect) that it is as well to review briefly what is known of his life, character and connections to offset the hostile caricature so successfully disseminated by his opponents. The fullest accounts of Theobald's life are given by Peter Seary, both in his *Lewis Theobald and the Editing of Shakespeare* (1990) and in the *Oxford Dictionary of National Biography*, but even Seary's meticulous research leaves many aspects of Theobald's life untouched.[1] Seary records that his attorney father Peter died in 1690, two years after the birth of Lewis, who was raised in the household of his godfather, John Monson, later created Earl of Rockingham, but there is no record of his mother Mary's death. (Seary states that she had been housekeeper to the Rockingham family.) Theobald apparently married and left a son, Lewis junior, for whom employment was procured by Walpole in the Office of the Pells – the office of the Exchequer in which receipts written on parchments or 'pells' were housed; but nothing more

1 Seary, *Theobald*, especially chs 1 and 10. See also Seary, *ODNB*.

is known of either his wife or child. His own practice as a lawyer is shrouded in similar mystery.

Little detail is available about Theobald's friends and social circles, though it is known that the prompter at Lincoln's Inn Fields theatre, John Stede, was a lifelong friend; and that in the later 1720s, before he met William Warburton, Theobald was closely associated with the lawyer Matthew Concanen and a set that included John Dennis, James Moore-Smyth and Thomas Cooke – all literary opponents of Pope. Theobald did benefit from having influential connections, though his social grouping was never as star-studded as was Pope's. He refers, in the dedication to his translation of Aristophanes' *Clouds* (1715), in terms evoking the country-house ideal of domesticity, charity and profusion, to a gentleman with whom he lived for nearly a year. This was John Glanville of Broadhurston, Wiltshire, who protected him while, from April 1700, he received his education at a school in Isleworth, Middlesex. Also in 1715, in his translation of Sophocles' *Oedipus King of Thebes*, he expresses gratitude to the Earl of Rockingham for securing him 'against those Calamities, that might have crush'd me, thro' the Loss of a Father, and a decaying Fortune' (*Oedipus*, sig. A4ʳ). His dedication of *The Happy Captive* (1741) to Lady Monson expresses further gratitude for her father Lord Rockingham's part in helping him through the school where her brother, Lord Sondres, was also a pupil. The Boyles, earls of Orrery, were his other great patrons.

Curiously, Theobald's life and career seems in several respects to mirror that of his adversary Pope; and it is tempting to suggest that Pope may have seen him as a baleful alter ego, the kind of career hack-writer that he might himself have become if his star had not been more propitious. Theobald was baptized in Sittingbourne, Kent, on 2 April 1688, six weeks before Pope's birth in London. Both men were to die in 1744. Presumably lacking the necessary support, Theobald was not university educated: Pope was similarly deprived, though for the reason that he was excluded from attending university by penal anti-Catholic legislation. Although nominally Theobald worked in the legal profession, there is very little evidence that it occupied much of his time. From around 1708 onwards, he tried to make his living, as did Pope, as a professional man of letters in London, though he was much franker about it than was Pope, and would probably have admitted that he did not have Pope's genius for original composition. His life would be spent mainly in translation from the classics and in literary scholarship of the kind nowadays conducted principally by professional academics in universities.

Much of his literary career might seem to have been modelled on, or set up in response to, Pope's. In spring 1714, he came under contract to translate the *Odyssey* for the bookseller Bernard Lintot, who also published Pope's version of Homer. This was to be part of an immense project that would include several plays by Sophocles and some of the works of Horace (the latter would likewise occupy Pope in the 1730s), but only one book of the *Odyssey* appeared.[1] Neither did Theobald's lifelong ambition to publish a complete translation of the plays of Aeschylus ever bear fruit, though his works and correspondence are studded with references to it. He did, however, complete several translations from the Greek dramas of Sophocles and Aristophanes in the very busy years of 1714–15, when he was making a conscious attempt to be noticed by influential patrons and by the Whig literary-political establishment.

In Theobald's early writing career there are two currents of particular relevance to *Double Falsehood*. From 1714 onwards, he expresses an interest in being able to imitate Shakespeare; and some odour of forgery subsequently attaches to his work. His poem *The Cave of Poverty* (1715) is supposedly written in imitation of Shakespeare's *Venus and Adonis*, but although some scholars have found significant stylistic overlaps, it bears mainly

---

1   It is recorded in *ESTC* as printed for J. Roberts, 1717. See Seary, *Theobald*, 17n.

a formal relationship to that poem.[1] What perhaps *is* noteworthy about it, in view of the parallels between Theobald's career and Pope's, is that its representation of a cave inhabited by poor writers may have contributed to Pope's refiguring of poverty and dullness in the Goddess's cave in *The Dunciad*. Stanza 40 is one of several that are suggestive in those terms:

> Here, in small silent Dormitories, lay
> Clusters of Bards; who, when they struck the Lyre,
> Did thro' the Caverns Harmony convey;
> Awak'ning sprightly Love and gay Desire.
> > These did the World's vain Idol, Wealth, despise;
> > Panting for Fame, and the contested Prize.

In Theobald's poem, poverty is no disgrace. Far from it, it is the necessary spur to genuine creativity. If Pope stole a hint from Theobald, it would not be the only time in his career that he borrowed the clothes of those he would style 'dunces' for their pains.

Since some have suspected Theobald of having forged *Double Falsehood*, it is necessary to record that the stigma of plagiarism, if not of forgery, does attach to his name. The charge principally relates to his 1715 play *The Perfidious Brother* which, incidentally, features a character called Roderick, a name deployed again in *Double Falsehood* – and equally incidentally, but tellingly, has a title that alludes to Shakespeare's *The Tempest*.[2] After a performance at Lincoln's Inn Fields on 21 February 1716, a watchmaker called Henry Mesteyer claimed that he had put the entire script into the hands of Theobald, and he published

1 Thomas Lounsbury, in *The Text of Shakespeare* (New York, 1906), writes: 'The truth is that the production throughout adopts and reflects Shakespeare's phraseology. There is frequently in it a faint echo of his style, and of the peculiar melody of his versification. Such characteristics could have been manifested only by one who had become thoroughly steeped in his diction, and especially in that of his two principal poems. These were so far from being well known at that time that they were hardly known at all' (184). For a recent and meticulous assessment of the poem and its relationship to *Venus and Adonis*, see Pattison, 'King Tibbald', ch. 3.
2 See Prospero's lines: 'My brother, and thy uncle, called Antonio – / I pray thee mark me, that a brother should / Be so perfidious –' (*Tem* 1.2.66–8).

what purported to be his own original version of it in 1716. Theobald, in his preface to the play published in 1715 before it was performed, had already tried to pre-empt the eventuality of such an accusation, claiming that he had put in several months' work rendering Mesteyer's original stageworthy. Mesteyer published his version of the play with a furiously ironic dedication to Theobald:

> Your Fondness in Fathering of it, (tho' none of your own) is so uncommon a Piece of Generosity, as will find but few Followers in so degenerate an Age as this we live in . . . the major Part of the Authors of this Age are a Company of sly, cautious Plagiaries, pilfering here and there a Thought, or a Line, and so compounding an *Olio*, which they palm on the Town for their own.
>
> (Mesteyer, *Perfidious Brother*, sig. A2^{r-v})

Towards the end of his life, Theobald was again accused of being capable of taking the credit for the work of others – this time by William Warburton, future editor of Pope and of Shakespeare, with whom Theobald had corresponded amicably for several years prior to this quarrel. Warburton's own reputation in literary scholarship is certainly no higher than Theobald's, however; and Seary's account of their relationship makes it abundantly clear how untruthful Warburton could be (Seary, *Theobald*, ch. 7).

The Perfidious Brother is already heavily steeped in Shakespeare, depending for some of its jealousy-plot elements on *Othello*. Theobald's periodical *The Censor* refers epidemically to *Hamlet* and to *Othello*. Number 36 for 12 January 1717, for example, defends *Othello* from such earlier critics as Thomas Rymer who had ridiculed its flimsy plot. To Theobald, tragic plots work best if the fatal catastrophe is provoked by impetuosity of temper – a sponsorship of domestic tragedy. From 1719 onwards, however, after the appearance of his adaptation of *Richard II*, omitting the first and second acts in their entirety, Theobald's interest in Shakespeare is geared up to a higher plane. It is almost as if, having become involved in scriptwriting for John Rich's phenomenally successful pantomimes presented at Lincoln's Inn Fields in the 1720s – Theobald wrote *Harlequin a Sorcerer, with the Loves of Pluto and Proserpine* in 1725; and *The Rape of Proserpine, or the Birth and Adventures of Harlequin* in 1727 – he felt that he owed the stage and the scholarly world something better than that, or at least something that would guarantee his legitimacy and legacy as a writer despite his participation in a low form of entertainment. As an author of serious plays, he did not earn a great deal. Known figures suggest that he probably made £62 from *The Perfidious Brother* in 1716 and £71 from *Orestes* in 1731, whereas his last play, *The Fatal Secret*, was dismissed after the second night, netting some £28 for its one benefit.[1]

It was in dialogue with Pope and his Shakespeare edition that Theobald set out to become the leading Shakespearean scholar of the age. To forward this ambition, and to stake out this territory, *Shakespeare Restored* was published in 1726 and *Double Falsehood* followed in its wake, claiming an archival discovery that would establish Theobald's pre-eminence. Despite the whiff of unscrupulousness mentioned above, close study of his career does not suggest that Theobald was a likely forger. By the later 1720s, his overriding ambition was to make a lasting impression on Shakespearean scholarship. His chances of successfully passing off a forged play as authentically Shakespearean were remote, and the long-term consequences of failure would have been far too serious to risk. My view, outlined in the next section, is that Theobald did have a literary property that he at first considered to be a play composed solely by Shakespeare, but that he lost faith in it very soon after

1   See Judith Milhous and Robert D. Hume, 'Playwrights' remuneration in eighteenth-century London', *Harvard Library Bulletin* n.s. 10 (1999), 3–90. Theobald probably received modest flat fees for his pantomime work. Henry Fielding was the only dramatist to make a successful living from playwriting in the period 1708–60.

it was published, because he came to be convinced that it was, after all, far more likely to be a Shakespeare–Fletcher collaboration than pure Shakespeare.

THE PROBLEM OF AUTHORSHIP, OR WHAT DID THEOBALD KNOW, AND WHEN DID HE KNOW IT?

A small number of seventeenth-century documents, not all of which Theobald is likely to have seen, confirm the existence of a Cardenio play, probably written by Shakespeare and Fletcher, prior to the performance and publication of *Double Falsehood*. As noted earlier, two records of a play variously called 'Cardenno' and 'Cardenna' have come down to us from the King's Treasurer's accounts for 20 May and 8 June 1613, recording payments to the actor John Heminges (see Fig. 2 and n. 1, p. 9). These accounts are held to prove that a play based on the Cardenio story from *Don Quixote* was performed twice at court at the latter end of the 1612/13 theatrical season. This is entirely consistent with the bibliographical details surrounding the publication and translation of *Don Quixote* – as Theobald was at pains to establish, though with slight factual inaccuracy, in his second preface. The first part of *Don Quixote*, containing the Cardenio story, was published in Madrid in 1605, to immense and lasting acclaim, and was soon translated into other languages. Thomas Shelton, an Irish Catholic exile mainly resident in Brussels, produced an English translation in manuscript around 1607 which was finally published in London in 1612.[1] Even without Shelton's assistance, the appearance of Cervantes' masterpiece coincided with a general interest in England in all things Spanish, as James I negotiated peace at the Somerset House conference. At least some of the King's Men are known to have attended the conference in their

---

1 See Edwin B. Knowles, 'Thomas Shelton, translator of *Don Quixote*', *Studies in the Renaissance*, 5 (1958), 160–75.

livery: indeed, Shakespeare might have been one of them.[1]
The learning of Spanish for diplomatic and other purposes
increased accordingly (the first 'teach yourself Spanish' manual
printed in England for many years, Lewis Owen's *Key of the
Spanish Tongue*, appeared in 1605).

Don Quixote was the best-selling sensation of the hour when
James's grand English embassy reached Valladolid to ratify
peace terms in 1605, and the novel was clearly known, if only
by report, to some of Shakespeare and Fletcher's colleagues
in London as early as 1607. Some doubt attaches to the date
of composition of Beaumont's *The Knight of the Burning Pestle*
(printed in 1613), but its recent editor Michael Hattaway considers on the basis of internal evidence that it was first performed
around 1607 or 1608 (Hattaway, vii–ix). For the purposes of
this discussion, the important point is that in the introductory
epistle addressed to Robert Keysar, financier of the Children of
the Revels Company at Blackfriars from around 1606, Beaumont
writes: 'Perhaps it will be thought to be of the race of *Don
Quixote*: we both may confidently swear it is his elder above a
year; and therefore may (by virtue of his birthright) challenge
the wall of him' (Hattaway, 4).

Although it is not absolutely clear what Beaumont is claiming
here (does he claim to have anticipated the first Spanish edition
of *Don Quixote*, or the manuscript circulation of Shelton's translation, or its printed publication?), his boast of independence
from it testifies to the imaginative power wielded by *Quixote*.
Both Thomas Middleton and George Wilkins alluded to the
episode of Don Quixote's tilting at the windmills in *Your Five
Gallants* (1607) and *The Miseries of Enforced Marriage* (1607)
respectively. Jonson would himself allude to Don Quixote in

1 In August 1604 the Spanish Constable of Castile made an eighteen-day visit to
   London to negotiate peace with King James I. The King's Men were required to
   attend them throughout that period. Though they did not perform plays, they were
   required to wear their distinctive scarlet livery. See Gurr, *Shakespeare Company*, 51.

Epicene (1609) and *The Alchemist* (1610).[1] Shakespeare had used Iberian sources in translation before, and he and Fletcher would in any case have found it hard to ignore the immense impact of Shelton's version of *Don Quixote* on its publication in 1612. Modern Shakespearean scholarship establishes the likelihood that a play composed in the latter half of 1612 or early in 1613 would be a collaboration between Shakespeare and Fletcher, as were *The Two Noble Kinsmen* and *Henry VIII*, but in Theobald's time there was no awareness that Shakespeare worked in collaboration; and there might, for reasons we have considered, have been a strong vested interest in denying it.[2] Confirmation that the lost Cardenio play was a collaboration between Shakespeare and Fletcher comes, as I have noted, in the form of an entry in the Stationers' Register for 9 September 1653 made by the bookseller/publisher Humphrey Moseley (Fig. 7). Amidst a long list of playtexts that Moseley was recording as his own property occurs a reference to 'The History of Cardenio, by Mr. Fletcher. & Shakespeare.' It has been noticed that the full stop after Fletcher's name might suggest that Shakespeare's was added as an afterthought; and it has been surmised that this entry suggests the survival of at least one manuscript of the play down to the mid-seventeenth century (Freehafer, 504).

How much of this pre-history could Theobald have known? The earliest record of the above facts in the eighteenth century known to modern scholars is given in a 1782 Dublin revision of David E. Baker's *Biographia Dramatica, or a Companion to*

---

1 See Wilkins, *Miseries*, sig. F1ʳ; Middleton, *Works*, 626 (4.6.7–8); Jonson, *Epicene*, 4.1.51; *Alchemist*, 4.7.40.
2 See Bate, 79. McMullan, *Henry VIII*, puts the point very clearly and forcefully: 'The word "collaboration" itself can mislead. For one thing, since 1940 or thereabouts, it has been loaded with connotations of betrayal, of a catastrophic failure of integrity, a connection which in fact predates the Second World War, originating in romantic aesthetic obsessions with unity and individuality in the field of artistic/literary production . . . Collaboration, by definition, disperses the authority of the author, and . . . is not something that was welcomed by the dominant modes of textual interpretation in the twentieth century, dependent as they were on ideas of unity, integrity and creative independence' (181–2).

7   Humphrey Moseley's entry in the Stationers' Register for 9 September
1653, containing a reference to 'The History of Cardenio, by Mr. Fletcher.
& Shakespeare.' The entry is ten lines up from the bottom of the page.

the Playhouse. The distinguished Shakespeare scholar Edmond Malone (1741–1812) provided the entries:

> *Cardenio* – See *The History of Cardenio.* This play was acted at Court in the year 1613 ... *The History of Cardenio* A Play, by Mr. Fletcher and Shakespeare; entered on the books of the Stationers' Company Sept.9 1653; but I believe never printed. It has been suggested that this play may possibly be the same as *The Double Falshood*; afterwards brought to light by Mr. Theobald.
> (Malone, '*Cardinio*', 2.429, 155)

Until the late eighteenth century, then, the information that there once had been a Cardenio play had gone to ground; and, able scholar though he was, Theobald may not have known of it. It is not known for certain whether he ever consulted the Stationers' Register – there is only one authenticated reference to any consultation of the Register in this period – though Freehafer has argued, on the basis of the changes Theobald made to the date of Shelton's translation of *Don Quixote* between his first and second prefaces, that he may probably have done, and that he therefore probably did know the Moseley entry (Freehafer, 510). I believe it to be highly likely that Theobald *did* know it, though not on the grounds argued by Freehafer (see pp. 95–6). As to those changes, it is not necessary to argue that Theobald ever had to check the date of, or consult at all, Shelton's translation of *Don Quixote.* He knew Spanish well. His version of Webster's *The Duchess of Malfi*, published in 1735 as *The Fatal Secret*, for example, refers to Lope de Vega's *El Mayordomo de la Duquesa de Amalfi.* Commenting on this, Theobald writes:

> *I was in hopes to have glean'd something noble, and sprightly, from the* Spanish *Poet; but, to my Mortification, was heavily disappointed. There was but a single Thought, if I remember, that I could wish to have transplanted from his whole Play.* Antonio *standing confus'd to find himself*

alone with the Dutchess *in her Bedchamber, and she enquiring into the Reason of his Disorder, he replies:*

Si corriendo una cortina
Un Angel se descubriesse,
No era justo que temiesse
Ver su figura divina?
(*Fatal Secret*, sig. A5ʳ)[1]

The sale catalogue of Theobald's library specifies Spanish-language versions of *Don Quixote* corresponding to the first 1605 edition and another dated 1611. It does not list Shelton, suggesting that Theobald got his *Quixote* in the original and is therefore less likely to be responsible for the play's close verbal echoes of Shelton's translation.[2]

Better grounds for Theobald's knowledge of the Moseley entry are constituted by the existence in the Bodleian Library of an assignment made to Jacob Tonson the Younger on 5 April 1718 of those Moseley copyrights that had been sold on by him to the booksellers Thomas Cockerell and Dorman Newman. The manuscript (Bodleian MS Eng. misc. d. 493) is endorsed on its upper cover with the words 'Moseley's Copys. Assigned to me the fifth day of April 1718' (Fig. 8). There follows a catalogue of all the copyrights held by Moseley between 29 May 1630 and 8 August 1661, including the famous entry of 9 September 1653 listed on p. 30 as 'The History of Cardeino by Fletcher & Shakspear' amidst the same list that can be found in the

1 In translation: 'If in drawing back a curtain an Angel were revealed, was it not right that s/he should be fearful to see its divine face/countenance?' *Figura* is a word applied to Don Quixote when he is described in the original as 'The Knight of the Woeful Countenance'.
2 Corbett, items 28 and 193. Another item of Spanish interest is item 134: 'Lopez de Vego [*sic*], a Spanish Poet, with his Life in MSS. by Mr. Theobald'; and of general interest, item 460: 'One hundred ninety-five old English Plays in Quarto, some of them so scarce as not to be had at any Price; to many of which are Manuscript Notes and Remarks of Mr. Theobald's, all done up neatly in Boards, in single Plays'.

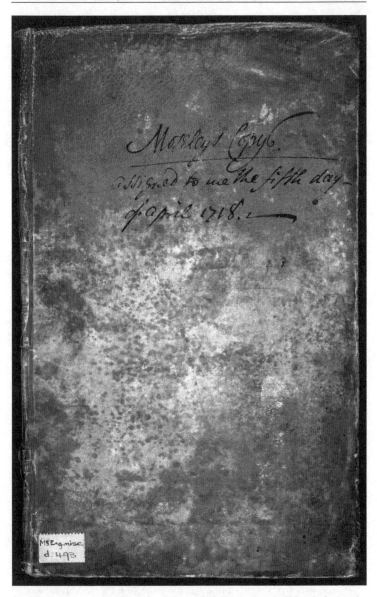

Moseley's Copy.

assigned to me the fifth day
of april 1718.

MSEng.misc.
d:493

8   The upper cover of Bodleian Library MS Eng. misc. d. 493, relating to the
copyrights held by Humphrey Moseley

Playes.
The Country Man
The Seige Cypres Davenant
The Jew of Venice & Tho: Decker
The woomon mistaken by Drew. & Davenpert
The History of Cardenio by Fletcher & Shakspear.
The Governer by Sr Cosm: Formido
The Kings mistresse
Beauty in a Trance by John Ford

Mens Distrubles Edited Woomen.

a Right woomon or womons
atward of woomans

no Witt no help like a Woomon by MV
The Puritan maide   Tho: Midleton
Modest wife
Wanton Widdaw

The Noble Chaire or y⁰ brater.

The Wandring Lovers or y⁰ Painter
The Jtalion night Piece or the
unfrtenete Pidly . . .

                                        H Mofeley?

9   Bodleian Library MS Eng. misc. d. 493, p. 30, containing the Moseley
    entry for 'The History of Cardeino by Fletcher & Shakespear'

Stationers' Register (Fig. 9).[1] After the list of copyrights, there is an 'Alphabeticall Table of Shop Copys which stand entred unto Mr. Humfry Moseley in the Register bookes of the Company of Stationers'. Here, 'History of Cardeino' is listed, but unlike some of the other entries, is not endorsed by a tick. On the final leaf is an agreement on the parts of John Sprint, Samuel Burrows and Elizabeth Bell to 'grant bargain sell assign or sett over' their right and title to 'one full moiety or half' the 'Copys of Books in the foregoing Book . . . which said Copys were purchased by us of Thomas Cockerill' in favour of Jacob Tonson. Sprint gained £100, and the others £50 each. The contract document, which is dated 5 April 1718, is witnessed by Benjamin Sprint and Robert Pollard – presumably for the sellers – and by Thomas Glenister, presumably for Tonson. The significance of the ticks with which some items, mainly literary properties, are endorsed, is not clear. (Does this mean that *Cardenio* was not one of the properties owned by Cockerell, and so not acquired by Tonson? Does it mean that there was no *actual* manuscript corresponding to the entry?) But it does at least suggest that the manuscript tantalizingly listed by Moseley in 1653 may still have been in existence.

It is true that the existence of this manuscript catalogue cannot prove beyond a doubt that in 1718 a copy of the Shakespeare–Fletcher *Cardenio* was extant and was acquired by the firm of publishers most closely associated with Shakespeare, the firm that commissioned both Rowe's and Pope's editions, and would go on to commission Theobald's. It is, however, a strong piece of circumstantial evidence, and might shed some light on an enigmatic reference to what might be the lost play in Charles Gildon's *The Postman Robbed of His Mail* (1719). Under the soubriquet 'Charles Dickson', Gildon writes to

---

1 I am greatly indebted to Richard Proudfoot, whose close scrutiny of the manuscript, concentrating on where the dot is placed over the minim of the letter *i* here and in the later index entry on fol. 38ᵛ, establishes that the spelling takes the form 'Cardeino'. This is closer to the Cardenno/Cardenna of the Chamber Accounts.

'Mr. Bickerstaff' of the *Tatler*, resenting the ignorant way in which the stage is run by a philistine management. The actor-managers have, for instance, rejected

> a valuable Jewel, lately brought to them by a Friend of mine, [that] might have had a Chance of obliging the Town with a noble Diversion. I mean, a Play written by *Beaumont* and *Fletcher*, and the immortal *Shakespear*, in the Maturity of his Judgment, a few Years before he dy'd. A Piece so excellent, that a Gentleman, who is allow'd a Master of the Stage, tells me, that after reading it seven times, it pleas'd and transported him, and that it is far beyond any of the Collegue Poets, and inferior to few of the other Poets which are in Print. There is infallible Proof that the Copy is genuine; yet this Rarity, this noble Piece of Antiquity, cannot make its way to the Stage, because a Person that is concern'd in it, is a Person, who of all Persons Mr. C[*ibber*] does not approve.
>
> (Gildon, 267–8)

Freehafer has argued that Gildon offered to the Drury Lane management the opportunity to produce *Cardenio*, which he had obtained from the sale of Betterton's library in 1710, part of an ingenious chain of speculations about the transmission of the three *Cardenio* manuscripts that Theobald had claimed he had in his possession. Freehafer thinks, taking into account what Theobald himself says in his first preface, that Sir William Davenant's prompter, John Downes, could have transcribed the play in 1661–7. Sir William's wife, Mary, Lady Davenant, who succeeded her husband as manager of the Duke's company, might have been the 'natural daughter' of Shakespeare mentioned, in the sense that she was the wife of the man rumoured to be Shakespeare's natural son. From her, Betterton might have acquired the play and might have contemplated staging it, as Theobald asserts (see Freehafer, 502). Whether Gildon was a later intermediary in the transaction by which Tonson might have come to possess *Cardenio*, or whether his was a separate copy, is not known; but Tonson seems the most immediately likely source for at least one of the *Cardenio* manuscripts deployed by Theobald in his adaptation.

If Tonson owned a copy of *Cardenio*, one wonders why he had not already put it at Pope's disposal before Theobald even entered the picture, given that Pope and Tonson had been collaborating on a new edition of Shakespeare since 1721, and both had placed an advertisement in the *Evening Post* for 21 October 1721 asking for 'old Editions of single Plays'. Perhaps, of course, he did do so, and Pope saw at once that whatever it was, it was not a single-authored play by Shakespeare. By 1726, however, Theobald's *Shakespeare Restored* had made two clear points to Tonson: first, the need for yet another edition of Shakespeare, as Pope's shelf-life would not be as lengthy as had been hoped; second, that no one but Theobald could be approached to perform the task. Tonson might have made the lost play available to him at that point. For his part, Theobald would have found it worth buying – worth, even, insisting that Tonson should sell it to him. What stronger endorsement of Theobald's claim to be the next in a succession of distinguished Shakespeare editors could be required than the ability to produce on the stage a play of Shakespeare's unknown for more than a hundred years? And this would be endorsement not only of Theobald, but also of a new kind of editor. Rowe and Pope were both distinguished men of letters, but they were not professional scholars – a species so newly emergent in the early century that they were still the objects of satire to such as Pope. *Double Falsehood* would be evidence of what Theobald could do for Shakespearean scholarship and of what the new methods of professional editing could achieve. Any forthcoming Shakespeare edition would be distinguished from all others by presenting a canon enlarged by a play to which the stigma of being apocryphal would not attach. It may be thought curious that, making such claims, Theobald would have mounted a production of a play *further adapted* by him, but David Scott Kastan makes the point that the relationship between Theobald's activity as an editor of Shakespeare and his activity as an adapter of him for the stage is a paradoxical one.[1] At the same time as adaptations for the stage became freer, textual editors tried to get closer than ever before to the text that Shakespeare actually composed. The performance and the printing of Shakespeare's plays were therefore increasingly disjunct. As Kastan writes:

> In the single figure of Lewis Theobald can be seen the era's schizophrenic relation to Shakespeare – always admiring, but, in one mode, presumptuously altering his plays for success on the stage, while, in another, determinedly seeking the authentic text in the succession of scholarly editions that followed Rowe's. The title page of Theobald's alteration – if that is what it is – of *Double Falsehood* economically makes the point, almost oxymoronically identifying it as 'Written Originally by *W.SHAKESPEARE*; And now Revis'd and Adapted to the Stage By Mr. Theobald, the Author of *Shakespeare Restor'd.*'
>
> (Kastan, 93)

It is also true that Theobald would have felt himself on stronger ground in claiming the proceeds from performances of a Shakespeare play he had adapted (and thus in some sense made himself the new author of) rather than of one he had merely bought. But it must be presumed that if *Cardenio* had survived into his edition of Shakespeare in 1733, it would have been printed in its original form unadapted by Theobald.

That it did not so survive is not surprising, though it has sometimes been used as an argument in favour of the view that *Double Falsehood* is entirely a forgery. Harriet C. Frazier takes this view. Writing before Stephan Kukowski and others

---

1 The point is also strongly made by Dobson, 8–11.

had conclusively demonstrated the hand of Fletcher in the play, she insists that Theobald forged the whole script himself. Inconsistently, she believes that Theobald was familiar with both the seventeenth-century references to a Shakespeare–Fletcher *Cardenio* play, though she can produce no evidence of this, but she still argues that he chose to base his alleged forgery on the Cardenio plot primarily to exploit Cervantes' popularity in eighteenth-century England. She is particularly struck by the high percentage of echoes of *Hamlet* in the text as it stands, noting the detailed work which Theobald had recently been doing on its early texts in *Shakespeare Restored* (Frazier, *Voices*, 35–7 and ch. 5 *passim*). A more recent proponent of the view that Shakespeare had no hand in what survives of *Cardenio* is Robert Fleissner, who is equally suspicious of the many echoes of *Hamlet* in *Double Falsehood*, though, unlike Frazier, Fleissner concedes that *Double Falsehood* is based on a genuine Fletcher dramatization of the Cardenio story. He discredits, however, Moseley's ascription of *Cardenio* as a collaboration with Shakespeare, and claims that Theobald himself must likewise have come to believe that *Cardenio* was solely written by Fletcher, making much of its non-appearance in Theobald's Shakespeare edition in 1733.

In 2004, the 'outright forgery' hypothesis is again represented in an edition of the play produced by Jeffrey Kahan:

> Given his problematic story concerning the play's discovery, the unexplained loss of the manuscripts, Theobald's interest in creating a 'classical' Shakespeare, Theobald's own plays and poems and his propensity to use other names to protect his own, it is logical to conclude that the play is not a Shakespeare/Fletcher.
>
> (Kahan 2004, 159)

There are, as Kahan rightly asserts, difficulties in accounting for the unremarked endurance of a literary property relating to the lost Shakespeare–Fletcher play. If Betterton possessed it during the Restoration period, why does no mention of it occur in any record and why did he not try to stage it? When Rowe began work on his Shakespeare edition, why did Betterton not put it at his disposal before the edition's publication (and Betterton's own death) in 1709?[1] Kahan's scholarly standards, regrettably, are not such as to inspire confidence in his views on such matters. Theobald nowhere claims, *pace* Kahan (160), that the oldest manuscript is in Shakespeare's own hand. Kahan writes that 'in 1728, Theobald transferred the rights to the *Double Falsehood* manuscripts to John Watts, who published the play twice that same year, and then reprinted the second edition in 1767' (161). There is no evidence that any *manuscripts* were conveyed to Watts – would that there were! And by 1767, Watts had been dead for nearly forty years. Reading on, we are told 'with certainty' that the 'Cardenno' and *Double Falsehood* are both based on chapter 9 of Cervantes' *Don Quixote* (163) – hardly a demonstrable contention in respect of the lost play. There follows a list of ten examples of parallel passages: extracts from *Double Falsehood* are compared with extracts from *Timon of Athens*, *Titus Andronicus*, *Cymbeline* and *The Rape of Lucrece*. In the absence of verbal similarities, Kahan bases his claims on 'parallels of dramatic intention' (165). As we have repeatedly seen, supposed allusions (even where they are convincing), can as easily support the forgery hypothesis as its opposite.

When, on p. 169, Theobald is credited with a play entitled *Harliquin* [*sic*] *a Sorcerer, with the Loves of Pluto and Persephine* [*sic*], the reader begins to wonder how well Kahan knows his author. He is wrong about the payment made by Watts for the copyright to *Double Falsehood* (170). What does one make of the statement that in 1715, when Theobald wrote *The Cave of*

---

1 Kahan's account of the difficulty in believing that there would not be more clamour in the press and elsewhere about a Shakespeare play said to exist during the period 1653–1727 is, as Edmund King argues in a paper given to the Cardenio Colloquium in Wellington, New Zealand, in May 2009, largely anachronistic (King, 'Theobald'). The Colloquium is further discussed on pp. 158–60.

Poverty, 'another work appeared that, although anonymous, has been repeatedly attributed to Theobald: "What D'Ya Call it?"' (174). This appears to be a reference to *The What D'ye Call It: A Tragi-Comi-Pastoral Farce. By Mr. Gay* – a work published by Lintot and owned as Gay's work on the title-page. Despite Kahan's footnote in which we learn that 'Pope attributed the work to Theobald in 1735', Pope knew perfectly well that Theobald did not write this hilarious parody because he and Arbuthnot both contributed material. Pope's ascription of it to Theobald was a typically Popean joke.

In his final paragraphs, Kahan uses Theobald's description of *Double Falsehood* as an '*Orphan* Play' to develop the beginnings of a conceit that makes Theobald the play's father. This line of thinking has been developed, with considerable elegance, by Neil Pattison. In May 2009 at the Queens' Arts Seminar in Queens' College, Cambridge, Neil Pattison gave a paper entitled '"O Brother! We shall sound the Depths of Falshood"', not yet in print as I write this, in which he made a suggestively brilliant argument in favour of forgery. Pattison spoke of the play's 'attestation of the ways in which the bad faith of the abject son can be made good by reparative sacrifice to the will of the father', and argued that 'in a certain sense the play itself represents Theobald's failed attempt at exactly such oblation' (Pattison, 'Brother'). Rehearsing some familiar and some less familiar evidence for Theobald's own acts of literary malfeasance, the most suggestive being Theobald's struggle with Pope in 1728–9 for 'rights of heredity in the works of their literary father' Wycherley, Pattison argued that a play about the search for the lost father is a quasi-allegorical figuration of Theobald's own anxieties. Possessing special political significance in the context of 1727/8 and the breach between George II and his errant son Frederick, given private autobiographical pathos by Theobald's desire for a more satisfactory paternity than life bestowed upon him, this Shakespearean adaptation is argued by Pattison to be 'a flawed forgery, a forgery that wants to be known as such; a forgery which only crudely, failingly, sublimates the concerns of its forger, who has marked the text with his anxieties, with his own barely withheld expressive purposes'. Pattison takes his place as one of the most engaging proponents of the outright forgery contention that we have seen espoused at various times in the history of the *Cardenio/Double Falsehood* conundrum. This contention does not convince: others, such as Freehafer and, more recently, Macdonald P. Jackson (see pp. 159–60), make the case for at least one hand prior to Theobald's own existing in the surviving text. It behoves us, however, to remain cautious.

It seems overwhelmingly likely that Theobald did not persist in the belief that Shakespeare was the sole author of the Cardenio play. He toughed it out in his first preface, but showed some signs of weakening in the second; and once the seeds of doubt were planted they must have grown. Nowadays it is common knowledge that collaboration was a fundamental, perhaps *the* fundamental, condition of authorship in Shakespeare's day. Brian Vickers's study of Shakespeare as co-author cites a statement made by G.E. Bentley to the effect that

> as many as half of the plays by professional dramatists in the period incorporated the writings at some date of more than one man. In the case of the 282 plays mentioned in Henslowe's diary . . . nearly two-thirds are the work of more than one man.
>
> (Vickers, 19–20)

Theobald, however, caught up in early-phase uncritical admiration for Shakespeare, was interested only in single authorship, and might have thought it hardly worth promoting *Cardenio* at all if he had believed from the outset that it was collaborative. He may also have come to suspect by 1733 that the manuscript or manuscripts he held, though substantially derived from an authentic Jacobean play, had already been subjected to some post-Restoration adaptation before even coming into his possession – a hypothesis which a close examination of *Double Falsehood* tends to support, as I suggest (pp. 54–5). There would have been no question, one assumes, of reprinting the play as part of the Shakespeare canon in 1733 if Theobald had significant doubts about its status as an unaided and unaltered work by Shakespeare, though in any case the final decision would have been Tonson's, and Tonson seems to have been more conservative than Theobald about the edition's potential scope. Seary argues that the agreement that Tonson and Theobald made to issue a re-edited Shakespeare, which survives as Bodleian MS Rawl. D.729, grants Theobald the rights only to the critical apparatus that he compiled and not to the contents of the edition, in which he would have had no say (Seary, *Theobald*, 215–18).

The question of why Theobald did not include *Double Falsehood* in his 1733 Shakespeare edition is discussed by Edmund King in a University of Auckland doctoral thesis. King reviews the 'copyright extension' argument propounded by Seary and further extended by Don-John Dugas, that Tonson used the Copyright Act to enable his editors to devise, and then sign over to him, 'a constant stream of new dedications, prefaces, notes, glossaries, and indices' and would thus have been able to create a perpetually self-renewing right in Shakespeare.

> In order to preserve this unbroken chain, Theobald would have been directed to use as the basis for his own text the most recent in the sequence, Pope's 1728 edition, and thus the boundaries of Pope's canon came to determine those of his own.
>
> (King, 'Shakespeare', 148)[1]

---

1 For the argument regarding the stranglehold gained on Shakespeare by the Tonsons through the manipulation of copyright, see Margreta de Grazia, *Shakespeare Verbatim: The Reproduction of Authenticity and the 1790 Apparatus* (Oxford, 1991), 191–202; Seary, *Theobald*, ch. 8; and Dugas, 190–2.

In fact there are some signs in the edition that Theobald's own enthusiasm, given its head, might have resulted in a larger canon. In the Preface to his seven-volume edition of *The Works of Shakespeare* (1733), he asserts that there are thirty-six genuine plays in the canon, 'to throw out of the Question those Seven, in which his Title is disputed: tho' I can, beyond all Controversy, prove some Touches in every one of them to come from his Pen' (1.vii).[1]

Fully three years before the articles were drawn up in October 1731 to publish Shakespeare, Theobald had sold *Double Falsehood* to Watts for a sum of money sufficient, one imagines, to recoup his investment in the project while it was still worth something (see p. 17). King reinforces Seary's supposition that Tonson was behind the acquisition – Watts was his printer after all – though he is less sure that the purchase would have included all of Theobald's manuscript holdings ('Shakespeare', 150). By that time, Theobald himself must have come to regard it as an embarrassment that the greatest Shakespearean scholar of the age, who bristled with such certainty in putting down Pope, could not at first sight distinguish the work of Shakespeare from that of Fletcher, and perhaps the work of both from a Restoration adapter such as Davenant or Betterton. If confessed, it would have been a humiliation on the scale of Lord Dacre's, when he failed to recognize the Hitler diaries as an obvious fraud.[2] King (152–7) stresses Theobald's fear of Pope's cultural

1   Theobald is referring here to the plays which Rowe, following the Third Folio, had added to the canon set by the First, i.e. *Pericles, The London Prodigal, Thomas, Lord Cromwell, Sir John Oldcastle, The Puritan, A Yorkshire Tragedy* and *Locrine.* Despite the conservatism in this regard of both Pope's edition and Theobald's (neither of which included even *Pericles*), the boundaries of the Shakespeare canon, and in particular the popular sense of what constituted Shakespearean comedy, were still flexible when *Double Falsehood* first appeared: Drury Lane theatre had advertised a performance of *The Puritan* as 'Written by William Shakespear, in the reign of King James the First' as recently as 1714.

2   In April 1983, the German news magazine *Stern* published extracts from what purported to be the diaries of Adolf Hitler, known as the *Hitler Diaries*, which were subsequently exposed as forgeries. Sir Hugh Trevor-Roper, Lord Dacre, was the Oxford historian and expert on the Second World War who erroneously authenticated the diaries.

power as the main reason why he dropped *Cardenio* – the action of a diffident man whose self-confidence was destroyed.

Scholars who examined the play in the period close to Theobald's own lifetime were unconvinced by it. The eminent Malone annotated a copy of the second issue, which survives in the Bodleian Library (Malone, *DF*). The annotations show his distrust, revealing that Malone considered Theobald to be working from a manuscript; and since he believed that the play was by Massinger, Malone must have thought that it was a manuscript in Massinger's hand that Theobald had open in front of him. Where, for example, the Dramatis Personae lists 'Duke *Angelo*', Malone notes: 'I believe this was an interpolation of Theobald's, to countenance his fraud. I suppose in the MS this person was only called *Duke*.' He notes, as did Richard Farmer (31), that Theobald himself claimed to be the author of Henriquez's lines 1.3.10–14: 'Strike up, my masters . . . convert to attention': 'Theobald asserted that he was the author of these five lines, & they were the only lines in the play that he wrote. I believe both these assertions to have been false.' In further notes, Malone identifies borrowings from Shakespeare and Massinger, including the line 'Throw all my gay comparisons aside' (1.3.73), which he identifies as taken from Shakespeare's *Antony and Cleopatra*,[1] and 'inserted by Theobald to give a colour to the imposition that he meant to put upon the publick' (sig. B6ᵛ).

Double Falsehood has continued to inspire diffidence in many Shakespearean scholars, reluctant to commit themselves too wholeheartedly to a view on its authenticity given the avowedly rewritten nature of the text that survives; but over the last hundred years a definite consensus has emerged among those who have studied the evidence thoroughly, to the effect that Theobald's adaptation is indeed what remains of an otherwise lost Shakespeare–Fletcher collaboration once called *Cardenio*. Proponents of the view that *Double Falsehood* bears partial

1 See 1.3.73n.

witness to an at least part-Shakespearean original have been arguing their case since the earliest days of the modern academic journal and the university-subsidized edition – see, for example, Gamaliel Bradford Jr's essay in *Modern Language Notes* in 1910, and the series of three articles published in *Notes and Queries* by E.H.C. Oliphant in 1919. Independently of Bradford, Oliphant came to the conclusion that from 3.3 onwards, 'a new voice became audible' and a 'firmer hand' apparent ('Double Falsehood', 61). Oliphant goes on to argue that Acts 4 and 5 are punctuated by speeches reminiscent of Fletcher; but the 'new voice' and the 'firmer hand' are unmistakeable in the first two speeches of 1.1; in 1.2, 1.3, 2.1, 2.2 and 3.1; in the first four speeches of 3.2 and again in the passage of action after the stage direction in which the scene opens out to a large hall; and finally in the three speeches of 4.1 that succeed Julio's entry (28–36, 40–50, 51–61). Oliphant ends by admitting, as Muir was to do later, that he has recanted an earlier scepticism and now does believe that the firmer hand is Shakespeare's. Oliphant suggested to Walter Graham that he should produce an edition of the play; and the introduction to Graham's 1920 Ohio edition recycles Oliphant's arguments with the addition of some valuable stylistic comparisons between Theobald's other adaptations and *Double Falsehood*, showing that the latter is very different from the rest.[1]

The tide turned decisively in favour of the view that *Double Falsehood* harbours an authentic Jacobean layer only after the publication of John Freehafer's influential essay in 1969. Freehafer's essay is, in my opinion, a remarkable piece of work, one of the finest essays, it may not be too sensational to assert, I have ever read on any literary subject. An inspired mixture of scholarship and speculation, the essay provides a genealogy for the manuscript that Theobald says is in Downes's hand: from Shakespeare himself to Davenant and Betterton, to Gildon, to

1 Graham 1920. See also Oliphant, *Beaumont and Fletcher*, 282–302; and Harbage.

Theobald's patron Orrery and thence to Theobald. His essay lays the groundwork for my own editorial conviction that *Double Falsehood* is a further redaction of an adaptation made in the Restoration of a collaborative play called *The History of Cardenio* by Shakespeare and Fletcher. There are some matters of detail on which I disagree with Freehafer, and I have added some new evidence: in particular, the evidence that Tonson may have been more instrumental than Gildon in the text's transmission, and the political and cultural context of Theobald's interest in Shakespeare and quarrel with Pope. But Freehafer's work is the more notable because shortly before the publication of this landmark essay, Frazier had begun to mount her challenge to the authenticity of Theobald's play in an article in *Comparative Drama* that was renewed at book length in 1974.[1] She reasons that Theobald somehow learned of the early performances of *Cardenio*, or of the Moseley entries, at about the time of Richard Knaplock's reissue in 1725 of Shelton's translation.[2] Swayed by his desire to link Shakespeare and Cervantes, and by commercial motives, he set about a deliberate forgery, the main evidence for which is the epidemic borrowing from *Hamlet*.

Given that challenge, the change of position recorded by the distinguished English Shakespearean Kenneth Muir between 1960 and 1970 is indicative of Freehafer's immense persuasive power. In 1960, in his book *Shakespeare as Collaborator*, Muir identified 'at least two passages that strike the reader as genuinely Elizabethan, though not Fletcherian' (1.2.63ff. and 1.2.106ff.), but he concluded that

> it is clearly impossible to come to any definite conclusions about *Double Falsehood* . . . But one can understand the desire to relieve Shakespeare of all

---

1 Frazier, 'Revision' and *Voices*; see also 'Forger'. Frazier does not discuss the part played by Fletcher, which is perhaps why she finds it possible to be persuaded by outright forgery as an explanation for the entire episode.

2 In 1725, a consortium of printers headed by Richard Knaplock published a reissue of Shelton's 1620 quarto edition of his translation of *Don Quixote*.

responsibility for a play which, at least in its present form, can add nothing to his reputation.

(148–60)

A year after the publication of Freehafer's essay, however, Muir, introducing a facsimile edition of the play, seemed to be more inclined to accept the presence of Shakespeare's hand, noticing

> a trick of Shakespeare's later style, which Fletcher also uses but not so frequently . . . internal rhyme in the same or adjacent lines . . . As this stylistic trick seems not to have been noticed by any previous critic, it would seem to support the view that Theobald really did have an authentic manuscript.[1]

Another powerful and crucial intervention in the debate was made in 1989 by G. Harold Metz, who had earlier signified his scholarly interest in non-canonical Shakespeare through an annotated bibliography of work on *Edward III*, *Sir Thomas More*, *The Two Noble Kinsmen* and *Cardenio* (Metz, *Four Plays and Sources*). Metz undertakes a meticulous and full account of all preceding scholarship on the issue (enabling me to avoid going over all the same ground) and raising crucial objections to those scholars, mainly Frazier and Paul Bertram, who had stressed Theobald's malfeasance.[2] Metz writes as follows:

> The evidence adduced and interpreted by the generality of scholars leads to the conclusion that there was a Shakespeare–Fletcher manuscript of a play entitled *The History of Cardenio*. This manuscript was the one that Moseley entered on the *Stationers' Register*. It found its way, along with an adapted version in Downes's hand, to Theobald. The Downes

1 Muir 1970. He cites 1.2.70–1; 1.3.67–8; 2.2.34–5, 41–5; and 2.3.21.
2 Bertram devotes ch. 4 of his book to the *Cardenio* problem (180–96). Bertram supports an argument that *Kinsmen* was written solely by Shakespeare with the hypothesis that *Cardenio* was not collaborative either. Shakespeare, he thinks, had nothing to do with it.

97

manuscript is likely to have been entitled *Double Falshood*, the title Theobald consistently employs, and may also have included other Restoration features of the play as it has come down to us. He revised it for the contemporary stage, the result being a drastic alteration of the first half and a less comprehensive editing of the last. In essence, *Double Falshood* is mainly Theobald, or Theobald and an earlier adapter, with a substantial admixture of Fletcher and a modicum of Shakespeare.

(Metz, *Sources*, 283)

This view is largely endorsed in this edition. Further support is found for it in recent years, albeit somewhat eccentrically expounded, by Henry Salerno, whose monograph *'Double Falshood' and Shakespeare's 'Cardenio': A Study of a 'Lost' Play* (2000) supports its arguments for the veracity of Theobald's claims for *Double Falsehood* with minutely compiled tables of phraseological echoes of other Shakespeare plays and of spellings unusual in 1728 but common in the First Folio, and further notes the play's unusually frequent use of hendiadys, a figure of speech Shakespeare had especially employed in *Hamlet*.[1]

The most telling recent evidence in favour of the play's authenticity has been provided by scholars more interested in the presence of Fletcher and of Shelton in the surviving text than in that of Shakespeare. In 1991 Stephan Kukowski's 'The hand of John Fletcher in *Double Falsehood*' identified a whole range of distinctively Fletcherian tricks of spelling, versification, vocabulary, phraseology, imagery and syntax in the latter half of the play (noting in passing that in this section of the

---

1 Echoes of Shakespearean phraseology, however, have been dismissed by earlier, hostile commentators as evidence merely of a diligent attempt at pastiche. Salerno, eccentrically, finds more Shakespeare in the latter half of the play than in the former – he reprints Acts 4 and 5 accordingly – and has little to say about Fletcher's co-authorship, finding the style of what he regards as the play's non-Shakespearean passages more reminiscent of Massinger. On the topic of hendiadys, see G.T. Wright's seminal essay 'Hendiadys and *Hamlet*', *PMLA*, 96 (1981), 168–93.

play there is a preference for the word 'has' to 'hath', a form largely confined to those earlier passages most often attributed to the more 'hath'-prone Shakespeare). Arguing that just such Fletcherian passages would have been most likely to survive Restoration and eighteenth-century adaptation, Kukowski concluded that their presence vindicated Theobald's honesty, if not his literary judgement:

> Although it is somewhat obscured by revision, the evidence we have is that the metre, the collocation of certain words, and the stylistic mannerisms of large parts of the play are distinctively Fletcherian. This does more than suggest Fletcher's presence in the play: it makes it clear that the play cannot be a forgery (unless, that is, Theobald had inadvertently forged the wrong writer); if the play is not a forgery, then the case for it being a relic of *Cardenio* is very strong.
>
> (Kukowski, 89)

This view has been endorsed by Jonathan Hope, whose analytical technique is more mindful than is Kukowski's of the complexity in respect of possible further adaptation by Theobald.[1] Hope describes his approach as 'socio-historical linguistic'. Calculated to recognize language as a changing process and to take into account the known facts about an author's background and social positioning, Hope's method is designed to use linguistic features impervious to scribal or compositorial interference. His evidence is derived from the use of the auxiliary 'do' and from relative markers ('who', 'which', 'that'), on the basis of which he finds clear indications of 'the presence of two hands in the text' (97), a very strong counter-argument to the forgery hypothesis. As for assignation of individual scenes, Hope feels reasonably confident in ascribing 1.2 to Shakespeare and 2.3, 4.1 and 5.2 to Fletcher. Greater emphasis on Fletcher in the work of Kukowski and Hope leads Fleissner to throw babies out with bathwater, however, arguing at article length that Fletcher

---

1 See also Bertram, 180–96.

was the sole author of *Double Falsehood*. 'To prolong the agony of misascription', opines Fleissner, 'would do justice neither to the British nor the Spanish genius' (227).

Coming at this from a different angle, A. Luis Pujante finds even more echoes of Shelton's *Don Quixote* in the play than had been recognized by earlier commentators (and no echoes of the subsequent translations which Theobald himself possessed). Pujante regards this circumstance as further evidence in favour of Theobald's having adapted a genuine collaborative 1612–13 Fletcher–Shakespeare *Cardenio*, itself probably still more closely based on Shelton's translation of Cervantes (which Pujante imagines open at the writers' elbows) than the surviving *Double Falsehood* lets on. The most 'scientific' approach to the authorship problem is that taken by Robert A.J. Matthews and Thomas V.N. Merriam, who apply to it the heavy artillery of 'a pattern recognition technique inspired by neurological research' (Matthews & Merriam, 203). They arrive at two networks – the Merriam-based and the Horton-based (devised by T.B. Horton in a 1987 University of Edinburgh doctoral thesis) – that provide algorithms for applying to the texts. Although the mathematics of this is too advanced to paraphrase, the results are broadly in line with earlier humanistic scholarship: 'this finding appears to add evidential weight to the view that, despite being the product of an eighteenth-century adaptation, *The Double Falsehood* [*sic*] has considerable Fletcherian characteristics' (209). Trained on individual acts, their method of analysis (which they recognize to be less reliable at that level of the text) finds Shakespeare more prominent in Acts 1, 2 and 4 and Fletcher in 3 and 5.

Without wishing to retread the ground already explored by such expert analysts, it is worth offering the reader some of the fruits of my own observation. Cyrus Hoy's pioneering work on Fletcher published in three articles in *Studies in Bibliography* in the 1950s established a checklist of characteristic Fletcherian usages by which one might distinguish his style from that of his collaborators (Hoy had Massinger particularly in mind). Most saliently, Fletcher has a decided preference for *has* over *hath* and for *does* over *doth*. Typically, he uses *ye* and *'em* (for 'them'), and has a fondness for the contractions *i'th'*, *o'th'*, *h'as* (for 'he has') and *'s* (for 'his'). Methodologically, Hoy has been superseded, but these usages are still deployed (for example by Kukowski) as a valuable indicator of Fletcher's stylistic presence. Tabulating their occurrence in *Double Falsehood* produces the result shown in Table 1.

The other most prominent identifier of Fletcher's style is his addiction to the feminine ending.[1] Tabulating their occurrence in the verse portions scene by scene produces the result shown in Table 2.[2]

What can be inferred from the combination of these two tables is limited. As McMullan has pointed out in a valuable discussion of attribution in collaborative playwriting, there are limits to what even very sophisticated forms of stylistic analysis (such as Hope's) can achieve:

> the quest for a stable 'fingerprint' which will be applicable to a given playwright, even one which takes into account the social and contextual construction of his 'style', conflicts with the basic instabilities and practicalities of the playwriting process in the early modern period.
>
> (McMullan, *Henry VIII*, 196)

So much the more complex will be a case such as the one now being considered, where we are trying to identify Shakespeare's hand, Fletcher's, Theobald's and possibly that of an unknown Restoration adapter. Due warning having been given, the analysis can be taken to support Fletcher's dominance of the writing from 3.3 onwards. This is close

---

1   An iambic pentameter line ending with an extra, unstressed syllable is designated a 'feminine' ending. Violante's line at 3.3.118, 'I would your brother had but half your virtue!', is an example. This contains eleven syllables, the final one unstressed.

2   I am grateful for Richard Proudfoot's assistance in compiling the table.

Table 1   Fletcherian usages in *Double Falsehood*

Act/scene	1.1	1.2	1.3	2.1	2.2	2.3	2.4	3.1	3.2	3.3	4.1	4.2	5.1	5.2
hath	2	2							4		2			
has		5			1	4			2	6	8	3	5	15
doth	1	1	1											
does			1	1		1			1	1	3			
ye						2				1				
'em		1	1				2	1	1		1			3
i'th'											2			
o'th'									1					1
~'s [= his]											2			
Sh'as/H'as[a]						1			1					

[a] *Sh'as* and *H'as* are modernized to *She's* and *He's* in this edition.

Table 2   Feminine endings in *Double Falsehood*

Act/scene	Verse lines	Feminine endings	
		Total	Percentage
1.1	48	17	35.4
1.2	124	44	35.5
1.3	77	33	42.9
2.1	32	3[a]	9.4
2.2	34	15	44.1
2.3	120	40	33.3
2.4	39	10	25.6
3.1	42	21	50
3.2	169	68	40.2
3.3	154	76	49.4
4.1	189	69	36.5
4.2	116	54	46.6
5.1	82	36	44
5.2	257	115	44.7

[a] Note that in this, as in other scenes, it would be possible to calculate the number of feminine endings differently. No two readers would necessarily count alike. Lines 13, 15 and 30 end with unstressed syllables. Some might consider 29, 'The time and place and opportunity', to have a feminine ending. It is, though, an entirely regular iambic pentameter, so I have not counted it. The pronunciation of proper names is another factor that radically affects the count.

to the consensus that has developed from Bradford and Oliphant to Muir about the way the collaboration worked and the division of labour in individual acts, but is not in agreement with the result produced by Matthews and Merriam. Although the idea that collaborators in the early seventeenth century worked simultaneously on scenes is not one that finds favour in the scholarly literature on the topic, it does seem likely that Fletcher may have retouched scenes drafted by Shakespeare. He is certainly not absent from the early scenes. Act 3 scene 2 is an interesting case. There are lexical items ('hoarded', 91; 'vassal', 128) found in Shakespeare's *oeuvre* but not in Fletcher's, as recorded in the commentary.[1] It is a scene very rich in allusion to Shakespeare's plays. On the Hoy checklist, however, Fletcher has some presence in the scene. *Pace* Matthews and Merriam, a commonsense view might be that Fletcher would not have been excluded from the writing of Act 4, because he was a pioneering writer of pastoral tragicomedy in *The Faithful Shepherdess* of 1608. Hope's confidence that 4.1 and 5.2 can be ascribed to Fletcher is reflected in my own analysis.

Moving towards the year 2000, the genuine basis of *Double Falsehood* in a Renaissance predecessor is endorsed by leading Shakespearean scholars. In *The Genius of Shakespeare*, Jonathan Bate writes: 'The inference has to be that Theobald's play is indeed a version of *Cardenio*, which Shakespeare and Fletcher must have written while Thomas Shelton's 1612 translation was new and popular' (80). The metaphor of *Double Falsehood* containing the 'ghost' of *Cardenio* is developed by Jennifer Richards and James Knowles in their introduction to *Shakespeare's Late Plays: New Readings*, where they argue that

> It is the appearance of a text, however mutilated, attributed to Shakespeare at a point when his collaborations were unrecognised and the existence of *Cardenio* unknown, which makes the possibility that *Double Falshood* embodies the *ghost* of Shakespeare and Fletcher's play so likely.
>
> (Richards & Knowles, 19)

Richard Proudfoot, in *Shakespeare: Text, Stage and Canon*, expresses 'little doubt that in *Double Falsehood* we have a text that may be characterized as "The Ghost of *Cardenio*"' (81). In

---

1 Other words used by Shakespeare but not Fletcher in the play include: bosom'd (1.1.30), peremptorily (1.2.31), disprize (1.2.95), dismission (1.3.56, 3.2.127), taxation (3.1.24), vermilion (4.1.79), coil (4.1.145). Words used by Fletcher but not by Shakespeare include: scoff (1.2.154), cringes (2.3.81). The lists are probably not exhaustive.

an unpublished essay, furthermore, Michael Wood, concurring with Kukowski that *Double Falsehood* genuinely derives from a Shakespeare–Fletcher *Cardenio*, identifies two songs by the lutenist Robert Johnson as leftovers from the original Jacobean play, finding echoes of Shelton's *Don Quixote* in their lyrics. The conclusion of Wood's research on songs that possibly derive from *The History of Cardenio* deserves to be quoted:

> Robert Johnson's song 'Woods rocks and mountaynes' was evidently written (by Fletcher?) for Shakespeare and Fletcher's *Cardenio*. It fits well with what we know of the King's Men's repertoire and their use of music 1612–1613; it shows how Shelton's Cervantes was used by, and inspired, the dramatists and their composer; it gives us a small but precious insight into the way the show might have been staged. And last, but not least, it confirms that Theobald's *Double Falshood* of 1728 was indeed, as he claimed, based on a genuine text of the lost play.
>
> (Wood, 9)[1]

See Appendix 5 for further discussion and for scepticism expressed about the song's provenance.

STAGE HISTORY

As I have noted, the stage history of the play begins in records of two performances of *Cardenio* at court. The first comes in the Treasurer's account for the 1612–13 season:

> Itm̄ paid to Iohn Heminges vppon lyke warrᵗ: dated att Whithall | ixᵒ die Iulij 1613 for him soelf and the

---

1 Christopher Goodwin argues that the imagery and diction of 'Woods, Rocks, & Mountaynes' is 'suspiciously close to that of *Away delights* (words by Beaumont and Fletcher) and *Care-charming sleep* (by Fletcher)' (Goodwin, 141). This would only be 'suspicious' if *Cardenio* were thought to be a single-authored play by Shakespeare. As a collaboration by Shakespeare and Fletcher, one might expect such similarities as Goodwin detects.

rest of his fellowes | his Ma^{tes} servauntes and Players
for presentinge a playe | before the Duke of Savoyes
Embassadour on the viij^{th} daye | of Iune 1613 called
Cardenna the some of | vj^{li} xiij^{s} iiij^{d}.

Later in the same account, we find, under Court (Greenwich):

Itm̄ paid to the said Iohn Heminges vppon the lyke
warr^{t}: | dated att Whitehall xx° die Maij 1613 for
presentinge | sixe severall playes viz one playe called
a badd beginninge | makes a good endinge, One
other called ye Capteyne, One | other the Alcumist.
/ One other Cardenno. / One other | The Hotspurr:
/ And one other called Benidicte and | Betteris All
played w^{th}in the tyme of this Accompte viz. | p^{d} -
Fortie powndes, And by waye of his Ma^{ts} rewarde |
twentie powndes In all | lx^{li}. /[1]

Although these are the only documented performances in
Shakespeare's lifetime, Metz comments (though without citing
his authority) that 'it was undoubtedly presented at Blackfriars
and possibly at the Globe' (Metz, *Sources*, 290).

About the initial run of the play in its adaptation as *Double
Falsehood*, a good deal has been said above, so we can cut to the
1740 revival at Covent Garden.[2] Very little is known about this
performance, other than the information supplied in the *London
Stage*.[3] Presumably it is more than coincidental that the play
was acted on the same date – 13 December – as the premiere
in 1727: perhaps the decision to present it was arrived at by
looking through old playbills for equivalent dates in past years.
The play was equipped with a new prologue (no longer extant)
and this, along with Peg Woffington's appearance as Violante,

1   Bodleian MS A. 239, fol. 47^{r–v}. The transcripts are kindly furnished by Richard
    Proudfoot.
2   The section on the play's stage history is based on more extensive information to be
    found in Hammond, 'Performance'.
3   *London Stage*, Part 2 (1700–29) vol. 2, ed. Emmett L. Avery (Carbondale, Ill., 1960).

ensured that it did reasonable business, taking around £130. Box-office takings slumped badly, however, on the second night (15 December: around £35), so that the play was not acted again until the tail end of the season, on 15 May 1741. If the public had lost confidence in the play, its sponsor apparently had not. The performance of 15 May was by royal command of the Prince and Princess of Wales, though in the event they did not attend. Consequently, the financial result to Theobald, whose benefit it was, was not more than £100 minus house costs of £50. His attempts to raise an audience for this performance are recorded in a letter to the Duke of Newcastle, in which he complains:

> I am once more encouraged to address your Grace on an Emergency. The Situation of my Affairs upon a Loss & Disappointment, obliging me to embrace a Benefit at this late & disadvantageous Season, it lays me under a Necessity of throwing Myself on the Favour of the Publick, & the kind Assistance of my Friends & Well-wishers. If your Grace can be so good as to honour me with your Presence, & to engage a few of your noble Friends . . .[1]

By this stage in Theobald's life, after the publication in 1737 of William Hogarth's print *The Distrest Poet* in which Theobald, easily identifiable through the verses he is depicted composing, is associated with poverty and hack-writing, his financial hardship was well known.[2]

Some years later, in 1767, the play was again revived at Covent Garden, now under the administration of John Beard, the celebrated tenor. It was given on two nights, Friday 24 April for William Gibson's benefit – he played Camillo and made around £70 after deduction of £66 5s. house charges – and Wednesday 6 May as a benefit for the actor Thomas Hull, who

1 BL Add. MS 32696, fol. 513ʳ.
2 See Seary, *Theobald*, 203ff., for Theobald's continuing financial hardship.

played Roderick and did better than Gibson, at a little over £80. Contemporary newspaper advertisements are openly disbelieving of the play's claims to Shakespearean ancestry. The *British Chronicle* for 27–9 April 1767 acidly declares that 'whoever will give himself the trouble to examine this Play, will be puzzled to find the least marks of Shakespeare's judgment, stile or manner'. 'The Rosciad', as the *Chronicle*'s critic called himself, echoed the generally sceptical attitude towards *Double Falsehood* earlier expressed in David E. Baker's *Companion to the Playhouse* (1764), which remarks that:

> This Piece *Theobald* endeavoured to persuade the World, was written by *Shakespeare.* – How true his Assertion might be, I cannot pretend to determine, but very few I believe gave any Credit to it. The Play, however, was acted with considerable Success.
>
> (Baker, 2.92)

A poem published in the *Public Advertiser* for Friday 1 May catches the general tone of knockabout scepticism pervading audience reaction to, as the poem's title puts it, '*the Play of* Double Falsehood, *or* The Distress'd Lovers, *unnecessarily said to have been written originally by* Shakespeare'. Theobald's supposed parasitism upon Shakespeare's genius is derided in the brief satire:

> A Painter once, a Hollander,
> With Genius blest, and Fame,
> To see a Rival in his Art
> To this our Island came . . .
>
> He learn'd the Englishman's Abode,
> And sought it Day by Day: –
> 'What still abroad? – and go I still
> 'Ungratified away?

'Must I my native Shore review
'Ere I my Brother find? –
'Let me, at least, a Token leave
'Of kindred Art behind.'

On the stretch'd Canvas glow'd a Face
With Virgin Beauty's Hue;
When on the Velvet Cheek a Fly
With curious Touch he drew.

Our Englishman return'd at last,
Sir, here has been – 'Forbear!
'I need but look upon his Lines,
'And know the Master there.'

The 1767 revival was certainly successful enough to spawn a 'third edition' of the play (actually the second London edition, since that edition designated the 'second' is strictly a second issue of the first edition), published by Thomas Lowndes in Fleet Street, and advertised in the *British Chronicle* for 4–6 May as 'now acted with great Applause, at the Theatre Royal in Covent Garden'.

Double Falsehood's next appearance on stage was at Drury Lane three years later, on Saturday 31 March 1770 and again on Friday 11 May. It was the season in which David Garrick's Stratford Shakespeare Jubilee had aroused unusual interest in the Bard, and doubtless that shrewd impresario thought the time ripe for another showing of a curious piece of Shakespeareana – 'Acted but Once these Forty Years', as the playbill for 11 May (Fig. 10) declares, conveniently forgetting the Covent Garden revivals. A prompt copy for the performance of 11 May exists in the Furness Shakespeare Library of the University of Pennsylvania, which is a rich source of information about this particular production. The copy is Lowndes's 1767 edition, inscribed throughout with two distinct sets of markings that give various kinds of information. There are actor warnings (names and numbers that remind the prompter to cue particular actors),

By Defire. [Acted but Once thefe Forty Years.]
For the BENEFIT of
Mrs. BRADSHAW, and Mrs. DORMAN.
At the Theatre-Royal in DRURY-LANE,
This prefent Friday, May 11, 1770,
DOUBLE FALSEHOOD;
Or, The DISTRESS'D LOVERS.
Written by SHAKESPEARE, and Revis'd by THEOBALD.
Julio by Mr. REDDISH,
Henriquez by Mr. AICKIN,
Roderick by Mr. PALMER,
Mafter of the Flocks Mr. MOODY, Camillo Mr. HURST,
Don Bernard by Mr. PARSONS, Duke by Mr. WRIGHTEN,
Violante by Mrs. JEFFERIES,
Leonora by Mifs YOUNGE.
In Act IV. The Original Song [New Compofed by Mr. HOOK.]
By Mifs RADLEY.
Act III. A Comic Dance by Sieur Daigville, and Sig' Vidini.
After the Play will be prefented (by Particular Defire, and for that Night only)
The Three OLD WOMEN Weather-Wife.
Cramp by Mr. HARTRY,
Twitch by Mrs. BRADSHAW, Rheum by Mrs. DORMAN.
To which will be added the Comic Opera of
The PADLOCK.
Leander by Mr. VERNON,
Don Diego by Mr. BANNISTER,
Mungo by Mr. DIBDIN,
Urfula by Mrs. DORMAN,
Leonora by Mifs RADLEY.
To-morrow, CYMON, (for the laft Time this Seafon) with The MINOR.
For the Benefit of Mr. FAWCETT, and Mrs. JOHNSTON.

10   Playbill for the Drury Lane revival of *Double Falsehood*, May 1770

entrance door notes, shop labels for the scenery to be used accompanied by instructions for the grooves in which to mount the flats (for example, the opening gives 'Stone Palace 4 gr'), props needed and music cues. The last two pages of the printed text are missing and have been replaced by an inserted leaf on which the final speeches have been written (minus the stage directions). Cuts in the text are indicated in pencil and one fairly insignificant textual change is inked in. Lowndes's 1767 edition supplies printed cast lists for the 1727/8 Drury Lane production and the 1767 Covent Garden revival (see pp. 172, 175). The prompt copy also has a handwritten cast list in the left-hand margin, identical to that given on the playbill for the production of 11 May 1770, except that Bransby is down to play the Duke and Mrs Baddeley to play Violante. The changes are significant. Astley Bransby was reaching the end of his career in 1770, a safe pair of hands compared to the fledgling James Wrighten whom he replaced, even if he was heavily satirized in Charles Churchill's *The Rosciad* for his monotonous roaring. The role of Violante, the romantic heroine, was normally taken by the leading actress of the company. The playbill lists Mrs Jefferies, the pretty Sarah Jefferies who had performed the role on 31 March. It was a bold step to replace her by Sophia Baddeley, who by May 1770 had reached the height of her notoriety. Her marriage to the actor Robert Baddeley had become so open as to cause David Garrick's brother George to challenge the careless husband to a duel on 17 March. Shortly after her appearance in *Double Falsehood* she had separated from her husband and was living in Ireland with an army officer. The production copy helps us to sense that Garrick was pulling out the stops in this performance.[1]

There are two distinct hands at work in the marking of the copy, which may be identified as those of Garrick himself and of William Hopkins, his prompter. Presumably, Garrick went over the script first, pencilling in cuts and changes (the one textual change in Garrick's hand is the cast list), roughly marking all entrances and exits and indicating changes of scenery where these occurred to him. Some shop labels are in Garrick's

---

1   See *The London Stage 1660–1800, Part 4, 1747–1776*, ed. George Winchester Stone, Jr (Carbondale, Ill., 1962), 1476, for playbill casts; and see *BDA*, 2.310–12, 16.286, 8.141–2, 1.202–8 for entries on the four performers concerned.

hand – doubtless whenever he recalled a suitable set as being in stock. Any special difficulties in the staging are also indicated by Garrick. The script was then delivered to Hopkins, who put in all the cues and recorded all the final decisions regarding entrances and exits, scenery and the like. Fig. 11 illustrates two typical pages from the prompt copy. The cuts Garrick indicates in Violante's lines on page 38 are perhaps intended to remove some of the declamatory abstractions. Throughout, the tendency of the cuts is to update the play by excising some of the abstract nouns, and to lower the emotional temperature. The instruction 'drop Landskip' at the end of the third act, inked in by Hopkins, is interesting. In general, curtains were not employed during performances at this time, but after 1750 painted scenes on rollers may have been used in a front position as act divides.[1] As in the case of the 'Landskip' indicated here, they often depicted a conventionalized rural or urban prospect.[2] Clearly, the purpose here is to give Violante time to don her 'Shepherd's Habit', and the fourth act opening is marked with an instruction to get her ready. Garrick has faintly indicated the scene to be used – 'Bank', which Hopkins has particularized to 'Sheep Hills and Bank', and the entrance is to be from the prompt side (PS). The circle is a conventional symbol meaning scene change; elsewhere in the copy the symbol W is employed, perhaps because the scene changers were normally cued by a whistle. Julio is cued to stand by for his entrance some thirty lines later. Throughout, Hopkins cues the actors about a page before their entrance.

1   Judith Milhous (private communication) expresses scepticism that scenes on rollers were used at this time. She does not recollect any such equipment being listed in stage inventories. In her view, the need to cover scene changes is a later (nineteenth-century) phenomenon. If a curtain were used slightly upstage at the position of the first wings, leaving a narrow space for acting while the scene was shifted, it would be as troublesome as closing the front curtain. The point of the wings and shutters system was to enable scene changing without closing the curtain.
2   On this point, see Allardyce Nicoll, *The Garrick Stage* (Manchester, 1980), 127–9.

112

Once again the play seems to have been popular in performance, whatever was thought of its literary merit. The *Gazetteer* for Monday 26 March 1770 comments:

> So great has been the demand for the Play of Double Falshood, or the Distress'd Lovers (to be acted on Saturday next at the theatre Royal in Drury-lane for the first time these forty years) that a new edition of this supposed relick of the immortal Shakespeare, was published on Saturday last, by Mr. Lowndes in Fleet-street.

This newspaper continued to plug the performance every day of the week until the 31st, when the advertisement gave a cast list and pointed out that that song 'Fond Echo, forego thy light Strain' (4.2.16–23) had been newly set by James Hook. Lowndes's edition is also advertised, along with the fascinating information that 'the original Manuscript of this play is now treasured up in the Museum of Covent-Garden Playhouse'.[1]

When the play had its last professional London performance at Covent Garden on 6 June 1791, it was thought to be in need of some gingering up. Several new songs were included and 'Fond Echo' was again given a new setting, this time by William Shield. As well as the London productions, there is some evidence of provincial interest in the play. At Bath's fashionable Theatre Royal, Orchard Street, it was given three performances in 1780, one in 1781, one in 1784, and two in 1793 (see Fig. 12). The *Bath Chronicle* for 17 May 1781 advertises the performance on the 19th, supplying the information that 'for the Benefit of Mrs. Keasberry, on Saturday the 19th of May will be performed a play called Double Falshood, or the Distressed Lovers (Written by Shakespear)', with Dimond as Julio, Blisset as Camillo, Didier as Roderick, Miss Wheeler as Violante and the celebrated

---

1 This tantalizing reference to a 'Manuscript' does not make clear whether the reference is to Theobald's manuscript of his adaptation, or to one of the originals on which this was said to be based. See further Hammond, *Cheat*.

113

38   DOUBLE FALSHOOD; *or,*

Say more than This ; and yet that Man was falſe.
Thou'lt not be ſo, I hope.

    Serv. By my Life, Miſtreſs,———

    Viol. Swear not ; I credit thee. But pry'thee tho'
Take heed, thou doſt not fail ; I do not doubt thee :
Yet I have truſted ſuch a ſerious Face,
And been abuſed too.

    Serv. If I fail your Truſt,———

    Viol. I do thee Wrong to hold thy Honeſty
At Diſtance thus : Thou ſhalt know all my Fortunes.
Get me a Shepherd's Habit.

    Serv. Well ; what elſe ?

    Viol. And wait me in the Evening, where I told thee ;
There thou ſhalt know my farther Ends. Take heed—

    Serv. D'ye fear me ſtill ?

    Viol. ————————No ; This is only Counſel :
My Life and Death I have put equally
Into thy Hand : Let not Rewards, nor Hopes,
Be caſt into the Scale to turn thy Faith.

    Be honeſt but for Virtue's Sake, that's all ;
    He, that has ſuch a Treaſure, cannot fall.   [*Exeunt.*

Thb Drop Landskip

      End of the Third Act.

11   Marked-up prompt copy for the close of Act 3 and opening of Act 4 of the May 1770 Drury Lane revival. The hands may be those of Garrick and his prompter William Hopkins. Marginal rules have been added to indicate cuts made in pencil on the original copy

The DISTREST LOVERS.   39

Dreßing Violante

Dreßing

Sheep Hill to Bank PS 1ᵗ Entr

ACT IV. SCENE I.

SCENE, *A Wide Plain, with a Prospect of Mountains at a Distance.*

Enter Master of the Flocks, three or four Shepherds, and Violante in Boy's Cloaths.

1 *Shep.* WELL, he's as sweet a Man, Heav'n comfort him ! as ever these Eyes look'd on.

2 *Shep.* If he have a Mother, I believe, Neighbours, she's a Woe-woman for him at this Hour.

Mast. Why should he haunt these wild unpeopled Mountains,
Where nothing dwells but Hunger, and sharp Winds ?

1 *Shep.* His Melancholy, Sir, that's the main Devil does it. Go to, I fear he has had too much foul Play offer'd him.

Mast. How gets he Meat ?

2 *Shep.* Why, now and then he takes our Victuals from us, tho' we desire him to eat ; and instead of a short Grace, beats us well and soundly, and then falls to.

Mast. Where lies he ?

1 *Shep.* Ev'n where the Night o'ertakes him.

2 *Shep.* Now will I be hang'd, an' some fair-snouted skittish Woman, or other, be not at the End of this Madness.

1 *Shep.* Well, if he lodg'd within the Sound of us, I knew our Musick would allure him. How attentively he stood, and how he fix'd his Eyes, when your Boy sung his Love-Ditty. Oh, here he comes again.

Mast. Let him alone ; he wonders strangely at us.

D 4   1 *Shep.*

2 Julio

11   *cont.*

115

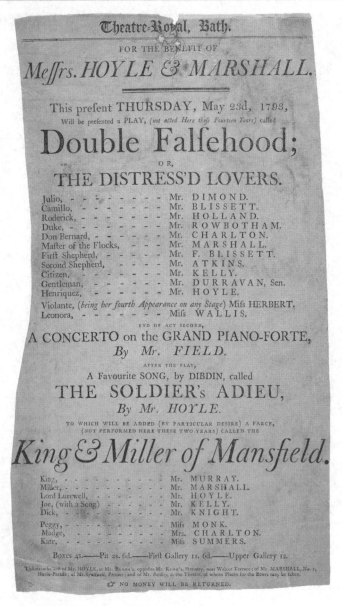

12   Playbill for a May 1793 performance, Theatre Royal, Bath

Mrs Siddons herself as Leonora. This was Sarah Siddons's third acting season in Bath and fourth appearance in the role of Leonora.[1] The performance given in Bath on 5 July 1793 was the last known professional production.

All recorded productions of *Double Falsehood* since the eighteenth century until very recently have been by amateurs. In the eighteenth century too, the play was used for private entertainment, as a prompt copy owned by the Folger Shakespeare Library attests.[2] This copy is Watts's 1728b edition, marked with handwritten emendations to the text and giving some directions on scenery and music. It belonged to Juliana Noel, whose name is endorsed on the endpaper along with a date – 10 March 1742, N.S.[3] She was the third daughter of Baptist Noel, fourth earl of Gainsborough, Lord Lieutenant of the County of Rutland from 1732 onwards. The performance recorded in this copy relates to a private production given by and for family and friends, probably at the family home, Exton, County Rutland.[4] Written beside the Dramatis Personae are the names of those who took part in the show. Some are illegible, but Henriquez was taken by 'Ld G.' (Baptist Noel), Don Bernard by 'Mr. Brown', Julio by a male member of the family, perhaps Juliana's uncle James Noel, Leonora by 'L.^{y} . I.N.' (Lady Jane Noel, Juliana's older sister), and Violante by Juliana. Duke Angelo and Camillo were also cast. Judging by the cuts made in the copy and the fact that no names appear against them in the Dramatis Personae, Roderick, the Master of the Flocks and Shepherds were not cast and the parts relating

1 See Belville S. Penley, *The Bath Stage* (London, 1892), 59.
2 Folger Shakespeare Library Prompt D36.
3 N.S. means 'new style' and refers to the change in the calendar from the Julian to the Gregorian, with a difference of ten days and 1 January becoming the first day of the year. Since this was not adopted in Britain until as late as March 1751 (Catholic countries accepted the new style calendar long before Protestant states did), the fact that N.S. is recorded by Juliana Noel is probably a defiantly Catholic act.
4 For the genealogy of the Noel family, see Emilia F. Noel, *Some Letters and Records of the Noel Family* (1910), 5–6; and for their country seats, see *Victoria History of the Counties of England: A History of Rutland*, ed. William Page, 3 vols (1908–36), vol. 2, entry for Luffenham Manor.

to them were not performed, for reasons of moral propriety or perhaps simply to make economies. The production was simpler than the professional ones examined above – closer, perhaps, to the makeshift staging invented by Jane Austen for the Mansfield Park production of *Lovers' Vows*. Stage sets are simplified to 'Grove' and 'The Street', but much care is taken over the music; so that for the marriage scene in 3.2 the copy is marked 'Musick' and 'symphony in Solomon', presumably referring to Handel's oratorio *Solomon*. If so, the performance must postdate the Covent Garden premiere of *Solomon* in March 1749. Juliana was fifteen years old in 1750, Jane seventeen. The song in Act 4, 'Fond Echo', is marked 'accompany'd by a Violin con Sordini' (mutes), which must have made a haunting sound. Great care has been taken with cutting, where the principle at work is not so much aesthetic as moral. With the girls' father playing Henriquez, difficulties arise over what it is proper for a peer to say and to have said to him by his daughters. This accounts for the heavy cutting and rewriting on the page illustrated in Fig. 13. Other cuts are more straightforward bowdlerizations. The lines on pages 56–7 that read

> The Voice of Parents is the Voice of Gods:
> For to their Children they are Heav'n's Lieutenants:
> Made Fathers, not for common Uses meerly
> Of Procreation; (Beasts and Birds would be
> As noble then as we are) but to steer . . .

become 'The Voice of Parents is the Voice of Gods: / By Heaven appointed to direct and steer'. As a whole, then, this prompt copy provides some insight into matters of contemporary taste and staging, as well as a little more knowledge of *Double Falsehood*'s popularity in its own time.

One amateur production is recorded in the nineteenth century, at the no longer standing Olympic Theatre in Wych Street, Drury Lane, on Saturday 27 November 1847. It was mounted

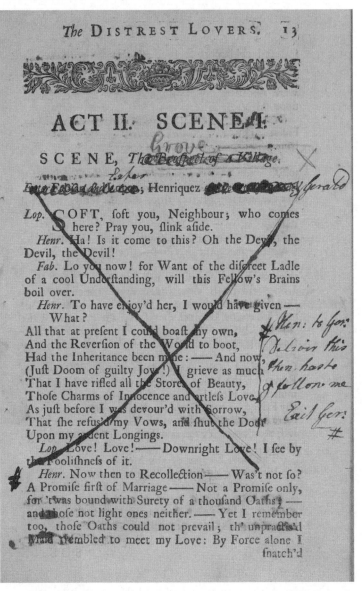

13 Opening of Act 2, marked up for a private performance (Juliana Noel's copy)

with great enthusiasm by a cast who believed themselves to be discovering a lost work of Shakespeare's. The producer, W.C. Day, left a detailed account of the play in his memoir *Behind the Footlights* (1885), which is exploited fully in a recent article by Howard Marchitello who gives an account of this hapless occasion (Marchitello). The press reaction was sceptical. The *Theatrical Journal* published the following review:

> On Monday an amateur performance took place for the purpose, it was said, of producing a play of Shakespere's, his last production, which was discovered in M.S. of the hand-writing of Downs, a celebrated prompter, sixty years after his death, by Lewis Theabold [*sic*] and by him presented to His Majesty George the First, in 1726. It is entitled 'The Double Falsehood'. Now as to the above statement, it may be true or false; we are not in a position either to prove its authority or otherwise – we can only give an opinion as to what we saw and heard. If the play in question is from the pen of our immortal bard, we think those who admire his recognized plays would have done well not to have brought the one in question to light at all. We cannot recognize a single feature of the wonderful style of our great poet; no, not even a line, a sentence, a thought, or situation. 'The Double Falshood' is properly named, for the man that could write the plays of 'Hamlet', 'Macbeth', 'Othello' and fifty others of the like, could never be so wanting at any period of his life as to use such common-place language – such vulgar sayings – such fulsome dialogue – as that which was brought forward on this occasion. As for plot, the stuff has none; the only scene of any interest throughout the play was one very similar to that of the mad scene in 'The Mountaineers', where Octavian appears in the wood, and this indeed fell very far short of it. The piece had evidently been taken pains

> with in the getting up; the scenery was appropriate, and the dresses very good.[1]

The reviewer praises most performances, but not that of Mrs Graham (playing Leonora), whom

> we would fain omit making any observations upon; we could have wished some friend had hinted to her to have been a little more animated – we were fearful she was not well – she appeared to be well acquainted with the dialogue, as she frequently prompted others.

Although the audience was not numerous, it was spirited. The *Manchester Evening Chronicle* for 22 April 1932 refers to this production, telling the story of a 'wag in the pit' who raised the cry of 'Author', whereupon an actor carried onstage a life-size plaster bust of Shakespeare. The *Chronicle* credits the claim that Shakespeare wrote the play. In the 1950s, two productions were mounted by amateur groups – the Nottingham Theatre Club on 7–10 December 1955 and the Northampton Drama Club in the same year.[2] The *Nottingham Evening Post* for 29 November previewed the play perceptively until the odd final paragraph, which writes of *Double Falsehood* surviving 'the deterioration, lack of understanding, fires, Puritan attacks, and negligence which took heavy toll of Elizabethan records'; and both the *Post* and the *Nottingham Evening News* reviewed it on 8 December, commenting on the large audience attracted by this curio and on the iridescent silks and brocades used for the costumes. About the play, the reviewer is less enthusiastic: 'if Shakespeare wrote it, or even parts of it, the world has lost little by its absence from the stage for so many years'. We have come a long way since the 'Universal Applause' Theobald claimed for the 1727 premiere.

---

1   *Theatrical Journal*, 8 (1847), 380–1. 'The Mountaineers' referred to in the review is George Colman's play *The Mountaineers* (1794), and the scene in which Octavian runs mad does bear some resemblance to Julio's scene in *Double Falsehood*, perhaps because the play is a dramatization of 'The Captive's Tale' from the same area of *Don Quixote*.

2   'Newspaper cuttings: Shakespeare's plays 1927– Apocryphal plays', Birmingham Central Library Shakespeare Collection. See the *Northampton Chronicle and Echo*, 20 August 1956, for the production in Northampton.

AN 'AGREEABLE CHEAT'?

How does the story of *Double Falsehood* end? Given that the manuscripts of Shakespearean provenance that Theobald claimed he owned never seem to have been independently published or otherwise authenticated, there has been a temptation to dismiss the whole affair as, in Theobald's words to his patron Dodington, an 'agreeable cheat' – bluntly, a forgery (see p. 20). As we have seen, the reference in the 1728 Preface to 'the Reception [the play] found from those Great Judges, to whom I have had the Honour of communicating it in Manuscript' and Theobald's letter to the Countess of Oxford offering her the chance 'to read the play in manuscript' are not conclusive because the 'manuscript' referred to could be that of Theobald's version in his own hand. They were being offered, that is to say, a preview of Theobald's play rather than a glimpse of the 'dear Relick' that he spoke of to Dodington. While I hope to have persuaded the reader that there is a great deal more to the story than an 'agreeable cheat', only discovery of Theobald's manuscripts or reliable external evidence that they existed can clear his name altogether of the stigma of forgery. I cannot claim to have found the manuscripts, but to the documentary story it is possible to add a widow's mite.

The newspaper report in the *Gazetteer* for 31 March 1770, referred to above, advertises Lowndes's edition of the play, along with the fascinating information that 'the original Manuscript of this play is now treasured up in the Museum of Covent-Garden Playhouse'. It is very tempting to conclude that this reference is to a manuscript that predates any writings of Theobald's, since Theobald's own holograph would scarcely be worth treasuring up. It is not clear that there was a museum in the modern sense in the Covent Garden theatre, but most certainly there were libraries which contained, inter alia, production copies of plays. If one of the original manuscripts on which *Double Falsehood* was based really was in safe keeping in Covent Garden, its fate would have been sealed on the sad night of 19 September 1808, when the theatre building burned down, destroying irreplaceable manuscripts by, amongst others, Handel and Arne. Henry Saxe Wyndham's *The Annals of Covent Garden Theatre* quotes James Boaden's account of a visit to the hapless manager, John Kemble, the day after the fire:

> Yes, it has perished – that magnificent theatre. It is gone with all its treasures of every description. That library, which contained all those immortal productions of our countrymen prepared for the purpose of representation . . .
>
> (Saxe Wyndham, 1.327)

Perhaps the story of one of Theobald's three playscripts terminates in these ashes, but the story of *Cardenio* does not, quite. No unaltered copy of this Cardenio play is now known to survive, but something called *Cardenio* gained a Frankenstein monster's existence when in 1994 Charles Hamilton argued at book length that the lost play and *The Second Maiden's Tragedy*, a manuscript play that most commentators consider to be by Thomas Middleton, are one and the same.[1] Hamilton's attribution argument eccentrically involved the renaming of the characters from the Cardenio plot in *Don Quixote* – the Wife narrative in the play is actually from the story of the Curious Impertinent. *The Second Maiden's Tragedy*, entitled *The Lady's Tragedy* and in its censored form *The Ladies' Tragedy*, in the complete Middleton edition published in 2007, was performed under the title of *Cardenio* in many places around the world in the 1990s and into the present century (see Briggs, *Lady's*

---

1 Hamilton's perversely ingenious arguments (which include the claim that the manuscript of *The Second Maiden's Tragedy* is in Shakespeare's hand) have convinced no scholars to date (see for example Irvin Leigh Matus's review, *Times Literary Supplement*, 5 August 1994: 'Unfortunately, [Hamilton] says nothing that is new and credible about *Cardenio, Double Falsehood* or Theobald'). They have, however, occasionally been accepted by student and fringe theatre directors, with the inconvenient and misleading result that there have been a few recent revivals of *The Second Maiden's Tragedy* under the title *Cardenio*. The one real link between this play and *Cardenio* is that its subplot is a version of the 'Tale of the Curious Impertinent', told at the inn during the interstices of the Cardenio plot in *Don Quixote*.

Tragedy). This is testimony to the remarkable upsurge of interest in Shakespeare's missing play. Once the preserve of a very few enthusiasts, a subject that Shakespeare scholars themselves knew comparatively little about, it has gained increasing prominence. Marchitello (984) notes that there was a production of *Cardenio/Double Falshood* in Los Angeles in August 2002 by the Lone Star Ensemble at 2100 Square Feet; though actually, this was the Hamilton-ascribed *Second Maiden's Tragedy* – by now capable, in its Spenserian shape-changing, of confusing scholars and the public alike.[1]

Finding *Cardenio* has become something of a Holy Grail. If finding the play proves impossible, the next best thing might be to write it oneself. Apart from the misleading packaging of Middleton's play as *Cardenio*, recent years have witnessed two major ways of dealing with the tantalizing fact of the play's shadowy existence and the natural desire to flesh that out. Both approaches take *Double Falsehood* as a basis, going on either to supply the scenes presumed missing, or to adapt the play more radically. Leading scholars and critics have been tempted to offer their own conjectural reconstructions of *Cardenio* in dramatic form. Gary Taylor's version, entitled *The History of Cardenio*, was given a private reading in New York in March 2006, and several public readings since; and a first fully staged performance in Wellington, New Zealand, in May 2009 (see Fig. 14 and pp. 156–8). Interpolation of material written by Taylor himself is justified thus in an unpublished introduction to his version:

> Because Theobald adapted *Cardenio* into *Double Falshood*, I have to unadapt *Double Falshood* in order to reconstruct *Cardenio*. This means that I have become, inevitably, a special kind of collaborator in this text. What follows is a play written by William Shakespeare

---

1   Marchitello (984, n. 32) notes that this production was reviewed in the *Los Angeles Times* by Kathleen F. Foley on 16 August 2002.

Shakespeare's Lost Play

The History of

CARDENIO

by William Shakespeare & John Fletcher
a creative reconstruction
by Gary Taylor
directed by David Carnegie

14   Programme for the production of *The History of Cardenio* staged at
Victoria University of Wellington, New Zealand, May 2009

and John Fletcher in 1612–13, with help from Gary Taylor in 2005. Taylor's contribution tries to be imperceptible; when the hole occurs in Shakespeare's portion of the play, it has been filled with images and rhythms and words Shakespeare might have written in 1612–13, and when the hole occurs in Fletcher's portion of the play it has been filled with images and rhythms and words Fletcher might have written in 1612–13. You can call this pastiche, or transparent forgery, or artistic imitation . . . my contributions to the following text of *Cardenio* have been guided by, and can be defended by reference to, all the available contemporary scholarship on the language and style of Shakespeare (and Fletcher). If I have succeeded, then an astute reader or playgoer, familiar with both dramatists, should be able to identify what is Shakespeare and what is Fletcher, but should not be able to tell which lines I have added. The result is not authentic (it could never be), but it is at least, I hope, authentish.

Reconstituting *Cardenio* poses another thorny problem besides that of having to write Shakespearean or Fletcherian dialogue: whether to restore, or not to restore, Don Quixote himself. I have already canvassed some of the scholarly arguments, mainly against this way of proceeding (see p. 43), revolving around the pragmatic question of how collaborative work was done in the period. Multiple plotting in Jacobethan drama, especially in tragicomedy or comedy, offered the advantage that two writers could work concurrently from different source books. Taking both plots from the same book would negate this possibility, though of course both Shakespeare and Fletcher needed Shelton for *Cardenio*, so that this is not a definitive argument against putting Quixote back, and, as we have seen, he does appear in Guillén de Castro's play explored by Roger Chartier and discussed earlier (pp. 34–5). Taylor has taken the decision to stage the Don. Introducing Quixote under one of his original names, Quesada, Taylor's *Cardenio* gets the Don and Sancho involved in the denouement of the main plot – the business with the coffin is extended and staged. He also goes back to Cervantes to involve Violante (he sticks with this name) posing as the Princess Micomicon to effect the dehumouring of the Don – freeing him, that is, from his delusions. She has to agree to pose as the Princess before she is reunited with (in this version) Don Ferdinando, a slightly awkward psychological proposition for the audience to accept. Taylor sees the need, as anyone reading *Double Falsehood* must, to do more with Violante's seduction by Don Ferdinando, so here she is tricked out of her virtue by a fake marriage ceremony. Lucinda in this version does pronounce the words 'I will' in the interrupted marriage scene, as she does in Cervantes but not in Theobald. 'Woods, Rocks, & Mountaynes', the song discovered by Michael Wood, is performed in this version, as it is also in the Bernard Richards version discussed below. Reconstructing *Cardenio* requires much new writing, as well as Theobald-style improvements to *Double Falsehood* itself: Taylor's is a courageous and imaginative attempt by a scholar who knows the period as well as anyone alive.

In some ways even more audacious, Richards's conjectural reconstruction of missing scenes was produced under the title *Cardenio* in early March 2009 at Queens' College, Cambridge, under the auspices of BATS, the Queens' dramatic society (see Fig. 15). This version is Theobald's *Double Falsehood* plus six additional scenes written by Richards. Those additions to Acts 1 and 4 fill gaps in the plot, but two scenes, the new 1.6 and 4.3, do much more than this. The first stages Henriquez's rape of Violante – in Richards's version there is no doubt that it is a rape, justified by Henriquez through a Volpone-like rhetoric of atheistical self-sufficient sensuality:

> Virtue is for cowards.
> When we're conjoined we shall define virtue
> In our own terms, and not those of the world's.

15   Violante (Katie Alcock) and Henriquez (Ben Blyth), in Bernard Richards's reworking of Shakespeare's lost *Cardenio*, presented at Queens' College, Cambridge, directed by Laura 'Pixie' Hounsom, March 2009

> We are the touchstones that test vice and virtue;
> We are the glasses in which lesser beings
> Trim and trick out themselves.
>
> (Richards, from 1.6, p. 13)

Shortly after the rape, Henriquez points to a statue of the Virgin Mary, claiming that 'This holy image is witness to my faith, / And sanctifies our union 'fore Heaven'. Such an overt Catholicization of the play points forward to the other major addition, 4.3, in which Henriquez enters Leonora's cell in the convent where she has taken refuge by impersonating a holy friar. Modelled, perhaps, on the Duke in *Measure for Measure*, Henriquez's blasphemy is far more overt and objectionable. By means of a perverted celebration of Holy Communion, Henriquez administers the sacraments to Leonora, but they contain a drug. He reveals himself to her in the cruellest possible way, ending the scene by dumping her in a coffin. Dramatically the scenes are very effective, but they do raise questions. Explicit onstage sexual acts were not, of course, permissible in Shakespeare's day or Theobald's. Richards's introduction alludes to the Act to Restrain Abuses of Players of 1606 that forbade all such inclusion of religious elements as feature in his nunnery scene. Arguably there is something confused about reconstructing a lost original in a form in which one knows it could never have existed: a little like producing an identikit portrait of someone who does not look like the criminal. Compounding Henriquez's villainy in this way makes the final resolution of his marriage to Leonora more difficult to accept, though it is perhaps no more problematic than Angelo's intended miscreancy in *Measure for Measure*. Richards's version inscribes 'Woods, Rocks, & Mountaynes' as the Act 4 song,& replacing Gouge's 'Fond Echo', as does Taylor's. He writes that the original song's 'jaunty and not entirely appropriate rhythms have, to ears attuned to early music, an eighteenth-century air to them' (vii). With this I disagree. Gouge's setting deliberately, in my view, tries to capture some of the plaintive quality of earlier music; it is anything but 'jaunty'.

Exemplifying the adaptation approach that does not involve writing any quasi-Shakespearean dialogue, Stephen Greenblatt has co-written a play with Charles Mee – also called *Cardenio* – boasting part of *Double Falsehood* as a play-within-a-play.[1] Greenblatt and Mee's *Cardenio* (2008) is in fact, like Middleton's *The Second Maiden's Tragedy*, based on the 'Tale of the Curious Impertinent' (the story in *Don Quixote* that had the most pervasive influence on playwrights in Shakespeare's period), though set among present-day rich East Coast Americans visiting an Umbrian villa for the wedding day of Anselmo and Camila, along with best man Will. Anselmo's parents, who in this version of the story are strolling players, arrive at the wedding celebration of Anselmo and Camila bearing a copy of *Cardenio* – in practice, *Double Falsehood* with Cervantes' character names restored – which some of the cast become involved in rehearsing. Life imitates art as, through the rehearsal process, Camila (Luscinda) and Will (Cardenio) discover the power of their mutual love; meanwhile, Anselmo finds that he truly loves Susana, an opera-trained actress who has actually been intended to play the part of Luscinda. The main scenes that are incorporated, with a little rewriting and rearrangement, are from 1.2 and to a lesser extent 4.1. This heavy reliance on 1.2 is in accordance with the view expressed by the play's characters, that although Theobald was a 'charlatan' Shakespeare wrote the early acts of *Cardenio* and Fletcher the later. The characters in the play, especially the odious Cassandra-figure Doris, find the excerpts from *Double Falsehood* tedious: when Will and Carmila are actually seen to be falling in love through their intense acting in the inset play, it is pastiche written (I presume) by the authors, not Theobald's play, that shows the quality and power of their relationship. This version of *Cardenio* is an audacious mix of Shakespeare's

1 I am indebted to Stephen Greenblatt for permitting me to read a rehearsal copy of the play (Greenblatt & Mee, *Cardenio*), from which the description is taken.

own plots, including that in *Cymbeline* where Posthumus (here, Anselmo) requests that Iachimo (here, Will) should test his newly wed wife's love; and the performance of the Albanian carpenter Rudi is suggestive of Bottom. It also derives something from the subgenre of wedding films and from those works in which 'real life' action imitates the action of an inset work of art (Carlos Saura's 1983 *Carmen* would be an example). The lyrical and philosophical quality of some of the writing reminds me of the verse dramas of T.S. Eliot.

As I write this, I am learning from the Shakespearean scholar Jonathan Bate and Gregory Doran, Chief Associate Director of the Royal Shakespeare Company, about plans to workshop a reconstruction of *Cardenio* in association with the Almagro Festival. It is hoped that this will be an Anglo–Spanish collaboration and will be a mix of Cervantes, Shelton and Theobald under the title of *Cardenio*.[1] Doran informs me that this reconstruction will tell the Cardenio story, focusing attention on that exclusively, without risking any possible muddying of waters by introducing the Don himself.

The play has also featured in the contemporary novel. *Cardenio* makes a cameo appearance in Jasper Fforde's amusing *Lost in a Good Book* (2002). In Fforde's world, there is a need for the LiteraTecs, division 27 of Special Operations whose role is to investigate serious literary fraud. Improbably, they are based in Swindon and their leading operative is Thursday Next. In the passage quoted below, Thursday and her partner Bowden Cable are investigating the story of one Mrs Hathaway that she has found a copy of Shakespeare's lost play *Cardenio*:

'Would you like a cup of tea?' asked Hathaway.

'No thank you, ma'am. You said you had a copy of *Cardenio*?'

---

1 'It . . . will be a mix of Theobald, Shelton and Cervantes, and will definitely include the Johnson songs (one of Michael Wood's best bits of work, that). It'll be worked up with Spanish as well as British actors, in an attempt to re-Spanishize the feel of Shelton and Theobald' (Gregory Doran, private communication, 23 July 2007).

'Of course!' she enthused, then added with a wink: 'Will's lost play popping up like a jack-in-the-box must come as quite a surprise to you, I imagine?'

I didn't tell her that a *Cardenio* scam was almost a weekly event.

(Fforde, *Lost*, 30)

As it will turn out, the manuscript that they are asked to inspect is written on lined paper with a ballpoint pen, and has Cardenio seeking Lucinda [*sic*] in a Range Rover. Even more recently, David Nokes introduces *Double Falsehood* into his novel *The Nightingale Papers* (2005) to set the scene for a story that plays with ideas of the forged and the genuine in literary production:

He turned back to his bookshelves, searched past the stacks of paperbacks to some handsome mock-leather bindings, removed a book and showed it to her. The spine said *The Double Falshood* by William Shakespeare.

'Know it?' he asked, and Gillian shook her head.

'I'm not surprised,' he said. 'No one does. The play turned up mysteriously in the eighteenth century, discovered by Lewis Theobald, Pope's chief dunce in the *Dunciad*. Pope and Theobald were both editing Shakespeare . . . You get the idea,' he said. 'Theobald claimed to have three copies of this play, by Shakespeare. The only trouble was that, according to him, they weren't very good. So he thought the best thing was to tidy them up prior to publication. So . . .'

He opened up the title page of the volume and Gillian read:

'*The Double Falshood*, A tragedy, by Lewis Theobald and William Shakespeare. What happened to the manuscripts?'

'Good question. They just mysteriously disappeared'
. . .

> Gillian turned over the pages of the book, murmuring 'The Double Falshood . . .'
>
> 'Neat title,' said Carstairs, 'and quite appropriate, really.'
>
> (Nokes, Papers, 20–1)

It is hoped that readers of this introduction may know a little more about the mysteries wrapped up in the *Double Falsehood*, and that they may not think the title quite so 'appropriate'.

For the writer of fiction, finding *Cardenio* has not always proved to be easier than for the scholar. Jean Rae Baxter's 2008 novel *Looking for Cardenio* has as its heroine Dr Deirdre Gunn, an academic at a fictional Canadian University called Melrose. Having lost her opportunity to gain tenure as a result of seducing a student, Dr Gunn is approached by her sometime classmate at King's College London, the odious George Pinkus. This loathsome character has found the manuscript of '*Cardenio*' hidden in the stacks of King's College Library and offers to make a Faustian bargain with Dr Gunn. Through the vagaries of plot rather than through hard work, Dr Gunn is rewarded with an endowed Chair of Shakespeare Studies, during the tenure of which, it is to be hoped, she will arrive at a more profound verdict on the Cardenio story than that expressed early in the novel: 'So far, one big yawn was all the story was worth' (Baxter, *Cardenio*, 71). The enormous success of Dan Brown's *The Da Vinci Code* (2003) has spawned various attempts at emulation, and one such murder-mystery thriller, J.L. Carrell's *The Shakespeare Secret* (2007), turns on the finding of the lost play. What is perhaps of most interest to the scholarly reader in her book is less the plot that revolves around the serial killer's devotion to protecting the Stratfordian against the Oxfordian hypothesis about Shakespeare's identity, than the lines quoted from *Double Falsehood* – 'passages that drifted across the ear with a loveliness almost too sweet to bear':

> Have you e'er seen the phoenix of the earth,
> The bird of paradise? . . .

I have, and known her haunts, and where she built
Her spicy nest; till, like a credulous fool,
I show'd the treasure to a friend in trust,
And he hath robb'd me of her.
    (4.1.49–50, 51–4; quoted in Carrell, *Secret*, 185)

In those lines a contemporary thriller writer hears genuine Shakespeare, and I am not the one to gainsay it.

TEXT

Double Falshood; Or, the Distrest Lovers was entered in the Stationers' Company Register by the printer John Watts on 29 December 1727.[1] It was published soon afterwards in octavo in early January 1728 at a retail price of 1s. 6d. How many copies Watts printed – the size of the edition – is unknown. Comparisons drawn from the ledgers of a rival printer, William Bowyer, suggest that, although 1,000 copies was a popular press run for plays, there could be enormous variation.[2] Bowyer printed more duodecimo editions than octavos of playtexts, and duodecimos could be printed in very high numbers of copies: single plays by Shakespeare, for example, were printed in runs of 10,000 copies, while in 1735 Sir George Etherege's *Man of Mode*, William Congreve's *Old Bachelor* and Cibber's *Careless Husband* were all published in editions of 6,000. In February 1731, Bowyer printed no fewer than 2,500 octavo copies of *Philotas* by Theobald's friend Philip Frowde.[3] Perhaps Theobald would have had reason to anticipate at least similar levels of demand.

1 National Archives, SP/44/363, pp. 129–31.
2 See Keith Maslen, 'Edition quantities for *Robinson Crusoe*, 1719' in *An Early London Printing House at Work: Studies in the Bowyer Ledgers* (New York: Bibliographical Society of America, 1993), 57–62. Maslen points out that plays could at times be produced in much larger numbers: *Three Hours after Marriage*, by John Gay and others, was produced in a run of 2,500 in 1716, for example.
3 The information is taken from *The Bowyer Ledgers: The Printing Accounts of William Bowyer Father and Son*, ed. Keith Maslen and John Lancaster (London and New York: Bibliographical Society and Bibliographical Society of America, 1991). See the Topical Index under 'Plays'.

Some two months after the January 1728 edition was published, further copies were printed of what is called on the new title-page a 'second edition'. Since all libraries that hold copies of the play accept this designation in their catalogues, it is useful to state the bibliographical position more accurately. On the basis of examining individual copies, it can be established that this is not truly a second edition. Copies of the first edition provide variants in signatures and press marks suggesting that they were not all printed in a single impression. The later print run of copies is very likely to have been produced from standing type,[1] but with some resetting in quire A to accommodate Theobald's revision of the Preface (see pp. 22–4); and the slight change in the title-page that proclaims a second edition. Properly, this is a new *issue* in that it constitutes a consciously planned print run intended for publication as a unit that is different in clearly discernible respects from the original print run. It is likely also to be a fresh impression, on the evidence of the variant press figure '5' in quire E and of minor displacement of ornaments, catchwords and signatures in other quires. Though a fresh impression of the whole book to produce the later print run may have taken place, the material evidence furnished by such minor variations as are noted in the next section does not provide conclusive proof of this.

Although the text of the first edition was prefaced with the panoply and fanfare of a royal licence (see pp. 15–17), it is not especially well printed, having a degree of fuzziness about the inking, several careless errors and some examples of crowding of text which suggest that the copy was not as carefully cast off as it might have been. The year 1728 also saw a duodecimo edition published by J. Hyde in Dublin, which certainly

---

1 Standing type is type that has previously been set and printed, and retained for future use (see further p. 141).

followed the second issue because it has the revised form of
the Preface.[1]

What is particularly striking about the printed version of
the play is the lineation. When Pope was attacking Theobald in
The Dunciad Variorum of 1729, he noticed that verse and prose
are inadequately separated in at least one scene. Although
Henriquez's speech at the opening of 2.1 is set out as verse
– and it is, indeed, written in relatively regular iambic pentameters – his remaining speeches in the scene are set out as prose.
The words 'unpractis'd', 'snatch'd' and 'prevail'd', in lines 25,
26 and 28, are marked as elisions in 1728a, suggesting strongly
that those lines, though arranged as prose, were originally verse.
Pope noticed that there are what might be termed verse 'fossils'
in the speeches set out as prose. Resetting a selection of the
lines as verse (2.1.52–5), Pope could not resist the temptation
to have a dig at Theobald by further *editing* the text, coming up
with the conjectural emendation of Theobald's 'Feaver' to his
own 'fervor' and Theobald's 'indeed' to 'in deed'. Under the
heading 'ACT 2. SCENE 1.' he writes:

All the verse of this Scene is confounded with prose.
   – O that a man
   Could reason down this *Feaver* of the blood,
   Or sooth with *words* the tumult in his heart!
   Then *Julio*, I might be *indeed* thy friend.
Read
   – this *fervor* of the blood,
   Then *Julio* I might be in *deed* thy friend.
marking the just opposition of deeds and words.

(Pope, Poems, 5.181–2)[2]

1 British Library 11774 aaa.28(6). The collation is A–C¹²; 58 pp., 36 leaves. Although
the text is taken from the second impression Preface, the correction from 'it' to 'the
Play' on the first page of the Preface made by Watts is not made in this edition. There
is no printed cast list.
2 See Appendix 1 for further examples of the kind.

In a later scene, 2.3, although Don Bernard begins the scene speaking regular iambic verse, by lines 54–7 this has broken down entirely and there is no longer any iambic rhythm to his speech. Something similar happens to the Citizen in 3.1, and in 4.1 the Master of the Flocks speaks a mixture of prose and verse in the same passage of action. The differentiation of prose and verse is again a difficult problem for the editor in 5.2, the more so because the typography of the 1728 edition itself seems to reflect a degree of uncertainty as to how to set it out. At times the layout seems designed to occlude the problem. Early eighteenth-century practice dictated that all the speech prefixes be on the same line as the speeches that follow, and the margins appear to have been set to conceal any clear distinction. The conventions of the Arden series require the editor to make a clear separation between verse and prose (by printing prose speeches on the same line as the speech prefix, whereas verse speeches starting with a full verse line begin below the prefix). In this play as we have it, such a clear distinction can be difficult to draw. My guiding principle has been to liberate as much verse as possible from the 1728 copy-text, including everything that is clearly indicated as verse therein and emancipating additional consecutive verse lines where these are demonstrably iambic and decasyllabic.

From the point of view of eighteenth-century metrical norms, the text of *Double Falsehood* makes uncomfortable reading. Searching for iambic pentameters, one finds a very high percentage of feminine endings: roughly averaged, just under 40 per cent of all verse lines have feminine endings (see p. 103). Several lines can be read as alexandrines. Many lines require elisions to render them metrical, and the proper names of the leading characters are especially manipulable in this respect – Henriquez and Leonora in particular can be scanned in a variety of ways depending on the metre of the verse line in which they occur. (Much of the time, it appears that Henriquez should be disyllabic, pronounced as 'Henricks', while Leonora is sometimes given her full four-syllable weight but often elided to three.) Julio is almost always elided to two syllables,[1] and so probably is Roderick (sometimes printed 'Rod'rick'). Any search for consistency – any attempt, for example, to allocate prose and verse to characters on the basis of social status or of a sense, expressed by stylistic register, of the nobility or otherwise of their sentiments – is doomed to failure. If one comes at the metre from the Renaissance end – with reference, say, to the printed texts of the early Beaumont and Fletcher plays – the unclear metrical situation seems more familiar. Act 4 scene 2 of *A King and No King* (1611), for example, presents in the first printed quarto of 1619 just such an inconsistent arrangement, with lines set out as verse that are either too long or too short to be properly pentameters, and with characters toggling between prose and verse in the same passage of action.[2] This is the standard situation in Middleton's plays also. It seems to me that Theobald's failure to regularize this prosodic confusion – to tidy it up so that verse and prose are more clearly distinguished, and to impart more regular iambic rhythms to passages where he could easily have done so along Pope's lines – is one additional strand of evidence for the authenticity of his exemplars and against the hypothesis that the entire project is a forgery.

---

1 A point worth noting is that if Julio's name was ever Cardenio, there would have had to be a wholesale rewriting of the text to accommodate the new scansion.

2 As the play's recent editor Lee Bliss writes: 'While Q1's lineation is often unsatisfactory . . . editors solve Q1's patches of irregular or broken verse in different ways, ways sometimes based less on the lines themselves than on assumptions about verse drama, about Beaumont and Fletcher's in particular, or about the linguistic decorum appropriate to a character's social status.' Francis Beaumont and John Fletcher, *A King and No King*, ed. Lee Bliss (Manchester, 2004), 41–2.

Collation and examination of copies

Copies of the first edition of *Double Falsehood* are not exceptionally rare, though copies of what is called on the title-page the 'second edition', but what is actually, as stated above, a second issue, with revised title-page, are harder to acquire. So too is the 1728 Dublin reprint of that second issue. The British Library has two copies of the first issue (1728a) and one of the second (1728b), as well as one of the Dublin reprint (1728c). The Bodleian Library has the richest collection in the UK, with four copies of the initial issue and a copy of the second that has extensive, if somewhat desultory, annotation by Edmond Malone. Some use has been made of this copy in the section on authorship above (see p. 94). The Library of the Faculty of English of Oxford University has another first-issue copy, while two further copies are to be found in the library of Worcester College, both bound as parts of collections of items. Eleven additional copies of the first issue are recorded by Copac as being held in UK libraries,[1] with only one additional copy of the second issue and two of the Dublin reprint being recorded. Copies in UK libraries that have been examined include those in the Birmingham Central Library and in the John W. Crow collection (bequeathed to the Library of the University of Kent, Canterbury). Major libraries elsewhere in the world have copies, the most significant being the Folger Shakespeare Library, which has a copy of the second issue marked up as a prompt copy for amateur performance (see pp. 117–18). Folger also possesses two copies of the Dublin reprint. Although copies of the 'third edition' of 1767 are not relevant for this edition, there is a significant copy in the Furness Library of the University of Pennsylvania. This is a prompt copy, possibly marked up for a production by David Garrick. It is further discussed above (pp. 109–12).

1   The Copac National, Academic, and Specialist Library Catalogue provides access to the merged online catalogues of major university, specialist and national libraries in the UK and Ireland, including the British Library.

Other major American libraries holding copies of the first issue include the Library of Congress (two copies); the Houghton Library at Harvard University; the Beinecke Rare Book Library at Yale University; the Huntington Library; the Clark Library, UCLA; the University of Illinois; the Chapin Library of Williams College; and the Princeton College Library. In 1769, a further duodecimo edition of the play was printed in Dublin for Charles Ingham. Copies are rare, but two have been seen, in the Bodleian Library and in the Birmingham Central Library.[1] Copies of all three 1728 'editions' in the possession of Richard Proudfoot have also been consulted.

It has not been an aim of this edition to undertake a thorough bibliographical analysis of the printing of *Double Falsehood* by J. Watts in 1728. However, as a record has been compiled of variations noted in an examination of twenty-three individual copies of the first issue, and four of the second, undertaken by the editor and by the general editor for this volume, Richard Proudfoot, it seems appropriate to offer it as an invitation to further exploration. Variations between 1728a and 1728b are textually and critically significant only in respect of Theobald's revision of his preface. The copy-text (1728a) for this edition is BL 841.d.32(7) (*ESTC* T034858). The title-page is reproduced as Fig. 6. The second issue (1728b) title-page differs from the first only in adding the words '*The* SECOND EDITION.' followed by a rule after the motto from Virgil. It appears clear, despite this claim, that the so-called 'second edition' is in fact a second issue (as discussed above), with substantial additions and minor corrections, all in quire A: there is no evidence of resetting of the type elsewhere in the book. Clearly the changes to the Preface were newly set, but with minimum effect on the pagination and in such a way as to make no difference to the overall collation. Some variants between the issues are listed

1   Birmingham 356730; Bodleian Vet. A5 f.1128 (11).

below, but these do not entail resetting any individual line of print.

Dash lengths, hyphenation, running titles and catchwords all seem to be identical. Spaces between words, where these are unusually wide, are identical in length in copies from both issues. Examples of identical spacing include the distances between 'Suspicion' and 'Thou' on sig. B1^v (0.5mm in both); between 'strain'd' and 'Petition' on B1^v (0.2mm in both); between 'absolute;' and 'they' on B2^r (0.4mm in both); while the gap in 'for, this Hour' on B2^r is likewise identical.

Errors, such as the lack of a space between the words 'Eyes' and 'shake' (D6^v) of the first edition ('Eyesshake'), or the anomalous speech prefixes 'Rhod.' for 'Rod.' (D8^r) and 'Roder.' for 'Rod.' (E3^r), or the misprinted 'Passiom' for 'Passion' (E8^r), are not corrected in the 'second edition', as they would presumably have been if type had been reset. This implies that the printer kept the type set for the first edition standing, which he would have done only if it was expected that more copies might very shortly be called for. The general practice at this time was to distribute type after use, and reset the text if and when more copies were needed. Compositors themselves much preferred the latter procedure, because they were paid for the job; so did the master printer. To keep fourteen octavo formes of set type standing took a substantial quantity of type out of use, so that it would have been awkward at a time when even a large printing house had only so much type of any one size and kind in stock. The implication of the second issue is that extra demand for the text was to be expected, and soon: the decision to keep the type standing afforded Theobald the opportunity to revise his preface.[1]

The main variants between the two issues, based on the individual copies inspected, are listed in Table 3.

---

1 It is always possible, however, that the 'second edition' could be a marketing device by which a smallish number of copies are printed, followed by a second small number (with minor revisions) to give the impression of demand.

Table 3   Main variants between 1728a and 1728b

1728a	1728b
A5ʳ l. 8 ro	or
A5ᵛ l. 67 lick	lick.
A6ʳ	*endpiece ornament changed*
A8ʳ	*endpiece ornament moved slightly to left*
A8ᵛ l. 10 Bridgewater. [. *high*]	*position of full stop partially rectified*
B3ʳ catchword You, *comma high*	*position of comma rectified*
B6ᵛ	*endpiece ornament moved slightly to left*
C1ʳ catchword Thro'	Thro,
D3ᵛ	*endpiece ornament moved slightly to left*
D4ʳ catchword *Shep.*	*Shep*
E3ʳ signature	*moved slightly to right*
E4ʳ signature	*moved slightly to left*
E5ᵛ l. 111 Preferment!	Preferment!–
E8ʳ Tho'	tho

The following press figures also occur – significant because, alongside the lateral movements of signatures and ornaments, they may reflect reimposition of formes and thus offer a potential basis for more precise conclusions about the size and sequence of impressions of the play in the early weeks or months after publication:

1728a	1728b
B7ᵛ press figure 3 or none	none
E5ᵛ press figure 4 or none	press figure 5

Some copies of the first issue have the press figure '3' on B7ᵛ; it is not present in the second issue; but where the first issue sometimes has '4' on E5ᵛ and sometimes no press figure, all copies of the second issue examined bear the press mark '5'. The only unequivocal evidence for machining of extra copies relates, therefore, to sheet E and the addition of the press figure '5', though the slight evidence for lateral movement of signatures and ornaments already described might extend this to include A, B, C and D as well. If fresh text sheets were needed to make up the second issue in addition to the replacement sheets of quire A with the revised Preface, the first issue must have sold well before the revisions were made, to the point of actual or near exhaustion of stocks.

In the copies of 1728a examined, the incidence of press figures is as shown in Table 4.

Table 4   Incidence of press figures in 1728a

Page	Figure	Copies
B7^v	3	Bhm, BL, Bod2, 3, 4, Chapin, Clark, F2, Harv, Ill, Kent, LC1, OUSE, Pr1, Worcs1, 2 (16 in all)
	None	Bod1, HN, LC2, Newb, Pr2, RP, Yale (7 in all)
E5^v	4	Bhm, BL, Bod1, 3, Clark, F2, HN, LC1, 2, Newb, OUFE, Pr1, 2, Yale, Worcs1, 2 (16 in all)
	None	Bod2, 4, Chapin, Harv, Kent, Ill, RP (7 in all)

All have at least one of the press figures '3' and '4', six only on B7^v, nine only on E5^v, and eight on both pages. Copies with press figures '3' on both B7^v and '4' on E5^v are: Bhm, BL, Bod 3, Clark, F2, LC1, Pr1, Worcs1, 2 (nine in all). Copies with press figure '3' on B7^v only are: Bod2, 4, Chapin, Harv, Ill, RP (six in all). Copies with press figure '4' on E5^v only are: Bod1, HN, Kent, LC2, Newb, OUFE, Pr2, Yale (eight in all). Table 5 gives the full list of copies examined.

Table 5 Copies of *Double Falsehood* examined

1728a	
UK	
Bhm	Birmingham Central Library 2767
BL	841.d.32 (7)
Bod1	G Pamph. 63 (3) [G = Godw.]
Bod2	8°. F. 259(4) Linc
Bod3	M. adds 108 e.12
Bod4	Harding D2122
Kent	J.W. Crow Collection, University of Kent Library, Canterbury
OUFE	English Faculty Library, Oxford University Faculty of English, XL77.70 [Dou.]
RP	Copy in the library of Richard Proudfoot
Worcs1	Worcs 1: 22.9.11
Worcs2	L. L. 3.6

USA	
Chapin	Chapin Library, Williams College
Clark	W.A. Clark Library, UCLA: PR 3729 T5 D7 *
F2	Folger Shakespeare Library: PR 2858 copy 2
Harv	Houghton Library, Harvard University: Bookplate of Harvard College Library. 'From the Gift of the Department of English'
HN	Henry E. Huntington Library: HN 143329
Ill	University of Illinois Library: X 822.33 Zth
LC1	Library of Congress: PR 2858. A1 1728
LC2	Library of Congress: John Davis Batchelder Collection [lacks D1–8]
Newberry	Newberry Library, Chicago: Y S864.728
Pr1	Princeton College Library: Ex 3600. 308 c.1
Pr2	Princeton College Library: from Library of Henry N. Paul
Yale	Yale University Library

1728b	
Bhm	Birmingham Central Library: 466549
BL2	11774.aaa.28 (6)
Bod5	Bodleian Library: Mal. 171 (8)
RP	Copy in the library of Richard Proudfoot

This sample is too narrow to afford a basis for broad conclusions, but it suggests that both formes inner B and inner E were printed with about 66 per cent of sheets bearing the press figure and 33 per cent without it. As the sheets were collated and bound at random as they happened to be placed in the pile for each quire, figured and unfigured copies are bound together without significance for the sequence of their printing. The absence of the press figure from B7^v in the second issue may further suggest that the numbered sheets preceded the unnumbered. Copies of the 'second edition' examined have no press figure on B7^v and '5' on E5^v: these include Bhm, BL2, Bod5 and RP.

One of the two copies in the Library of Congress was printed on large paper. LC1 measures 142×214mm as against a standard size of approximately 120×197mm. In addition, it omits the price from A1^r. It would appear, accordingly, that a limited number of presentation or de luxe copies, having wide margins, was printed as a variant state within the first issue. Regrettably, this copy provides no indication of ownership.

The third and fourth editions

In May 1767, a further edition of the play was published by Lowndes of Fleet Street, presumably to accompany the Covent Garden revival of Friday 24 April. The title-page is very similar in appearance to the previous printings, though it refers to the Covent Garden production and deals with authorship by claiming that the play was 'written originally by W. Shakespeare; and revised by Mr. Theobald'. The play is here described as in a third edition, which is an accurate description if the 1728 Dublin edition is regarded as the second. There are a number of insignificant changes in accidentals and three substantive changes in the text at 1.1.43, 1.3.63 and 2.4.30 SD (see textual notes) designed to clarify points in the dramaturgy (though leaving most of the real confusions unaddressed). This edition was set from the second issue (1728b), following its octavo format and reprinting paginally. It has five press figures (C5^r, D4^v: '2'; C5^v, D8^r: '4'; E7^r: '5'). If this implies the use of three presses, it could suggest some haste in printing, probably as a result of the 1767 revival at Covent Garden. John W. Kennedy has suggested (in his digitized edition of the play) that this edition was set from a copy of the second impression that had been used as a prompt copy.

As noted above, copies of what will count as the fourth edition, printed by Charles Ingham in Dublin in 1769, seem to be rare. Those examined in the Bodleian Library and in the Birmingham Central Library are printed in half-sheet duodecimo. This edition appears to have been printed directly from 1728a as it has the Preface unrevised. It corrects some, but not all, of the more obvious misprints, but retains the incorrect italics for *Citizen* in the exit stage direction at 3.3.70. Since 1767 corrects this to roman, the conclusion follows that this edition does not use 1767.

This edition

Double Falsehood has been edited four times in the last hundred years. Walter Graham's edition was published in Cleveland, Ohio, in 1920 as part of the Western Reserve Studies series (Graham 1920). Graham's text is unmodernized, does not have textual notes and reproduces the text of the first edition. Obvious typographical errors are silently corrected (e.g. 'passion' in 5.2.263); I have adopted no readings from Graham. In 1970 the Cornmarket Press published a facsimile edition reprinted from the copy of 1728a in the Birmingham Central Library (S359.1728) with a brief introduction by Kenneth Muir (Muir 1970).

The year 2004 was a good one for editions of the play: two appeared. Jeffrey Kahan's edition, published as part of a three-volume collection, argues in its introduction that Theobald was a forger (see pp. 88–90 above). The edition is modernized and there are a few notes, though some are decidedly eccentric.

Glossing the word 'bearn' in 5.2, for example ('bairn' in my text, 5.2.21), Kahan writes: 'Béarn is a region encompassing mountainous regions of the southwestern French department of Pyrénées-Atlantiques. Camillo may be asking, in effect, "Wouldn't you want your daughter to marry someone with land?"' (Kahan 2004, 228). His list of parallel passages between *Double Falsehood* and Shakespeare's plays (237–41) might inspire more confidence if it included any verbal echoes and if the names of the characters Lavinia and Posthumus were spelt correctly. The forgery hypothesis renders equally eccentric his introduction of various 'new readings'. He argues that some of these are inferable from the printed text, which he alleges to be cramped in places, so failing to represent authorial intentions. In general, though, anyone committed to the view that *Double Falsehood* is a forgery must regard such flaws as it displays as deliberately built-in imperfections. The most logical course of action for an editor who thinks Theobald is a forger must be to reproduce the play exactly as in the copy-text. For that reason, and because of its shaky scholarly standards (as instanced on pp. 89–90 above), I have not adopted any readings from Kahan's edition.

John W. Kennedy's online edition, also published in 2004 (Kennedy), is a digitized version of the second issue (1728b). The text, like Graham's, is unmodernized, and though it does not have a full apparatus it represents a considerable advance on any previous edition. He provides a more comprehensive list of dramatis personae than was hitherto available, which has formed a basis for the List of Roles in my edition. Kennedy's text, though more conservative in its lineation than mine, completes a large number of half-lines not marked as such in his copy-text. From his collation of some ten eighteenth-century copies he has compiled the first available set of variant readings; I have incorporated these in the textual notes, and added others unnoticed by Kennedy.

This Arden edition is the first to be thoroughly edited, addressing the various questions raised by the state of the text, by documentary evidence bearing on the issue of authorship and by recent scholarship in the field. The commentary represents a full attempt to assess the range and scale of Shakespearean and Fletcherian allusion, as well as to gloss lexical and other difficulties.

Modernization has its major effects on punctuation and on capitalization. The number of colons, semicolons and commas has been vastly reduced in accordance with modern standards. Eighteenth-century print conventions required the capitalization of nouns. Capitals are retained in this edition only for the beginnings of verse lines and for the occasional instance of personification and the like. These changes are made silently. The copy-text has far more dashes than has my modernized edition. Dashes serve a typographical function, indicating the presence of divided verse lines. Those are redundant in this edition. Dashes also related, however, in the later seventeenth and eighteenth centuries, to performative aspects of the playtext. They frequently indicate that the speaker is gesturing, being interrupted, moving or pausing in a semiotically significant way. Their use intensifies when a speaker is in a heightened emotional state. Don Bernard's speeches are rich in dashes, to indicate the emotionally unstable and vehement nature of his character, for example at 3.3.74–80. The Master's realization, at 4.1.168–71, that the disguised Violante's hand is that of a woman is rendered thus in the original text:

> Come, come, all this is not sufficient, Child,
> To make a Fool of me.– This is a fine Hand,
> A delicate fine Hand,– Never change Colour;
> You understand me,– and a Woman's Hand.

The dashes here serve the typographical function of indicating the beginnings and ends of asides, but they are also, I would contend, a marker of an agitated psychological condition. I have tried to strike a balance between the retention of dashes that signify in this way, and the production of a text that does not look too outlandish to modern readers.

The following practices adopted in the text and textual notes should be brought to the reader's attention. I have preserved all the original elisions in verse (*int'rest*, *wav'ring*) because they are an integral aspect of this text and usually have a role to play in the metre. Readers used to working with the third series of the Arden Shakespeare will find that this edition differs from other texts in one respect: the final *-ed* in past tense and participial forms of verbs is left in its elided form as *-'d* rather than being spelled out in full. Despite his hostility to it as a disfigurement, Jonathan Swift's comment on elision in his *Proposal for Correcting, Improving and Ascertaining the English Tongue* (1712) provides a context for this practice:

> There is another Set of Men, who have contributed very much to the spoiling of the English Tongue; I mean the Poets, from the Time of the Restoration. These Gentlemen, although they could not be insensible how much our Language was already overstocked with Monosyllables, yet to save Time and Pains, introduced that barbarous Custom of abbreviating Words, to fit them to the Measure of their Verses . . . What does your Lordship think of the Words, *Drudg'd, Disturb'd, Rebuk'd, Fledg'd*, and a Thousand others, every where to be met in Prose, as well as Verse? Where, by leaving out a Vowel to save a Syllable, we form so jarring a Sound, and so difficult to utter, that I have often wondered how it could ever obtain.
>
> (Swift, 4.11)

In attributing this linguistic practice only to the post-Restoration period Swift may be revealing his ignorance, but his sense that this is a characteristic orthographic practice of his day has helped to shape my decision to retain it. On some occasions the first edition fails to make elisions required by the metre, whether of final *-ed* or of other syllables. In the interests of consistency, and to avoid confusing the reader, I have elided final *-ed* where required by the metre (as recorded in the textual notes), but have usually left other non-elided forms as they stand, since these could reflect the state of the manuscript copy that the printers were setting.

The first edition uses the singular '*Enters*' in SDs for the entrance of a single character (with the exception of '*Enter Gerald*' at 4.1.243.1). I have regularized this throughout as '*Enter*', as indicated in the commentary (1.2.0.1n.). Asides in the first edition are placed at the end of the speech to which they apply. In my edition the SD '*aside*' precedes the speech to which it applies and its original position is noted. Where, to assist readers and performers, I have inserted some SDs not present in the original, they are in square brackets and their origin in this edition is recorded in the textual notes. Expansion of the original forms *tho'* and *thro'* to *though* and *through* is not recorded. *Pr'ythee* becomes *prithee*. *Can'st* is silently altered to *canst*; other forms ending in *-st* are similarly altered, such as *didst, hadst, shouldst, wouldst, couldst, mayst, mightst*. The apostrophe is retained for forms such as *depend'st*, where there is a true elision. Other forms silently modernized include: *'till* (a mistaken or superfluous form of 'until'), corrected to *till* throughout; word divisions no longer accepted, such as *my self, one's self, any thing, ev'ry thing* and *no body*. Hyphenated words no longer hyphenated in modern usage are also modernized. The only new hyphenation introduced is at 5.2.44: *sev'nty-one*.

Spelling is a very complicated matter in respect of *Double Falsehood*. It is immediately clear that much of the spelling of the first edition was already, if not quite archaic, at least going out of fashion in Theobald's own time. This is an important aspect of the immediate impression the play makes on the modern reader of the first edition: that it has a seventeenth-century document underlying it. Many spellings are shown by the *Oxford English Dictionary* to have been widely current from the late sixteenth or early seventeenth century, even if some of them did survive into the eighteenth century. Among these are entire categories: *-ck* endings for words that now end in *-c* (e.g. *publick*); non-standard *-our/-or/-er* usage (e.g. *Taylour*, *Souldier*); past participles ending in *-t* rather than *-ed*; *-ie* rather than *-y* endings (*jealousie*) and *ye* for *ie* (*dye*). Many particular early spellings, such as *strait*, *chuse*, *wooe*, *shew*, *feaver*, *risque* and *perswade*, were already in process of change by the 1720s. Spelling might seem to offer potential evidence of the date of origin of *Double Falsehood*, were it not that Theobald's own orthography appears to have been somewhat antiquated: in consequence, many of the word forms and lexical items that one might select as clearly antiquated by the 1720s were in fact adopted by Theobald elsewhere in his *oeuvre* as his preferred forms (e.g. *humane*, *traytor*, *confest*, *sooth* (for 'soothe'), *faln*). In the textual notes, I have collated only such spellings as were certainly current in the early seventeenth century and are used by Theobald only in *Double Falsehood*, or at most only rarely elsewhere.

As suggested above, the opening scene of Act 2 is a useful point at which to observe the relationship between the first edition and my practice in this edition, as illustrated in Fig. 16. The printer's ornament introducing a new act renders the page distinctive in ways that modern editions do not reproduce. Several other aspects of the original text contribute to its eighteenth-century appearance. Most obvious and immediate to the modern reader is the use of the long *s* in Lopez's words 'soft' and 'slink'. Capitalization of nouns in the copy-text produces a very different visual effect from the modernized text in which those capitals have been reduced. Such contractions as 'enjoy'd', 'devour'd' and 'refus'd', because they greatly increase the frequency of the apostrophe, are characteristic of the eighteenth-century playscript page. Period orthography – words

ACT II. SCENE I.

SCENE, *The Prospect of a Village.*

Enter Fabian *and* Lopez; Henriquez *on the Opposite Side.*

Lop. SOFT, soft you, Neighbour; who comes
here? Pray you, flink afide.

Henr. Ha! Is it come to this? Oh the Devil, the
Devil, the Devil!

Fab. Lo you now! for Want of the difcreet Ladle   5
of a cool Underftanding, will this Fellow's Brains
boil over.

Henr. To have enjoy'd her, I would have given ——
What?
All that at prefent I could boaft my own,
And the Reverfion of the World to boot,   10
Had the Inheritance been mine : —— And now,
(Juft Doom of guilty Joys!) I grieve as much
That I have rifled all the Stores of Beauty,
Thofe Charms of Innocence and artlefs Love,
As juft before I was devour'd with Sorrow,   15
That fhe refus'd my Vows, and fhut the Door
Upon my ardent Longings.

Lop. Love! Love! —— Downright Love! I fee by
the Foolifhnefs of it.

Henr. Now then to Recollection —— Was't not fo? 20
A Promife firft of Marriage —— Not a Promife only,
for 'twas bound with Surety of a thoufand Oaths; ——
and thofe not light ones neither. —— Yet I remember
too, thofe Oaths could not prevail; th' unpractis'd
Maid trembled to meet my Love: By Force alone I   25
snatch'd

16 Opening of Act 2 of the first edition of *Double Falsehood* (British Library
841.d.32). Line numbers have been added

14   DOUBLE FALSHOOD; *or,*

snatch'd th' imperfect Joy, which now torments my
Memory. Not Love, but brutal Violence prevail'd;
to which the Time, and Place, and Opportunity,
were Acceffaries moft difhonourable. Shame, Shame
upon it!   30

Fab. What a Heap of Stuff's this——I fancy, this
Fellow's Head would make a good Pedlar's Pack, Neighbour.

Henr. Hold, let me be fevere to my Self, but not
unjuft. —— Was it a Rape then? No. Her Shrieks, 35
her Exclamations then had drove me from her. True,
fhe did not confent; as true, fhe did refift; but ftill
in Silence all. ——'Twas but the Coynefs of a mo-
deft Bride, not the Refentment of a ravifht Maid.
And is the Man yet born, who would not rifque the 40
Guilt, to meet the Joy?——The Guilt! that's true
——but then the Danger; the Tears, the Clamours of
the ruin'd Maid, purfuing me to Court. That, that,
I fear will (as it already does my Confcience) fome-
thing fhatter my Honour. What's to be done? But 45
now I have no Choice. Fair *Leonora* reigns confeft the
Tyrant Queen of my revolted Heart, and *Violante*
feems a fhort Ufurper there. —— *Julio's* already by my
Arts remov'd.——O Friendfhip, how wilt thou anfwer That? Oh, that a Man could reafon down this 50
Feaver of the Blood, or footh with Words the Tumult in his Heart! Then, *Julio,* I might be, indeed,
thy Friend. They, they only fhould condemn me, who
born devoid of Paffion ne'er have prov'd the fierce
Difputes 'twixt Virtue and Defire. While they, who 55
have, like me,

The loofe Efcapes of youthful Nature known.
Muft wink at mine, indulgent to their own.
                                                       [*Exit* Henriquez.

Lop. This Man is certainly mad, and may be mif-
chievous. Pr'ythee, Neighbour, let's follow him; 60
but at fome Diftance, for fear of the worft.
                                                       [*Exeunt, after* Henr.
            3   SCENE

such as 'ravisht', 'risque' and 'Feaver' – creates the exoticism of historical pastness.

Moving away from the visual, but always keeping in mind the effect of any modification on the page's appearance, we appreciate that Lopez's dialogue with Fabian is not intended to be overheard by Henriquez. His soliloquy is delivered apart, though this is not indicated by SDs in the first edition. I have, therefore, interpolated the necessary SDs. The modern editor has to consider the function of every punctuation mark. The comma after Fabian's 'Understanding' is not necessary by modern standards, but what of the colon followed by a dash in Henriquez's speech, l. 11? Such use of the colon does not form part of the modern practice of punctuation, but the dash could be retained as marking an abrupt transition in the character's focus of attention. I have not retained it. To satisfy modern punctuation standards while retaining the function of dashes as motivating a sudden thought (with the possibility of some accompanying gesture or action on the actor's part), I have altered the brackets enclosing 'Just Doom of guilty Joys!' to dashes. I have preserved the exclamation mark because the sentiment is exclamatory and is commenting on, rather than forwarding, Henriquez's confession. The reader may notice that there are far more dashes on this printed page and on the next one than would be found in a modern text. Those seem to be mimetic of Henriquez's restless, self-exculpating frame of mind: they are possibly even prompts for movement – pacing across the stage as he tries to rationalize his brutish behaviour. They seem to be directed at performance. The editor has, however, greater problems than that of how to respond to the dashes because, as Pope observed, there is verse here that is set as prose.

Difficulties in identifying and setting out the verse are of several kinds. The editor is looking for verse lines that are both iambic and pentameters, but the iambic pentameter is at best a norm from which the lines frequently depart. 'Now then to Recollection – Was't not so?' *is* actually an iambic pentameter, but what follows it, down to 'neither', does not have any kind of regular iambic rhythm and is best represented as prose. I have normally treated singly occurring lines of iambic verse as prose, but where two or more consecutive lines occur they are usually lined as verse. When the iambic rhythm returns at lines 23–4, it returns in a line that has twelve syllables rather than the desired ten: 'Yet I remember too, those Oaths could not prevail'. Is there any elision that could regularize the line? Answer 'no', so the line must stand as an alexandrine. The following line, if regular, demands an accent on the second syllable of the third word: 'tremblèd'. In stage delivery, the emphasis would doubtless come on the first syllable, the departure from the iambic rhythm adding extra effect. Things now proceed fairly straightforwardly until 'were Accessaries most dishonourable' (29), which calls for elision to 'dishon'rable' to avoid a feminine ending. Very many lines in the play do have feminine endings, so I have not chosen to mark an elision in my edition. 'Shame, Shame upon it!' is a short line, but again, there are many such in the play. Henriquez's next speech is as it stands a mixture of prose and verse and the editor could make differing decisions about how to arrange it. As an example, I have set lines 53–4 as follows:

> They, they only should condemn me,
> Who, born devoid of passion, ne'er have prov'd
> (56–7)

where 56 is unsatisfactorily short and could perhaps have 'Who' at its close, but that word makes 57 a regular iambic line.

I hope that the above serves to give the reader a clear idea of the decisions with which the editor of this curious play is faced. How Theobald compiled the manuscript copy that he sold to the printers is a much deeper enigma. If this edition has not solved that puzzle, it has at least provided foundations upon which later readers and scholars can build.

EPILOGUE

Interest in the *Cardenio* enigma, already deeply embedded in popular culture as we have seen above, continues to develop. In May 2009, a production of Gary Taylor's 'creative reconstruction' entitled *The History of Cardenio* was staged by theatre students at Victoria University of Wellington, New Zealand, under the direction of David Carnegie and Lori Leigh. If allowances are made for the difficulties of having old men played by young students, and ancillary characters who surround Don Quixote such as Sancho (a boy in this version) and Master Nicholas the Barber played by women, this production presented spirited performances from all of the principals, particularly Paul Waggott playing Cardenio, whose madness in the manner of 'Poor Tom' (see Fig. 17) was dramatically exciting. Late Shakespearean tragicomic patterning was inclined here towards the comic. Dominated by the stark image of the coffin brought on at the play's opening and claimed by the Duke for his own eventual resting place, Taylor's *Cardenio* deployed that coffin as a surprise device. The audience has observed Lucinda being concealed inside it to effect her escape from the convent. In 5.1, she rises from the coffin 'in the habit of a novice'. It appears again in the final scene (5.3), where it teases the audience as to the identity of its occupant before being prised open to reveal the Don himself. Notes of farcical comedy were thereby introduced. The rape scene, using Violante's waiting-woman Leonela as a cod priest to perform a fake marriage, was greeted with more audience laughter than seemed entirely appropriate. When the maddened Cardenio meets the Don in Act 4, the clashing types of delusion on display made for interesting theatre. In other respects, though, the introduction of Quixotic material from the original source was not so successful. Using Violante, costumed lavishly as the Princess Micomicon, to dehumour the Don, did not work. 'Dehumouring' (see p. 127) is already a difficult concept for modern audiences to understand. This, combined with the clash of dramatic functions in asking Violante to perform

17 Paul Waggott as Cardenio and Elle Wootton as *Violante* in Gary Taylor's 'creative reconstruction' of *The History of Cardenio*, directed by David Carnegie and Lori Leigh at Victoria University of Wellington, New Zealand, May 2009

an essentially comic role before she has had satisfaction for her own wrongs, introducing the new and unfamiliar character of the Princess, taxed audience comprehension. The thrust stage at Studio 77 made for appropriate intimacy and involvement, intensified by the shared lighting between actors and audience – though this could have been usefully diversified to create differing atmospheres for the Court, the quotidian world inhabited by the Don and his acolytes, and the hilly desert inhabited by the raving Cardenio and forlorn Violante.

Around the production David Carnegie, Professor of Theatre at Victoria University of Wellington, had constructed an academic colloquium at which several absorbing papers were delivered. Those will appear in a forthcoming volume, but it seems appropriate to indicate some of the new directions in which the scholars present will develop work on the play. From Taylor and Carnegie, new insight was gained as to how Theobald may have gone about adapting an original source. Carnegie's work on *The Fatal Secret*, Theobald's adaptation of Webster's *Duchess of Malfi*, showed how he simplifies his source to observe the unities and to eliminate the unseemly Jacobean horror and improper sexuality. Typically, scene and act endings would interpolate stretches of Theobald's own writing, inflated with rhyming couplets. There is a wholesale reascription of lines said by some characters to other characters. All of those features Taylor believes to be characteristic also of the *Double Falsehood* adaptation. Here too, he claims, Theobald has removed subplot material now considered unseemly (relating to Don Quixote) and has reascribed lines: in Taylor's view, Henriquez's speeches in 2.1 are interpolated by Theobald. The uncomfortable presence of Fabian and Lopez as overhearers in that scene he considers to be material displaced from action involving Cardenio/Julio rather than Henriquez.

Interesting and lively work relating to the representation of gender in *Double Falsehood* was presented by Huw Griffiths and the production's assistant director, Lori Leigh. Griffiths traces the silhouette of a lost friendship between Henriquez and Julio that he believes must have been in the source play. (Many students of the play have felt the absence of some developed relationship between the pairings of men and women who are central to its action. All the reconstructions considered above build up this vestigial element of the surviving play.) That friendship must have taken an earlier, homoerotic form much more typical of friendships in *The Two Gentlemen of Verona* and *The Two Noble Kinsmen*: less directed towards the domestic, heterosexual and familial patterns imposed by Theobald and more in line with the passionate relationships between men countenanced by earlier drama. This intelligent account of how Theobald's eighteenth-century sensibility is imposed on the earlier play is supplemented and at times counterpointed by Leigh's study of Violante as a cross-dressed heroine. Speculating that Violante may be etymologically related to 'violation' as well as to the violet flower through which defloration may be indicated, Leigh argues that Violante becomes a frail, victimized and relatively entrapped disguised female – typical of Fletcher's, rather than of Shakespeare's, spirited cross-dressed heroines. Leigh brings out Henriquez's horror, at the play's denouement where he is accused of having commerce with one 'Florio', of being taken for a homosexual: the word 'minion' (5.2.188) carrying much semantic weight here. At this point, her analysis complements that of Griffiths.

A major focus of interest was, naturally, the authorship hypothesis. Would any speaker's work dislodge the consensual view expressed in this edition that the play is a radical adaptation of a Shakespeare–Fletcher collaboration probably already subjected to a layer of adaptive revision in the Restoration period? Two keynote lectures had a bearing on this. Macdonald P. Jackson's painstaking and meticulous textual analysis took its starting point in E.H.C. Oliphant's ascriptions of authorship (see p. 95 above), subjecting these to sophisticated forms of stylometric testing based partly on pause patterns resulting from a change of speaker within a shared line of verse, partly on 'links' (phrases or collocations found only in one of the three relevant authors), and partly on passages where Shakespeare's presence is most convincing. Jackson's provisional conclusions do not dislodge the authorship hypothesis expressed above, but they are even handed and inclined towards a degree of scepticism. He confirms that there is overwhelming evidence for the hand of Fletcher – so the play is not an outright forgery. The evidence for Shakespeare's hand is, as we know, much scantier – in truth very scanty. Nowhere do we have the continuous passages of Shakespeare that render his style easy to identify in, for example, *The Two Noble Kinsmen*. Yet the concentration of diverse Shakespearean characteristics in, for example, 1.3.53–6 brings Jackson out on the side of his presence in the play. Jackson reserves the right, however, to test a hypothesis that what Theobald owned was a collaboration between Beaumont and Fletcher rather than Shakespeare and Fletcher. There is no reason, though, why this should rule Shakespeare out. As we have seen (p. 85), Gildon reports the play as the work of all three authors. Neither, perhaps, is there a clearer case for testing Beaumont's authorship than that, say, of Massinger. Beaumont ceased to write for the theatre after his marriage – and possibly a debilitating stroke – in the year 1613. If he had a hand in *Cardenio*, it would have been one of the last writing tasks he accomplished.

Tiffany Stern's keynote lecture was the most openly sceptical contribution. Her study of the various ways in which plays could be plotted in Shakespeare's period – in particular her contention that co-writing might not actually involve two hands being present in the finished article because one of the authors might be responsible only for the 'plot' or summary of the narrative content – paves the way for saying that both Shakespeare's and Fletcher's hands need not be found in a collaborative play by them. (This is not, of course, the textual situation in the other extant collaborations between the two writers.) Combined with a sceptical account of how Theobald composed his dramatic work – his fixation on impersonating the writers whom he admired – Stern built up a case convincing enough to render any editor of the play cautious. And 'cautious' is what I hope this edition has been.

THE HISTORY OF CARDENIO

by
William Shakespeare and John Fletcher

Adapted for the eighteenth-century stage as

DOUBLE FALSEHOOD
OR
THE DISTRESSED LOVERS

by
Lewis Theobald

ROYAL LICENCE

George the Second, by the grace of God, King of Great
Britain, France and Ireland: Defender of the Faith &c. To
all to whom these presents shall come, greeting. Whereas
our trusty and well-beloved Lewis Theobald, of our city of
London, Gent., hath, by his petition, humbly represented to us   5
that he having at a considerable expense purchased the
manuscript copy of an original play of William Shakespeare
called *Double Falsehood, or The Distressed Lovers*; and, with
great labour and pains, revised and adapted the same to the
stage; has humbly besought us to grant him our royal privilege   10
and licence, for the sole printing and publishing thereof, for
the term of fourteen years: we, being willing to give all
due encouragement to this his undertaking, are graciously
pleased to condescend to his request; and do therefore, by
these presents, so far as may be agreeable to the statute in that   15
behalf made and provided for us, our heirs, and successors,
grant unto him, the said Lewis Theobald, his executors,
administrators, and assigns, our royal licence, for the sole
printing and publishing the said play, in such size and manner
as he and they shall think fit, for the term of fourteen years, to   20
be computed from the date hereof; strictly forbidding all our
subjects within our kingdoms and dominions to reprint
the same, either in the like, or in any other size or manner
whatsoever; or to import, buy, vend, utter or distribute any
copies thereof, reprinted beyond the seas, during the aforesaid   25
term of fourteen years, without the consent or approbation of
the said Lewis Theobald, his heirs, executors and assigns,
under his or their hands and seals first had and obtained; as
they will answer the contrary at their peril. Whereof the
commissioners, and other officers of our customs, the Master,   30
Warden and Company of Stationers are to take notice, that the
same may be entered in the register of the said company, and
that due obedience be rendered thereunto. Given at our court
at St James's, the fifth day of December, 1727; in the first
year of our reign.   35

By His Majesty's command,
HOLLES NEWCASTLE

ROYAL LICENCE Theobald's licence was granted on 5 December 1727, and the work was entered in the Stationers' Company records by the printer John Watts on 29 December 1727 (National Archives SP/44/363, 129–31). The act of procuring a royal licence for a work was relatively unusual, though not absolutely without precedent. The most authoritative account is given by Rogers. Rogers's bibliography lists 189 items for his period. Three licences, including Theobald's, were granted in 1727; there were 22 grants in the entire decade of the 1720s. Perhaps the best known is that granted on 13 January 1742, to Charles Rivington, Samuel Richardson and John Osborn for 'Pamela, or Virtue rewarded'. Petitioners had to offer reasons why a licence ought to be granted, normally having to demonstrate some social or moral benefits that would accrue. Since no such case is put in Theobald's licence, one assumes that the recovery of a lost play by Shakespeare was regarded as self-evidently valuable. The standard cost of procuring such a licence granted to a single holder was £8 1s. (see Rogers, 143, for further detail). In addition, a fee of 6d. was payable to the Stationers' Company for entry of the published work (see 31–2n.) and nine copies needed to be submitted. In the case, therefore, of multi-volume sets, the procedure of obtaining a royal licence could be expensive and must have been regarded as highly prestigious.

3, 15 **these presents** legal language meaning 'the present document or writing'

6 **at . . . expense** This was a formula that appears in most royal licences, so it does not prove anything about Theobald's acquisition of the manuscripts.

10 **privilege** here used in the technical sense of *OED n.* 8a: 'A grant to an individual, corporation, community, etc., of a legal or (esp.) commercial right, esp. to the exclusion or prejudice of the rights of others; a franchise, monopoly, or patent'

12 **fourteen years** By the 1710 Act of 8 Anne, authors (more usually publishers) were entitled to sole publishing rights for a period of 14 years. Royal licences did not grant any additional rights but they did prevent the distribution and sale of imported editions, and works publicized in this way must have been more difficult to pirate, though the existence of a 1728 Dublin duodecimo reprint of *DF* suggests clear limitations to that proposition.

14 **condescend** assent, without the modern pejorative inflection of the word

18, 27 **assigns** those to whom a property or right is legally transferred

24 **utter** 'To put (goods, wares, etc.) forth or upon the market; to issue, offer, or expose for sale or barter; to dispose of by way of trade; to vend, sell' (*OED v.*[1] 1a)

31–2 **Company . . . register** The Guild of Stationers was formed in 1403, and gained its royal charter in 1557, becoming a livery company of the City of London. The Stationers' Company had control over the publishing industry, and its members asserted ownership of a text by entering it in the entry book or the Stationers' Company Register. The Register still continued to function even after the passing of the 1710 Copyright Act.

37 HOLLES NEWCASTLE Thomas Pelham-Holles, Duke of Newcastle-upon-Tyne (1693–1768), appointed Lord Chamberlain in 1717, one of whose offices was to supervise censorship of literary works and the granting of licences. By 1724, he was Secretary of State for the southern department, in charge of British foreign policy, and a strong ally of Sir Robert Walpole, the Prime Minister.

[DEDICATION]

To the Right Honourable George Dodington, Esq.

Sir:
Nothing can more strongly second the pleasure I feel, from the
universal applause which crowns this orphan play, than this
other which I take in presuming to shelter it under your   5
name. I bear so dear an affection to the writings and memory
of Shakespeare that, as it is my good fortune to retrieve
this remnant of his pen from obscurity, so it is my greatest

Dedication

1 **George Dodington** George Bubb
Dodington, Baron Melcombe
(1690/91–1762), was a wealthy and
powerful patron of Whig writers.
Hanham in *ODNB* refers to the tre-
mendous expense of maintaining his
grand estate designed by Sir John
Vanbrugh at Eastbury, Dorset, and
comments: 'The Eastbury "palace"
was to cost Dodington more than
£140,000 to complete and was a drain
on his pocket throughout most of
his career. Its purpose was to fulfil
Dodington's soaring, if buffoonish,
aspirations to rank among the foremost whig grandees, and though loving nothing better than to ridicule
and snipe at his colleagues in power,
his pressing financial needs required
the cushioning of salaried office. This
weakness in his position, coupled
with his naturally orotund personality, portly appearance, and sententious
humour, ensured that he remained
a political lightweight, a slightly
ridiculous larger than life character,
blinkered, vain, and with little principle.' On George II's accession in
1727, Dodington distanced himself
somewhat from the Walpole faction
though he remained a member of
the administration. Alexander Pope's
lines (231–44) on the self-satisfied
patron 'Bufo' (toad), in the *Epistle to
Dr Arbuthnot* (1735), are thought to

have him in their sights: 'Proud, as
Apollo on his forked hill, / Sate full-
blown *Bufo*, puff'd by ev'ry quill; /
Fed with soft Dedication all day long,
/ *Horace* and he went hand in hand in
song. / His Library, (where Busts of
Poets dead / And a true *Pindar* stood
without a head) / Receiv'd of Wits
an undistinguish'd race, / Who first
his Judgment ask'd, and then a Place:
/ Much they extoll'd his Pictures,
much his Seat, / And flatter'd ev'ry
day, and some days eat: / Till grown
more frugal in his riper days, / He
pay'd some Bards with Port, and
some with Praise, / To some a dry
Rehearsal was assign'd, / And others
(harder still) he pay'd in kind' (Pope,
Poems, 4.112–13). He was among the
subscribers to Theobald's edition of
Shakespeare in 1733, specifying that
his copy was to be printed on 'Royal
Paper', which (before being folded
into leaves or pages) normally meas-
ured 25 inches by 20 inches.

3 **second** support, encourage

4 **orphan play** in the sense that it has
no known 'parents' (authors). John
Heminges and Henry Condell, in their
dedicatory epistle to Shakespeare's
First Folio (1623), used the same metaphor: 'We haue but collected them [the
plays], and done an office to the dead,
to procure his Orphanes, Guardians.'
Theobald may have been echoing this
consciously.

ambition that this piece should be received into the protection
of such a patron; and I hope future times, when they mean to   10
pay Shakespeare the best compliment, will remember to say,
'Mr Dodington was that friend to his remains, which his own
Southampton was to his living merit.'

It is from the fine discernment of our patrons that we can
generally best promise ourselves the good opinion of the   15
public. You are not only a distinguished friend of the
Muses, but most intimately allied to them: and from
hence it is I flatter myself, that if you shall think fit to
pronounce this piece genuine, it will silence the censures of
those unbelievers who think it impossible a manuscript of   20
Shakespeare could so long have lain dormant; and who are

12–13 **Mr ... merit** Theobald's flattery
is carefully pitched to appeal to the
portly and sententious Dodington's
ambitious vanity: the comparison of
Dodington to an earl is particularly
well chosen, given Dodington's notorious longing for a peerage.

13 **Southampton** Henry Wriothesley,
third earl of Southampton (1573–
1624), courtier and literary patron, to
whom *VA* (a poem that Theobald imitated in his 1715 *The Cave of Poverty*)
was dedicated in 1593 and *Luc* in the
following year. Notoriously, the 1609
Sonnets were ambiguously dedicated
to 'Mr W.H.'. Southampton's reputation for generosity stood high at the
time, thanks to a questionable story
– also in part addressed to contemporary patrons – retailed in Nicholas
Rowe's edition of Shakespeare in 1709:
'There is one Instance so singular in
the Magnificence of this Patron of
Shakespear's, that if I had not been
assur'd that the Story was handed
down by Sir William Davenant, who
was probably very well acquainted
with his Affairs, I should not have

ventur'd to have inserted, that my
Lord Southampton, at one time, gave
him a thousand Pounds, to enable
him to go through with a Purchase
which he heard he had a mind to. A
Bounty very great, and very rare at
any time, and almost equal to that pro-
fuse Generosity the present Age has
shewn to French Dancers and Italian
Eunuchs' (Rowe, *Shakespeare*, 1.x). For
modern discussion of this anecdote,
see Duncan-Jones & Woudhuysen, 13;
and on Southampton, 26–31.

17 **intimately allied** Dodington married Katherine (d. 1756), daughter
of Edmund Beaghan of Sissinghurst,
Kent, in 1725, though the marriage
was not openly acknowledged until
1742. It is not altogether clear what
Theobald means here, unless he means
the network of poets whom Dodington
patronized. In 1726 Dodington had
published a poem, *An Epistle to the
Right Honourable Sir Robert Walpole*,
a scarcely disguised appeal for promotion which argues that loyalty among
politicians deserves greater reward
than merit.

blindly paying me a greater compliment than either they
design, or I can merit, while they cannot but confess
themselves pleased, yet would fain insinuate that they are
imposed upon. I should esteem it some sort of virtue, were I   25
able to commit so agreeable a cheat.

But pardon me, sir, for a digression that perverts the very
rule of dedications. I own, I have my reasons for it. As, sir,
your known integrity and honour engages the warmest wishes
of all good men for your prosperity, so your known distinction   30
in polite letters, and your generous encouragement of those
who pretend to them, obliges us to consider your advancement
as our own personal interest; and as a good omen, at least, if
not as the surest means of the future flourishing condition of
those humane arts amongst us which we profess, and which   35
you adorn. But neither your modesty nor my inability will
suffer me to enter upon that subject. Permit me therefore, sir,
to convert panegyric into a most ardent wish that you would
look with a tender eye on this dear relic, and that you would
believe me, with the most unfeigned zeal and respect, sir,   40

Your most devoted and obedient humble servant.
Great Russell Street, 21st December, 1727
LEWIS THEOBALD

27–8 **digression . . . dedications** The usual 'rule' of dedications was to praise and flatter the dedicatee, not to seek personal favours.

31 **polite letters** refined, elegant arts

37 **suffer** permit, enable

39 **relic** 'An object invested with interest by reason of its antiquity or associations with the past' (*OED* A. *n.* 5). Some of the religious associations of *n.* 1a adhere to this usage also, however: 'Some object, such as a part of the body or clothing, an article of personal use, or the like, which remains as a memorial of a departed saint, martyr, or other holy person, and as such is carefully preserved and held in esteem or veneration'. Theobald played his part in the 18th-century process of elevating Shakespeare's status to that of quasi-religious icon.

42 **Great Russell Street** Theobald lived in Wyan's Court, off Great Russell Street in Bloomsbury, which, in his time, was the site of such great houses as Montagu House and Bedford House. Great Russell Street ran into Southampton Row to the east (as it still does), and there was a road nearby called Theobald's Row (now Road).

43 LEWIS] (*LEW.*)

PREFACE OF THE EDITOR

The success which this play has met with from the town in the representation (to say nothing of the reception it found from those great judges to whom I have had the honour of communicating it in manuscript) has almost made the purpose of a preface unnecessary; and therefore what I have to say is   5
designed rather to wipe out a flying objection or two, than to labour at proving it the production of Shakespeare.

It has been alleged as incredible that such a curiosity should be stifled and lost to the world for above a century. To this my answer is short: that though it never till now made its   10
appearance on the stage, yet one of the manuscript copies which I have is of above sixty years' standing, in the handwriting of Mr Downes, the famous old prompter; and as I am credibly informed, was early in the possession of the

---

1 **success** The play had its premiere on Wednesday 13 December 1727, with further performances on 14–16, 18–22 and 26 December, and was performed again on 9 January 1728. At a time when many plays did not reach a third performance (and when the profits from every third performance went directly to the author), a run of 10 consecutive nights can reasonably be claimed as a success.

town the fashionable society of London, living in its fashionable areas

3–4 **great . . . manuscript** We do not know to whom Theobald refers, but there is a letter from Theobald to the Countess of Oxford dated 10 December 1727 that encloses 'twelve box tickets' for the performance and has a postscript that reads 'If your Honour has any mind to read the play in manuscript, upon the earliest intimation of your pleasure you shall command it' (see Cadwalader). Theobald could of course be referring to the manuscript of his own revised version. Clearly, others must have seen this:

John Watts the printer, for example, and Colley Cibber who, along with Barton Booth and Robert Wilks, was in charge of the Drury Lane theatre. Booth created the role of Julio (see Original Cast 1727–8, 6n.), so it would be surprising if he and Watts, at least, did not ask to see the manuscripts that Theobald claimed to possess.

12 **above . . . standing** This would date it to the early 1660s.

13 **Downes** John Downes (d. ?1712). Kewes writes in *ODNB* that: 'According to the lord chamberlain's records, Downes was sworn as a comedian in the Duke of York's Company on 27 June 1664, and as a comedian in the King's Company successively on 12 January 1688, 22 February 1695, and about 20 April 1697. Some time in the 1660s he became prompter to the Duke's Company. Following the merger of the Duke's and the King's companies in 1682 he worked for the United Company until the split of 1694; thereafter he was a member of Betterton's Company at Lincoln's Inn Fields and, from 1705, at the

celebrated Mr Betterton, and by him designed to have been   15
ushered into the world. What accident prevented this purpose
of his, I do not pretend to know; or through what hands it had
successively passed before that period of time. There is a
tradition (which I have from the noble person who supplied
me with one of my copies) that it was given by our author, as   20
a present of value, to a natural daughter of his, for whose
sake he wrote it, in the time of his retirement from the stage.

Haymarket, until his retirement in October 1706.' Although stage fright put an early end to his acting aspirations, he produced, in *Roscius Anglicanus, or An Historical Review of the English Stage* (1708), the first theatre history in English.

15–16 **Betterton ... world** Thomas Betterton (bap. 1635, d. 1710), actor and theatre manager, the leading actor of his age. In November 1660 he became a member of the Duke's Company, for which troupe he played leading roles in Shakespeare, both comic and tragic. He masterminded the building of the Dorset Garden theatre which opened in 1671, and was behind the uniting of the two theatrical companies (the King's and the Duke's) in 1682, before forming his own group yet again, appearing in Lincoln's Inn Fields theatre from 1695. His final move was into Vanbrugh's Haymarket theatre from 1705. Betterton could therefore have been responsible, as Theobald implies here, for a stage-adapted version of an earlier play in which Shakespeare had a hand. He had continued to act almost to his death, and by 1727 had become a near-legendary figure, the personification of a former great age of English theatre.

19–22 **tradition ... stage** On this, see Freehafer (502–4), who argues that although Shakespeare did not have a 'natural daughter', Sir William

Davenant was rumoured to be his natural son, so Davenant's (third) wife Henrietta might be regarded as his natural daughter. Of the story that Shakespeare and Davenant's mother had sexual relations while he was a lodger with the family in their Oxford tavern, Edmond writes in *ODNB*: 'The notion that Shakespeare and his Oxford hostess shared a bed in the "painted chamber" of the tavern, and that William was the result of their union, is highly improbable. There is no compelling reason to reject near-contemporary reports that Shakespeare stood *god*father when young William was baptized at St Martin's, Carfax, on 3 March 1606.' 'Son' could be purely figurative, as in 'Sons of Ben [Jonson]'. Another possibility, suggested to me by Neil Pattison, is that the comma after 'his' in 'natural daughter of his' is erroneous and that the phrase should run 'natural daughter of his for whose sake he wrote it'. This would have the consequence that Shakespeare wrote the play not for his own natural daughter but for his patron's natural daughter.

20 **it** In 1728b, 'it' is altered to 'this Play', with the intention, one assumes, of making the number of copies that Theobald claimed to have in his possession less ambiguous. Even in the altered form, it is still not absolutely certain how many copies he is claiming to have in total (see 23n.).

20 it] this Play *1728b*

Two other copies I have (one of which I was glad to purchase at a very good rate) which may not, perhaps, be quite so old as the former; but one of them is much more   25
perfect, and has fewer flaws and interruptions in the sense.

Another objection has been started (which would carry much more weight with it, were it fact) that the tale of this play being built upon a novel in *Don Quixote*, chronology is against us, and Shakespeare could not be the author. But it   30
happens that *Don Quixote* was published in the year 1611, and Shakespeare did not die till April 1616, a sufficient interval of time for all that we want granted.

Others again, to depreciate the affair, as they thought, have been pleased to urge that though the play may have   35
some resemblances of Shakespeare, yet the colouring, diction and characters come nearer to the style and manner of Fletcher. This, I think, is far from deserving any answer. I submit it to the determination of better judgements; though my partiality for Shakespeare makes me wish that   40

---

23 **Two** The various unclarities in Theobald's story have led to confusion as to whether he is claiming a total of *three* manuscript copies, or *four*. As Metz points out, it is unclear from Theobald's formulation whether the copies are (1) the Downes copy, (2) the copy of the 'noble person', and (3) and (4) 'Two other copies'; or whether (1) and (2) are identical, as the ensuing phrase 'not . . . quite so old as the former' would imply. Metz comments that whereas Chambers was unsure whether to count three or four manuscripts, Muir in his facsimile edition (1970) states plainly that there were four. See Metz, *Sources*, 261–2 and n. 15.

29 **novel** here in the sense of 'interpolated story'
30–3 **But ... granted** In 1728b, Theobald took the opportunity to correct the chronology here. Scholars have argued that Theobald's erroneous claim that *Don Quixote* was published in 1611 may be based on the fact that Shelton's translation was entered in the Stationers' Register on 19 January 1612, though not published until later in 1612. This would imply that Theobald had consulted the Register, an important assumption in the overall discussion of authorship (see pp. 22–3).
34 **depreciate** lessen the value of
36 **colouring** overall character or tone; style

29, 31 *Quixote*] *(Quixot)*   31 that . . . was] that the *First* Part of *Don Quixot*, which contains the Novel upon which the Tale of this Play seems to be built, was *1728b*   32–3 1616 . . . all] 1616; an Interval of no less than Eleven Years, and more than sufficient for All *1728b*

everything which is good or pleasing in our tongue had been owing to his pen.

As to the performance of the respective actors concerned in this play, my applauding it here would be altogether superfluous. The public has distinguished and given them a   45
praise much beyond any that can flow from my pen. But I have some particular acknowledgements to make to the managers of this company, for which I am glad to embrace so fair an opportunity.

I came to them at this juncture as an editor, not an author,   50
and have met with so much candour and handsome treatment from them, that I am willing to believe the complaint which has so commonly obtained, of their disregard and ill behaviour to writers, has been more severely urged than it is justly grounded. They must certainly be too good judges of   55

---

41 **in our tongue** In 1728b, Theobald amended these words (see t.n. and p. 23). To some scholars, this is evidence that the degree of certainty about Shakespeare's *sole* authorship has weakened, even if he concedes very little in this rephrasing.

42–3 **pen. As** In 1728b a passage of 19 lines is interpolated here (see t.n.) in which Theobald indicates that he is working on a complete edition of Shakespeare, which was published in seven volumes in 1733.

48 **this company** i.e. at the Theatre Royal, Drury Lane

53–8 **ill ... hands** Cibber in particular was constantly upbraided for his conservatism in refusing to take on new work. He had recently rejected

Philip Frowde's tragedy *The Fall of Saguntum*, which was performed at the rival theatre in Lincoln's Inn Fields, where it ran for 11 nights between 16 and 28 January 1727. Since Theobald wrote the Prologue for Frowde's play and vice versa, we might speculate that Frowde became somewhat disaffected when his tragedy was refused while Theobald's play was accepted. Frowde's play did reasonably well financially, except that he had twice to make up the house charge of £50. (See Hume, *Fielding*, 24.) If he continued to complain to Theobald about rejection, it is perhaps no wonder that the latter became impatient. Perhaps this is a coded suggestion to Frowde to stop whingeing. See further Prologue 0.1n.

---

41 our tongue] that other great Poet *1728b*   42–3 pen. / As] pen. I had once design'd a *Dissertation* to prove this Play to be of *Shakespeare*'s Writing, from some of its remarkable Peculiarities in the *Language*, and Nature of the *Thoughts*: but as I could not be sure but that the Play might be attack'd, I found it adviseable, upon second Consideration, to reserve *that* Part to my *Defence.* That Danger, I think, is now over; so I must look out for a better Occasion. I am honour'd with so many powerful Sollicitations, pressing Me to the Prosecution of an Attempt, which I have begun with some little Success, of *restoring* SHAKESPEARE from the numerous Corruptions of his Text: that I can neither in Gratitude, nor good Manners, longer resist them. I therefore think it not amiss here to promise, that, tho' *private Property* should so far stand in my Way, as to prevent me from putting out an *Edition* of *Shakespeare*, yet, some Way or other, if I live, the Publick shall receive from my Hand his *whole* WORKS corrected, with my best Care and Ability. This may furnish an Occasion for speaking more at large concerning the present *Play*: For which Reason I shall now drop it for another Subject. / As *1728b*

their own interest not to know that a theatre cannot always
subsist on old stock, but that the town requires novelty at
their hands. On the other hand, they must be so far judges
of their own art and profession as to know that all the
compositions which are offered them would never go down   60
with audiences of so nice and delicate a taste, as in this age
frequent the theatres. It would be very hard upon such a
community, where so many interests are concerned, and so
much merit in their business allowed, if they had not a
privilege of refusing some crude pieces, too imperfect for the   65
entertainment of the public. I would not be thought to infer
that they have never discouraged what they might, perhaps,
afterwards wish they had received. They do not, I believe, set
up for such a constant infallibility. But if we do but fairly
consider out of above four thousand plays extant, how small a   70
number will now stand the test; if we do but consider too,
how often a raw performance has been extolled by the
partiality of private friendship; and what a clamour of injury
has been raised from that quarter upon such performance
meeting a repulse; we may pretty easily account for the   75
grounds upon which they proceeded in discountenancing
some plays, and the harsh things that are thrown out upon
their giving a repulse to others. But I should beg pardon for
interfering in this question, in which I am properly neither
party nor judge. I am only throwing out a private opinion,   80
without interest or prejudice, and if I am right in the notion,
valeat quantum valere potest.

61 **nice and delicate** discriminating and
sophisticated
67–8 **discouraged . . . received** By the
time the play was published, John
Gay's *The Beggar's Opera* had begun
its triumphant run at Lincoln's Inn
Fields, on 29 January 1728. Gay had
offered the play to Drury Lane but

Cibber turned it down, and his rival
John Rich profited.
82 *valeat . . . potest* 'let it pass for what it
is worth' (sometimes translated as 'Let
the plea avail as far as is proper', or 'It
shall have effect as far as it can have
effect'), a Latin tag still popular with
lawyers

66 public.] *(*Pub-/lick*)*

DRAMATIS PERSONAE
AND
ORIGINAL CASTS

DRURY LANE 1727–8

Men

Duke Angelo	Mr Corey	
Roderick, *his elder son*	Mr Mills	
Henriquez, *his younger son*	Mr Wilks	
Don Bernard, *father to Leonora*	Mr Harper	
Camillo, *father to Julio*	Mr Griffin	5
Julio, *in love with Leonora*	Mr Booth	
	Mr Williams	
	(1st to 4th nights)	
Citizen	Mr Oates	
Master of the Flocks	Mr Bridgwater	
First Shepherd	Mr Norris	
Second Shepherd	Mr Ray	10

Women

Leonora	Mrs Porter
Violante	Mrs Booth

DRURY LANE 1727–8 The original cast is included in the list of Dramatis Personae in 1728a.

1 **Mr Corey** John Corey (*fl. c.* 1699–1735). He had played the Duke in Thomas D'Urfey's *Don Quixote* while working for Rich at Lincoln's Inn Fields. In the 1720s Corey acted at Drury Lane and at the booth stages during summer fairs. His most popular role was Lucius in Joseph Addison's *Cato*. Shortly before playing the Duke in *DF*, he had played King Edward IV in Rowe's *Jane Shore* at Bartholomew Fair (August 1727).

2 **Mr Mills** John Mills (d. 1736) was an actor of considerable versatility. His career stretched back to the 1690s. He had a reputation for personal morality and honesty. *BDA* notes that in the 1721–2 season Mills played around 50 different roles in 70 plays acted at Drury Lane, appearing in 12 different roles in 12 nights; and he probably performed on 160 out of 192 nights the theatre was open (*BDA*, 10.249). His Shakespearean parts at Drury Lane in this decade included Julius Caesar, Buckingham in *R3*, Gloucester in *KL* and Wolsey in *H8*.

3 **Mr Wilks** Robert Wilks (*c.* 1665–1732), actor and manager, was part of the triumvirate (with Cibber and Booth) who managed Drury Lane theatre, and was the natural successor to the aged Betterton in both comic and tragic acting. He played a vast range of leading parts in both genres, though his reputation was for vanity and temperament. In the season preceding the premiere of *DF*, for example, Wilks objected to Cibber's

suggestion that he give the role of Constant in Vanbrugh's *The Provoked Wife* to Booth, and a well-documented row followed. Wilks was advanced in age for taking on a juvenile leading part such as Henriquez, but in this period it was customary for leading actors to 'own' roles, and Wilks was already identified with rakish characters. Other acting responsibilities in the 1720s embraced modern rakes such as Horner in William Wycherley's *The Country Wife* and Dorimant in Sir George Etherege's *The Man of Mode*, as well as major Shakespearean characters including Hamlet, Mark Antony in *JC*, and Macduff. He also played a number of Fletcher parts at this time: Valentine in *WWM*, the elder Loveless in *SL*, John in *Cha* and the Copper Captain in *Rule*.

4   **Mr Harper** John Harper (d. 1742) joined the Drury Lane troupe in 1721–2, playing Sir Epicure Mammon in Ben Jonson's *The Alchemist*. Given his success in roles such as Falstaff, Sir Tunbelly Clumsy and Henry VIII, he may have been a corpulent man.

5   **Mr Griffin** Benjamin Griffin (?1680–1740), actor and playwright. A short, slight man, he specialized in low comic roles, and does not appear to have been well treated by the Drury Lane management. One of his roles was Justice Silence.

6   **Mr Booth** Barton Booth (?1679–1733), actor and manager. After his triumph as Cato in Addison's play in 1713, Booth became a partner in the Drury Lane theatre management together with Cibber and Wilks. With some reputation for indolence, and dogged by ill health in the later 1720s, Booth had Charles Williams understudy him for the role of Julio. Williams performed the role on the first night. Booth returned for the fifth to the twelfth nights, and gave his final performance on any stage as Julio on 9 January 1728. Included in his repertoire were the roles of Lear, Brutus and Henry VIII.

Mr Williams Charles Williams

(1693–1731). A Drury Lane actor from 1718, who also worked extensively during the summer season at the fairs, he aspired to such roles as Laertes and Banquo, but was not a leading player.

7   **Mr Oates** James Oates (d. 1751) began with the Drury Lane company in 1717–18, but never aspired to large roles in the main house. His other roles around this time included Poins in *2H4* and Pedro in Sir Samuel Tuke's *The Adventures of Five Hours*.

8   **Mr Bridgwater** Roger Bridgwater (d. 1754). Though a relatively young man in 1727, he played both mature and younger roles, and was somewhat inclined towards bombast. He specialized at this time in young rakes such as Archer in George Farquhar's *The Beaux' Stratagem*, but in tragedy sometimes took older roles such as Ghost in *Ham* and Banquo in *Mac*.

9   **Mr Norris** Henry Norris (1665–1731), a veteran actor, mainly of comic and character parts, who worked at Drury Lane from 1708 to 1730. The First Shepherd is a curious role for such an experienced actor, but by then in his sixties, Norris may have been looking for less tiring work. His nickname was 'Jubilee Dicky' after the role he played in Farquhar's *A Trip to the Jubilee*. He was notorious for ad-libbing.

10 **Mr Ray** John Ray (d. 1752) was known for his singing. His career did not develop at Drury Lane, and in 1727–9 he was playing mostly minor roles such as the Second Shepherd. His other roles at this time, all minor, included the Second Gravedigger in *Ham*.

11 **Mrs Porter** Mary Porter (d. 1765) must have been approaching the age of 50 when she played Leonora. She had been acting professionally since the late 1690s, and at Drury Lane regularly since 1710, despite having advantages neither of beauty nor of voice. She had considerable stage presence, however, and excelled in passionate tragic roles. Dignity and injured propriety were her stock in trade. Aaron Hill comments on her habit of 'extending

her arms to emphasize her shape' when acting tragic roles (*BDA*, 12.95), which included Queen Katherine in *H8* and Gertrude in *Ham*.

12 **Mrs Booth** Hester Booth, née Santlow (*c.* 1690–1773), second wife of Barton Booth. A mistress in her early years of James Craggs, who would become Secretary of State, and possibly even of the Duke of Marlborough, Booth conformed to some of the stereotypes of the actress-whore of the period.

There was some surprise when Barton Booth married her in 1719. Known for her dancing, she played both tragic and comic parts successfully. When her husband became ill and quit the stage after *DF* her own career also slowed down, and there is some evidence that even in 1728 she was no longer at the height of her powers. Her Shakespearean roles at this time included Ophelia in *Ham* and Lady Percy in *1H4*.

COVENT GARDEN 1767

Men

Duke Angelo	Mr Clarke	
Roderick, *his elder son*	Mr Hull	
Henriquez, *his younger son*	Mr Smith	
Don Bernard, *father to Leonora*	Mr Walker	
Camillo, *father to Julio*	Mr Gibson	5
Julio, *in love with Leonora*	Mr Ross	
Citizen	Mr Perry	
Master of the Flocks	Mr Buck	
First Shepherd	Mr Bennet	
Second Shepherd	Mr Cushing	10
Gentleman	Mr Gardner	
Servant	Mr R. Smith	

Women

Leonora	Mrs Mattocks
Violante	Miss Macklin

COVENT GARDEN 1767 The original cast is included in the list of Dramatis Personae in 1767.

1   **Mr Clarke** Matthew Clarke (d. 1786) 'stepped directly from the obscurity of a City tradesman's shop into leading roles in one of the great patent theatres of London, a unique occurrence in the annals of British theatricals' (*BDA*, 3.305), in 1755. He became a stalwart at Covent Garden for over 30 years, playing roles such as Antonio in *MV* and Belarius in *Cym*.

2   **Mr Hull** Thomas Hull (1728–1808) made his debut at Covent Garden in 1759, performing there for the next 48 winters. By the mid-1760s he aspired to some leading roles, including Mark Antony in *JC* and Edgar in *KL* around the time of his appearance as Roderick. Francis Gentleman in *The Dramatic Censor* (1770) refers to his 'tender

sensibility' (1.477), important for the role of Roderick. He was a writer and theatre manager as well as an actor.

3   **Mr Smith** William Smith (1730–1819). Educated at Eton and Cambridge (from which he was removed for snapping an unloaded pistol at a proctor), Smith drifted into the theatre after his father's financial ruin, making his theatrical debut in 1753. He married an older woman of aristocratic family in 1754, and his rakish manners must have qualified him very well for the role of Henriquez. He was already playing Iago and Cassius, as well as Antony in John Dryden's *All for Love*. The *Theatrical Review* referred in 1758 to his eyes that 'have naturally a rakish leer, which suits very well the modern fine gentleman and the agreeable debauché' (*BDA*, 14.177).

11 Gentleman] *1767*   12 Servant] *1767*

4   **Mr Walker** John Walker (1732–1807). Prior to joining the Covent Garden troupe in 1762, he had experience at Drury Lane and in Birmingham and Bristol. He normally played senior figures such as Claudius in *Ham* and Kent in *KL*, though he played Brutus in the same season as he played Don Bernard. His clear articulation and pronunciation were praised in his own time.

5   **Mr Gibson** William Gibson (1713–71). His career as an actor was virtually over by the time he played Camillo, having begun at Covent Garden in 1739. He was by then exclusively playing older characters such as Claudius in *Ham* and Brabantio in *Oth*. His latter days were spent campaigning for a large theatre to be erected in Liverpool, where he was already a theatre manager.

6   **Mr Ross** David Ross (1728–90). He offended his father irrevocably by taking to the stage. In 1751 he made his debut at Covent Garden, and after a spell at Drury Lane rejoined in 1757. His reputation was for charm, good looks and elegance, but several contemporary reviews stress his negligence and refusal to work at his art. In the season after appearing as Julio, he moved into theatre management in Edinburgh.

8   **Mr Buck** William Buck (d. 1777). The Master would have been a good role for this minor actor who otherwise aspired to supporting roles such as the First Murderer in *Mac* and the Second Gravedigger in *Ham*.

13 **Mrs Mattocks** Isabella Mattocks, née Hallam (1746–1826). Born of a theatrical family, she was a child actress who made her first 'adult' appearance as Juliet in *RJ* at Covent Garden in 1761, and by 1767 (after her elopement with and marriage to George Mattocks in 1765) was playing such roles as Cordelia in *KL*, Jessica in *MV* and other glamorous female leads. She was a fine singer but as an actress she does not appear to have been regarded as first rate and was often criticized for affected distortion of the features.

14 **Miss Macklin** Maria Macklin (*c.* 1733–81). Illegitimate daughter of the famous actor Charles Macklin, she was tutored by her father and had her first substantial part at Drury Lane in 1745, followed by her adult debut at Covent Garden in 1751. She was an exceptionally accomplished person and performer, with considerable musical talent that must have shone through as Violante. After working at Drury Lane with David Garrick, she joined Rich's Covent Garden troupe in 1760, appearing as Juliet in *RJ*. Somewhat overshadowed by Susannah Maria Cibber, she was admired for her Rosalind in *AYL* but never achieved the exalted status of such stars as Cibber, Ann Barry or Margaret (Peg) Woffington.

DOUBLE
FALSEHOOD
OR
THE DISTRESSED
LOVERS

LIST OF ROLES

DUKE Angelo

RODERICK *his elder son*

HENRIQUEZ *his younger son*

DON BERNARD *father to Leonora*

LEONORA   5

CAMILLO *father to Julio*

JULIO *in love with Leonora*

VIOLANTE *a maid, in love with Henriquez*

CITIZEN

MASTER of the Flocks   10

SHEPHERDS

FABIAN

LOPEZ

GERALD *servant to Henriquez*

MAIDS   15

SERVANTS

Churchman

GENTLEMEN

Attendants, Courtiers, Musicians

Scene: the province of Andalucia in Spain   20

---

11 SHEPHERDS] First Shepherd, Second Shepherd *1728a*   12 FABIAN] *Fabian,* a Clown *Kennedy*   13
LOPEZ] *Lopez,* another *Kennedy*   14 GERALD *servant to Henriquez*] *Kennedy*   15 MAIDS] Maid to
Leonora, Maid to *Violante / Kennedy*   16 SERVANTS] Servant to *Henriquez,* Servant to *Violante*
/ Kennedy   17 Churchman] *Kennedy*   18 GENTLEMEN] *Kennedy*   19 Attendants] Attendants to
Leonora / Kennedy   Courtiers] *this edn*   Musicians] *Kennedy*   20 *Andalucia] (Andalusia)*

178

1 DUKE **Angelo** named Ricardo in Shelton (3.10.221). The name is specified only in the List of Roles, not used in the text, where he is always referred to as 'the Duke' by other characters. *Index* lists 10 entries for Angelo, most prominently Ben Jonson, *The Case Is Altered* (1597); George Chapman, *May Day* (1602); Shakespeare, *CE* (1592) and *MM* (1604); Fletcher with ?Beaumont, *Capt* (1612); and Fletcher and Massinger, *SC* (1622).

2 RODERICK The name may derive from a note in Shelton (3.13.267; see p. 365 below), though it arises in the form Rodorick in John Dryden's *The Rival Ladies* (1664), a play written in the Spanish fashion of Sir Samuel Tuke's *The Adventures of Five Hours* (1663). Theobald had himself used the name Roderick in his 1715 play *The Perfidious Brother*. The Spanish form Roderigo is common throughout the 16th and 17th centuries. In *DF*, the name is first spoken at 1.1.10; it probably requires elision to two syllables (Rod'rick), and is sometimes printed as such.

3 HENRIQUEZ named Fernando in Shelton (3.9.215). It is used by Fletcher and Massinger in *SC*, in the form Henrique. Tuke's *Five Hours* has a character called Enrique, and Dryden's *Don Sebastian* (1690) has one called Enriquez. In *DF*, the name is first spoken at 1.1.15; it frequently requires pronunciation as two syllables rather than three, i.e. 'Henricks'.

4 DON BERNARD The name Bernard appears only in two obscure plays in Shakespeare's period, though there is a Barnardo in *Ham*. The form Bernardo is found in Philip Massinger's *The Great Duke of Florence* (1627) and in James Shirley's *The Gentleman of Venice* (1639). In *DF*, the character is referred to occasionally as 'Bernardo' (2.3.32, 132) or 'Bernard' (5.2.219), and elsewhere as 'Don Bernard'.

5 LEONORA named Luscinda in Shelton (3.10.220). The name has seven entries in *Index*, the closest in date to 1613

being John Webster, *The Devil's Law Case* (1619); Shirley, *The Gamester* (1633); and Massinger, *A Very Woman* (1634). In *DF*, the name is first spoken at 1.2.23; it often requires pronunciation as three syllables rather than four, i.e. 'Le'nora'.

6 CAMILLO The name is used in *WT* for Leontes' wise old retainer, and by Webster in *The White Devil* (1612). Before that, Jonson deploys it in *The Case is Altered* (1597). Later users include Fletcher and Massinger in *DM* (1620), Fletcher in *WM* (1624), Massinger in *The Guardian* (1633) and John Ford in *The Fancies* (1635). In *DF*, the name is first spoken at 1.1.34.

7 JULIO named Cardenio in Shelton (3.10.220). The name had a long history of deployment in the period 1560–1660. *Index* lists 22 entries. Amongst the most prominent are John Marston, *Antonio's Revenge* (1600); Webster, *White Devil* and *Law Case*; Fletcher with ?Beaumont, *Capt*; Ford, *Fancies*; and plays by Massinger and Shirley. In *DF* the name almost always requires pronunciation as two syllables, i.e. Jul-yo.

8 VIOLANTE named Dorotea in Shelton (4.1.291). This name is not especially common in pre-1660 plays, which may impart significance to those in which it does occur. It is found as '*Violenta*' in the First Folio, used of a minor character in *AW* 3.5. The first time the name Viola is found in F is as '*Violenta*' in *TN* 1.5. It is found in Fletcher and Massinger's *SC*, Shirley's *Gamester*, John Crowne's *Sir Courtly Nice* (1685), Dryden's *Don Sebastian*, and Susanna Centlivre's *The Wonder! A Woman Keeps a Secret* (1714). The name was topical in 1727–8, because there was a celebrated rope-dancer who went under the stage name of Mrs Violante, and the newspapers of the period advertised her benefit performances. In *DF*, the name is first spoken at 1.3.37.

10 MASTER of the Flocks named 'Master' in Shelton (4.1.299)

8 a . . . Henriquez] this edn

12 FABIAN The name is found in *TN* and in Jonson's *The Devil Is an Ass* (1616). It is not spoken in *DF*.

13 LOPEZ The name is found in Fletcher's *WPl* and in Fletcher and Massinger's *SC*. It is not spoken in *DF*.

14 GERALD The name does not appear elsewhere as a character name in Shakespeare's period, but there is a Gerrold as used for the Schoolmaster in *TNK*. In *DF*, it is first spoken at 2.2.9.

17 **Churchman** A clergyman is specified thus functionally in Thomas Dekker's *Match Me in London* (1611) and in Webster's *The Duchess of Malfi* (1614).

DOUBLE FALSEHOOD
OR
THE DISTRESSED LOVERS

PROLOGUE

Written by Philip Frowde, Esq.
and spoken by Mr Wilks

As in some region where indulgent skies
Enrich the soil, a thousand plants arise
Frequent and bold; a thousand landscapes meet

TITLE The play was first printed under the title *Double Falshood; Or, The Distrest Lovers*. Since the missing play by Shakespeare and Fletcher was entered in the Stationers' Company Register under the title *The History of Cardenio* (see Fig. 9, p. 83), this title is a later invention. English play titles containing the word 'double' are not found before 1660, gaining popularity after Dryden's *The Spanish Friar, or The Double Discovery* (1681) and William Congreve's *The Double Dealer* (1694). *DF* may have gained its title in the Restoration period. Successful plays by Mary Pix (*The Double Distress*, 1701) and Colley Cibber (*The Double Gallant*, 1707) may, however, have suggested the title to Theobald. It is possible that Pope parodies the omitted '*e*' in the spelling of *Falshood* in his opening footnote to the title of the 1729 edition of *The Dunciad Variorum*. This deals with the spelling of the poem's name: 'The *Dunciad, Sic* M.S. It may be well disputed whether this be a right Reading. Ought it not rather to be spelled *Dunceiad*, as the Etymology

evidently demands? *Dunce* with an *e*, therefore *Dunceiad* with an *e*' (Pope, *Dunciad Variorum*, 175). Pope goes on to refer to the fact that Theobald ('That accurate and punctual Man of Letters, the Restorer of *Shakespeare*', 175) always includes both letters *e* in the spelling of Shakespeare's name. Kahan (2004, 1.238) considers that the play's title is 'clearly built around' *TC* 3.2.185–91.

PROLOGUE In the 18th-century theatre, a prologue, often commissioned from a friend of the playwright, was usually spoken to introduce the first performance of a new play.

0.1 **Philip Frowde** (1678/9–1738). See pp. 64–6 Sambrook in *ODNB* further underlines Frowde's Williamite and Whig family connections. Like Theobald, he trained as a lawyer and seems not to have begun professional writing until he was in his forties.

0.2 **Mr Wilks** See Original Cast 1727–8, 3n.

1 **indulgent** lenient; avoiding harshness

1–6 This opening owes something to Alexander Pope's *Windsor-Forest* (1713): 'Here hills and vales, the wood-

Our ravish'd view, irregularly sweet:
We gaze, divided, now on these, now those;   5
While all one beauteous wilderness compose.
Such Shakespeare's genius was. Let Britons boast
The glorious birth, and, eager, strive who most
Shall celebrate his verse; for while we raise
Trophies of fame to him, ourselves we praise: 10
Display the talents of a British mind,
Where all is great, free, open, unconfin'd.
Be it our pride to reach his daring flight,
And relish beauties he alone could write.
Most modern authors, fearful to aspire,   15
With imitation cramp their genial fire;
The well-schemed plan keep strict before their eyes,
Dwell on proportions, trifling decencies;
While noble nature all neglected lies.

---

land and the plain, / Here earth and water, seem to strive again; / Not *Chaos* like together crush'd and bruis'd, / But as the world, harmoniously confus'd: / Where order in variety we see, / And where, tho' all things differ, all agree' (11–16; *Poems*, 1.149–50). Likening Shakespeare's art to a verdant natural landscape (implicitly or explicitly contrasted to the narrowly formal gardens cultivated by his modern successors, as in ll. 15–28) was a commonplace of 18th-century poetry and criticism, and would remain so. Samuel Johnson's formulation is typical: 'The work of a correct and regular writer is a garden accurately formed and diligently planted, varied with shades, and scented with flowers; the composition of *Shakespeare* is a forest, in which oaks extend their branches, and pines tower in the air, interspersed sometimes with weeds and brambles, and sometimes giving shelter to myrtles and to roses; filling the eye with awful pomp, and gratifying the mind with endless

diversity' (Johnson, 2.105–6).

11 **British mind** Shakespeare is used as a symbol of British freedom of expression, implying a contrast with France and Spain.

15–18 Behind this lies the debate, brought to new prominence by controversies over Pope's translation of Homer, that juxtaposed Virgilian rule-bound composition and the more purely imaginative expression of Homer, to which the word 'fire' was often applied. Since French critics such as Nicolas Rapin and Nicolas Boileau were often regarded as prescriptive and rule-bound, the lines continue the implied critique of absolutist France. To 'dwell on proportions' is to attend to the purely technical aspects of poetical composition, as an architect might attend to the dimensions and measurements of his building, to the detriment of its imaginative inspiration.

19–24 Frowde picks up on characterizations of Shakespeare as a wild, untutored genius that began as early as John

17–19] *marked with brace as rhyming triplet 1728a*

Nature, that claims precedency of place,   20
Perfection's basis, and essential grace!
Nature so intimately Shakespeare knew,
From her first springs his sentiments he drew;
Most greatly wild they flow, and when most wild, yet
   true.
While these, secure in what the critics teach,   25
Of servile laws still dread the dangerous breach,
His vast, unbounded soul disdain'd their rule,
Above the precepts of the pedant school!
O, could the Bard, revisiting our light,
Receive these honours done his shade tonight,   30
How would he bless the scene this age displays,
Transcending his Eliza's golden days!
When great AUGUSTUS fills the British throne,
And his lov'd consort makes the muse her own,
How would he joy to see fair merit's claim   35
Thus answer'd in his own reviving fame!
How cry with pride – 'Oblivion I forgive;

Milton's memorial sonnet of 1630, printed in the 1632 Second Folio. In 'L'Allegro', Milton has 'Then to the well-trod stage anon, / If Jonson's learned sock be on, / Or sweetest Shakespeare fancy's child / Warble his native wood-notes wild' (131–4) (Milton, 188).

20 **precedency** precèdency

24 The triplet (grouping of three rhyming lines) is rounded off here with an alexandrine (12-syllable line).

25 **these** the *modern authors* (15)

26 **dangerous** The metre requires elision to two syllables.

31 **the scene** political landscape, but referring also to the playhouse itself – its scenery and the health of its repertoire

32 **Eliza** Queen Elizabeth I

33 AUGUSTUS George Augustus (1683–1760), Duke of Brunswick-Lüneberg (Hanover) and King George II of Great Britain and Ireland, crowned only a few months earlier. The coincidence between his middle name and that of the great Roman Emperor Augustus (63 BCE–14 CE) enables poets to praise him or, like Pope in his *Imitations of Horace Epistle II.i: To Augustus* (1737), to use the comparison as the basis of subtle irony.

34 **lov'd consort** Queen Caroline of Brandenburgh-Ansbach (1683–1737). To refer to her as *lov'd consort* is to take a pro-Whig political position. She had considerable interest in the arts and sciences, especially in matters of theology.

35 **fair merit's claim** the just demands made by dramatists of real ability

22–4] marked with brace as rhyming triplet 1728a

This my last child to latest times shall live:
Lost to the world, well for the birth it stay'd;
To this auspicious era well delay'd.'   40

[*Curtain rises.*]

1.1   *A royal palace*

DUKE Angelo, RODERICK *and Courtiers* [*discovered*].

RODERICK
My gracious father, this unwonted strain

---

38 **last child** Frowde's metaphor, in which the play becomes a lost child rediscovered at last, seems at once to take up Theobald's claim that the play had been bequeathed to an apocryphal daughter and to cast *DF* as Perdita in *WT* or Marina in *Per*.

39 **stay'd** waited; was deferred or postponed

40 SD *Curtain rises* The rising of the curtain is deduced from the fact that 1728a has '*Curtain falls*' at the end of the text. Normal practice in the period would be for the curtain to rise after the introductory music, either before or after the Prologue, and to remain up throughout the entire action of the play. There was no interval in the modern sense, though 'act music' was played for a few minutes between acts.

1.1

0 SD *A royal palace* This and other indicators of setting, such as those in 1.2 and 2.1, either go back to the Restoration or are, presumably, Theobald's own additions. They call for back shutters that would be in stock in scenery stores of the period. Since the first Drury Lane theatre had been built in 1663, the stage had been equipped with perspective scenery, something Fletcher and Shakespeare could have seen only in court masques.

Such indications at the start of scenes as to where they are taking place – common to most Restoration and 18th-century playtexts, and to 18th-century editions of Shakespeare from Nicholas Rowe's (1709) onwards – imply the use of painted back shutters, of which that depicting the interior of a palace was absolutely standard, particularly in tragedy.

0.1 *discovered* In modern stage directions, the term means that the characters are disclosed onstage in a particular position or state as the curtain rises (*OED* 3d, 1993 additions). The earliest usage in this sense recorded in *OED* 3a is 1716, in a letter from Lady Mary Wortley Montagu to Pope: 'The stage was built over a . . . canal, and, at the beginning of the second act, divided into two parts discovering the water.' In the drama of Shakespeare's period, 'discovery' scenes involved either the revelation of true identity by the removal of a disguise or the revelation of a hidden scene by the opening of a curtain or a door. Dessen & Thomson (70) record more than 90 such scenes in drama between 1580 and 1642.

1–19 **My . . . reclaim** There is nothing in Cervantes to anticipate this launching of the story from the point of

---

1.1] *(ACT I SCENE I.)   Curtain rises] this edn   0 SD A] SCENE, A 1728a   0.1 discovered] this edn*

Visits my heart with sadness.

DUKE   Why, my son?
Making my death familiar to my tongue
Digs not my grave one jot before the date.
I've worn the garland of my honours long   5
And would not leave it wither'd to thy brow
But flourishing and green; worthy the man
Who with my dukedoms heirs my better glories.

RODERICK
This praise, which is my pride, spreads me with blushes.

view of the Duke, calmly meditating on his own death while considering the succession of his elder son and keeping a watchful eye on the moral failings of his younger. Most commentators on the play, whether they attribute this element to Shakespeare or to Theobald, find here an echo of Shakespeare's late romances, and some find the Duke reminiscent of Vincentio in *MM*, despite his being given the name of Angelo. The motif introduced in this dialogue, however, is very little developed elsewhere in the adaptation, and may well have suffered from cutting.

1–2 **My . . . sadness** This opening, *in medias res* as it is, will certainly remind the reader of Shakespearean openings where inexplicable melancholy is at issue. For example *MV*, where Antonio begins 'In sooth, I know not why I am so sad'; or *TN*, where Orsino's mood is echoed by the sad 'strain' of the music he hears; or *AW* 1.2, where courtiers show solicitude towards a sick king all too stoically aware of his mortality. The key words used in Roderick's opening – *unwonted*, *strain*, and *Visits* deployed as a transitive verb – are all Shakespearean usages. In *Tem* 2.1.194–5, when Alonso finds himself inclined to sleep, Sebastian advises: 'Do not omit the heavy offer of it. / It seldom visits sorrow'.

3–4 Speaking about death does not hasten it.

8 who, as well as inheriting my titles and lands, is the inheritor of my moral achievements. This usage of *heirs* as a transitive verb to mean 'inherits' is not found in Shakespeare, though it has struck some commentators as Shakespearean. *OED* heirs *v.* a provides an example from George Chapman's translation (*c.* 1611) of Homer's *Iliad*, v. 161: 'Not one son more / To heir his goods'. *TC* demonstrates that Shakespeare knew Chapman's text. As Palmer, the editor of the second Arden edition of the play, writes: 'It is . . . likely that [Shakespeare] knew Chapman's *Seaven Books of the Iliades* (1593), which afforded him Books I, II, VII–XI . . . Those who argue for the use of Chapman point out that matter from Chapman's Books corresponds to what we find in the play in Acts I–IV . . . and that what Chapman omits . . . is also omitted by Shakespeare. The argument is persuasive' (Palmer, 33–4). Theobald again uses 'heir' as a verb in his adaptation of *The Duchess of Malfi* called *The Fatal Secret* (1735): 'We are content you hold it, till requir'd, / In our young Nephew's Right, who heirs her Dukedom' (Act 4, p. 35).

9 **spreads me** This impersonal and transitive use of the verb 'spread', meaning 'causes me to spread', is found only in *DF*. It does not occur in Fletcher or Shakespeare.

DUKE

Think not that I can flatter thee, my Roderick,   10
Or let the scale of love o'erpoize my judgement.
Like a fair glass of retrospection, thou
Reflect'st the virtues of my early youth,
Making my old blood mend its pace with transport;
While fond Henriquez, thy irregular brother,   15
Sets the large credit of his name at stake,
A truant to my wishes and his birth.
His taints of wildness hurt our nicer honour
And call for swift reclaim.

RODERICK   I trust my brother
Will, by the vantage of his cooler wisdom,   20

11 **o'erpoize** overbalance or outweigh.
Shakespeare uses the word 'poise' to
mean 'weigh in the balance' on several
occasions, e.g. *MM* 2.4.68 (though as
a noun rather than a verb), when
Angelo, persuading Isabella to yield
her body in exchange for her brother's
life, says 'Pleased you to do't at peril
of your soul, / Were equal poise of sin
and charity'. In *Mist's Weekly Journal*
for 27 April 1728, Theobald cited *RJ*
1.2.96–7 as follows: '*Pho! pho! you saw
her fair, none else being by;* Her self
poiz'd with her self in either Eye.' (See
Appendix 3 for the context of this reference: Theobald's response to Pope's
ridicule of 3.1.17, 'None but itself can
be its parallel'.)
12 **glass of retrospection** mirror capable
of surveying past times. *OED* retrospection 4 gives 'The action or fact of
looking back upon, or surveying, past
time', but records no instance predat-
ing 1697. Glasses in Shakespeare, like
this one, are more often figurative than
literal, often serving a moral purpose.
In *Ham* 3.4.18–19, the protagonist sets
up for his mother a 'glass / Where you
may see the inmost part of you'. This
is an established tradition in medieval

literature.
14 **transport** rapture, ecstasy
15 **fond** 'infatuated, foolish, silly' (*OED*
A *adj.* 2), tending towards the stronger
meaning 'mad'
irregular unruly; not living in accordance with rules or moral principles
16 gambles with his reputation. The
Duke's censure upon his errant
son's behaviour will call to mind the
relationship between Henry IV and
Prince Hal. In the famous speech in
which the Prince tries to extenuate his
faults to his father, he speaks of 'some
things true, wherein my youth / Hath
faulty wandered and irregular' (*1H4*
3.2.26–7). The good elder brother/bad
younger brother motif is fundamental
also to the Gloucester plot of *KL*.
18 **nicer** more scrupulous
19 **reclaim** 'The act of recalling, or state
of being recalled, to right conduct'
(*OED n.*[1] 2a). An older meaning is 'the
act of recalling a hawk' (1a). Given
the Duke's reference to his son's *wildness*, some of those connotations may
remain. Theobald does not use the
word elsewhere in his works, but the
usage persists from Shakespeare's time
through the 18th century.

11 o'erpoize] *(o'er-poize)*

Erewhile redeem the hot escapes of youth
And court opinion with a golden conduct.

DUKE

Be thou a prophet in that kind suggestion!
But I, by fears weighing his unweigh'd course,
Interpret for the future from the past;   25
And strange misgivings why he hath of late
By importunity and strain'd petition
Wrested our leave of absence from the Court
Awake suspicion. Thou art inward with him;

21 **escapes** transgressions, especially sexual lapses. *OED n.*[1] 7 notes that Shakespeare sometimes uses this word to refer to more serious crimes than do his contemporaries, for whom it is almost synonymous with 'peccadilloes'. Cf. *Tit* 4.2.115; but the word 'scape' is used by the Old Shepherd to refer to a sexual transgression when he finds the abandoned infant Perdita (*WT* 3.3.71–3). Cf. *DF* 2.1.60 (see n.).

22 **court opinion** procure a favourable account of one's abilities. Foster has used this phrase to support the view that there must be something genuine behind *DF*. As part of an argument that *A Funeral Elegy* (1612), attributed to one W.S., is by Shakespeare, he points out that the collocation 'court opinion', using the noun without an article or possessive pronoun, is very rare, but occurs twice in the poem. He further observes that it occurs in *DF* (Foster, 1084). This is, however, a somewhat circular argument, as the elegy in question is now attributed to John Ford. Nevertheless, the occurrence of the phrase in any text dated 1612 may be relevant to the question of what lies behind *DF*.

23 **Be . . . prophet** Cf. *TC* 3.2.178, 'Prophet may you be!'

24 **by . . . course** 'using my anxieties to measure his unconsidered conduct'. This is reminiscent of one of Polonius's verbal mannerisms: cf. 'By indirections find directions out' (*Ham* 2.1.63).

26–7 **why . . . petition** Frazier (*Voices*, ch. 6) points to *Ham* 1.2.58–9: 'He hath, my lord, wrung from me my slow leave / By laboursome petition'. The hendiadys of 'By importunity and strain'd petition', the vocabulary and the content here are certainly all reminiscent of *Ham*, on which Theobald had been working very closely in the period immediately before *DF* appeared.

29 **inward** This word occurs three times in *Ham* (1.3.13, 2.2.6, 4.4.27), though not in this sense of 'belonging to the inner circle of one's acquaintance or friends' (*OED adj.* 3). Shakespeare uses the noun form in *MM* 3.2.125, 'I was an inward of his'. 'Inward' is a very frequent word in the Fletcher canon, usually connoting depths or substance hidden from view. The Fletcher–Rowley play *Maid* offers an example of similar usage. When Lisauro accuses Pedro of bringing a foppish tailor into their party, he replies: 'No, I assure ye on my word, I am guiltlesse, / I owe him too much

21 Erewhile] *(E'er-while)*

187

And, haply, from the bosom'd trust canst shape   30
Some formal cause to qualify my doubts.

RODERICK

Why he hath press'd this absence, sir, I know not;
But have his letters of a modern date,
Wherein by Julio, good Camillo's son
(Who, as he says, shall follow hard upon,   35
And whom I with the growing hour expect),
He doth solicit the return of gold
To purchase certain horse that like him well.
This Julio he encounter'd first in France,
And lovingly commends him to my favour;   40
Wishing, I would detain him some few days,
To know the value of his well-plac'd trust.

to be inward with him' (3.2.7–8). The lexis in this passage – the earlier words *truant* and *kind* – calls *Ham* strongly to mind, however. Horatio informs Hamlet of his 'truant disposition' (time-wasting or delinquent) at 1.2.168. Hamlet's opening line in the play is the bitter 'A little more than kin, and less than kind' (1.2.65).

30 **bosom'd** The word occurs in *KL* 5.1.13, where Regan reminds Edmund that he has 'bosomed' with Goneril. It is not found in Fletcher. Ford and Thomas Heywood use it, but it is more common in 18th-century drama, especially towards the latter half of the century.

31 **qualify** moderate, mitigate, render less violent (*OED* II 9a)

32 **press'd** insisted on, executed quickly

33 **modern** recent. *OED* finds this usage of the adjective in the late 16th century. Shakespeare and Fletcher both use it, the former most notably in Jaques's famous speech in *AYL* 2.7, 'Full of wise saws and modern instances' (157). The phrase 'modern

date', however, was current in the later 17th and 18th centuries and not before.

35 **follow hard upon** Cf. Horatio, 'Indeed, my lord, it followed hard upon' (*Ham* 1.2.178).

36 **growing hour** advancing time. This phrase is not found before 1660.

37 **return** remittance

38 **horse** For the collective plural, *OED n.* 1(b) cites *Tit* 2.2.18: 'Come on then, horse and chariots let us have'.
like him well Pope's note to the 1729 *Dunciad* 3.272 comments '*Horse* that *like him well*, is very absurd.' In this passive sense meaning mounts that suit him or that he likes well, the phrase is uncommon, but it occurs mostly in the early period. Cf. the rhyming *Mar-Martine* pamphlet of 1589, attributed in *EEBO* to Thomas Nashe: 'And if his horseplay like him well' (n.p.); and *The History of Philip de Commines* (1596): 'some such newes as he thought would like him well' (de Commynes, 125).

42 well-plac'd] *(*well-placed*)*

DUKE

O, do it, Roderick; and assay to mould him
An honest spy upon thy brother's riots.
Make us acquainted when the youth arrives.   45
We'll see this Julio, and he shall from us
Receive the secret loan his friend requires.
Bring him to court.   *Exeunt.*

1.2   *Prospect of a village at a distance*

Enter CAMILLO *with a letter.*

CAMILLO   How comes the Duke to take such notice of my
son that he must needs have him in court and I must

---

43 **assay to mould** 'attempt [the difficult task of] making him into'. The
locution 'assay to' does not occur
in Shakespeare, but is found in the
drama of the period. Cf. Fletcher,
rev. Massinger, *RDN* (1617) 3.1.398:
'Assay to forget death.' The play is also
called *The Bloody Brother*.
44 **An honest spy** This proposal to
recruit Julio as part of the Duke's sur-
veillance of Henriquez, which comes
to nothing and has no precedent in
Cervantes, is highly reminiscent both
of Polonius's deployment of Reynaldo
to watch Laertes (*Ham* 2.1) and his
subsequent placing of himself and
Claudius to watch Hamlet's encounter
with Ophelia in 3.1, when Claudius
describes them as 'lawful espials' (F
Ham 3.1.32).
   riots 'Wanton, loose, or wasteful living; debauchery, dissipation, extravagance' (*OED n.* 1a).
47 **requires** The meaning is closer here
to the Latin root of 'asks for' rather
than the more modern 'needs'.
48 Ending scenes with a half-line is characteristic of late Shakespeare.

1.2
0.1 1728a uses '*Enters*' when noting
the entry of a single character (with
the exception of '*Enter* Gerald' at
4.1.243.1), which this edition mod-
ernizes to '*Enter*'. This is Theobald's
normal practice in his plays. Similar
modernizations occur at 1.2.11.1,
178.1; 2.2.0.1; 2.3.0.1, 151.1; 2.4.13.1;
3.2.0.1, 21.1; 3.3.0.1, 10 SD, 46.1, 60
SD, 73.1, 128.1; 4.1.27.1, 147.1, 188.1,
212.1; 4.2.37.1; 5.2.31 SD, 36.1, 129.1.
1–11 Camillo will call to mind other
Shakespearean fathers who make a
point of treating their sons without
much ceremony: Polixenes in *WT*
(which has a character called Camillo),
Polonius in *Ham* and Gloucester
in *KL*. Very close is the scene in
R2 5.2, where York demands to see
Aumerle's letter and uncovers a con-
spiracy. Perhaps the strongest overall
similarity in stagecraft is between the
early part of this scene and *TGV* 1.3.
Proteus has a letter from his friend
Valentine who is attending upon the
emperor at court. His father Antonio
determines that Proteus shall also go

43] 'I have, upon *Henriquez*' strong Request, / Sent for this *Julio* – Thou assay to mould him'
1767   **1.2**] *(SCENE II.)*   5 practis'd] *(practised)*

send him upon the view of his letter? Horsemanship!
What horsemanship has Julio? I think he can no more
but gallop a hackney, unless he practis'd riding in   5
France. It may be he did so, for he was there a good
continuance. But I have not heard him speak much
of his horsemanship. That's no matter. If he be not a
good horseman, all's one in such a case – he must bear.
Princes are absolute; they may do what they will in   10
anything, save what they cannot do.

Enter JULIO.

O come on, sir; read this paper. [*Gives him the letter.*]
No more ado, but read it. It must not be answer'd by
my hand, nor yours, but in gross, by your person, your
sole person. Read aloud.   15

---

to court: 'Tomorrow be in readiness
to go. / Excuse it not, for I am peremptory' (70–1). Camillo sends Julio
to court, pointing out that Henriquez
has urged it 'peremptorily' (1.2.31).
Equally blunt fathers are to be found
in Beaumont and Fletcher plays written around this time. In *KNK*, for
example, Ligones, father of Spaconia,
is a disagreeable parent who affects to
treat his daughter as a whore.

4–5 **he . . . hackney** The most he can do
is get up to full speed on a workaday
walking horse (a hackney, as opposed
to a racehorse or warhorse, was used
for journeys, and tended to be slow
and comfortable). Camillo's references
to *horsemanship* and to *riding in France*
in this speech would certainly contain
sexual innuendo in plays by Beaumont
and Fletcher or Shakespeare. It is
possible, but less certain, that they do
so here.

6–7 **good continuance** substantial
length of time. Cf. *1H6* 2.5.105–6,
'cloyed / With long continuance in a

settled place'.

8–9 **If . . . bear** Even if he is not a good
rider, it makes no difference under
these circumstances – he must obey
(i.e. regardless of his horsemanship,
he must *bear* like a horse). Again,
this would probably be a sexual pun
in Shakespeare. The concentration
of such terms in this passage, even
if an 18th-century actor would not
have marked them in delivery, does
suggest a survival from an earlier
version.

10–11 **Princes . . . do** a comically inane
and sententious remark about the
extent of monarchs' legal prerogatives
which perhaps belongs more obviously to the period after the Hanoverian
succession than to the era of the
Stuarts

14 **in gross** Camillo here puns on the
term 'gross', meaning (1) in summary
and (2) in large letters (*OED* gross *adj.*
1c). There may be a play on the verb
'engross', meaning to write in large letters on a legal document (*OED v.* 1a).

12 SD] *this edn*

JULIO   Please you to let me first o'erlook it, sir.

CAMILLO   I was this other day in a spleen against your new
   suits. I do now think some fate was the tailor that hath
   fitted them, for this hour they are for the palace of the
   Duke. Your father's house is too dusty.   20

JULIO (*aside*)   Hem! To court? Which is the better, to serve
   a mistress, or a duke? I am sued to be his slave, and I
   sue to be Leonora's.

CAMILLO   You shall find your horsemanship much prais'd
   there. Are you so good a horseman?   25

16 Some of Julio's lines in the opening
section of this scene (see also 26–7,
38) are iambic pentameters and could
therefore be printed as verse. In the
first edition, it is impossible to tell
whether this line is represented as
verse or prose; similarly 38. Lines
26–7, however, are certainly presented
as verse. On balance, I have preferred
to print prose throughout, rather than
toggling from one to the other for no
clear advantage.
Please 1728a has an apostrophe
before 'Please', indicating omission
of a word or words such as 'Would it'
or 'I'. See 1.2.190n. for a similar construction in respect of 'till'; 3.2.2–3n.
for 'He' and 'Maybe'; and 3.2.29n. for
'Would'.
17 **in a spleen** in a gloomy, irritable ill
humour or passion with. This particular use of the word 'spleen' suggests that the passage is Theobald's
own, since in Shakespeare and
Fletcher the spleen is associated
much more with laughter or caprice
than with ill nature and depression, i.e. 'melancholy': cf. *TS* Ind.
1.136, *1H4* 5.2.19, *LLL* 5.2.117,
WPl 1.3.30. The sense employed by
Camillo was far more prevalent in
the early 18th century: cf. the Cave

of Spleen in Pope's *Rape of the Lock*
(1714).
18 **suits** Camillo here puns on at least
three different senses of the word: (1)
pursuit or purpose; (2) wooing or pursuing of a woman; (3) dress or garb.
There may also be some sense of the
word in feudal law, where it means the
attendance by a tenant at the court of
his lord.
fate goddess of fate, or destiny
21 SD 1728a, following 18th-century
convention, places this SD after the
speech rather than before, to indicate
that all of its content is addressed to
the audience rather than to Camillo.
Later asides are modernized on this
basis (see p. 150). A director might
decide that only part of the speech
should be delivered as an aside.
21 **Hem!** indicates a nervous cough
or throat-clearing, as in *Oth* 4.2.29,
'Cough, or cry hem, if anybody come'.
Fletcher uses this ejaculation often:
several times, for example, in *BB*.
22–3 **sued . . . Leonora's** Camillo's earlier remark that princes are *absolute*
(10) is taken up in a different register;
Julio is positioned between erotic and
political subjection. He puns on two
meanings of the verb 'sue': pursue
(*OED v.* 3a); woo or court (15).

16 Please] ('Please) 18 tailor] (*Taylour*) 21 SD] *this edn; after* Leonora's. 23 1728a 24, 29
prais'd] (praised)

JULIO I have been ere now commended for my seat, or
mock'd.

CAMILLO Take one commendation with another, every
third's a mock. Affect not therefore to be prais'd.
Here's a deal of command and entreaty mix'd. There's   30
no denying – you must go; peremptorily he enforces
that.

JULIO (*aside*) What fortune soever my going shall
encounter cannot be good fortune. What I part withal
unseasons any other goodness.   35

CAMILLO You must needs go; he rather conjures than
importunes.

JULIO (*aside*) No moving of my love suit to him now –

CAMILLO Great fortunes have grown out of less grounds.

JULIO (*aside*) What may her father think of me, who   40
expects to be solicited this very night?

CAMILLO Those scatter'd pieces of virtue which are

---

26 *ere This is printed as 'E'er' in 1728a
but it means 'before', not 'ever'. This
emendation is made also at 1.2.70,
194; 2.3.164; 3.2.101; 3.3.36; 5.2.95.
Throughout his *oeuvre*, Theobald used
e'er indiscriminately to mean 'ever'
and 'before'. It is a secure identifier of
his hand here.
seat manner of sitting on horseback
28–9 **Take ... mock** Shakespeare uses
the word 'mock' as a noun in *WT*
2.1.14, where Mamillius, in response
to the waiting-lady's claim that her
eyebrows are blue, says: 'Nay, that's
a mock'.
31 **peremptorily** confidently or emphat-
ically (*OED* 3). The word occurs in
1H4 2.4.417–18, where Falstaff says
of himself: 'peremptorily I speak it:
there is virtue in that Falstaff'. It
could also have the legal meaning of
OED 1a, 'By, as, or in obedience to a
peremptory order or writ; without (the

possibility of) delay or postponement'.
Fletcher does not use the word, nor
does Theobald elsewhere.
34 **withal** with. The phrase *part withal*
occurs in *Ham* 2.2.210–12, when
Polonius announces that he will take
his leave and Hamlet replies: 'You
cannot take from me anything that I
will not more willingly part withal –
except my life, except my life, except
my life.'
35 **unseasons** deprives of seasoning or
relish. *OED* cites this passage, but also
has examples from 1590 and *c.* 1600.
'Unseason'd' is a popular adjective
with Fletcher; it occurs in *Val* 1.3.30
('unseason'd fooles'), *Phil* 2.4.104
('unseason'd houres') and *WGC* 1.2.15
('unseason'd Country').
36 **conjures** 'to charge or appeal to sol-
emnly' (*OED v.* II), with some sense
of being on oath or of being asked to
swear by something sacred

---

26 ere] *(E'er)*   26–7 *this edn; 1728a lines* been, / mock'd./   33 SD] *this edn; after* Goodness.
1728a   38 SD] *this edn; after* now? – *1728a*   40 SD] *this edn; after* Night? *1728a*

in him, the Court will solder together, varnish and
rectify.

JULIO (*aside*) He will surely think I deal too slightly, or   45
unmannerly, or foolishly, indeed – nay, dishonestly, to
bear him in hand with my father's consent, who yet
hath not been touch'd with so much as a request to it.

CAMILLO Well, sir, have you read it over?

JULIO Yes, sir.   50

CAMILLO And consider'd it?

JULIO   As I can.

CAMILLO If you are courted by good fortune, you must
go.

JULIO So it please you, sir.   55

CAMILLO By any means, and tomorrow. Is it not there the
limit of his request?

JULIO It is, sir.

CAMILLO I must bethink me of some necessaries without
which you might be unfurnish'd, and my supplies shall   60
at all convenience follow you. Come to my closet by and
by; I would there speak with you.   *Exit. Julio remains alone.*

---

44 **rectify** In the context, here, of the
technical terms *solder* and *varnish*, this
has the force of putting right or setting
to rights an instrument or a piece of
equipment. Camillo sees his son as a
malfunctioning instrument or apparatus.

47 **bear . . . hand** 'to assure, to lead (one)
to believe, to delude, abuse with false
pretences' (*OED* bear *v.*[1] 3e). Two
of *OED*'s citations for this phrase
are from Shakespeare: *MA* 4.1.302–3,
'What, bear her in hand until they
come to take hands'; *Cym* 5.5.43, 'Your
daughter, whom she bore in hand to
love'.

56 **there** i.e. in the Duke's letter

59 **some necessaries** Cf. *TGV* 2.4.185–
6, 'I must unto the road to disembark
/ Some necessaries that I needs must
use'.

60 **supplies** provision of funds

61 **closet** a private inner room, often
serving the purposes of an office or
study. There is a splendid example
of such a room in the Little Castle
at Bolsover, Derbyshire, home of the
Cavendish family.

61–2 **by and by** Camillo wants Julio at
once, straight away, rather than at his
convenience or at his leisure. There
may be an echo of the exchange
between Hamlet and Polonius in
F *Ham* 3.2.372–6, when Hamlet is
summoned to his mother's closet:
'HAMLET Then will I come to my
mother by and by. [*aside*] They fool
me to the top of my bent. – I will
come by and by. / POLONIUS I will say
so. *Exit.* / HAMLET [*aside*] "By and
by" is easily said.'

45 SD] *this edn; after* it. *48 1728a*   62 SD] *(Exit Camillo. / Manet Julio solus.)*

JULIO

I do not see that fervour in the maid
Which youth and love should kindle. She consents,
As 'twere, to feed without an appetite;   65
Tells me she is content and plays the coy one,
Like those that subtly make their words their ward,
Keeping address at distance. This affection
Is such a feign'd one as will break untouch'd;
Die frosty ere it can be thaw'd; while mine,   70
Like to a clime beneath Hyperion's eye,

63–73 Unless this is what was on Julio's mind on his entry, before his encounter with Camillo, this soliloquy about Leonora's inadequate enthusiasm seems something of a non sequitur in the adaptation as it stands. Castle (196–7) concluded that this scene was composed of material derived from two separate scenes in the original *Cardenio*.

65 **appetite** Cf. *TNK* 1.3.87–90, where Emilia has denied that she will ever love a man, and Hippolyta responds: 'I must no more believe thee in this point, / Though in't I know thou dost believe thy self, / Than I will trust a sickly appetite / That loathes even as it longs'.

66 **plays . . . one** The phrase occurs only here and in a 1749 translation of Horace by Philip Francis. The word 'coy' itself, meaning shy or retiring, occurs in e.g. *VA* 96: ''Tis but a kiss I beg; why art thou coy?' It is much used by Fletcher, e.g. in *FSh* 4.4.110, and three times in Beaumont and Fletcher's *SL*: 1.1.155, 254; 5.4.3.

67 **ward** in fencing, a way of parrying one's opponent's thrust; a defensive posture. In *1H4*, Falstaff uses the term when describing to the Prince his supposed heroics during the supposed robbery: 'Thou knowest my old ward' (2.4.187–8). The phrase *words their ward* is unique to Theobald, but the 1726 play *The Fatal Extravagance* by

Aaron Hill and Joseph Mitchell has the line 'And, by fair Words, to ward the threaten'd Blow' (1.3, p. 30).

68–9 **This . . . untouch'd** The buried metaphor here may be of sculpted sugar, as in decorative sugar flowers; the following metaphor of frost would make a natural transition from this. Imagery of ice and thawing is to be found in the opening scene of *TNK*, e.g. 1.1.106–8, where the Third Queen sues to Hippolyta: 'Oh, my petition was / Set down in ice, which by hot grief uncandied / Melts into drops'. Equally, however, the imagery invokes damage to plants caused by late frost, as in *Son* 18.3, 'Rough winds do shake the darling buds of May'; and the ripe mulberry as in *Cor* 3.2.79–80: 'the ripest mulberry / That will not hold the handling'.

70 *ere See 26n.

71 **clime** climate; tract or region of earth **beneath Hyperion's eye** i.e. in the full glare of the sun. Hyperion was one of the 12 Titans, son of Gaia and Uranus. He fathered the sun, moon and dawn on his sister Theia. The name is often used to mean the sun itself. In Shakespeare, the most famous occurrence is in *Ham* 1.2.139–40, where Hamlet compares his father to Claudius in the terms 'So excellent a king, that was to this / Hyperion to a satyr'.

---

70 ere] *1767;* e'er *1728a*

Burns with one constant heat. I'll straight go to her,
Pray her to regard my honour – but she greets me –

Enter LEONORA *and Maid.*

See how her beauty doth enrich the place!
O, add the music of thy charming tongue,   75
Sweet as the lark that wakens up the morn,
And make me think it paradise indeed.
I was about to seek thee, Leonora,
And chide thy coldness, love.

LEONORA   What says your father?

JULIO

I have not mov'd him yet.

LEONORA   Then do not, Julio.   80

JULIO

Not move him? Was it not your own command
That his consent should ratify our loves?

LEONORA

Perhaps it was: but now I've chang'd my mind.
You purchase at too dear a rate, that puts you
To woo me and your father too. Besides,   85

---

73 **Pray . . . honour** entreat her to pay
his feelings the respect due to his
rank; ask her to place more faith in
his professions of love. The metre
here is irregular, an alexandrine at
best. One might propose the elision
of 't'regard'.

73.1 *and Maid* This non-speaking maid,
of whom no other character in the
scene takes any notice and who is given
nothing to do, was probably added
in the adaptation in the interests of
decorum: some 18th-century theatre-
goers would have looked askance at a
heroine willing to converse with her

suitor while alone in the fields.

74–7 These lines presumably continue
the soliloquy as an aside before Julio
addresses Leonora directly at 78, but
since they are not marked as such in
1728a the possibility remains that they
could be played to Leonora (in which
case her own first line would seem even
more pointed).

76 The commonplace imagery of 'Sweet
as the lark' resembles that in *Cym*
2.3.20–25, where the musicians in
Cloten's employment sing the song
'Hark, hark, the lark at heaven's gate
sings'. See further 1.3.1–27n.

85 woo] *(wooe)*

As he perchance may say you shall not have me,
You who are so obedient must discharge me
Out of your fancy. Then, you know, 'twill prove
My shame and sorrow, meeting such repulse,
To wear the willow in my prime of youth.   90

JULIO

O do not rack me with these ill-plac'd doubts,
Nor think though age has in my father's breast
Put out love's flame, he therefore has not eyes,
Or is in judgement blind. You wrong your beauties.
Venus will frown if you disprize her gifts,   95
That have a face would make a frozen hermit
Leap from his cell and burn his beads to kiss it;

87 **discharge** 'To dismiss, send away, let go' (*OED v.* 5b)
90 **wear the willow** The willow, perhaps because of its drooping stance, was a symbol of grief for unrequited love or for the death of a mate. In *3H6*, the phrase appears twice: at 3.3.228 and 4.1.100. Desdemona, before her murder, sings a ballad that has the refrain 'Sing all a green willow' (*Oth* 4.3.40). Another singer of the willow song is the maddened Jailer's Daughter in *TNK* 4.1.79–80: 'Then she sung / Nothing but "Willow, willow, willow"'. Amoret in *FSh*, rejected by Perigot, asks, 'Come thou forsaken willowe winde my head, / And noyse it to the world, my love is dead' (4.4.114–15). Aspatia sings a mourning song in *Maid's*, with the lyrics 'Lay a garland on my hearse / Of the dismal Yew, / Maidens willow branches beare, / Say I died true' (2.1.72–5).
prime of youth The phrase also occurs in *3H6* 2.1.23. It is well known from the title of the elegiac poem written by Chidiock Tichborne, Catholic conspirator against Elizabeth I, in 1586 and set to music by Richard Alison in 1606, 'My prime of youth is but a frost of cares'.

93–4 **eyes . . . judgement**   In Shakespeare, the juxtaposition of the eyes and the judgement is a common motif. See for example *MND* 1.1.56–7: 'HERMIA I would my father look'd but with my eyes. / THESEUS Rather your eyes must with his judgement look'; and *Cym* 4.2.301–2, where Imogen says, seeing Cloten's corpse, 'Our very eyes / Are sometimes like our judgements, blind.'
95 **disprize** devalue, disparage or slight. In F *Ham*, the word occurs in the famous 'To be, or not to be' soliloquy at 3.1.72, 'The pangs of disprized love'. Shakespeare uses 'disprizing' in *TC* 4.5.75. The word is found in a late 1680s but is rarely found later; Fletcher does not use it.
96–7 Cf. *LLL* 4.3.237–9: 'She passes praise; then praise too short doth blot. / A withered hermit, five-score winters worn, / Might shake off fifty, looking in her eye'. The phrasing is closer, however, to the more venal late 17th- and 18th-century versions of this sentiment. Cf. Aaron Hill, *Elfrid; Or, The Fair Inconstant* (1710): 'she has Charms / Would make a bearded Hermit quit his Cell' (3.1, pp. 22–3)

91 ill-plac'd] *(*ill-placed*)*

Eyes, that are nothing but continual births
Of new desires in those that view their beams.
You cannot have a cause to doubt.

LEONORA   Why, Julio?   100
When you that dare not choose without your father
And where you love you dare not vouch it; must not,
Though you have eyes, see with 'em. Can I, think you,
Somewhat, perhaps, infected with your suit,
Sit down content to say you would but dare not?   105

JULIO

Urge not suspicions of what cannot be.
You deal unkindly – misbecomingly
I'm loath to say, for all that waits on you
Is grac'd and graces. No impediment
Shall bar my wishes but such grave delays   110
As reason presses patience with, which blunt not

101–2 The syntax of this, and to a lesser
extent of Julio's responding speech, is
coagulated in ways that call to mind that
of Leontes in *WT*. Leonora is upbraid-
ing Julio for reproaching her with having doubts, when it is he who refuses
to follow his heart and press his suit
without paternal consent; 'you would
but dare not', however, recalls Lady
Macbeth in *Mac* 1.7.44–5: 'Letting "I
dare not" wait upon "I would," / Like
the poor cat i'th'adage?'

104 **infected** diseased; less strongly,
tainted or stained. Prospero says
of Miranda's instant attraction to
Ferdinand, 'Poor worm, thou art
infected!' (*Tem* 3.1.31).

106 **Urge not** do not press

107 **misbecomingly** unfittingly. The
word occurs in *TNK* 5.3.53–5: 'Those
darker humours that / Stick misbecomingly on others, on them / Live in
fair dwelling.' Kukowski (86) considers
this line typically Fletcherian.

108–9 **all . . . graces** Cf. *WT*, where the

word 'grace' is a keyword, attaching to
Hermione and Perdita.

109 **impediment** The religious connotations of this passage are reinforced by the
use of a term taken from the Anglican
marriage service in *BCP*. Shakespeare
uses the term drawing on that context in
Son 116.1–2, 'Let me not to the marriage
of true minds / Admit impediments';
and in the scene of Hero's interrupted
marriage in *MA* 4.1.10.

111–12 **blunt . . . loves** Frazier (*Voices*)
invokes *Ham* 3.4.107–8, where the
Ghost tells Hamlet that 'This visi-
tation / Is but to whet thy almost
blunted purpose.' Frazier uses this in
support of her thesis that Theobald
has forged the play: 'In no other
canonical play does Shakespeare
combine the words *whet* and *blunt*
or *blunted* in a single line, and their
combination in *Hamlet* renders
Kenneth Muir's citation of the *DF*
lines as Shakespearian somewhat less
than sagacious' (132).

---

107 misbecomingly] *(mis-becomingly)*   109 grac'd] *(graced)*

But rather whet our loves. Be patient, sweet.

LEONORA

Patient! What else? My flames are in the flint.

Haply to lose a husband I may weep;

Never to get one. When I cry for bondage,   115

Let freedom quit me.

JULIO   From what a spirit comes this?

I now perceive too plain you care not for me.

Duke, I obey thy summons, be its tenor

Whate'er it will. If war, I come thy soldier;

Or if to waste my silken hours at court,   120

The slave of fashion, I with willing soul

Embrace the lazy banishment for life,

113–16 **Patient ... me** a passage much cited as evidence of Shakespeare's hand, even by comparative sceptics such as Muir (see Muir, *Shakespeare*, 145)

113 **flames ... flint** not yet kindled or sparked. Cf. *Tim* 1.1.23–5, 'The fire i' th' flint / Shows not till it be struck, our gentle flame / Provokes itself'. In *Val*, Proculus refers to the virtuous Lucina whom the Emperor has raped thus: 'Ile melt a Christall, / And make a dead flint fire himselfe, ere they [such virtuous women] / Give greater heate, then now departing embers / Gives to old men that watch 'em' (3.1.16–19).

115–16 **When ... me** The paradoxical juxtaposition of freedom and bondage is found in *TNK* 2.1.34–5, where the Jailer's Daughter describes Palamon and Arcite as captives who 'with such a constant nobility enforce a freedom out of bondage'. A similar paradox occurs in *Tem* 3.1.88–9, when Ferdinand agrees to marry Miranda: 'Ay, with a heart as willing / As bondage e'er of freedom'. *Maid* 1.3.71–2 has this word-play: 'There is no blessednesse but in such bondage: / Give me that freedom (Madam) I beseech ye.' The motif is very common in several plays of the Restoration period. See for example Katherine Philips,

Pompey (1663): 'As Bondage first, let's Freedom next bestow' (4.1, p. 40). Dryden, *The Indian Emperor* (1667): 'Freedom and bondage in her choice remains' (3.1, p. 20). Theobald uses the collocation again in *Perfidious Brother*: 'I wonder not that Libertines, like thee, / Should dread Restraint from Vice, and term it Bondage: / Thou count'st it Freedom, uncontroul'd to range' (3.1, p. 25).

116 **spirit** 'The disposition, feeling, or frame of mind with which something is done, considered, or viewed' (*OED n*. 8b). The current phrase 'That's the spirit!' captures this sense. An elision here to 'spir't' or 'sprite' is likely.

118 **tenor** general meaning, substance, purport, import. The word is used three times in *TNK*, at 1.1.90, 3.5.122 and 3.6.133.

120 **silken** 'effeminate, luxurious' (*OED* 8). The word is used by Shakespeare in this sense, though it is more common from the mid-17th century.

122 **lazy** sluggish, slothful. Used by Shakespeare and by Fletcher, notably in the latter's *FSh* where it occurs four times (2.4.53; 4.4.3, 117; 5.5.183). Neither uses the adjective to qualify an abstract noun as here, but Fletcher does use it of an inanimate noun in *FSh* 2.4.53, 'lazy mistes'.

Since Leonora has pronounc'd my doom.

LEONORA

What do you mean? Why talk you of the Duke?
Wherefore of war, or court, or banishment?   125

JULIO

How this new note is grown of me, I know not,
But the Duke writes for me. Coming to move
My father in our bus'ness, I did find him
Reading this letter; whose contents require
My instant service and repair to court.   130

LEONORA

Now I perceive the birth of these delays,
Why Leonora was not worth your suit.
Repair to court? Ay, there you shall perhaps,
Rather past doubt, behold some choicer beauty,
Rich in her charms, train'd to the arts of soothing,   135
Shall prompt you to a spirit of hardiness,

125 **Wherefore** why
126 **note** Julio puns on the *note* in his hand and *note* as notability, attention paid to him or focused on him.
128 **bus'ness** This word appears to have a special significance in the text. As well as occurring in the Preface, l. 64 (clearly Theobald's usage), it occurs no fewer than 15 times in the text, the other instances being at 1.2.181, 193, 222; 2.2.15, 20; 2.3.75, 178; 3.2.4, 6, 43, 130, 144; 4.1.213; 5.2.69. On two occasions – here, and at 3.2.43 – the word is printed in 1728a in the elided form 'bus'ness'. On all other occasions it is given in the full form 'business', although on some of those occasions the metre calls for elision. This edition adopts the form that appears in 1728a. Shakespeare and Fletcher employ this word very frequently. The latter, in particular, uses it epidemically: no fewer than 19 times in *KNK*, 11 in *Rule*, 9 in *Phil*, 6 in *Maid's*. Awkwardly for any conclusions on authorship, Theobald is also very fond of it. His translations of 1714–15 from Aristophanes of *Plutus* and *The Clouds*

and of Sophocles' *Electra*, for example, use the word a total of 30 times. It also occurs in his original works.
129 **contents** contènts
130 **repair** the act of going or making one's way to a place
131–41 **Now . . . inherit** The exchange is very close in texture to that between Florizel and Perdita at the opening of *WT* 4.4. Perdita argues that Florizel will not be constant to her if his father favours a woman of higher birth. Florizel replies that he will not desert her to obey his father (35–6). The resemblance continues in 369–72 and 474–92.
134 **past doubt** beyond doubt. Shakespeare uses the expression in *Cor* 2.3.255 and *WT* 1.2.268. The phrase continues to occur in the Restoration and into Theobald's period.
135 **soothing** flattering, blandishing
136 **Shall** who shall
   hardiness boldness, daring, audacity. Shakespeare and Fletcher both use the word, the former in *H5* 1.2.221 and *Cym* 3.6.22; the latter in *Maid* 4.2.126.

To say, 'So please you, father, I have chosen
This mistress for my own.'

JULIO   Still you mistake me.

Ever your servant I profess myself;
And will not blot me with a change, for all   140
That sea and land inherit.

LEONORA   But when go you?

JULIO

Tomorrow, love – so runs the Duke's command,
Stinting our farewell kisses, cutting off
The forms of parting and the interchange
Of thousand precious vows with haste too rude.   145
Lovers have things of moment to debate
More than a prince, or dreaming statesman, know:
Such ceremonies wait on Cupid's throne.

---

137 **So . . . father** Beatrice is similarly
ironic about filial obedience in *MA*
2.1.46–7: 'it is my cousin's duty to
make curtsy, and say, "Father, as it
please you."'
138 **Still** always, incessantly
140 **blot me** deface, disfigure or stain me.
Julio may here be using the term either
in the sense of *OED* blot *v.*[1] 3a, 'To cast
a blot upon (good qualities or reputation); to tarnish, stain, sully', or in sense
4, 'To make a blot over (writing) so as to
make it illegible; to obliterate, efface'.
change here, an inconstant act
141 In 1728a, this is lineated as verse,
'inherit. / you?' It may be that here,
and at 149, the printer has failed to
indicate half-lines with a long dash sig-
nifying indentation. At several other
points in the text, lines are lineated as
prose that either should be lineated as
verse, or reveal verse possibilities. In
such cases, I have relineated as verse.
See 1.3.61; 2.1.24–31, 40–3, 52–9;
3.1.31; 3.3.60, 63, 82, 105, 129–34,
137, 140, 144, 147; 4.1.136; 4.2.25–6,
31; 5.1.5, 59; 5.2.58, 66, 84, 103, 114,

118, 197, 231, 275; and t.nn. Kennedy
has picked up the point about lineation
of half-lines in his edition.
inherit come into possession of; cf.
Tem 4.1.153–4, 'the great globe itself,
/ Yea, all which it inherit'.
143–5 Muir (*Shakespeare*, 155–6) reads
this as a paraphrase of *TC* 4.4.32–47.
The lines themselves are not especially
close, but there is a similarity of dramatic situation in that Cressida is to
be required to leave Troy and Troilus
immediately, just as Julio must leave
his home and Leonora. Freehafer (507)
argues that the source in Shelton, with
its 'thousand oathes and promises', is
closer (Shelton, 3.10.222).
145 **thousand** the first of several uses of
this both general and specific number;
see also 2.1.22; 2.2.32; 2.3.34, 109;
2.4.34; 3.2.25. This usage is very common indeed in Shakespeare.
146 **things of moment** important matters. The phrase occurs in three plays
by Fletcher: *MT* 3.3.25, *LPi* 2.4.66
and *Cha* 1.1.16.
148 **Cupid** god of erotic love

141] *Kennedy; prose 1728a*   143 farewell kisses] *(Farewell-kisses)*

Why heav'd that sigh?
LEONORA   O Julio, let me whisper
What but for parting I should blush to tell thee.   150
My heart beats thick with fears, lest the gay scene,
The splendours of a court, should from thy breast
Banish my image, kill my int'rest in thee,
And I be left, the scoff of maids, to drop
A widow's tear for thy departed faith.   155

JULIO

O let assurance, strong as words can bind,
Tell thy pleas'd soul I will be wondrous faithful;
True, as the sun is to his race of light,
As shade to darkness, as desire to beauty:
And when I swerve, let wretchedness o'ertake me   160
Great as e'er falsehood met, or change can merit.

LEONORA

Enough; I'm satisfied, and will remain
Yours, with a firm and untir'd constancy.

149–55 **O . . . faith** Leonora's last-minute confession of love to a departing suitor to whom she has previously been cold is reminiscent of Julia's behaviour in *TGV* 1.2 and 2.2.

151 **thick** in close or rapid succession, i.e. very fast
gay scene No instance of this phrase is found in literature before 1690. In the depreciatory sense of *gay* as 'airy' or vapid (*OED adj.* 3d), this is mainly an 18th-century usage.

154 **scoff** As a noun meaning object of contempt or scorn, *OED n.*[1] 2 first records the word in 1640. It is predominantly late 17th century and later. Nevertheless, Fletcher uses the term in his 1621 play *WGC*, 'His Person made a publique Scoff' (3.1.168), and the word is used as a verb 10 lines later.

drop let fall

155 **departed** both torn apart and gone away

157 **wondrous** This adverbial usage is found in several of Shakespeare's plays, e.g. *Tem* 2.1.198, *Per* 2.5.35, *AW* 3.6.107, 5.3.304; and in Fletcherian parts of *TNK*: 2.2.148, 151, 2.5.20.

158 **race of light** the daily or annual course of the sun through the heavens. The phrase occurs in Thomas Southerne's *Oroonoko* (1696): 'like the Sun, / That rises from the Bosom of the Sea, / To run his glorious Race of Light anew' (Act 5, p. 75). No instance of the phrase is found in literature prior to 1664.

160 **swerve** deviate from the right path, especially morally; transgress. *OED v.* 3d draws attention to *Cym* 5.4.129, Posthumus's 'But, alas, I swerve'.

149] *Kennedy; prose 1728a*   157 wondrous] *(wond'rous)*

Make not your absence long; old men are wav'ring,
And sway'd by int'rest more than promise giv'n.   165
Should some fresh offer start when you're away,
I may be press'd to something which must put
My faith, or my obedience, to the rack.

JULIO

Fear not but I with swiftest wing of time
Will labour my return. And in my absence,   170
My noble friend, and now our honour'd guest,
The Lord Henriquez will in my behalf
Hang at your father's ear and with kind hints
Pour'd from a friendly tongue secure my claim
And play the lover for thy absent Julio.   175

LEONORA

Is there no instance of a friend turn'd false?
Take heed of that: no love by proxy, Julio.
My father –

Enter DON BERNARD.

DON BERNARD   What, Julio, in public? This wooing is too
    urgent. Is your father yet mov'd in the suit, who must   180
    be the prime unfolder of this business?

164–8 Leonora shows considerable pre-
    science both here and at 176–8, in
    anticipating that some other suitor
    may be pressed upon her.
168 **faith** fidelity (to you)
    rack literally, an instrument of tor-
    ture; hence, painful trial
170 **labour** to work at; to take great pains
    with (a matter) (*OED* I 5a). This usage
    does not occur in Theobald's writing.
    It is rarely found in either Shakespeare
    or Fletcher: e.g. *R3* 1.4.244–5, 'swore
    with sobs / That he would labour my
    delivery'; *Pilg* 2.2.370, 'And how he
    labour'd him'.

173 **Hang . . . ear** recalls 'hang a pearl in
    every cowslip's ear', *MND* 2.1.15
174 **friendly tongue** The phrase is
    found in Chapman's 1602 play *The
    Gentleman Usher*, 3.2.178.
179 **public** perhaps a reference to the
    presence of the Maid, who entered
    with Leonora
181 **prime unfolder** *OED* cites this pas-
    sage as the sole example of the term
    'unfolder', with a very unhelpful defini-
    tion. The word certainly occurs, how-
    ever, in texts of the late 16th century.
    Don Bernard means that Camillo must
    take the lead in proposing the marriage.

179 wooing] *(Wooeing)*   180 mov'd] *(moved)*

JULIO

> I have not yet, indeed, at full possess'd
> My father whom it is my service follows,
> But only that I have a wife in chase.

DON BERNARD   Chase! Let chase alone. No matter for that.   185
> You may halt after her whom you profess to pursue, and
> catch her too. Marry, not unless your father let you slip.
> Briefly, I desire you (for she tells me my instructions
> shall be both eyes and feet to her) no farther to insist
> in your requiring till, as I have formerly said, Camillo   190
> make known to me that his good liking goes along with
> us. Which but once breath'd, all is done; till when, the
> business has no life, and cannot find a beginning.

JULIO

> Sir, I will know his mind, ere I taste sleep.
> At morn you shall be learn'd in his desire.   195
> I take my leave – O virtuous Leonora,
> Repose, sweet as thy beauties, seal thy eyes.
> Once more, adieu. I have thy promise, love;
> Remember, and be faithful.   *Exit.*

DON BERNARD   His father is as unsettled as he is wayward   200

---

182 **possess'd** briefed, i.e. put Camillo in possession of the facts

184 **in chase** in prospect. Julio initiates the somewhat unsavoury hunting metaphor that Don Bernard develops in the following lines.

186–7 **You . . . slip** Even if you only limp (*halt*) after Leonora, whom you claim to be chasing, you may still catch her (such is her willingness); but you may not marry her unless with your father's permission.

187 **Marry** There could be a pun here on 'marry' as an emphasizing interjection, and the verb 'to marry'. Shakespeare puns thus in *RJ* 1.3.63–4: Lady Capulet's 'Marry, that marry is the very theme / I came to talk of.'

let you slip liberate you, with the sense of loosing a hound from the leash in order to begin the chase. Don Bernard is as blunt as is Camillo in his way of addressing his putative son-in-law.

190 **requiring** request, or desired request. Caliban uses the word in *Tem* 2.2.176–7, 'No more dams I'll make for fish, / Nor fetch in firing at requiring', where it has a stronger meaning, closer to 'by order'.
***till** 1728a prints the word with an apostrophe preceding it, denoting 'until'.

192 **breath'd** uttered, declared

194 ***ere** See 26n.

200 **he** i.e. Julio

200–1 **wayward . . . disposition** Don Bernard, here and at 215, where he

190 till] ('till)   194 ere] (e'er)   199 SD] (*Ex.* Julio.)

203

in his disposition. If I thought young Julio's temper
were not mended by the metal of his mother, I should
be something crazy in giving my consent to this match.
And, to tell you true, if my eyes might be the directors
to your mind, I could in this town look upon twenty   205
men of more delicate choice. I speak not this altogether
to unbend your affections to him; but the meaning of
what I say is, that you set such price upon yourself to
him as many, and much his betters, would buy you at
(and reckon those virtues in you at the rate of their   210
scarcity), to which if he come not up, you remain for a
better mart.

LEONORA   My obedience, sir, is chain'd to your advice.

DON BERNARD   'Tis well said, and wisely. I fear your lover
is a little folly-tainted; which, shortly after it proves so,   215
you will repent.

LEONORA   Sir, I confess I approve him of all the men I

---

expresses his sense that Julio is a little *folly-tainted*, shares his daughter's
prescience.

202 **mended** improved, or the modern
sense of repaired
metal 1728a has 'Mettal'. It is unclear
whether this should be modernized to
'metal' or 'mettle'.

203 **crazy** Bernard's use here suggests 'of
unsound judgement', rather than 'of
unsound mind'. *OED*'s first citation
for the latter sense (*adj.* 4a) is 1617; the
word is not used by Shakespeare or by
Fletcher. Neither, however, is it used
elsewhere in Theobald's writing.

207 **unbend** slacken or weaken. *OED* I
2 notes that the word appears in *Mac*
2.2.44, where Lady Macbeth says to
her husband, 'You do unbend your
noble strength'.

208–12 **you . . . mart** You place a value
upon yourself in your dealings with
him that many others, and better than

him at that, would be willing to accept
you at (valuing your good qualities
the more highly for their rarity); if
he doesn't match you in this, you can
still make a better bargain elsewhere.
Not an easy sentence for an actor to
make immediately clear in performance. Don Bernard's advice to Leonora
to set a high price on her hand is reminiscent of Polonius's advice to Ophelia
to 'Set your entreatments at a higher
rate / Than a command to parle' (*Ham*
1.3.121–2). There is perhaps a faint
echo of Rosalind's (opposite) advice to
Phoebe in *AYL* 3.5.61, 'Sell when you
can, you are not for all markets'.

215 **proves so** turns out to be the case

217 **approve** think (him) worthy of
approval. Given the earlier reference
to 'metal/mettle', the verbs *proves*
(215) and *approve* may pun on the
proving of metal: the establishing of
it as genuine.

202 metal] *(*Mettal)*;* Metal *1767*

know; but that approbation is nothing till season'd by
your consent.

DON BERNARD   We shall hear soon what his father will do,   220
and so proceed accordingly. I have no great heart to the
business, neither will I with any violence oppose it, but
leave it to that power which rules in these conjunctions,
and there's an end. Come, haste we homeward, girl.   *Exeunt.*

1.3   *Enter* HENRIQUEZ *and* Servants *with lights.*

HENRIQUEZ
Bear the lights close. Where is the music, sirs?
SERVANT
Coming, my lord.
HENRIQUEZ   Let 'em not come too near.

218 **season'd** flavoured, as in food; or
matured, as in timber, cf. 35.
223 **that power** destiny. The lines are
probably delivered to Leonora, but
equally could be delivered directly to
the audience.
conjunctions The primary meaning
is sexual unions (*OED* 2b), with a reference also to the astrological sense of
the proximity of the planets governing
such unions and making them successful or otherwise (*OED* 3).
1.3 No scene is specified here. This balcony scene could have been played in
front of the scenery back shutter for
1.2 – the perspective painting of the
'prospect' of a distant village; but it
seems more likely that this was shut-
tered off during 1.3. See further 27.1n.
0.1 1728a makes no provision for the
Musicians to enter or to exit. Bringing
a group of musicians on at this point
would be somewhat cumbersome,
requiring the expense of costumes.
The music, which is instrumental
rather than sung, is presumably played
offstage. Not much is known about the
exact constitution of theatre orches-

tras in the first half of the 18th century. Stage appearances such as this one
would probably call for a group of four
or five string players. The Musicians
might have been visible from behind
a wing opposite Violante's balcony,
or invisible behind the wing. It is also
possible, but less likely given the need
for Henriquez to communicate with
them, that they played from a stage
box on the third level.
1–27 There are strong resemblances in
situation between this scene and *TGV*
4.2, where Proteus, having already
been false to his friend Valentine, is
using Turio and his musicians to reach
Silvia. The serenading scene also calls
to mind the opening of *Cym* 2.3, where
Cloten uses musicians to woo Imogen,
though Henriquez does not descend
to Cloten's obscenity and, given that
Imogen does not respond to the musical invitation, the scene is dissimilar in
its stagecraft.
1 **Bear . . . close** Bring the torches
closer.
Where . . . music Where are the
musicians. See 0.1n.

1.3] *(SCENE III.)*   2–3 Let . . . maid] *this edn; one line 1728a*

[*aside*] This maid,
For whom my sighs ride on the night's chill vapour,
Is born most humbly, though she be as fair   5
As nature's richest mould and skill can make her,
Mended with strong imagination.
But what of that? Th'obscureness of her birth
Cannot eclipse the lustre of her eyes,
Which make her all one light.
[*to Musicians*]   Strike up, my masters,   10
But touch the strings with a religious softness;
Teach sound to languish through the night's dull ear,
Till melancholy start from her lazy couch
And carelessness grow convert to attention.   *Music plays.*
[*aside*] She drives me into wonder when I sometimes   15

6   **mould** 'Rotting earth considered as the material of the human body' (*OED n.*[1] 2a); including also the meaning given as *n.*[3] 4b, 'The body of a living creature, esp. considered as something that has been shaped'

7   **imagination** six syllables

10–14 **Strike . . . attention** Henriquez addresses the Musicians directly here, which could be done even if they are offstage. Freehafer (506) cites an anecdote found in Richard Farmer's *An Essay on the Learning of Shakespeare* (1767) to the effect that these lines were particularly admired in contemporary performance, and that Theobald claimed them as his own. Actually, the story predates Farmer. The clergyman William Dodd, who was hanged for forging and cashing a bill of exchange supposedly from Lord Chesterfield (and to save whom Samuel Johnson mounted a campaign), produced a long-popular compilation of *The Beauties of Shakespear* (1752), where it is stated that 'A gentleman of great judgment happening to commend these lines

to Mr *Theobald*, he assured him, he wrote them himself, and only them, in the whole play; if this be true, they are the best lines Mr *Theobald* ever wrote in his life' (Dodd, 1.70). In the 'Life' of Theobald included in *The Lives of the Poets of Great Britain and Ireland, by Mr Cibber, and other hands* (1753), it is said that 'The ingenious Mr Dodd, who has lately favoured the public with a judicious collection of the beauties of Shakespeare, has quoted a beautiful stroke of Mr Theobald's, in his double Falsehood, upon music' (*Lives*, 5.286). The lines are quoted as in Dodd, and followed by the anecdote (but not the critical remark).

12   **night's dull ear** The phrase occurs in *H5* 4.0.10–11: 'Steed threatens steed, in high and boastful neighs / Piercing the night's dull ear'.

13   **lazy couch** transferred epithet, i.e. melancholy is lazy, rather than her couch. The phrase occurs in Aphra Behn's 1683 play *The Young King, or The Mistake*: 'Then, when he [sleep] ties thee to thy lazy Couch' (4.3, p. 43).

3 SD] *this edn*   10 SD] *this edn*   15 SD] *this edn*

Hear her discourse. The Court, whereof report
And guess alone inform her, she will rave at,
As if she there sev'n reigns had slander'd time.
Then, when she reasons on her country state,
Health, virtue, plainness and simplicity,   20
On beauties true in title, scorning art,
Freedom as well to do as think what's good;
My heart grows sick of birth and empty rank,
And I become a villager in wish.
[*to Musicians*] Play on – she sleeps too sound. Be still,
       and vanish.   [*Exeunt Servants.*]
A gleam of day breaks sudden from her window: 26
O taper, graced by that midnight hand!

VIOLANTE *appears above at her window.*

VIOLANTE
Who is't that woos at this late hour? What are you?

18 **slander'd time** This elliptical phrase means something like 'vilified the reports (of people) carried by time', or more simply 'shamefully wasted' time. It is the kind of pithy phrase one might expect from Shakespeare. It is not to be found in his canon exactly, though cf. *Ham* 1.3.132–3, where Polonius advises Ophelia not to 'so slander any moment leisure / As to give words or talk with the Lord Hamlet'.

19 **reasons on** discourses about, talks about, considers. The idiom occurs in *H5* 3.7.35–6: 'my horse is . . . a subject for a sovereign to reason on'.

20 **plainness** of dress and/or manners

25 **Be still** Cease playing. If the Musicians are onstage, this line provides the cue for their exit. If they are offstage, they may stop playing or slowly fade. 1728a does not make provision for the exit of the Servants carrying lights. Violante's *taper* (27) may offer enough light.

27 **graced** gracèd

27.1 The stagecraft here will put the audience in mind of the balcony scene in *RJ* 2.2, when Juliet enters above. Romeo's 'what light through yonder window breaks?' (2) is close to Henriquez's 'A gleam of day breaks sudden from her window' (26). However, as Freehafer (507) points out, the equivalent situation in Shelton's translation of *Don Quixote* has Fernando (Henriquez) catching his first sight of Luscinda (Leonora) 'by the light of a candle, at a window' (3.10.225). Information about the interior architecture of the Drury Lane theatre in the 1720s is not plentiful. Violante probably appeared in the small stage box immediately above the stage-left proscenium door, with Henriquez onstage near the door, the Servants to the right and the Musicians offstage right. In the Jacobean theatre, balcony scenes such as this would have been played on the tiring house gallery upstage.

25 SD1, 2] *this edn*

HENRIQUEZ

 One who for your dear sake –

VIOLANTE   Watches the starless night!

 My lord Henriquez, or my ear deceives me.   30

 You've had my answer, and 'tis more than strange

 You'll combat these repulses. Good my lord,

 Be friend to your own health; and give me leave,

 Securing my poor fame, nothing to pity

 What pangs you swear you suffer. 'Tis impossible   35

 To plant your choice affections in my shade,

 At least for them to grow there.

HENRIQUEZ   Why, Violante?

VIOLANTE

 Alas sir, there are reasons numberless

 To bar your aims. Be warn'd to hours more wholesome;

 For these you watch in vain. I have read stories   40

---

29 an alexandrine
Watches keeps watch over, stays awake for/during. Cf. *watch* (40). See also 31n.
starless Cf. 39–40, 53 (*unseasonable*), suggesting that the absence of any form of light renders Henriquez's action especially ambivalent.

30 Cf. *TGV* 4.2.84–7, where Silvia first recognizes Proteus by the sound of his voice.

31 **You've . . . answer** If so, this action was not shown. Given the way Violante completes Henriquez's earlier line 'One who for your dear sake' with 'Watches the starless night!' (29), it is possible that she is echoing an earlier attempt to charm her.

33 **Be . . . health** Here, and at 39, Violante advises Henriquez to consider his health in staying out late at night. This could be a general health warning, but in Shakespeare the night is spoken of as particularly dangerous, e.g. *JC* 2.1.264–5, where Portia warns Brutus of the 'vile contagion' and the 'rheumy and unpurged air' of night.

34 **Securing . . . fame** protecting my reputation

35 **What** whatever

36 **choice affections** most powerful emotions (of love). The collocation is found as early as 1624, but is not common until after the Restoration. In a sermon by Benjamin Keach, for example, printed in 1698, humans are said to be 'the Objects of [God's] most choice Affections', here meaning the object of His particular care and concern (Keach, 236).
shade Violante's metaphor figures her humble rank as a shady spot in a garden, where the delicate plants of Henriquez's high status (*choice affections*) cannot grow well.

39 **bar** prevent (the fruition of)

40–6 **I . . . contempt** Kukowski (86) quotes Muir's comment that 'this passage recalls not only Aspatia's lament [in *Maid's*], but all the laments of Fletcher's numerous "ruin'd maids", who typically see themselves as exempla for future dramas' (*Shakespeare*, 153). Muir presumably has *Maid's*

(I fear too true ones), how young lords like you
Have thus besung mean windows, rhym'd their
    suff'rings
E'en to th'abuse of things divine, set up
Plain girls, like me, the idols of their worship,
Then left them to bewail their easy faith   45
And stand the world's contempt.

HENRIQUEZ   Your memory,
Too faithful to the wrongs of few lost maids,
Makes fear too general.

VIOLANTE   Let us be homely,
And let us too be chaste, doing you lords no wrong,
But crediting your oaths with such a spirit   50
As you profess them; so no party trusted
Shall make a losing bargain. Home, my lord!
What you can say is most unseasonable; what sing,
Most absonant and harsh. Nay, your perfume,

2.1.40–56 in mind. Resemblances are equally strong, however, to *TGV* 4.2.92–5, where Silvia asserts that she will not be seduced by Proteus's deceptive flattery. She also wishes to send her lover back to his own bed.

42 **besung** sung about or to; celebrated or serenaded. This participial form of 'besing' is not listed in *OED* prior to the 19th century. It appears to be unique to *DF*.
    rhym'd This perfect-tense construction is similar to the passive construction used by Shakespeare in *AYL* 3.2.172, where Rosalind complains of being 'berhymed' by Orlando.

43 **th'abuse . . . divine** to the point of idolatry

45 **easy faith** too trusting confidence, with the religious undertones persisting

46 **stand** endure, with a hint, perhaps, of public humiliation

48–9 **Let . . . chaste** The connection made

by Violante between homeliness and chastity is the one also made, in a comic context, by Audrey in *AYL* 3.3.34–5.

49 an alexandrine

50 **spirit** See 1.2.116n.

51–2 **so . . . bargain** Since neither will trust the other, no one will be the loser.

53–6 **What . . . breath** This is perhaps the passage in *DF* that has been most widely regarded as unadulterated Shakespeare; see e.g. Muir, *Shakespeare*, 145; Bate, 81.

54 **absonant** harsh and discordant, or abhorrent to reason. The word does not occur elsewhere in the Shakespeare canon or in Fletcher. Theobald does not use it elsewhere. *OED* finds examples of the word dating from around 1600, but gives no example between 1657 and 1864. There are examples, however, of the word occurring in translations from Livy and Plutarch in 1600 and 1603.
    perfume perfùme

42 rhym'd] *(rhymed)*   suff'rings] *(Sufferings)*   43 E'en] *(Ev'n)*

Which I smell hither, cheers not my sense   55
Like our field-violet's breath.

HENRIQUEZ   Why, this dismission
Does more invite my staying.

VIOLANTE   Men of your temper
Make ev'rything their bramble. But I wrong
That which I am preserving, my maid's name,
To hold so long discourse. Your virtues guide you   60
T'effect some nobler purpose.   *Exit.*

HENRIQUEZ   Stay, bright maid!
Come back, and leave me with a fairer hope.
She's gone – who am I, that am thus contemn'd?
The second son to a prince? Yes. Well, what then?
Why, your great birth forbids you to descend   65
To a low alliance. Hers is the self-same stuff
Whereof we dukes are made, but clay more pure;
And take away my title, which is acquir'd
Not by myself, but thrown by fortune on me,
Or by the merit of some ancestor   70
Of singular quality – she doth inherit

---

55 **Which . . . hither** which I smell even
from here
56 **our** This possessive construction with
respect to flowers is characteristically
Shakespearean. It occurs, for example,
in *WT* 4.4.82, 'our carnations and
streak'd gillyvors'.
dismission 'The sending away of
a person; permission to go, leave to
depart; often in earlier use, formal
leave-taking' (*OED* 2a). Shakespeare
uses the word in this sense in *AC*
1.1.27 and *Cym* 2.3.53. Although the
word enters the language earlier, it is
particularly common between 1600
and 1610, though Fletcher does not
use it. See 3.2.127.
57–8 **Men . . . bramble** Men motivated

as is Henriquez will use any excuse to
stay around. A parallel for the force of
the metaphor is found in *MM* 4.3.176,
Lucio's 'Nay, friar, I am a kind of burr,
I shall stick.'
60 **Your** may your
66 **alliance** normally denotes a union by
marriage. Henriquez is giving reasons
why he cannot contemplate a marriage
to Violante.
66–72 **Hers . . . me** This traditional
argument about the dubious nature of
elevated rank is found in various plays
of Shakespeare, e.g. *AW* 2.3.118–45.
71 **inherit** Henriquez is making the point
that Violante derives her superior
quality or character from her progeni-
tors by natural descent (*OED* 2b). He

---

58 ev'rything] *(ev'ry Thing)*   61] *Kennedy; prose 1728a*   SD] *(Ex. Violante.)*   63 She's gone –]
'She's gone: – No matter! I have brib'd her Woman, / And soon shall gain Admittance. –' *1767*   66
Hers] *(Her's)*

Deserts t'outweigh me. I must stoop to gain her;
Throw all my gay comparisons aside
And turn my proud additions out of service,
Rather than keep them to become my masters.   75
    The dignities we wear are gifts of pride,
    And laugh'd at by the wise, as mere outside.   *Exit.*

End of the first act

2.1   *The prospect of a village*

Enter FABIAN *and* LOPEZ; HENRIQUEZ *on the opposite side.*

LOPEZ [*to Fabian*]   Soft, soft you, neighbour; who comes
here? Pray you, slink aside. [*They withdraw.*]

HENRIQUEZ   Ha! Is it come to this? O the devil, the devil,
the devil!

FABIAN [*to Lopez*]   Lo you now, for want of the discreet   5

may simply mean that she possesses such a character, without any connotation of legacy, as in *OED* 3. *OED* gives examples of both meanings in Shakespeare.

72 **Deserts** excellences; good qualities
stoop to assume a position below one's rightful dignity; perhaps with overtones of hawking, where to stoop is to descend on prey

73 **gay comparisons** splendid trappings. In *AC* 3.13.26, Antony requests Caesar to 'lay his gay comparisons apart'. (See p. 94 above.) The word appears to be a corruption of 'caparison' meaning dress and ornament.

74 **additions** 'Something annexed to a man's name, to show his rank, occupation, or place of residence, or otherwise to distinguish him; "style" of address' (*OED n.* 4). Examples are cited from *KL* and *Oth.*

76–7 The same convention – an indented couplet ending the act – is used at

the ends of Acts 2, 3 and 4. This practice must postdate Shakespeare and Fletcher. Thomas Betterton could have been responsible, or Theobald. See also 5.2.281–2n.

2.1
0 SD Unlike 1.2, the scene is not here specified as a village '*at a distance*'. It is likely that this is a differently painted back shutter with a closer view of the village. Its function is to identify an open-air location where Henriquez can plausibly be overheard.

0.1 FABIAN *and* LOPEZ The fact that these supernumerary characters have names is possible evidence of a subplot that has been excised.

2 **slink** move stealthily; cf. 4.1.113. Both Shakespeare and Fletcher deploy the word. See, for example, *AYL* 3.1.245, 'Slink by and note him.'

5–7 **discreet . . . over** might refer to adding cold water to already boiling liquid, or to an action of skimming

77 mere] *(meer)*   **2.1**] *(*ACT II. SCENE I.*)*   1 SD] *this edn*   2 SD] *this edn*   5 SD] *this edn*

ladle of a cool understanding will this fellow's brains
boil over!

HENRIQUEZ

To have enjoy'd her, I would have given – what?
All that at present I could boast my own,
And the reversion of the world to boot　　　　　　　　10
Had the inheritance been mine. And now –
Just doom of guilty joys! – I grieve as much
That I have rifled all the stores of beauty,
Those charms of innocence and artless love,
As just before I was devour'd with sorrow,　　　　　　15
That she refus'd my vows and shut the door
Upon my ardent longings.

LOPEZ [*to Fabian*]　Love! Love! Downright love! I see by
the foolishness of it.

HENRIQUEZ　Now then to recollection – was't not so?　A　　20
promise first of marriage – not a promise only, for 'twas
bound with surety of a thousand oaths – and those not
light ones neither.
Yet I remember too, those oaths could not prevail.
Th'unpractis'd maid trembled to meet my love.　　　　25

8–17 Henriquez's sentiments of ardent
desire in the prospect of sexual
gratification with Violante, followed
by guilt and self-disgust afterwards,
might call to mind Shakespeare's *Son*
129, 'Th'expense of spirit in a waste
of shame'. The sentiment is shared
by Florizel in *WT* and by Ferdinand
in *Tem*, though in honourable contexts.

8　**enjoy'd** could perhaps mean married or possessed, since he has already
enjoy'd her carnally

10　**reversion** right of succession

13　**rifled . . . stores** Cf. *Luc* 692, 'Pure
Chastity is rifled of her store'. This

line has been adduced as a kind of
forger's signature (as has the play's
title): a clue to a forger's actions left
for the attentive reader. Kahan (2004,
1.239) echoes this suggestion.

18　**Downright love!** The only recorded
instance of the ejaculation prior to
Theobald's use is in Colley Cibber's
comedy *The Refusal, or The Ladies
Philosophy* (1721): 'this is downright
Love in a Tragedy!' (Act 5, p. 68).

20–64　In 1728a, this section is set as
prose. There are, however, as Pope
noticed (see pp. 51, 315), lines within
it that scan as regular verse.

25　**unpractis'd** inexperienced

18 SD] *this edn*　24–31] *this edn; prose 1728a*

By force alone I snatch'd th'imperfect joy,
Which now torments my memory. Not love,
But brutal violence prevail'd; to which
The time and place and opportunity
Were accessories most dishonourable.   30
Shame, shame upon it!

FABIAN [*to Lopez*]   What a heap of stuff's this? I fancy
this fellow's head would make a good pedlar's pack,
neighbour.

HENRIQUEZ Hold, let me be severe to myself, but not   35
unjust. Was it a rape then? No. Her shrieks, her
exclamations then had drove me from her. True, she
did not consent: as true, she did resist; but still in
silence all.

'Twas but the coyness of a modest bride,   40
Not the resentment of a ravish'd maid.

And is the man yet born, who would not risk
The guilt to meet the joy? The guilt! That's true.

But then the danger, the tears, the clamours of the
ruin'd maid, pursuing me to court. That, that, I fear   45
will (as it already does my conscience) something
shatter my honour. What's to be done? But now I have
no choice. Fair Leonora reigns confessed the tyrant
queen of my revolted heart and Violante seems a short

---

26 **imperfect** because it lacked Violante's
full consent. The phrase *imperfect joy*
occurs in plays of the Restoration
period, e.g. Davenant's *The Distresses*
(1673), Act 5, p. 59; and in two plays by
Mary Pix, *The Double Distress* (1701),
Act 5, p. 53, and *The Different Widows*
(1703), Act 4, p. 45, in the latter of
which it occurs in an amatory context.
Cf. 8n.

29 **time . . . opportunity** Cf. *Luc* 876–
931, an extended meditation on the
outrages enabled by Opportunity in

conjunction with Night and Time.

30 **accessories** àccessòries

33 **would . . . pack** because stored with
such disparate and miscellaneous
items

35–61 See 2.3.1–23n.

37 **had drove** would have driven

46 **something** slightly, somewhat (perhaps ironic with *shatter*)

49 **revolted** rebellious or insurgent;
treacherous. The phrase 'revolted
heart' does not occur in literature pre-
1640. The earliest recorded example is

32 SD] *this edn*   40–3] *this edn*; *prose 1728a*   48 confessed] *(confest)*

usurper there. Julio's already by my arts remov'd. O   50
friendship!
How wilt thou answer that? O, that a man
Could reason down this fever of the blood,
Or soothe with words the tumult in his heart!
Then, Julio, I might be indeed thy friend.   55
They, they only should condemn me,
Who, born devoid of passion, ne'er have prov'd
The fierce disputes 'twixt virtue and desire.
While they, who have, like me,
The loose escapes of youthful nature known,   60
Must wink at mine, indulgent to their own.

Exit Henriquez.

LOPEZ   This man is certainly mad, and may be mischievous.
Prithee, neighbour, let's follow him; but at some
distance, for fear of the worst.

Exeunt [Fabian and Lopez] after Henriquez.

---

in a poem by Thomas Carew, 'In the Person of a Lady to her Inconstant Servant' (1640): 'When on the Altar of my hand, / (Bedew'd with many a kisse, and teare;) / Thy now revolted heart, did stand / An humble Martyr' (Carew, *Poems*, p. 67, ll. 1–4). **short** short-lived

53 **fever . . . blood** A similar phrase occurs in *LLL* 4.3.94, where Berowne echoes Dumaine's complaint that he has a fever in his blood for love of Katherine: 'A fever is in your blood?' The emotional situation in which Henriquez finds himself is close to that of the speaker in the later sonnets, e.g. *Son* 147, 'My love is as a fever', in which 'reason is past care' (9).

57 **prov'd** 'To put (a person or thing) to the test' (*OED* prove *v.* 6a)

60 **escapes** 'An inconsistent transgression; a peccadillo, venial error' (*OED* n.[1] 7). Cf. *Tit* 4.2.115, 'Rome will

despise her for this foul escape', which here means 'an outrageous transgression'. Fletcher does not use the word in this sense, but cf. 1.1.21 (see n.).

61 **wink** turn a blind eye to

62–4 No use is subsequently made of the overhearing and pursuit of Henriquez. Hearers add little to the impact of soliloquy at this point. Lopez's remark somewhat spoils the effect of the couplet rhyme ending Henriquez's speech, even if such deflations are typical of tragicomedy.

64 **for . . . worst** The locution occurs in *MV* 1.2.93. It was popular in plays from the Restoration period to the early 18th century, e.g. Sir George Etherege, *The Comical Revenge* (1664), 3.5, p. 40; Dryden, *Sir Martin Mar-All* (1668), Act 3, p. 25; Southerne, *The Fatal Marriage* (1706), 5.1, p. 70); and Betterton, *The Amorous Widow* (1706), Act 5, p. 57.

52–9] *this edn; prose 1728a*   54 soothe] *(sooth)*   63 Prithee] *(Pr'ythee)*   64 SD *Fabian and Lopez] this edn*

214

2.2   *An apartment*

Enter VIOLANTE *alone.*

VIOLANTE

    Whom shall I look upon without a blush?
    There's not a maid whose eye with virgin gaze
    Pierces not to my guilt. What will't avail me
    To say I was not willing?
    Nothing, but that I publish my dishonour,   5
    And wound my fame anew. O misery,
    To seem to all one's neighbours rich, yet know
    One's self necessitous and wretched.

Enter Maid, *and afterwards* GERALD *with a letter.*

MAID

    Madam, here's Gerald, Lord Henriquez' servant.
    He brings a letter to you.   10

VIOLANTE

    A letter to me? [*aside*] How I tremble now!
    [*to Gerald*] Your lord's for court, good Gerald, is he not?

GERALD   Not so, lady.

VIOLANTE [*aside*]

    O my presaging heart! [*to Gerald*] When goes he then?

2.2
0 SD The alternating of interior and
   exterior scenes continues.
1–8 There is an iambic rhythm beneath
   this speech of Violante's, but as in 2.1,
   it breaks down into short lines. I have
   lineated this as in 1728a.
5 **publish** make public
6 **fame** reputation, honour
7 **yet know** I follow 1728a in placing
   this phrase at the close of 7, though
   there are arguments for allowing it to
   complete the sense and the metre of 8.
8 **necessitous**. 'Placed or living in a condition of necessity, want, or poverty;

having little or nothing to support oneself by; poor, needy' (*OED adj.* 2a). The
earliest example for this sense cited is
1611. The word does not appear in the
Shakespeare or Fletcher canons.
14 **presaging** experiencing a presenti-
   ment of evil or misfortune. Recorded
   uses are found in *E3* and in 1619 and
   1622. It occurs in Dryden's poem
   Sigismonda and Guiscardo (1700), l. 721;
   in Nathaniel Lee's *The Massacre of Paris*
   (1690), 3.3, p. 25; and in Pope's 1715
   translation of Homer's *Iliad*, 6.462.
   Theobald reuses it in his own *Perseus
   and Andromeda* (1730), Act 1, p. 2.

2.2] *(SCENE II.)*   11 SD] *this edn*   12 SD] *this edn*   14 SD1, 2] *this edn*

GERALD

His business now steers him some other course.   15

VIOLANTE

Whither, I pray you? [*aside*] How my fears torment me!

GERALD   Some two months' progress.

VIOLANTE   Whither, whither, sir, I do beseech you? Good
heav'ns, I lose all patience. Did he deliberate this, or
was the business but then conceiv'd when it was born?   20

GERALD   Lady, I know not that, nor is it in the command I
have to wait your answer. For the perusing the letter I
commend you to your leisure.   *Exeunt Gerald [and Maid]*.

VIOLANTE

To hearts like mine suspense is misery.

Wax, render up thy trust: be the contents   25
Prosp'rous or fatal, they are all my due.

(*Reads.*)   *Our prudence should now teach us to forget
what our indiscretion has committed. I have already made
one step towards this wisdom, by prevailing on myself to bid
you farewell.*   30

17–20 1728a lines as verse here. The
degree of irregularity in the verse lines
so created (half-line; 13 syllables; 12
syllables if 'Business' is two; 8 syllables) is so extreme that, unusually, this
edition sets as prose.

19 **deliberate** take time to consider; pre-
plan. There is only one usage of 'deliberate' as a verb in Shakespeare, in *TGV*
1.3.73, when Proteus asks his father
Antonio to consider a little longer about
sending him to court: 'Please you deliberate a day or two'. See 1.2.1–11n. and
149–55n., further supporting the view
that *TGV* is influential on *DF*.

24–46 The stagecraft here, the use of soliloquy to announce the impending disappearance of a leading female character,
is deployed by Shakespeare, for example in *AW* 3.2.99–129, when Helena
sets out to take fate into her own hands
and effect a cure for the King of France.

25 **Wax . . . trust**   As discussed in
Appendix 1 (pp. 309, 311), Theobald
was heavily criticized for this line. But as
he himself pointed out in *Mist's Weekly
Journal* for 27 April 1728, Edgar makes
a very similar appeal to a letter in *KL*
4.6.254 – 'Leave, gentle wax' – before
he reads Goneril's self-incriminating
letter. He also pointed to Imogen's sol-
emn address to a letter in *Cym* 3.2.35–6,
'Good wax, thy leave: blest be / You
bees that make these locks of counsel!'
There is also the admittedly egregious
Malvolio, who likewise asks leave of the
wax seal before reading the supposed
letter from Olivia in *TN* 2.5.91.
contents contènts

26 **my due** intended for me only; my
deserts

28 *our indiscretion* Henriquez here
implies Violante's shared responsibility for her fall.

---

16 SD] *this edn*   17–20] *this edn; 1728a lines* Sir, / Patience. / Business / born? /   23 SD *Exeunt*]
Exit 1728a   *and Maid*] *this edn*

O, wretched and betray'd! Lost Violante!
Heart-wounded with a thousand perjur'd vows,
Poison'd with studied language, and bequeath'd
To desperation. I am now become
The tomb of my own honour, a dark mansion 35
For death alone to dwell in. I invite thee,
Consuming desolation, to this temple,
Now fit to be thy spoil. The ruin'd fabric,
Which cannot be repair'd, at once o'erthrow.
What must I do – but that's not worth my thought. 40
I will commend to hazard all the time
That I shall spend hereafter. Farewell, my father,
Whom I'll no more offend; and men, adieu,
Whom I'll no more believe; and maids, adieu,
Whom I'll no longer shame. The way I go 45
As yet I know not – sorrow be my guide. *Exit.*

32 **Heart-wounded** This phrase does not occur in Shakespeare or Fletcher, though it is commonplace from their period onward and is particularly prevalent as a compound in Restoration drama. Theobald introduces the compound adjective to describe Richard II in his 1720 version of the play: 'See, your disconsolate, heart-wounded Lord, / With folded Arms, and down cast Eyes, approaches' (Act 4, p. 44). It also appears in another play of 1720, John Leigh's *Kensington Gardens, or The Pretenders* (1720), Act 3, p. 44.

33 **studied language** a reflection, perhaps, on *our indiscretion* at 28

35 **tomb . . . honour** Cf. *AW* 2.3.140–1, 'Where dust and damn'd oblivion is the tomb / Of honour'd bones indeed.' It is significant that the King's speech to Bertram which is here echoed is one in which he is exhorting Bertram to disregard Helena's low social status. Henriquez's speech at the close of 1.3 encompasses both sides of the debate: see 1.3.63–77. Cf. also *R2* 5.1.12–13, 'Thou map of honour, thou King Richard's tomb, / And not King Richard!'

35–7 **mansion . . . temple** in the ecclesiastical sense of the body as a dwelling-place for the soul. Cf. *TGV* 5.4.7–8, 'O thou that dost inhabit in my breast, / Leave not the mansion so long tenantless'; and *Cym* 3.4.66–7: 'I draw the sword myself, take it, and hit / The innocent mansion of my love, my heart'. See 5.1.34 and n.

38 **spoil** 'Goods . . . taken from an enemy or captured city in time of war . . . in more general sense, any goods, property, territory, etc., seized by force' (*OED n.* 1)

40 The dash here suggests that Violante might be repudiating a suicide attempt.

41, 45–6 Cf. *WT* 3.2.166–7, 'to the certain hazard / Of all incertainties', and 4.4.497–8: 'let myself and fortune / Tug for the time to come'. Violante's

39 o'erthrow] *(o'er-throw)* 46 SD] *(Exit* Violante.)

2.3   *Prospect of a village, before Don Bernard's house*

Enter HENRIQUEZ.

HENRIQUEZ

Where were the eyes, the voice, the various charms,
Each beauteous particle, each nameless grace,
Parents of glowing love? All these in her
It seems were not, but a disease in me
That fancied graces in her. Who ne'er beheld   5
More than a hawthorn shall have cause to say
The cedar's a tall tree, and scorn the shade
The lov'd bush once had lent him. Soft! Mine honour
Begins to sicken in this black reflection.
How can it be that with my honour safe   10

---

sudden departure, throwing herself on the mercy of fortune, resembles Florizel's action in *WT* 4.4.667 and Helena's action at the end of *AW* 3.2.

2.3

0 SD A back shutter representing the exterior of Don Bernard's house is presumably used to create the scene here.

1–23 This soliloquy recalls Henriquez's self-serving and pragmatic self-defence, hair-splitting about whether he has raped Violante, in 2.1.35–61. Both speeches are reminiscent of Proteus's soliloquy in *TGV* 2.6.1–43, in which he justifies his own double treachery towards his intended Julia and his friend Valentine, resulting from the transfer of his affections to Valentine's mistress Silvia. Proteus's 'At first I did adore a twinkling star, / But now I worship a celestial sun' (9–10) performs the same rhetorical function as Henriquez's comparison of a hawthorn and a cedar (5–8). Proteus's sense of perfidy to himself, to Valentine and to Silvia is echoed in Henriquez's sentiments at 12–16. Shakespeare uses paired soliloquies to effect a radical transition of feeling

in *TGV* and in other plays, e.g. *MM*, where the twin soliloquies that conclude 2.2 and 2.4 achieve the change in Angelo's attitude towards Isabella. Henriquez's abandoning of a moral position in 18–19 is even more sudden and to an extent bathetic than the same volte-face performed by Proteus, perhaps because his concerns are as much social as moral.

2 **particle** small part or portion of the whole person

5 **fancied** imagined
Who whoever

9 looks sickly in this dark mirror-image of it. This reading engages *OED* reflection 3a, 'The action of a mirror or other polished surface in exhibiting or reproducing the image of an object'; but *reflection* could mean, as in *OED* 8a, 'The action of turning (back) or fixing the thoughts on some subject; meditation, deep or serious consideration'. In this reading the line means 'begins to seem sick when I think of it in this dark way'. 'Reflection' as a way of thinking is not a meaning current in Shakespeare's day.

10 **my honour safe** my reputation intact

2.3] *(SCENE III.)*

I should pursue Leonora for my wife?
That were accumulating injuries,
To Violante first, and now to Julio;
To her a perjur'd wretch, to him perfidious,
And to myself in strongest terms accus'd   15
Of murd'ring Honour wilfully, without which
My dog's the creature of the nobler kind.
But Pleasure is too strong for Reason's curb,
And Conscience sinks o'er-power'd with Beauty's
          sweets.
Come, Leonora, auth'ress of my crime,   20
Appear and vindicate thy empire here;
Aid me to drive this ling'ring Honour hence,
And I am wholly thine.

Enter to him DON BERNARD *and* LEONORA.

DON BERNARD
Fie, my good lord, why would you wait without?
If you suspect your welcome, I have brought   25
My Leonora to assure you of it.
HENRIQUEZ (*Salutes Leonora.*)
O kiss, sweet as the odours of the spring,
But cold as dews that dwell on morning flow'rs!

---

11 **Leonora** three syllables
16–22 **Honour . . . Pleasure . . . Reason
. . . Conscience . . . Beauty . . .
Honour** personifications. Henriquez
at this point imagines himself involved
in a quasi-allegorical struggle between
his better and worse natures.
16 **without which** which, if I were without
18 **curb** Henriquez may be thinking specifically of the strap connected to a
horse's bit used to restrain an unruly

animal; or, the meaning may be the
figurative restraint or check.
20 **auth'ress . . . crime** sophistry comparable with that of Richard's wooing
Lady Anne in *R3* 1.2: perhaps even
greater, because Henriquez is trying to
convince himself
24 **without** outside
27–8 Cf. *Phil* 3.1.201–2, where Philaster
says of Arathusa: 'Is she not parrallesse? Is not her breath / Sweet as
Arabian winds, when fruits are ripe?'

27 SD] *this edn;* Henr. *salutes* Leon. *after it* 26 *1728a*

Say, Leonora, has your father conquer'd?
Shall Duty then at last obtain the prize,   30
Which you refus'd to Love? And shall Henriquez
Owe all his happiness to good Bernardo?
Ah no! I read my ruin in your eyes;
That sorrow, louder than a thousand tongues,
Pronounces my despair.

DON BERNARD   Come, Leonora,   35
You are not now to learn this noble lord
(Whom but to name restores my failing age)
Has with a lover's eye beheld your beauty,
Through which his heart speaks more than language
      can.
It offers joy and happiness to you,   40
And honour to our house. Imagine then
The birth and qualities of him that loves you,
Which when you know, you cannot rate too dear.

LEONORA

My father, on my knees I do beseech you
To pause one moment on your daughter's ruin.   45
I vow my heart e'en bleeds that I must thank you
For your past tenderness, and yet distrust
That which is yet behind. Consider, sir,
Whoe'er's th'occasion of another's fault,
Cannot himself be innocent. O, give not   50

30–1 **Duty . . . Love** See 16–22n.
31 **Henriquez** The exact metre requires two syllables (Henricks), as also at 98.
36 **You . . . learn** you already know. The phrase is commonly used in Shakespeare and Fletcher's period but not by them. John Wilmot, Earl of Rochester, introduces it in his 1685

alteration of Fletcher's *Valentinian* (Wilmot, *Poems*, 5.4, p. 448).
37 **failing age** Rowe uses the phrase in *The Tragedy of Jane Shore* (1714): 'I have known more plenteous Days / Than those which now my failing Age affords' (1.2, p. 7).
47 **distrust** be wary of
48 **yet behind** yet to transpire

46 e'en] *(ev'n)*

The censuring world occasion to reproach
Your harsh commands, or to my charge lay that
Which most I fear, the fault of disobedience.

DON BERNARD   Prithee, fear neither the one, nor the other.
I tell thee, girl, there's more fear than danger. For my   55
own part, as soon as thou art married to this noble lord,
my fears will be over.

LEONORA

Sir, I should be the vainest of my sex
Not to esteem myself unworthy far
Of this high honour. Once there was a time   60
When to have heard my lord Henriquez' vows
Might have subdued my unexperienc'd heart,
And made me wholly his. But that's now past:
And my firm-plighted faith by your consent
Was long since given to the injur'd Julio.   65

DON BERNARD   Why then, by my consent e'en take it
back again. Thou, like a simple wench, hast given thy
affections to a fellow that does not care a farthing for
them; one that has left thee for a jaunt to court, as who
should say, 'I'll get a place now; 'tis time enough to   70
marry, when I'm turn'd out of it.'

---

51 **censuring world** The phrase, meaning censorious society, is found in *Maid's* 2.1.332. The expression had something of a vogue in the 1680s, when it is found in several works written by Behn, Lee, Elkanah Settle and others.

54–7 Don Bernard switches abruptly into prose at this point.

60–3 **Once . . . his** This possibly indicates some background to the relationship between Henriquez and Leonora, perhaps an orphan of a previous version of the play; or she may simply be saying that before her heart was won by Julio, she might have been susceptible to Henriquez's advances. In *MA* 2.1.253–8, there is a similarly ambiguous hint of a previous relationship between Beatrice and Benedick which is nowhere developed: 'DON PEDRO Come, lady, come; you have lost the heart of Signor Benedick. / BEATRICE Indeed, my lord, he lent it me awhile, and I gave him use for it, a double heart for his single one. Marry, once before he won it of me with false dice; therefore your grace may well say I have lost it.'

62 **unexperienc'd** *OED* gives a range of dates for this form of the word 'inexperienced' spanning 1569–1860. The phrase, however, occurs in literature only in Davenant's play *The Man's the Master* (1669), Act 3, p. 37; in Theobald and in later poems.

70 **place** sexual innuendo on place as 'vulva'. See Williams, 237.

HENRIQUEZ

So, surely, it should seem, most lovely maid.
Julio, alas, feels nothing of my passion:
His love is but th'amusement of an hour,
A short relief from business, or ambition,   75
The sport of youth and fashion of the age.
O, had he known the hopes, the doubts, the ardours,
Or half the fond varieties of passion
That play the tyrant with my tortur'd soul,
He had not left thee to pursue his fortune,   80
To practise cringes in a slavish circle
And barter real bliss for unsure honour.

LEONORA

[*aside*] O, the opposing wind,
Should'ring the tide, makes here a fearful billow.
I needs must perish in it. [*to Henriquez*] O my lord,   85
Is it then possible you can forget
What's due to your great name and princely birth,
To friendship's holy law, to faith repos'd,
To truth, to honour and poor injur'd Julio?
O think, my lord, how much this Julio loves you;   90
Recall his services, his well-tried faith;
Think too, this very hour, where'er he be,
Your favour is the envy of the Court
And secret triumph of his grateful heart.
Poor Julio, how securely thou depend'st   95

73–85 **Julio . . . it** Kukowski (85) marks this passage out as having many of the characteristic mannerisms of Fletcher's style: he refers to listing in threes (77), 'short-cuts' (78) and the image of billowing (84).

75 **business . . . ambition** Probably the first word has two syllables and the second has three.

77–9 Cf. F *Ham* 2.2.554–6, 'What would he do / Had he the motive and the cue for passion / That I have?'

81 **cringes** The word does not appear in Shakespeare, but Fletcher uses it in *EB* 3.3.37 and in two collaborations with Massinger, *FMI* (1626) 3.1.30 and *SV* 3.1.372.

82 **real** two syllables

95 **securely** with full Shakespearean sense of carelessness, overconfidence

83 SD] *this edn*   85 SD] *this edn*   92 where'er] (where-e'er)

Upon the faith and honour of thy master.
Mistaken youth! This very hour he robs thee
Of all thy heart holds dear. 'Tis so Henriquez
Repays the merits of unhappy Julio.   *Weeps.*

HENRIQUEZ (*aside*)

My slumb'ring honour catches the alarm.   100
I was to blame to parley with her thus:
She's shown me to myself. It troubles me.

DON BERNARD   Mad, mad. Stark mad, by this light.

LEONORA

I but begin to be so. [*to Don Bernard*] I conjure you,
By all the tender interests of nature,   105
By the chaste love 'twixt you and my dear mother
(O holy heav'n, that she were living now!)
Forgive and pity me. O sir, remember,
I've heard my mother say a thousand times

---

98 **Henriquez** See 31n.
100–2 1728a has a brace around Henriquez's lines, indicating that they are all spoken aside.
102 **She's ... myself** Cf. Gertrude's similar conviction that Hamlet has shown her to herself, *Ham* 3.4.86–9.
103 **Stark ... light** The ejaculation or oath in this form, or as 'mad, by this light', is a late Restoration phrase. It occurs in Thomas D'Urfey's *Love for Money* (1691), 5.3, p. 52; and William Congreve's *The Old Bachelor* (1693), Act 5, p. 50; but not before that.
104–6 **conjure ... mother** *OED* conjure *v.* 3 gives 'To constrain (a person to some action) by putting him upon his oath, or by appealing to something sacred'. Leonora's invocation will recall other such 'conjurings' in Shakespeare; for example, Isabella's plea to Duke Vincentio in *MM* 5.1.51–4: 'O Prince, I conjure thee, as thou believ'st / There is another comfort

than this world, / That thou neglect me not with that opinion / That I am touch'd with madness.' The most extended example, somewhat similar in context to *DF* here, and also employing the phrase *holy law* to be found in Leonora's previous speech (88), is *Luc* 568–74: 'She conjures him by high almighty JOVE, / By knighthood, gentry and sweet friendship's oath, / By her untimely tears, her husband's love, / By holy human law and common troth, / And by heaven and earth, and all the power of both, / That to his borrowed bed he make retire, / And stoop to honour, not to foul desire.'
104 **conjure** The stress is of interest: it could be either on the first syllable, or on the second, as *conjùre* (cf. 2.4.16, 25). Shakespeare stresses 'conjùr'd' in *RJ* 2.1.26 and *Oth* 1.3.106, 3.3.298.
109–18 **I've ... wife** The dramatic situation here resonates with *TN* 2.4.110ff., where Viola tells the contrasting story of

---

100 SD] *this edn; after* me. *102 1728a*   100–2] *extent of 'aside' indicated by brace after lines 1728a.*   102 She's] Sh'as   104 SD] *this edn*

Her father would have forc'd her virgin choice,   110
But when the conflict was 'twixt love and duty,
Which should be first obey'd, my mother quickly
Paid up her vows to love and married you.
You thought this well, and she was prais'd for this.
For this her name was honour'd. Disobedience   115
Was ne'er imputed to her; her firm love
Conquer'd whate'er oppos'd it, and she prosper'd
Long time your wife. My case is now the same:
You are the father which you then condemn'd;
I what my mother was, but not so happy.   120

DON BERNARD   Go to, you're a fool. No doubt you have
old stories enough to undo you. What, you can't throw
yourself away but by precedent, ha? You will needs be
married to one that will none of you? You will be happy
nobody's way but your own, forsooth. But, d'ye mark   125
me, spare your tongue for the future – and that's using
you hardly too, to bid you spare what you have a great
deal too much of. Go, go your ways, and, d'ye hear, get
ready within these two days to be married to a husband
you don't deserve. Do it, or, by my dead father's soul,   130
you are no acquaintance of mine.

---

her 'sister', who would not speak about
her love: 'My father had a daughter lov'd
a man, / As it might be perhaps, were I a
woman, I should your lordship.'
110 **virgin choice** This unusual phrase
occurs only once before Theobald's
usage, in a 1703 poem by John
Oldmixon, *Amores Britannici*, Epistle
5.30. King Richard II is at this point
addressing Queen Isabella: 'Did you
for this ungrateful *England* chuse,
/ That thus she might your Virgin
Choice abuse.' Because this poem
is a dramatic monologue spoken by
Richard II, a king in whom Theobald

had much interest, it is easily possible
that he had read it.
120 **happy** lucky
125–6 **d'ye mark me** This ejaculation,
especially in the form 'mark me', is
very common in Beaumont and in
Fletcher, who sometimes uses it several times in the same play – on no
fewer than four occasions (sometimes
as 'mark me') in *WGC*, for example:
1.3.200, 2.3.82, 4.2.27, 4.3.19.
127–8 **what . . . of** an echo, perhaps, of
AW 3.2.90–1: 'The fellow has a deal
of that too much, / Which holds him
much to have'.

---

110 forc'd] *(forced)*   114 prais'd] *(praised)*   125 nobody's] *(no Body's)*

HENRIQUEZ

    She weeps. Be gentler to her, good Bernardo.

LEONORA

    Then woe the day! I'm circled round with fire;
    No way for my escape but through the flames.
    O, can I e'er resolve to live without   135
    A father's blessing, or abandon Julio?
    With other maids the choice were not so hard;
    Int'rest, that rules the world, has made at last
    A merchandise of hearts, and virgins now
    Choose as they're bid and wed without esteem.   140
    By nobler springs shall my affections move,
    Nor own a master but the man I love.   *Exit.*

DON BERNARD Go thy ways, contradiction. – Follow her,
    my lord, follow her, in the very heat. This obstinacy
    must be combated by importunity as obstinate.   145

                    Exit Henriquez after her.

    The girl says right; her mother was just such another. I
    remember two of us courted her at the same time. She
    lov'd neither of us, but she chose me purely to spite
    that surly old blockhead my father-in-law. Who comes
    here? Camillo? Now the refusing part will lie on my   150
    side.

                    Enter CAMILLO.

CAMILLO My worthy neighbour, I am much in fortune's
    favour to find you thus alone. I have a suit to you.

138–9 **made . . . hearts** The phrase 'to make a merchandise' means to make a deal or conclude a bargain. Leonora means that her love has become a commodity.

144 **the very heat** in the heat of the moment; at once. Although the phrase occurs in *1H4* 1.1.59–60, 'in the very heat / And pride of their contention', it is not there a self-contained utterance meaning 'immediately'. Used in that way, the locution is later, largely post-1660, and not very common.

142 SD] *(Exit Leonora.)*

DON BERNARD   Please to name it, sir.

CAMILLO   Sir, I have long held you in singular esteem, and   155
    what I shall now say will be a proof of it. You know, sir,
    I have but one son.

DON BERNARD   Ay, sir.

CAMILLO   And the fortune I am blest withal, you pretty
    well know what it is.   160

DON BERNARD   'Tis a fair one, sir.

CAMILLO   Such as it is, the whole reversion is my son's.
    He is now engag'd in his attendance on our master the
    Duke. But ere he went, he left with me the secret of his
    heart, his love for your fair daughter. For your consent,   165
    he said, 'twas ready. I took a night, indeed, to think
    upon it and now have brought you mine, and am come
    to bind the contract with half my fortune in present,
    the whole some time hence, and in the meanwhile my
    hearty blessing. Ha? What say you to't, Don Bernard?   170

DON BERNARD   Why, really, neighbour – I must own, I have
    heard something of this matter.

CAMILLO   Heard something of it? No doubt you have.

DON BERNARD   Yes, now I recollect it well.

CAMILLO   Was it so long ago, then?   175

DON BERNARD   Very long ago, neighbour – on Tuesday
    last.

CAMILLO   What, am I mock'd in this business, Don
    Bernard?

DON BERNARD   Not mock'd, good Camillo, not mock'd.   180
    But in love matters, you know, there are abundance of

---

159 **withal** with

162–70 Although this speech is printed
    as prose, as it is in 1728a, there are
    possible verse lines in *he left . . . heart,*
    / *his . . . consent,* / *he . . . indeed,* /
    to . . . mine (164–7).

164 ***ere** See 1.2.26n.

166 **a night** suggests that a single night
    separates Acts 1 and 2; and in dramatic
    terms, accentuates the inconstancy of
    Don Bernard

163 engag'd] *(engaged)*   164 ere] *(e'er)*   169 meanwhile] *(mean while)*   181 love matters] *(Love-matters)*

changes in half an hour. Time, time, neighbour, plays
tricks with all of us.

CAMILLO   Time, sir! What tell you me of time? Come, I
see how this goes. Can a little time take a man by the   185
shoulder and shake off his honour? Let me tell you,
neighbour, it must either be a strong wind, or a very
mellow honesty that drops so easily. Time, quoth'a?

DON BERNARD   Look'e, Camillo, will you please to put
your indignation in your pocket for half a moment   190
while I tell you the whole truth of the matter. My
daughter, you must know, is such a tender soul she
cannot possibly see a duke's younger son without
falling desperately in love with him. Now you know,
neighbour, when greatness rides post after a man of my   195
years 'tis both prudence and good breeding to let one's
self be overtaken by it. And who can help all this? I
profess, it was not my seeking, neighbour.

CAMILLO   I profess, a fox might earth in the hollowness
of your heart, neighbour, and there's an end. If I were   200
to give a bad conscience its true likeness it should be
drawn after a very near neighbour to a certain poor
neighbour of yours. Neighbour – with a pox!

DON BERNARD   Nay, you are so nimble with me you will
hear nothing.   205

CAMILLO   Sir, if I must speak nothing, I will hear nothing.
As for what you have to say, if it comes from your heart,
'tis a lie before you speak it. I'll to Leonora; and if I

---

188 **mellow** ripe and, by proverbial
association, soon rotten. See Tilley,
R133, 'Soon ripe, soon rotten', where
the association is made with the med-
lar as a fruit that is only good when
it has rotted and fallen off the tree.
That may be behind the metaphor
here.
quoth'a? did he say? (with an empha-

sis of derision)
195 **rides post** rides with post horses, i.e.
express; at high speed
199 **earth** hide, or burrow in the earth, as
foxes do. *OED v.* 4c cites Fletcher, *SC*,
for its earliest recorded instance.
204 **nimble** quick-witted, clever; but
with overtones here of haste, precipi-
tateness

189 Look'e] *(Look'ee)*

find her in the same story, why, I shall believe your wife
was true to you and your daughter is your own. Fare   210
you well.   *Exit, as into Don Bernard's house.*

DON BERNARD   Ay, but two words must go to that bargain.
It happens that I am at present of opinion my daughter
shall receive no more company today – at least no such   214
visits as yours.   *Exit Don Bernard, following him.*

2.4   *Changes to another prospect of Don Bernard's house.*

[*Enter*] LEONORA, *above.*

LEONORA
How tediously I've waited at the window,
Yet know not one that passes. Should I trust
My letter to a stranger whom I think
To bear an honest face (in which sometimes
We fancy we are wondrous skilful), then   5
I might be much deceiv'd. This late example
Of base Henriquez, bleeding in me now,

212 **two . . . bargain** proverbial; see Tilley, W827. Fletcher uses the saying in *WGC* 2.3.10.

2.4

0 SD The balcony scene here reprises 1.3, but against a different back shutter.

1–30 Scenes in which letters are posted by immured heroines from windows are common in Elizabethan and Jacobean plays such as Thomas Kyd's *Spanish Tragedy* (1592) and Ford's *'Tis Pity She's a Whore* (1633). Here, there is a resonance with Ophelia's dialogue with Hamlet in *Ham* 3.1.89–129, where she says, sadly, 'I was the more deceiv'd' (119). Pujante (98–9) argues that this scene is very closely modelled on the presumed source text, Shelton. (See pp. 48–58 above for further discussion of the source.) In 3.13.270, Cardenio (Julio) tells the story of how he has received a letter from Luscinda

(Leonora) and has ascertained the following from its bearer: 'a very beautifull Ladie did call him from a certaine window: Her eyes were all beblubbered with teares; and said vnto him very hastily: Brother, if thou beest a Christian, as thou appearest to be one, I pray thee for God's sake, that thou doe forthwith addresse this letter to the place and person that the supercription assigneth, (for they be well knowen) and therein thou shalt doe our Lord great seruice. And because thou mayest not want meanes to doe it, take what thou shalt finde wrapped in that Handkerchife: and saying so, she threw out of the window a handkerchife, wherein were lapped vp a hundred Rials, this ring of golde which I carie here, and that letter which I deliuered vnto you . . . and after perceiuinge the paines I might take in

214 today] *(to day)*   **2.4**] *(SCENE IV.)*   0.1 *Enter*] *this edn*   5 wondrous] *(wond'rous)*

From each good aspect takes away my trust,
For his face seem'd to promise truth and honour.
Since nature's gifts in noblest forms deceive,   10
Be happy you that want 'em! Here comes one.
I've seen him, though I know him not. He has
An honest face too – that's no matter – sir!

Enter Citizen.

CITIZEN   To me?

LEONORA

As you were of a virtuous matron born   15
(There is no doubt, you are), I do conjure you
Grant me one boon. Say, do you know me, sir?

CITIZEN

Ay, Leonora, and your worthy father.

LEONORA

I have not time to press the suit I've to you
With many words. Nay, I should want the words   20
Though I had leisure. But for love of justice,
And as you pity misery – but I wander
Wide from my subject. Know you Julio, sir?

CITIZEN

Yes, very well; and love him too as well.

LEONORA

O, there an angel spake! Then I conjure you,   25
Convey this paper to him: and believe me,
You do heav'n service in't, and shall have cause
Not to repent your pains. I know not what

---

bringing you it . . . and seeing by the indorsement, that you were the man to whom it was addrest. For Sir I know you verie well.'

8 **each good aspect** anyone who looks honest; aspect is stressed on the first syllable, which is never the case in Shakespeare. The word is very common in Fletcher who does sometimes

stress the first syllable: see for example *LPi* 3.2.325–6, 'Of what a full command she bears, how gracious / All her aspect shows; bless me from a feavor.'

11, 20 **want** lack

16, 25 **conjure** conjùre. See 2.3.104n.

18 **Leonora** could be three or four syllables, depending on the director's or actor's decision

Your fortune is – pardon me, gentle sir,
That I am bold to offer this.
   Throws down a purse with money.
DON BERNARD (*within*)   Leonora –   30
LEONORA

I trust to you; heav'n put it in your heart
To work me some relief.
CITIZEN

Doubt it not, lady. You have mov'd me so,
That though a thousand dangers barr'd my way,   34
I'd dare 'em all to serve you.   *Exit.*
LEONORA

Thanks from a richer hand than mine requite you!
DON BERNARD (*within*) Why, daughter –
LEONORA

I come. – O Julio, feel but half my grief,
And thou wilt outfly time to bring relief.
                        Exit Leonora from the window.

End of the second act

3.1   *The prospect of a village*

Enter JULIO *with a letter, and* Citizen.

CITIZEN

When from the window she did bow and call,
Her passions shook her voice, and from her eyes
Mistemper and distraction, with strange wildness,

---

39 **outfly** Shakespeare uses the word,
meaning outstrip or overtake, in *TC*
2.3.113. *OED*'s earliest citation for the
verb in this sense (2) is 1602, and its
period of common usage is predominantly later.

3.1
0 SD The scene here is the same as for
2.1.
3 **Mistemper** disorder, discomposure,
indisposition. *OED n.* cites this passage.

30 SD1] *Offers to throw down a Purse with Money. 1767*   30 Leonora] *this edn; prose 1728a*   35 SD]
(Exit Citizen.)   **3.1**] *(ACT III. SCENE I.)*   0 SD *The*] SCENE, *The 1728a*

Bespoke concern above a common sorrow.

JULIO

Poor Leonora! Treacherous, damn'd Henriquez!   5
She bids me fill my memory with her danger.
I do, my Leonora. Yes, I fill
The region of my thought with nothing else.
Lower she tells me here that this affair
Shall yield a testimony of her love   10
And prays her letter may come safe and sudden.
This pray'r the heav'ns have heard, and I beseech 'em
To hear all pray'rs she makes.

CITIZEN   Have patience, sir.

JULIO

O my good friend, methinks I am too patient.
Is there a treachery like this in baseness   15
Recorded anywhere? It is the deepest.
None but itself can be its parallel –
And from a friend profess'd! Friendship? Why, 'tis
A word forever maim'd. In human nature
It was a thing the noblest; and 'mong beasts   20
It stood not in mean place. Things of fierce nature
Hold amity and concordance. Such a villainy

4 **common sorrow** ordinary misfortune
5 **Leonora . . . Henriquez** As often with lines that include proper names, there are several possible ways of delivering this, depending on what weighting of syllables is given to the names; *Treacherous* may also be elided.
6–13 **She . . . makes** Pujante (101) remarks on the proximity between this passage and the equivalent passage in Shelton, 3.13.271: '*and the successe of this affaire shall let you to perceiue, whether I loue you well or no. I beseech Almighty God that this may arriue vnto your hands, before mine shall see it selfe in danger to joyne it selfe with his.*'
17 **None . . . parallel** See pp. 309–10, 311 and Appendix 3 for discussion of this ill-fated line.
18 **friend . . . Friendship?** Julio's sen-

timents are close here to those of Valentine in *TGV* 5.4.62–6: 'Thou common friend, that's without faith or love, / For such is a friend now! Treacherous man, / Thou hast beguiled my hopes. Naught but mine eye / Could have persuaded me. Now I dare not say / I have one friend alive'.
21 **stood . . . place** was not given a low value
22–5 **Such . . . enormous** This convoluted way of saying that 'no one would believe this if it were written in a play' is of a piece with the earlier circumlocution at 8, 'The region of my thought'. In *TN* 3.4.123–4, Fabian comments on Malvolio, 'If this were played upon a stage now, I could condemn it as an improbable fiction.'

A writer could not put down in his scene
Without taxation of his auditory
For fiction most enormous.

CITIZEN   These upbraidings   25
Cool time while they are vented.

JULIO   I am counsell'd.
For you, evermore thanks. You've done much for us
So gently press'd to't that I may persuade me
You'll do a little more.

CITIZEN   Put me t'employment
That's honest, though not safe, with my best spirits   30
I'll give't accomplishment.

JULIO   No more but this –
For I must see Leonora, and to appear
Like Julio, as I am, might haply spoil
Some good event ensuing. Let me crave
Th'exchange of habit with you: some disguise   35
May bear me to my love unmark'd and secret.

CITIZEN

You shall not want. Yonder's the house before us;

---

24 **taxation of** criticism by or from:
OED taxation 3, 'A charging with a
fault or offence; accusation; censure,
reproof, blame', and cf. *AYL* 1.2.83–4,
'You'll be whipped for taxation one
of these days.' In this sense, the word
is used only twice by Shakespeare;
it is not used at all by Fletcher or
Theobald. *OED* has no example after
1653.
auditory audience, assembly of listen-
ers; cf. *Tit* 5.3.95 and *FMI* 4.2.338.
Common in the drama of Shakespeare's
period – much liked by Jonson, for
example – the term is not used elsewhere by Theobald and is uncommon
in the 18th century, by which time it
would have seemed bookish.

25 **enormous** unnatural, monstrous
25–6 **These . . . vented**   Coriolanus
speaks of the plebeians and their griev-
ances in similarly dismissive phrasing,
in *Cor* 1.1.207–8: 'With these shreds /
They vented their complainings'.
28 **So gently press'd** with such mild
persuasion; so kindly when requested
me myself
29 **Put** if you put
32 The metre seems to call for the elision
't'appear', not made in 1728a, and for
elision of *Leonora* to three syllables.
34 **event** outcome
35–6 **some disguise / May** i.e. some
disguise that may
37 **the house** the Citizen's house, where
clothes may be exchanged

31] *Kennedy; prose 1728a*

Make haste to reach it.   [*Exit.*]

JULIO   Still I thank you, sir.

O Leonora, stand but this rude shock,

Hold out thy faith against the dread assault   40

Of this base lord, the service of my life

Shall be devoted to repay thy constancy.   *Exit.*

3.2   *Don Bernard's house*

Enter LEONORA [*in wedding attire*].

LEONORA

I've hop'd to th' latest minute hope can give.

He will not come. He's not receiv'd my letter.

Maybe some other view has from our home

Repeal'd his chang'd eye: for what business can

Excuse a tardiness thus wilful? None.   5

Well then, it is not business. O! That letter,

I say, is not deliver'd, or he's sick;

Or – O suggestion, wherefore wilt thou fright me? –

---

38 **Still** evermore; yet again
39 **rude shock** violent, impolite, offen-
sive blow; cf. *dread assault*, 40. The
term 'shock' in Shakespeare's time
might have had overtones of the clashing of armies or of jousting partners.
The more interiorized sense of a blow
that destroys one's psychic equilib-
rium is later.
40 **Hold . . . faith** a conditional: 'if you
hold . . .'. Julio's fidelity is conditional
upon Leonora's proper conduct.
41 **base lord** an oxymoron
42 an alexandrine
3.2
0 SD continuing the oscillation from
exterior to interior scenes
2–3 *****He . . . Maybe** 1728a prints an
apostrophe before 'He'; in 1728b, this

erroneous apostrophe is dropped and
placed before 'May be', to indicate the
elision of 'it'. See 1.2.16n. for other
similar elisions.
4 **Repeal'd** The sense here is 'recalled'
or 'brought back'. This figurative
use, with a concrete noun such as
'eye', is unusual. Shakespeare has a
similar expression (similar in that it
means the bringing back or restoring
of one of the senses) in *AW* 2.3.49–
50, 'this healthful hand, whose
banish'd sense / Thou hast repeal'd'.
Otherwise, the phrase 'chang'd eye'
is unique to *DF*.
8 **suggestion** 'Prompting or incitement
to evil; an instance of this, a temptation of the evil one': *OED n.* 1a, citing
KJ 3.1.218, 'giddy loose suggestions'

---

38 SD] *this edn*   42 SD] *this edn; Exeunt 1728a*   3.2] *(SCENE II.)*   0.1 *in wedding attire*] *this
edn*   1 hop'd] *(hoped)*   2 He] *('He) 1728a*   He's] *(H'as)*   3 Maybe] *'May be 1728b*

Julio does to Henriquez on mere purpose,
On plotted purpose, yield me up, and he   10
Hath chose another mistress. All presumptions
Make pow'rful to this point: his own protraction,
Henriquez left behind – that strain lack'd jealousy,
Therefore lack'd love. So sure as life shall empty
Itself in death, this new surmise of mine   15
Is a bold certainty. 'Tis plain and obvious,
Henriquez would not, durst not, thus infringe
The law of friendship, thus provoke a man
That bears a sword and wears his flag of youth
As fresh as he. He durst not. 'Tis contrivance,   20

9   **Julio . . . Henriquez** Both names may
have two syllables here.
  on mere purpose deliberately. This
adjectival use of 'mere', to mean
downright or nothing short of, is
deployed by Shakespeare and Fletcher
in their collaborative plays, on four
occasions in *H8* (3.1.112; 3.2.324,
329; 4.1.59); and five in *TNK* (1.2.42;
2.2.58; 4.2.26, 44, 52). Fletcher uses it
twice in *CR*, at 3.4.13, 145. It remains
common in the plays of Theobald's
time. Theobald uses it elsewhere, e.g.
in *Shakespeare Restored*.
11 **Hath chose** This form of the past
participle is used by Theobald in his
adaptation of Aristophanes' *Plutus*
(1715), p. 29 ('have rather chose');
in his version of *Richard II* (1720),
p. 26 ('has chose'); and in his later
play *Merlin* (1734), p. 11 ('have
chose'). The collocation was current
in Shakespeare's time e.g. *PP* 18.1,
'When as thine eye hath chose the
dame'. (This poem is not thought to
be Shakespeare's; see Duncan-Jones &
Woudhuysen, 85.)
12 **Make pow'rful** conduce strongly
  protraction delay. The word is a
curious one. It does not appear else-

where in Theobald, but neither does
it appear in Shakespeare or Fletcher.
It does, however, occur in this sense in
Shakespeare's period.
13 The line can scan as an alexandrine or
it may suggest an elision in *jealousy*.
  strain class or type of conduct.
The term is very commonly used to
describe individual (usually inherited)
character traits in Shakespeare and
in Fletcher, for example in *Maid's*
3.1.196–7, where the King says to
Evadne, of Amintor: 'is not his spirit,
/ Though he be temperate, of a valiant strain'. It is not commonly used
to refer to actions. See also 1.1.1–2n.,
3.3.23.
17, 20 **durst not** a collocation frequently deployed by Shakespeare and by
Fletcher. Theobald also uses it, however: for example in his translation from
Sophocles of *Electra* (1714), Act 4, p.
48; in *The Persian Princess* (1715), Act
3, p. 36; and in *Richard II*, Act 2, p. 13.
19 **wears his flag** displays the banner
of. This figurative usage of the term
'flag' with the verb 'wears' is unique
to *DF*.
20 **he** ambiguous between Henriquez and
Julio

15 Itself] *(*It self*)*

Gross-daubing 'twixt them both. But I'm o'erheard. *Going*

Enter JULIO, *disguised.*

JULIO

Stay, Leonora. Has this outward veil
Quite lost me to thy knowledge?   [*Reveals himself.*]

LEONORA   O my Julio!
Thy presence ends the stern debate of doubt
And cures me of a thousand heartsick fears   25
Sprung from thy absence, yet awakes a train
Of other sleeping terrors. Do you weep?

JULIO

No, Leonora. When I weep, it must be
The substance of mine eye. Would I could weep;
For then mine eye would drop upon my heart   30

21 **Gross-daubing** *OED* gross *a.* and *n.*[4] 16b gives, for this quasi-adverbial usage, a citation from Dryden's *Conquest of Granada, Part II* (1672): 'Love, like a Scene, at distance should appear; / But Marriage views the gross-daub'd Landscape neer' (3.1, p. 100). Marriage, that is, allows the viewer to get too close to the object and see the painter's technique – perhaps, by extension, the blemishes on matrimony. Landscapes should be viewed from a distance. Leonora here means that the supposed plan formed by Julio and Henriquez is so obvious as to resemble a poorly executed painting. For the verbal noun 'daubing', *OED vbl. n.* 1c offers 'Painting coarsely or inartistically; hence, a coarsely or badly executed painting', but all the examples postdate Shakespeare. This may be evidence of later recension, but Shakespeare does use the verb 'daub' in the sense of putting on a false show or dissembling, as in *KL* 4.1.55, Edgar's 'Poor Tom's a-cold. [*aside*] I cannot daub it further'.

21 SD presumably indicates Leonora's failure to recognize Julio
24 **stern debate** strict or severe interrogation. This locution does not occur in Shakespeare or Fletcher. It is found in Heywood's *The Four Prentices of London* (performed 1594, published 1615) and occasionally in early 17th-century texts; but is given currency by Dryden's translation of Ovid and by Pope's translation of Homer, where it occurs several times.
25 **heartsick** 'Sick at heart; *fig.* depressed and despondent' (*OED a.* 1). The word occurs in Shakespeare's period, but qualifying 'fears', is unique to *DF.*
29 **substance** Julio may mean the material out of which the eye is made (i.e. the eye itself), or that which the eye sees.
    *****Would** 1728a has an apostrophe before 'Would', indicating an omitted 'I'. See 4.1.167, 5.2.67, 237 for similar cases; and see also 1.2.16n. for other similar emendations.
30–1 **mine. . . there** The eye will drop quenching tears (or itself, in melted form) on the heart.

21 Gross-daubing] *(*Gross-dawbing*)*   23 SD] *this edn*   29 Would] *(*'Would*)*

And 'suage the fire there.

LEONORA   You are full possess'd
How things go here. First, welcome heartily;
Welcome to th'ending of my last good hour.
Now summer bliss and gaudy days are gone,
My lease in 'em's expir'd.

JULIO   Not so, Leonora.   35

LEONORA

Yes, Julio, yes; an everlasting storm
Is come upon me, which I can't bear out.
I cannot stay much talk; we have lost leisure.
And thus it is: your absence hath giv'n breeding
To what my letter hath declar'd, and is   40
This instant on th'effecting.   (*Flourish within*)
                     Hark! The music
Is now on tuning which must celebrate
This bus'ness so discordant. Tell me then
What you will do.

JULIO   I know not what. Advise me.
I'll kill the traitor.

LEONORA   O, take heed: his death   45
Betters our cause no whit. No killing, Julio.

JULIO

My blood stands still and all my faculties

34–5 **summer . . . expir'd** Cf. Antony's
'Let's have one other gaudy night' (*AC*
3.13.188); and *Son* 18.4, 'summer's
lease hath all too short a date.'

34 **gaudy** luxurious, festive. The meaning of the noun 'gaudy' as a festival or
merry-making is early, but the more
specific sense of a college gaudy, meaning 'a grand feast or entertainment; *esp.*
an annual dinner in commemoration of
some event in the history of a college'
(*OED n.* 5), is not attested before 1651.

35 **Leonora** three syllables

36–7 **everlasting . . . out** Cf. *Per* 4.1.18–
19, where Marina says, 'This world to
me is as a lasting storm, / Whirring me
from my friends'.

39 **breeding** opportunity (for development)

41 **on th'effecting** being put into effect

42 **on tuning** tuning up; this phrase is
unique to Theobald.

43 **discordant** inharmonious; jarring.
The word is not in the Shakespeare
or Fletcher canons, nor does Theobald
use it elsewhere.

---

31 'suage] (swage*)*   34 gaudy] (gawdy*)*   41 effecting.] *this edn;* effecting, *1728a*   SD] *this edn;*
after Musick *1728a*

Are by enchantment dull'd. You gracious pow'rs,
The guardians of sworn faith and suff'ring virtue,
Inspire prevention of this dreaded mischief!   50
This moment is our own; let's use it, love,
And fly o'th' instant from this house of woe.

LEONORA

Alas, impossible! My steps are watch'd;
There's no escape for me. You must stay too.

JULIO

What, stay, and see thee ravish'd from my arms?   55
I'll force thy passage. Wear I not a sword?
Ne'er on man's thigh rode better. If I suffer
The traitor play his part – if I not do
Manhood and justice honour – let me be deem'd
A tame, pale coward, whom the night owl's hoot   60
May turn to aspen leaf; some man take this,
  [*indicating his sword*]

---

50 **Inspire prevention** cause to be prevented
  mischief stronger than its modern sense: disaster or catastrophe
55–6, 67–8 **thee . . . thy . . . thy . . . you**
There is an upping of the emotional temperature in the change from the 'you' to the 'thou' form of the second-person pronoun. Such changes are characteristic of Jacobean texts. It is interesting to observe the pattern here. Leonora has been using *you*, but modulates into *thy* at 67, returning to *you* in the following line. She is perhaps conscious of being forward or over-intimate.
56 **thy passage** referring back to *escape* at 54. Julio will clear her way to escape.
56–7 **Wear . . . better** Dodd (for whom, see 1.3.10–14n.), in the two-volume compilation *The Beauties of Shakespear* (1752) draws attention to the similarity between this line and *Oth* 5.2.257–9: 'Lo! I have a weapon: / A better

never did itself sustain / Upon a soldier's thigh'. Accurately, the quotation begins 'Behold, I have a weapon'. Of the lines in *DF*, Dodd comments: 'whether *Shakespear*'s, or introduc'd by *Theobald*, I cannot pronounce' (2.174).
57–8 **If . . . part** if I permit Henriquez (*The traitor*) to be Leonora's husband (*play his part*)
58–9 **not . . . honour** i.e. do not honour manhood or justice
61 **turn . . . leaf** i.e. cause to tremble. The leaves of aspen trees turn and move in the wind, because they are attached to flattened stems. The comparison of the cowardly or the fearful to aspen leaves is commonplace in the plays of Shakespeare's period and continues to be in the Restoration. Shakespeare himself deploys the figure in *2H4* 2.4.106–7, where the Hostess asserts that she shakes 'and 'twere an aspen leaf'; and in *Tit* 2.3.44–7, in

60 night owl's] *(*Night-Owl's*)*   61 aspen leaf] *(*Aspen-leaf*)*   SD] *this edn*

Give me a distaff for it.

LEONORA   Patience, Julio,
And trust to me. I have forethought the means
To disappoint these nuptials.   (*Music within*)
                    Hark! Again!
These are the bells knoll for us. See, the lights   65
Move this way, Julio. Quick, behind yon arras
And take thy secret stand. Dispute it not;
I have my reasons – you anon shall know them.
There you may mark the passages of the night.
Yet more: I charge you by the dearest ties,   70
Whate'er you see, or hear, whate'er shall hap,
In your concealment rest a silent statue.
Nay, hide thee straight, or (*Shows a dagger.*) see – I'm
    arm'd, and vow
To fall a bleeding sacrifice before thee.
    Thrusts him out to the arras.
I dare not tell thee of my purpose, Julio,   75
Lest it should wrap thee in such agonies
Which my love could not look on.

Scene opens to a large hall. An altar prepared with tapers.

a tragic context, Marcus says of the
mutilated Lavinia: 'O, had the monster
seen those lily hands / Tremble like
aspen leaves upon a lute / And make
the silken strings delight to kiss them,
/ He would not then have touched
them for his life.'

62 **distaff** a cleft stick on which wool was
spun, symbolizing women's work. The
contrast between the sword or lance
and the distaff operates as a symbol of
contrasting maleness and femaleness
in several Shakespearean contexts.
Goneril uses the expression to make
the point to Edmund that Albany has
become effeminate in *KL* 4.2.17–18: 'I
must change names at home and give
the distaff / Into my husband's hands.'

65 **knoll** summon by the sound of a bell
(*OED v.* 3); cf. 3.3.68. The word con-
flates 'toll' and 'knell'. *OED*'s citations
include several from Shakespeare: *Mac*
5.9.16, *AYL* 2.7.115, *TNK* 1.1.134.

66 **arras** tapestry or woven wall-hanging,
called after the French town in which
such tapestries were made. The stagecraft here will inevitably recall the
concealment of Polonius behind an
arras in *Ham* 3.4.6, where he meets his
death some 17 lines later.

69 **passages** progress or transition;
phases (*OED n.* 3a)

75–7 The lines are in soliloquy rather
than delivered to the concealed Julio.

77 SD *Scene opens* This suggests that
a set of wings, or possibly the back

63 forethought] *(*fore-thought*)*   64 SD] *this edn; after* again; *1728a*   71 Whate'er] *(*What-e'er*)*
73 SD] *this edn; after* vow *1728a*

Enter at one door Servants with lights,
HENRIQUEZ, DON BERNARD *and Churchman.*
At another, Attendants to Leonora. Henriquez runs to her.

HENRIQUEZ

Why, Leonora, wilt thou with this gloom
Darken my triumph, suff'ring discontent
And wan displeasure to subdue that cheek   80
Where love should sit enthron'd? Behold your slave.
Nay, frown not, for each hour of growing time
Shall task me to thy service, till by merit
Of dearest love I blot the low-born Julio
From thy fair mind.

LEONORA   So I shall make it foul.   85
This counsel is corrupt.

HENRIQUEZ   Come, you will change –

LEONORA

Why would you make a wife of such a one,
That is so apt to change? This foul proceeding

shutters, part to discover a space for-
mally prepared with an altar and lights
for the carrying out of a marriage or
ceremony.

77.1–3 The stagecraft here is similar to that
found in various plays by Shakespeare.
In *MA* 4.1, there is an interrupted
wedding set in a church, when Hero is
cruelly exposed to ridicule by Claudio.
In 5.3, when restitution is made to
her, again in church, the SD reads
'*Enter* CLAUDIO, DON PEDRO, *and three
or four . . . with tapers.*' Similar formal-
ity is achieved in the Temple of Diana
at Ephesus in the closing scene of *Per*
(5.3); and in the chapel in Paulina's
house with which *WT* closes (5.3).

79 **triumph** public festival; joyous occasion – with, perhaps, some connotation
of the Roman historical sense of military triumph. The idea of Henriquez
as a successful general gaining her as
a spoil of war would be unwelcome to
Leonora.

80 **wan displeasure** The phrase is
unique to *DF*.

83 **task** This transitive usage is found in
Shakespeare and in Fletcher, e.g. in
Oth 2.3.38–9, Cassio's 'I am unfortu-
nate in the infirmity, and dare not task
my weakness with any more'; and in
Bon 2.1.43: 'Nor can *Rome* task us with
impossibilities'. See also *Cor* 1.3.35–8,
the inhuman imagery of 'His bloody
brow / With his mail'd hand then wip-
ing, forth he goes / Like to a harvest
man that's task'd to mow / Or all, or
lose his hire.'

85 **fair . . . foul** Cf. *Mac* 1.1.11, 'Fair is
foul, and foul is fair'; and Macbeth's
opening line in the play, 'So foul and
fair a day I have not seen' (1.3.38).

86 **counsel** both the advice and the person who offers it

88 **foul proceeding** The phrase occurs
in *Oth* 1.3.66, where the alleged seduction of Desdemona is characterized in
these terms.

239

Still speaks against itself and vilifies
The purest of your judgement. For your birth's sake   90
I will not dart my hoarded curses at you
Nor give my meanings language. For the love
Of all good things together, yet take heed
And spurn the tempter back.

DON BERNARD

I think you're mad. Perverse and foolish wretch!   95

LEONORA

How may I be obedient and wise too?
Of my obedience, sir, I cannot strip me,
Nor can I then be wise. Grace against grace!
Ungracious if I not obey a father,
Most perjur'd if I do. – Yet, lord, consider,   100
Or ere too late, or ere that knot be tied
Which may with violence damnable be broken,
No other way dissever'd – yet consider,
You wed my body, not my heart, my lord,
No part of my affection. Sounds it well   105
That Julio's love is Lord Henriquez' wife?
Have you an ear for this harsh sound?

HENRIQUEZ

No shot of reason can come near the place
Where my love's fortified. The day shall come

---

89 **vilifies** brings into disgrace, devalues
91 **hoarded** The word is not in the Fletcher canon, but Shakespeare uses it in *Cor* 4.2.11–12 where Volumnia curses Brutus: 'the hoarded plague o'th' gods / Requite your love!' *Cor* seems to be figuring in this section: see 83n. As a phrase, 'hoarded curse' occurs in a 1702 tragedy by Rowe, *The Ambitious Stepmother*, 4.3, p. 14.
92 **give . . . language** In the context of *curses* (91), the passage is reminiscent of *Tem* 1.2.364–5, Caliban's 'You

taught me language, and my profit on't / Is I know how to curse.'
96 **obedient** The metre requires three syllables here.
101 *ere See 1.2.26n.
103 **dissever'd** separated, divided. The verb is common in Shakespeare's period and in Theobald's; cf. 'The meeting points the sacred hair dissever' in Pope's *Rape of the Lock*, 3.153.
108–9 **No . . . fortified** The military imagery intensifies that of *triumph* (79).

101 ere . . . ere] *(e'er . . . e'er)*

Wherein you'll chide this backwardness and bless   110
Our fervour in this course.
LEONORA   No, no, Henriquez,
When you shall find what prophet you are prov'd,
You'll prophesy no more.
DON BERNARD   Have done this talking.
If you will cleave to your obedience, do't;
If not, unbolt the portal and be gone: 115
My blessing stay behind you.
LEONORA   Sir, your pardon.
I will not swerve a hair's breadth from my duty;
It shall first cost me dear.
DON BERNARD   Well then, to th'point.
Give me your hand.   [*Leonora gives her hand.*]
                                       My honour'd lord, receive
My daughter of me – nay, no dragging back,   120
But with my curses – whom I frankly give you,
And wish you joy and honour.

As Don Bernard goes to give Leonora to Henriquez,
  Julio advances from the arras, and steps between.

JULIO   Hold, Don Bernard.
Mine is the elder claim.
DON BERNARD   What are you, sir?
JULIO
A wretch that's almost lost to his own knowledge,
Struck through with injuries.

---

117 **hair's breadth** Although occasional
earlier usages can be found, this phrase
comes into its own from the 1680s
onward. It occurs in Dryden's *The
Spanish Friar* (1681), Act 1, p. 12,
and in plays by George Farquhar in
the first decade of the 18th century
(though cf. *Oth* 1.3.137).
118 **It . . . dear** I will pay a consider-

able price before I will (forsake my
duty). The audience may think that
Leonora's suicide is a possibility.
120 **dragging back** The audience must
wonder how Leonora construes her
duty at 117. Clearly, it does not involve
obeying her father without question.
124 **almost . . . knowledge** i.e. barely
knows himself

119 SD] *this edn*

241

HENRIQUEZ   Ha! Julio? – Hear you,   125
    Were you not sent on our commands to court?
    Order'd to wait your fair dismission thence?
    And have you dar'd, knowing you are our vassal,
    To steal away unprivileg'd and leave
    My business and your duty unaccomplish'd?   130

JULIO

    Ungen'rous lord! The circumstance of things
    Should stop the tongue of question. You have wrong'd
      me;
    Wrong'd me so basely, in so dear a point
    As stains the cheek of honour with a blush,
    Cancels the bonds of service, bids allegiance   135
    Throw to the wind all high respects of birth,
    Title and eminence; and in their stead
    Fills up the panting heart with just defiance.
    If you have sense of shame or justice, lord,
    Forego this bad intent, or with your sword   140
    Answer me like a man and I shall thank you.
    Julio once dead, Leonora may be thine;

---

127 **dismission** sending away. Julio has been told to stay at court. Shakespeare uses the word twice, in *AC* 1.1.27 and in *Cym* 2.3.53; Fletcher not at all. See 1.3.56n.

128 **vassal** commonly used in Shakespeare, the only connection with Fletcher being *TNK* 5.1.84–5: 'that mayst force the king / To be his subject's vassal', usually ascribed to Shakespeare

129 **unprivileg'd** unauthorized. The term reinforces *vassal* in the previous line, emphasizing Henriquez's superiority and Julio's subordinated position.

130 **unaccomplish'd** incomplete, unperformed. In its positive form, 'accomplish'd', the word occurs in

Shakespeare and in Fletcher (though in the different meaning of 'having personal attributes' in Fletcher). *OED* gives instances of the negative form pre-Shakespeare; and Theobald does not use the word elsewhere.

134 **stains . . . blush** a possible reminiscence of Hamlet's words to Gertrude in *Ham* 3.4.38–9, 'Such an act / That blurs the grace and blush of modesty'

136 **respects** regards, considerations (*OED n.* 13a)

142 This is a difficult line to scan; it could be an alexandrine if the full syllabic allocation is given to the two proper names; alternatively, *Julio* could have two syllables and *Leonora* three.

128 dar'd] *(dared)*

But living, she's a prize too rich to part with.

HENRIQUEZ

Vain man! The present hour is fraught with business
Of richer moment. Love shall first be serv'd.   145
Then, if your courage hold to claim it of me,
I may have leisure to chastise this boldness.

JULIO

Nay, then I'll seize my right.

HENRIQUEZ   What, here, a brawl?
My servants – turn this boist'rous sworder forth,
And see he come not to disturb our joys.   150

JULIO

Hold, dogs! Leonora! Coward, base Henriquez!
                        Julio is seized, and dragged out by
                        the Servants. Leonora swoons.

HENRIQUEZ

She dies upon me. Help!

DON BERNARD   Throng not about her,
But give her air.
        (*As they endeavour to recover her, a paper drops from her.*)

HENRIQUEZ   What paper's that? Let's see it.

---

143 **living** i.e. while alive
144 **fraught** loaded
145 **richer moment** greater significance
146 **it** i.e. combat or satisfaction
148 **What, here,** 1728a's punctuation, the commas before and after *here*, has been retained to give the sense of 'here' as 'in this place'. 'What's here' is a possible emendation.
149 **sworder** Enobarbus refers to Antony as a 'sworder' in *AC* 3.13.31. It carries overtones of the thuggish. The phrase *boist'rous sworder*, however, is unique to *DF*.
151 **Leonora** three syllables
    Henriquez probably two syllables
    SD *swoons* 1728a gives this SD after

Help!, 152. Hermione swoons at the climactic moment in *WT* 3.2 when the death of her son is announced and Leontes accepts his error; Hero swoons similarly at the moment of deepest intensity when she is wrongfully accused in *MA* 4.1; as does the disguised Julia in *TGV* 5.4. Another famous Shakespearean swooner (though a comic one) is Rosalind, who loses consciousness when she sees Orlando's bloody napkin brandished by Oliver in *AYL* 4.3.
153 SD 1728a gives this SD immediately after Leonora's swoon. The action of dropping the paper seems, however, to follow attempts to revive her.

151 SD *Leonora swoons*] *this edn; after* help! *152 1728a*   153 SD] *this edn; after swoons 151 SD 1728a*

It is her own handwriting.

DON BERNARD   Bow her head!

'Tis but her fright; she will recover soon.   155

What learn you by that paper, good my lord?

HENRIQUEZ

That she would do the violence to herself

Which nature hath anticipated on her.

What dagger means she? Search her well, I pray you.

DON BERNARD

Here is the dagger. O, the stubborn sex,   160

Rash e'en to madness!

HENRIQUEZ   Bear her to her chamber.

Life flows in her again. Pray, bear her hence,

And tend her as you would the world's best treasure.

                    Women carry Leonora off.

Don Bernard, this wild tumult soon will cease,

The cause remov'd, and all return to calmness.   165

Passions in women are as short in working

As strong in their effect. Let the priest wait.

Come, go we in. My soul is all on fire

And burns impatient of this forc'd delay.

                    Exeunt, and the scene closes.

3.3   *Prospect of a village at a distance*

                    Enter RODERICK.

---

154 **Bow** bend (transitive)

158 **anticipated** forestalled

160 **stubborn sex** The only other recorded literary usage of the phrase is in Theobald's own earlier play *The Perfidious Brother* (1715), Act 1, p. 3.

164 **tumult** commotion or uproar. The word may come from Shelton, 3.13.275: 'All the house was in a tumult for this sodaine amazement of *Luscinda*.'

3.3] *(SCENE III.)*

169 SD *scene closes* The wings or back shutters come together to form the village prospect required for the next scene. The scene has no couplet to mark the ending.

3.3

0 SD After the more spectacular interior staging of the latter part of 3.2, this scene returns to the back shutter used for 1.2.

RODERICK

> Julio's departure thus in secret from me,
> With the long doubtful absence of my brother
> (Who cannot suffer, but my father feels it),
> Have trusted me with strong suspicions
> And dreams, that will not let me sleep, nor eat,   5
> Nor taste those recreations health demands:
> But, like a whirlwind, hither have they snatch'd me
> Perforce, to be resolv'd. I know my brother
> Had Julio's father for his host: from him
> Enquiry may befriend me.

Enter CAMILLO.

>   Old sir, I'm glad   10
> To've met you thus. What ails the man? Camillo –

CAMILLO   Ha?

RODERICK

> Is't possible you should forget your friends?

CAMILLO

> Friends! What are those?

RODERICK   Why, those that love you, sir.

CAMILLO

> You're none of those, sure, if you be Lord Roderick.   15

RODERICK

> Yes, I am that Lord Roderick, and I lie not
> If I protest, I love you passing well.

---

2 **long doubtful** both lengthy in dura-
tion and for dubious reasons

4 **trusted** This very unusual transitive
usage of the verb 'trust' corresponds
most closely to *OED v.* 8, 'To place (a
person) in trust *with* property; to make
a trustee of'. Henriquez's suspicions
are, so to speak, invested in him. *OED*
has only one citation for the verb,
dated 1670.

suspicions pronounced as four syllables; the 'iön' form (as also at 29) is
familiar in Jacobean plays

6 **taste** try, sample

13 **forget your friends** If Roderick is
an old friend of Camillo's, as seems
to be established later in the scene
(34ff., where it appears that the Duke,
Roderick's father, was a close friend of
Camillo's), it has not appeared until
now. This may suggest an earlier version of the episode, but it may simply be a familiar dramatic convention,
avoiding lengthy exposition.

CAMILLO

    You lov'd my son too passing well, I take it:

    One that believ'd too suddenly his court-creed.

RODERICK (*aside*)

    All is not well.

    [*to Camillo*]   Good old man, do not rail.   20

CAMILLO

    My lord, my lord, you've dealt dishonourably.

RODERICK

    Good sir, I am so far from doing wrongs

    Of that base strain, I understand you not.

CAMILLO

    Indeed! You know not neither, o' my conscience,

    How your most virtuous brother, noble Henriquez   25

    (You look so like him, lord, you are the worse for't;

    Rots upon such dissemblers!), under colour

    Of buying coursers, and I know not what,

    Bought my poor boy out of possession

    E'en of his plighted faith. Was not this honour?   30

    And this a constant friend?

RODERICK   I dare not say so.

CAMILLO

    Now you have robb'd him of his love, take all;

    Make up your malice and dispatch his life too.

RODERICK

    If you would hear me, sir –

---

19 **court-creed** system of belief practised at court
20 **rail** be abusive
23 **strain** See 3.2.13n.
25 another line that presents metrical problems. The word *virtuous*
may be elided. Henriquez's name
may be pronounced as two syllables
(Henricks).
26 Cf. *WT* 2.3.95–7, 'It is yours; / And,
might we lay th' old proverb to your

charge, / So like you, 'tis the worse.'
27 **Rots upon** an unusual oath not found
elsewhere in Shakespeare, Fletcher or
Theobald, though Abraham Cowley
has it twice in *Love's Riddle* (1638),
Acts 1 and 5 in the singular form 'rot
upon': 'A rott upon you' and 'a rotte
upon your beasts' (n.p.)
28 **coursers** swift horses
29 **possession** four syllables; see 4n.
33 **Make up** complete

20 SD1] *this edn; after* well. *1728a*   SD2] *this edn*   30 E'en] *(Ev'n)*

CAMILLO   Your brave old father
  Would have been torn in pieces with wild horses   35
  Ere he had done this treachery. On my conscience,
  Had he but dreamt you two durst have committed
  This base, unmanly crime –
RODERICK   Why, this is madness –
CAMILLO
  I've done. I've eas'd my heart; now you may talk.
RODERICK
  Then, as I am a gentleman, believe me   40
  (For I will lie for no man), I'm so far
  From being guilty of the least suspicion
  Of sin that way that, fearing the long absence
  Of Julio and my brother might beget
  Something to start at, hither have I travell'd   45
  To know the truth of you.

Enter VIOLANTE *behind*.

VIOLANTE
  My servant loiters. Sure, he means me well.

---

35 **with** by
36 ***Ere** See 1.2.26n.
45 **start at** closest to *OED* start *v.* 15a,
'To cause to start or flinch; to startle'.
Here it means something more like to
occasion surprise or need for further
investigation. With the preposition
'at', the phrase occurs in Shakespeare
(e.g. *AW* 1.3.139); and in several of
Fletcher's single-authored and collaborative plays, e.g. *Capt* 1.1.11, 1.3.219.
46.1 '*behind*' indicates that Camillo and
Roderick are playing front stage, perhaps on the protruding apron area,
and Violante enters from behind them,
presumed to be approaching from the
'*village*' indicated by the back shutter.

At Drury Lane in 1727–8, there were
only two usual entrance points for
actors, the stage doors right and left,
though it is technically possible to
enter from the wings and even from
between the back shutters. The direction '*behind*' may therefore indicate
an entry from a wing position well
upstage, rather than from a downstage
wing position or from a stage door.
47 Violante refers presumably to the
Servant who will enter later, at 129,
whom she has taken with her for reasons of decorum. Her doubting that
he means her well perhaps reveals a
general distrust of the male sex caused
by Henriquez's treatment of her.

36 Ere] *(*E'er*)*   38] *Kennedy; 1728a lines* Crime, – / Madness. – /

[*Catches sight of Camillo.*] Camillo, and a stranger?
    These may give me
Some comfort from their talk. I'll step aside
And hear what fame is stirring.   (*Violante retires.*)

RODERICK   Why this wond'ring?   50

CAMILLO
    Can there be one so near in blood as you are
    To that Henriquez, and an honest man?

RODERICK
    While he was good, I do confess my nearness;
    But since his fall from honour he's to me
    As a strange face I saw but yesterday,   55
    And as soon lost.

CAMILLO   I ask your pardon, lord.
    I was too rash and bold.

RODERICK   No harm done, sir.

CAMILLO
    But is it possible you should not hear
    The passage 'twixt Leonora and your brother?

RODERICK
    None of all this.

                    Enter Citizen.

CAMILLO   How now?   60

CITIZEN
    I bear you tidings, sir, which I could wish
    Some other tongue deliver'd.

CAMILLO   Whence, I pray you?

CITIZEN
    From your son, sir.

CAMILLO   Prithee, where is he?

50 **fame** rumour, news   59 **passage** i.e. that which passed

48 SD] *this edn*   60] *this edn; prose 1728a*   63] *this edn; prose 1728a*

CITIZEN

    That's more than I know now, sir.

    But this I can assure you; he has left   65

    The city raging mad. Heav'n comfort him!

    He came to that curs'd marriage – the fiends take it!

CAMILLO

    Prithee, be gone, and bid the bell knoll for me.

    I have had one foot in the grave some time.

    Nay, go, good friend; thy news deserve no thanks.   70

                              Exit Citizen.

    How does your lordship?

RODERICK   That's well said, old man.

    I hope all shall be well yet.

CAMILLO   It had need,

    For 'tis a crooked world. Farewell, poor boy!

Enter DON BERNARD.

DON BERNARD

    This comes of forcing women where they hate.

    It was my own sin; and I am rewarded.   75

    Now I am like an aged oak, alone,

    Left for all tempests. I would cry, but cannot.

    I'm dried to death almost with these vexations.

    Lord, what a heavy load I have within me!

---

67 **curs'd** an expression of vexation: damned, confounded

68 **knoll** See 3.2.65n.

69 **one . . . grave** The idiom is not in Shakespeare but is found in Fletcher and Massinger's *LFL* 1.1.161 and in the latter's *The Guardian* (1633), 5.4.101 (Massinger, 4.192); as well as in plays by Thomas Shadwell: the Epilogue to *Bury Fair* (1689), l. 17; and *The Scowrers* (1691), Act 2, p. 16.

73.1 The staging here of an encounter between two grieving fathers has echoes of other such encounters in Shakespeare, e.g. Lear and Gloucester in *KL* 4.6, Prospero and Alonso in *Tem* 5.1.

74–80 **This . . . heart** Some would consider this to be a very sudden repentance on the part of Don Bernard, but it is no more so than, for example, the instantaneous regret expressed by Leontes in *WT* 3.2.144–5, when the death of the prince Mamillius is announced: 'Apollo's angry, and the heavens themselves / Do strike at my injustice'; or than Evadne's in *Maid's* 4.1.183–5, when her brother

My heart – my heart – my heart!

CAMILLO   Has this ill weather   80
Met with thee too?

DON BERNARD   O, wench, that I were with thee!

CAMILLO
You do not come to mock at me now?

DON BERNARD   Ha?

CAMILLO
Do not dissemble. Thou mayst find a knave
As bad as thou art to undo thee too.
I hope to see that day before I die yet.   85

DON BERNARD
It needeth not, Camillo; I am knave
Sufficient to myself. If thou wilt rail,
Do it as bitterly as thou canst think of,
For I deserve it. Draw thy sword and strike me
And I will thank thee for't. I've lost my daughter.   90
She's stol'n away; and whither gone, I know not.

CAMILLO
She has a fair blessing in being from you, sir.
I was too poor a brother for your greatness;
You must be grafted into noble stocks
And have your titles rais'd. My state was laugh'd at   95
And my alliance scorn'd. I've lost a son too,
Which must not be put up so.   (*Offers to draw.*)

Melantius makes her aware of her dishonour at the hands of the King: 'O my loaden soule, / Be not so cruell to me, choake not up / The way to my repentance.'

82–5 Frazier (*Voices*, ch. 6) adduces *Ham* 1.2.176 and 181–2, 'I prithee do not mock me . . . Would I had met my dearest foe in heaven / Or ever I had seen that day'.

87 **rail** be abusive

94 **grafted . . . stocks** The metaphor is from arboriculture: the process of inserting the shoots from one tree into another tree. The figure itself is commonplace; see e.g. *2H6* 3.2.213–14. In this phrasing, it occurs for example in *Bon* 1.1.172; and in several plays by Dryden, D'Urfey, Betterton, Shadwell and others from the late 1670s onwards.

82] *Kennedy; prose 1728a*

RODERICK   Hold; be counsell'd.
You've equal losses; urge no farther anger.
Heav'n, pleas'd now at your love, may bring again,
And no doubt will, your children to your comforts: 100
In which adventure my foot shall be foremost.
And one more will I add: my honour'd father,
Who has a son to grieve for too, though tainted.
Let your joint sorrow be as balm to heal
These wounds of adverse fortune.
DON BERNARD   Come, Camillo,   105
Do not deny your love; for charity
I ask it of you. Let this noble lord
Make brothers of us, whom our own cross fates
Could never join. What I have been, forget;
What I intend to be, believe and nourish.   110
I do confess my wrongs; give me your hand.
CAMILLO
Heav'n make thee honest – there.   [*Gives his hand.*]
RODERICK   'Tis done like good men.
Now there rests naught but that we part and each
Take sev'ral ways in quest of our lost friends.
Some of my train o'er the wild rocks shall wait you.   115
Our best search ended, here we'll meet again
And tell the fortunes of our separate travels.   *Exeunt.*
    Violante comes forward.
VIOLANTE
I would your brother had but half your virtue!

---

97 **be counsell'd** take advice; I advise you

101 **foot . . . foremost** Theobald uses 'foremost' in the sense of putting one's best foot foremost, or taking a leading part, in *Richard II*: 'I know, you will be foremost in that Quarrel' (Act 4, p. 41).

114 **friends** relatives, kindred

115 **wait** attend

118–55 The stagecraft here has many Shakespearean echoes: Helena following Bertram in *AW*; Imogen going in search of Posthumus in *Cym*; Violante's blunt address 'Art thou corrupted?' (133) to the servant

105] *Kennedy; prose 1728a*   106 love; for charity] *this edn;* Love, for Charity; *1728a*   112 SD] *this edn*   113 naught] *(*Nought*)*

Yet there remains a little spark of hope
That lights me to some comfort. The match is cross'd,   120
The parties separate, and I again
May come to see this man that has betray'd me
And wound his conscience for it. Home again
I will not go, whatever fortune guides me,
Though ev'ry step I went I trod upon   125
Dangers as fearful and as pale as death.
No, no, Henriquez; I will follow thee
Where there is day. Time may beget a wonder.

Enter Servant.

O, are you come? What news?

SERVANT

None but the worst. Your father   130
Makes mighty offers yonder by a crier,
To anyone can bring you home again.

VIOLANTE

Art thou corrupted?

SERVANT   No.

VIOLANTE   Wilt thou be honest?

SERVANT

I hope you do not fear me.

VIOLANTE

Indeed I do not. Thou hast an honest face;   135

---

echoing Hamlet's brief and blunt
exchanges with Polonius and
Rosencrantz and Guildenstern (2.2)
and Ophelia (3.1). Pathos is empha-
sized between Violante and the
Servant as it is between Julia and the
Host in *TGV* 4.2.
128 **Time . . . wonder** The metaphor
of time as a begetter is common; cf.
Tit 4.3.30 and *TS* 1.1.45. This is

close to proverbial expressions such
as 'Time reveals all things' and 'Time
tries all things' (Tilley, T333, 336),
both of which are used by Fletcher
and variants of which are used by
Shakespeare.
133 **Art thou corrupted?** Have you
been bribed?
135 **Thou hast** The metre requires elision to 'Thou'st'.

129–34] *this edn; prose 1728a*   132 anyone] *(any One)*

And such a face, when it deceives – take heed –
Is curs'd of all heav'n's creatures.
SERVANT   I'll hang first.
VIOLANTE
Heav'n bless thee from that end! I've heard a man
Say more than this – and yet that man was false.
Thou'lt not be so, I hope.
SERVANT   By my life, mistress –   140
VIOLANTE
Swear not; I credit thee. But prithee, though,
Take heed thou dost not fail. I do not doubt thee;
Yet I have trusted such a serious face
And been abus'd too.
SERVANT   If I fail your trust –
VIOLANTE
I do thee wrong to hold thy honesty   145
At distance thus. Thou shalt know all my fortunes.
Get me a shepherd's habit.
SERVANT   Well. What else?
VIOLANTE
And wait me in the evening where I told thee.
There thou shalt know my farther ends. Take heed –
SERVANT
D'ye fear me still?
VIOLANTE   No; this is only counsel.   150
My life and death I have put equally
Into thy hand. Let not rewards nor hopes

---

137 **curs'd** See 67n.
147 **shepherd's habit** In Act 1 of
Mucedorus (version published in 1610),
Anselmo offers Mucedorus a shepherd's 'Cassocke' (sig. A5ʳ). *Mucedorus*
was perhaps the single most popular
play of Shakespeare's period, especially after 1610 when reprints were issued

every couple of years. It has been
attributed to Shakespeare, though
without plausibility.
148 **wait me** wait for me; attend me
150 **D'ye ... still** i.e. why not confide
in me now
   counsel caution, good sense

137] *Kennedy; prose 1728a*   140] *Kennedy; prose 1728a*   144] *Kennedy; prose 1728a*   abus'd]
*(*abused*)*   147] *Kennedy; prose 1728a*

Be cast into the scale to turn thy faith.
　Be honest but for virtue's sake, that's all;　　　　154
　He that has such a treasure cannot fall.　　　　　*Exeunt.*

End of the third act

4.1　*A wide plain, with a prospect of mountains at a distance*

Enter MASTER of the Flocks, *three or four* Shepherds
and VIOLANTE *in boy's clothes.*

1 SHEPHERD　Well, he's as sweet a man, heav'n comfort
him, as ever these eyes look'd on.

2 SHEPHERD　If he have a mother, I believe, neighbours,
she's a woe-woman for him at this hour.

MASTER

Why should he haunt these wild unpeopled mountains　　5
Where nothing dwells but hunger and sharp winds?

1 SHEPHERD　His melancholy, sir, that's the main devil does

4.1

0 SD　The change of back shutter opens the play out scenically, departing from the pattern of village exteriors and interiors in the first three acts.

0.1 MASTER . . . **Flocks** The introduction of a new character in Act 4 resembles the stagecraft of e.g. *WT* where Autolycus makes his explosive entrance in 4.3. A closer situational parallel is *Per* 4.5, where Lysimachus appears as a new character, whose intentions towards Marina in the Mytilene brothel are at first ambiguous.

4　**woe-woman** grieving widow. *OED* does not record this term. In *TGV* 2.3.25–6, Lance says, 'Now come I to my mother: O, that she could speak now, like a wood woman!' Carroll points out that in F, 'wood woman' is given as 'would woman'. Theobald was the first editor to emend 'would'

to 'wood' meaning 'mad' or 'angry', a solution that Carroll accepts as being the most plausible. 'Woe-woman' in some manuscript form could be behind this crux in *TGV*.

5　**unpeopled** This relatively uncommon word occurs in *AYL* 3.2.122–3, in the sonnet hung by Orlando upon a tree and read by Celia: '*Why should this a desert be? / For it is unpeopled?*'; and in *AC* 1.5.81, 'Or I'll unpeople Egypt'.

7　**melancholy** 'Originally: a pathological condition thought to result from an excess of black bile in the body, characterized in early references by sullenness, ill temper, brooding, causeless anger, and unsociability, and later by despondency and sadness. Later: severe depression, melancholia' (*OED n.*[1] 2b). Amongst Shakespeare's best-known melancholics are Hamlet, Antonio in *MV* and Jaques in *AYL*.

155.1 *End*] *(The End)*　**4.1**] *(ACT IV. SCENE I.)*　0 SD *A*] SCENE, *A 1728a*

254

it. Go to, I fear he has had too much foul play offer'd
him.

MASTER

    How gets he meat?   10

2 SHEPHERD Why, now and then he takes our victuals from
    us, though we desire him to eat, and instead of a short
    grace, beats us well and soundly and then falls to.

MASTER

    Where lies he?

1 SHEPHERD E'en where the night o'ertakes him.   15

2 SHEPHERD Now will I be hang'd an some fair-snouted
    skittish woman or other be not at the end of this
    madness.

1 SHEPHERD Well, if he lodg'd within the sound of us I
    knew our music would allure him. How attentively he   20
    stood and how he fix'd his eyes when your boy sung his

8 **Go to** corresponds here to a modern
phrase such as 'I say' or 'oh dear!'

11 **takes our victuals** Pujante (102–3)
provides a list of eight passages from
Shelton that are paralleled in the action
that takes place in the mountains in *DF*
Acts 4 and 5. Only this first instance
is noted here; for fuller discussion, see
p. 100 above. Shelton's *History* has: 'we
did not see him a good many of daies,
vntill by chance one of our sheepheards
came by with our prouision of victuals,
to whom he drew neere, without speaking a word, and spurned and beate him
welfauourdly, and after went to the Asse
which carried our victuals, and taking
away all the bread and cheese that was
there, hee fled into the mountaine with
wonderfull speede . . . We requested
him likewise that whensoeuer he had
any neede of meat . . . he should tell
vs where wee might finde him and we
would bring it to him with great loue and
diligence . . .' (3.9.214–15).

13 **falls to** begins eating (with a ravenous
appetite)

16 **fair-snouted** pretty-nosed (though
the description is half-way between
a compliment and an insult: 'nose'
is perhaps more like 'mug' here).
The phrase 'fair-snouted skittish
woman', as Kukowski notes, 'can
almost be reconstructed from pieces
to be found elsewhere in Fletcher's
work' (87): 'some snout-faire piece'
in *Cox* 4.3.44 and 'a skittish Filly' in
SL 3.1.349.

17 **skittish** whimsical, frivolous, light.
The word occurs in *TN* 2.4.17–18,
where Orsino describes himself thus:
'For such as I am all true lovers are, /
Unstaid and skittish in all motions else'.
Fletcher too is fond of the adjective; it
features in *MT* 1.1.78 ('sketish'), *SL*
3.1.349 and *WGC* 2.3.11.

21 **your boy** The audience has not yet
heard Violante sing. This may be evidence of an earlier play, or we are
perhaps to assume that singing took
place offstage. Equally, however, the
allusion to *your boy* cues Violante's
male disguise and her later song in 4.2.

15 E'en] *(Ev'n)*   16 an] *(an')*

love ditty. O, here he comes again.

MASTER

Let him alone; he wonders strangely at us.

1 SHEPHERD   Not a word, sirs, to cross him, as you love
your shoulders.   25

2 SHEPHERD   He seems much disturb'd. I believe the mad
fit is upon him.

Enter JULIO.

JULIO

Horsemanship! Hell – riding shall be abolish'd.
Turn the barb'd steed loose to his native wildness;
It is a beast too noble to be made   30
The property of man's baseness. What a letter
Wrote he to's brother! What a man was I?
Why, Perseus did not know his seat like me;

24–5 **love your shoulders** because Julio
will belabour them with blows

28–36 Ludovico Ariosto's *Orlando
Furioso* (1516, first complete version
1532) is perhaps the most likely analogue for Julio's madness; it was first
translated into English by Sir John
Harington in 1591. Frazier (*Voices*,
ch. 6) points to general resemblances
to *Ham* that continue throughout 4.1,
but in some respects Julio's madness
is closer to the 'trial' scene in *KL* 3.6.
Like Lear's, Julio's form of madness
assumes that others have suffered in
an analogous way to himself. Bradford
(53) offers the insanity of the Jailer's
Daughter in *TNK* as an analogue for
Julio's 'mad fit'; she certainly has
much to say of an intelligent horse
at 5.2.45ff. Equally plausible would
be *KL* as suggested above, or the
temporary 'wildness' that overcomes

Maximus when he hears of his wife's
death in *Val* 3.1.282ff.

29 **barb'd steed** 'Of a horse: Armed
or caparisoned with a *barb* or bard;
properly "barded"' (*OED* barbed *ppl.
a.*[2]), where 'bard' means 'a protective
covering for the breast and flanks of
a war-horse, made of metal plates,
or of leather set with metal spikes or
bosses, but sometimes (*e.g.* in tourna-
ments) merely ornamental, and made
of velvet or other rich stuff' (*OED n.*[2]
1). The phrase occurs in *R3* 1.1.10,
'instead of mounting barbed steeds',
and in *R2* 3.3.117, 'His barbed steeds
to stables'.

33 **Perseus** According to Greek legend,
Perseus rode the winged horse
Pegasus, though in earlier forms of the
legend it was Bellerophon who did so.
know his seat understand horsemanship

22 love ditty] *(Love-Ditty)*

The Parthian, that rides swift without the rein,
Match'd not my grace and firmness. Shall this lord   35
Die, when men pray for him? Think you 'tis meet?

1 SHEPHERD [*to Julio*]   I don't know what to say. [*to Master
    and Second Shepherd*] Neither I, nor all the confessors
    in Spain, can unriddle this wild stuff.

JULIO

I must to court; be usher'd into grace   40
By a large list of praises ready penn'd!
O devil! What a venomous world is this,
When commendations are the baits to ruin.
All these good words were gyves and fetters, sir,
To keep me bolted there, while the false sender   45
Play'd out the game of treach'ry.
[*to Second Shepherd*]   Hold; come hither.
You have an aspect, sir, of wondrous wisdom,
And, as it seems, are travell'd deep in knowledge.
Have you e'er seen the phoenix of the earth,
The bird of paradise?

---

34 **Parthian** The Parthians occupied a territory stretching from the Euphrates to the Indus, with Ctesiphon as their capital (corresponding to modern eastern Iran, Afghanistan and Pakistan). Semi-nomads, their horsemanship was proverbial. Iachimo compares himself to them in *Cym* 1.7.20, 'Or like the Parthian I shall flying fight'; Palamon in *TNK* 2.2.48–50 also uses the comparison with the 'Parthian shot', the departing horseman's final arrow: 'No more now must we hallow, no more shake / Our pointed javelins whilst the angry swine / Flies like a Parthian quiver from our rages'. The Parthians feature three times in *Val*, at 1.3.40, 189; 4.1.137.

38 **confessors** similar, one assumes, to friars in Shakespearean plays such as *RJ* and *MM*. They are invoked here as cryptographers, or perhaps psychiatrists: or even as specialists in extracting information, such as under the Inquisition.

40–8 This continues to resonate with Lear's condemnation of the Court and its corruptions, and with his construction of Edgar and Poor Tom as wise justices, in *KL* 3.6.

44 **gyves** leg shackles. The term occurs in *TNK* 3.1.72, where Palamon requests Arcite to 'Quit me of these cold gyves', and again in 3.2.14.

45 **bolted** fastened down

48 **travell'd** experienced in travel, but also 'travailed' – learned, wearied by study. The phrase *travell'd deep* is unique to *DF*.

49 **phoenix** mythical bird with beautiful gold and red plumage. At the end of its life-cycle the phoenix builds itself

37 SD1] *this edn*   37–8 SD] *this edn*   46 SD] *this edn*   47 wondrous] *(*wond'rous*)*

2 SHEPHERD   In troth, not I, sir.   50
JULIO
I have, and known her haunts, and where she built
Her spicy nest; till, like a credulous fool,
I show'd the treasure to a friend in trust,
And he hath robb'd me of her. Trust no friend:
Keep thy heart's counsels close. Hast thou a mistress?   55
Give her not out in words, nor let thy pride
Be wanton to display her charms to view.
Love is contagious, and a breath of praise
Or a slight glance has kindled up its flame,
And turn'd a friend a traitor. 'Tis in proof,   60
And it has hurt my brain.

1 SHEPHERD   Marry, now there is some moral in his
madness, and we may profit by it.

a nest of cinnamon twigs to which it sets fire; from the ashes a new, young phoenix arises. The emblem was associated with Queen Elizabeth I, for example in the verses known as *The Phoenix and Turtle* (*PT*) that Shakespeare contributed to Robert Chester's *Love's Martyr* (1601). He uses the phoenix as an emblem of innocence, e.g. in *Cym* 1.7.17, where Imogen is described by Iachimo as 'th'Arabian bird'. In Fletcher's *Val*, the phoenix is a symbol that becomes attached to the virtuous Lucina, wife of Maximus, who is ruined by the Emperor (1.2.18, 3.1.195).

52 **spicy nest** of cinnamon twigs (see 49n.). Julio's complaint that his friend has robbed his nest is similar to *MA* 2.1.203–5, where Benedick accuses Don Pedro of having stolen Claudio's beloved: 'The flat transgression of a schoolboy, who, being overjoyed with finding a bird's nest, shows it his companion, and he steals it.'

52–4 **credulous . . . her** Similarly boastful men in Shakespeare, who cannot keep their lovers' virtues to themselves, include Collatine in *Luc*, Valentine in

TGV and Posthumus in *Cym*.

56 **Give . . . out** do not sing her praises, or advertise her

57 **wanton** ill-mannered, indecorous (*OED adj.* 1c, 2c)

58 **contagious** catching, as of a sickness. Shakespeare uses the word in *TN* 2.3, where Sir Andrew Aguecheek catches it from Sir Toby and is mocked by him for coupling it with 'sweet' (53–5). The word occurs six times in Fletcher's single-authored and collaborative plays. Theobald uses it in *Persian Princess* (Act 5, p. 52) and *Perfidious Brother* (Act 3, p. 31) (both 1715), though as here, without irony.

60 **'Tis in proof** it has been proved (in general and in this particular case)

61 **hurt my brain** reminiscent of Lear's 'I am cut to the brains', *KL* 4.6.189

62–3 **moral . . . madness** Cf. *Ham* 2.2.202–3, where Polonius says of Hamlet's alleged madness, 'Though this be madness yet there is method in't.' Julio's madness is, as the Shepherd notes, expressive of moral condemnation; Hamlet's is less overtly didactic.

MASTER

See, he grows cool, and pensive.

Go towards him, boy, but do not look that way.   65

VIOLANTE

Alas! I tremble –

JULIO   O, my pretty youth!

Come hither, child. Did not your song imply

Something of love?

1 SHEPHERD [*to Master and Second Shepherd*]   Ha, ha –

goes it there? Now if the boy be witty, we shall trace   70

something.

VIOLANTE   Yes, sir, it was the subject.

JULIO

Sit here then. Come, shake not, good pretty soul,

Nor do not fear me. I'll not do thee wrong.

VIOLANTE

Why do you look so on me?

JULIO   I have reasons.   75

It puzzles my philosophy to think

---

65 **towards** The metre requires elision to
'to'rds'.

that way in that direction, rather than
the more modern sense of urging her
not to look as afraid as she clearly feels,
though cf. 3.3.42–3, where Roderick
denies 'the least suspicion / Of sin
that way', i.e. 'of that kind' or 'in that
manner', a meaning closer to the more
modern one

66, 73 **pretty** The adjective reminds the
audience that Violante is female, but it
may also suggest some clairvoyance on
the 'mad' Julio's part: an ability to see
through the disguise. It is very common
in Fletcher's work, perhaps the closest
dramaturgical parallel being *Phil*, where
the adjective is repeatedly attached to
Euphrasia when she is disguised as
Bellario. Philaster speaks of her/his

'pretty helpless innocence' at 1.2.123.

70 **trace** 'To discover, find out, or ascertain by investigation; to find out step
by step; to search out' (*OED v.*[1] 8a).
This meaning, and 8b, 'To discover
evidence of the existence or occurrence of; to find traces of', postdates
Shakespeare and Fletcher, according
to *OED*. It occurs, however, in *Cym*
1.1.65.

74 **Nor do not** Theobald does not deploy
such a double negative construction in
his original writing.

76 **philosophy** similar to the sense in
which Hamlet uses the term to Horatio
in *Ham* 1.5.165–6: 'There are more
things in heaven and earth, Horatio, /
Than are dreamt of in your philosophy.'
The meaning is general: 'world view' or
'understanding of the world'.

69 SD] *this edn*

That the rude blast, hot sun and dashing rains
Have made no fiercer war upon thy youth,
Nor hurt the bloom of that vermilion cheek.
You weep too, do you not?

VIOLANTE   Sometimes I do.   80

JULIO

I weep sometimes too. You're extremely young.

VIOLANTE

Indeed, I've seen more sorrows far than years.

JULIO

Yet all these have not broken your complexion.
You have a strong heart, and you are the happier.
I warrant, you're a very loving woman.   85

VIOLANTE

A woman, sir? (*aside*) I fear he's found me out.

2 SHEPHERD [*to Master and First Shepherd*] He takes the
  boy for a woman. Mad again!

JULIO

You've met some disappointment, some foul play
Has cross'd your love. I read it in your face.   90

---

79 **vermilion** The term was used for the
bright red of cheeks from Shakespeare's
day to Theobald's. Shakespeare uses it
in *Son* 98.10; Theobald does not use
it elsewhere, and it does not appear in
Fletcher's work.

81 **extremely** This use of the adverb
to qualify an adjective is of interest. Shakespeare deploys the word,
but only as an adverb standing alone.
For Fletcher, it is a favourite word,
occurring no fewer than three times in
his portion of *TNK* (2.2.207, 2.4.15,
3.5.82), twice positioned after the verb.
It also occurs twice in a post-verbal
position in *H8* (2.1.33, Epilogue 6).
Again, though, Fletcher deploys it as
a free-standing adverb. Theobald uses
'extremely' to qualify an adjective in

Clouds (p. 53) and *Plutus* (p. 24). The
balance of evidence associates the line
with Fletcher. See further 4.2.74n.

83 **complexion** very often used by
Shakespeare and by Fletcher to denote
the appearance of the skin, as here.
The term is also used by Theobald in
that sense.

90 **cross'd your love** Cf. 3.3.120, where
Violante refers to the match between
Leonora and Henriquez as *cross'd*. The
repetition calls to mind the opening
Chorus of *RJ*, 'A pair of star-cross'd
lovers' (1.1.5). Salerno (41) suggests
Hermia's line from *MND*, 'If then true
lovers have been ever cross'd' (1.1.150).
Overall, though, this sequence between
Julio and Violante catches more the
atmosphere of *TN* 2.4.

86 SD] *this edn; after* out. *1728a* he's] *(ha's)*   87 SD] *this edn*

VIOLANTE

You read a truth then.

JULIO   Where can lie the fault?

Is't in the man, or some dissembling knave

He put in trust? Ho! Have I hit the cause?

VIOLANTE   You're not far off.

JULIO

This world is full of coz'ners, very full;   95

Young virgins must be wary in their ways.

I've known a duke's son do as great a knavery.

Will you be rul'd by me?

VIOLANTE   Yes.

JULIO   Kill yourself.

'Twill be a terror to the villain's conscience

The longest day he lives.

VIOLANTE   By no means. What?   100

Commit self-murder!

JULIO   Yes; I'll have it so.

1 SHEPHERD   I fear his fit is returning. Take heed of all

hands. [*to Julio*] Sir, do you want anything?

JULIO [*to Second Shepherd*]

Thou liest, thou canst not hurt me. I am proof

'Gainst farther wrongs. [*to Violante*] Steal close

---

95 **coz'ners** deceivers, cheats, impostors

97 **knavery** The metre here may require an elision to 'knav'ry'.

98 **Kill yourself** This unexpected line has some of the impact of Beatrice ordering Benedick to 'Kill Claudio' in *MA* 4.1.288. In *Maid's* 2.1.177–84, Evadne sets up a situation in which Amintor is sworn to kill whoever has wronged her, then says: 'Why, it is thou that wrongst me, I hate thee / Thou should'st have kild thy selfe' (182–3).

101 **Commit self-murder!** Violante's

horror is similar to that of Imogen when she discovers Posthumus's belief that she is unfaithful and urges Pisanio to kill her: 'Against self-slaughter / There is a prohibition so divine / That cravens my weak hand' (*Cym* 3.4.75–7).

104 **proof** Salerno (42) hears echoes of Autolycus in *WT* 4.4.842–3, asserting that he is no rogue: 'I am proof against that title'; and of *KL* 4.6.104, 'I am not ague-proof'. However, the word is not sufficiently rare to offer evidence of an allusion.

103 SD] *this edn*   anything] *(any thing)*   104 SD] *this edn*   105 SD] *this edn*

behind me, lady.   105
I will avenge thee.

VIOLANTE   Thank the heav'ns, I'm free.

JULIO

O treach'rous, base Henriquez! Have I caught thee?

Julio seizes on [Second] Shepherd.

Violante runs out.

2 SHEPHERD [*to First Shepherd and Master*]
Help! Help, good neighbours; he will kill me else.

JULIO

Here thou shalt pay thy heart-blood for the wrongs
Thou'st heap'd upon this head. Faith-breaker! Villain!   110
I'll suck thy life-blood.

1 SHEPHERD

Good sir, have patience; this is no Henriquez.

[First Shepherd and Master] rescue [Second] Shepherd.

JULIO

Well, let him slink to court and hide a coward.
Not all his father's guards shall shield him there;
Or if he prove too strong for mortal arm,   115
I will solicit ev'ry saint in heav'n
To lend me vengeance. I'll about it straight.
The wrathful elements shall wage this war;
Furies shall haunt him; vultures gnaw his heart

---

105 **lady** harks back to 83–5, where either
Julio has seen through Violante's disguise, or in his madness he sees her
as female
107 **SD1** This is brought forward from
its position after 108 in 1728a, since it
seems clear that Julio gets hold of the
Shepherd one line earlier.
110 **Faith-breaker** The term, meaning
a religious apostate or a sexual traitor, does not occur in Shakespeare or
Fletcher, but is found in the period in
Marston's version of the Sophonisba

story, *The Wonder of Women* (1606), 2.1
(n.p.), and in Ford's *The Broken Heart*
(1633), 3.1 (n.p.).
113 **slink** See 2.1.2n.
118 **wrathful elements** The phrase
'wrathful skies' occurs in *KL* 3.2.43.
119 **Furies** Romanized version of the
Erinyes or Eumenides, Greek personifications of revenge as female beings
vultures . . . heart A similar curse is
conferred by Ancient Pistol on the
Lord Chief Justice in *2H4* 5.3.139: 'Let
vultures vile seize on his lungs also!'

107 SD1] *Julio . . . Shepherd*] *this edn; after* else. *108 1728a   Second*] *this edn; the 1728a*   108 SD]
this edn   112 SD *First . . . Master*] *this edn; They 1728a   Second*] *this edn; the 1728a*

And nature pour forth all her stores of plagues   120
To join in punishment of trust betray'd.   *Exit.*
2 SHEPHERD Go thy ways, and a vengeance go with thee!
    Pray, feel my nose. Is it fast, neighbours?
1 SHEPHERD 'Tis as well as may be.
2 SHEPHERD He pull'd at it as he would have dragg'd a   125
    bullock backward by the tail. An't had been some men's
    nose that I know, neighbours, who knows where it had
    been now? He has given me such a devilish dash o'er
    the mouth that I feel I shall never whistle to my sheep
    again. Then they'll make holiday.   130
1 SHEPHERD Come, shall we go, for I fear if the youth
    return our second course will be much more against
    our stomachs.
MASTER
    Walk you afore; I will but give my boy
    Some short instructions, and I'll follow straight.   135
    We'll crash a cup together.
1 SHEPHERD   Pray, do not linger.

---

120 **stores** In the plural, the meaning is 'supplies'; it is possible that this is an error for singular 'store', where it would mean 'abundance'.
126 **An't** if it had
126–7 **some . . . knows** reference to destruction of the nose by venereal disease, with a continuing pun on *nose/knows*. This is one of relatively few such bawdy puns in the play.
128 **dash** blow; a Shakespearean usage
129–30 **never . . . holiday** released from his control, the sheep will go their own way; though the Second Shepherd seems to think of his sheep more as employees than as creatures in his charge. The expression 'make holiday' occurs in *JC* 1.1.31 and in *SV* 3.1.359.

132 **course** of a meal; here meaning next beating
132–3 **against our stomachs** literally, indigestible; in respect of a beating, against our inclinations or wishes
135 **straight** straight away
136 **crash a cup** presumably simply to drink, with some suggestion, perhaps, of dashing the vessels down in abandon afterwards; the similar phrase 'crush a cup' is found in *RJ* 1.2.82, when a servant issues an invitation to Romeo to 'crush a cup of wine'. Although in the Jacobean period it was customary to pass round a common cup, it would appear from Iago's song in *Oth* 2.3.65–70, 'And let me the cannikin clink', that clinking cups against one another was also customary.

121 SD] *(Exit Julio.)*   130 holiday] *(Holy-day)*   136] *Kennedy; prose 1728a*

MASTER

I will not, sirs.   [*Exeunt First and Second Shepherds.*]
This must not be a boy.
His voice, mien, gesture, ev'rything he does,
Savour of soft and female delicacy.
He but puts on this seeming, and his garb   140
Speaks him of such a rank as well persuades me
He plays the swain rather to cloak some purpose
Than forc'd to't by a need. I've waited long
To mark the end he has in his disguise,
But am not perfect in't. The madman's coil   145
Has driv'n him shaking hence. These fears betray him.
If he prove right, I'm happy. O, he's here.

Enter VIOLANTE.

Come hither, boy; where did you leave the flock, child?
[*Strokes her cheek.*]

VIOLANTE   Grazing below, sir. [*aside*] What does he mean,
to stroke one o'the cheek so? I hope I'm not betray'd.   150

MASTER

Have you learnt the whistle yet, and when to fold?

---

137 **must not** cannot possibly
139 **female delicacy** The phrase is recorded on only one previous occasion, in a defence of Christianity against scepticism by John Smith, published in 1675 (Smith, 82). 'Delicacy' in its earlier range of meanings signifies voluptuousness and luxury; the range of meanings having to do with female sensitivity or softness or propriety develops in the eighteenth century. The signification here is somewhere between *OED* delicacy 5 and 6, and is likely to postdate Shakespeare's period.
140 **seeming** outward appearance; see 4.2.70n.

141 **Speaks him** declares that he is
142 **plays the swain** acts the role of farm boy
144 **mark the end** observe the aim
145 **perfect in't** absolutely sure about it
   coil turmoil; disturbance. The famous 'To be, or not to be' soliloquy in *Ham* has the line 'When we have shuffled off this mortal coil' (3.1.66); the word is used also by Prospero to Ariel: 'Who was so firm, so constant, that this coil / Would not infect his reason?' (*Tem* 1.2.207–8). 'Coil' is not used by Fletcher.
147 **he . . . he's** respectively, Julio and the boy
151 **fold** enclose (the sheep) in a fold or pen

---

137 SD] *this edn*   138 ev'rything] (ev'ry Thing)   148 SD] *this edn*   149 SD] *this edn*

And how to make the dog bring in the strayers?

VIOLANTE

    Time, sir, will furnish me with all these rules.

    My will is able, but my knowledge weak, sir.

MASTER

    That's a good child. Why dost thou blush, my boy?   155

    (*aside*) 'Tis certainly a woman. [*to Violante*] Speak, my

      boy.

VIOLANTE [*aside*]

    Heav'n, how I tremble. [*to Master*] 'Tis unusual to me

    To find such kindness at a master's hand,

    That am a poor boy, ev'ry way unable,

    Unless it be in pray'rs, to merit it.   160

    Besides, I've often heard old people say

    Too much indulgence makes boys rude and saucy.

MASTER

    Are you so cunning?

VIOLANTE (*aside*)   How his eyes shake fire,

    And measure ev'ry piece of youth about me!

    [*to Master*] The ewes want water, sir. Shall I go drive

      'em   165

    Down to the cisterns? Shall I make haste, sir?

    (*aside*) Would I were five miles from him.

      [*Master seizes her.*]   How he grips me!

---

152 **strayers** straggling sheep

154 **will . . . weak** recalls the biblical 'the spirit indeed is willing but the flesh is weak' from Matthew, 26.41, in the King James version completed in 1611, just prior to the Shelton translation of *Don Quixote* and any presumed date of composition for *Cardenio*

155 **blush** Blushing, like swooning, is a sign of womanhood in Shakespeare; see e.g. *RJ* 2.2.85, 'Else would a maiden blush bepaint my cheek'.

163 **eyes shake fire** The phrase occurs on only one previous occasion, in a poem 'To the Ladies', by George Sewell, in 1720. Theobald may have been responsible for the line.

164 **piece of youth** youthful attraction

165 **want** need, lack

166 **cisterns** storage basins from which the sheep drink. Cf. *TNK* 5.1.46–7, 'him that makes the camp a cistern / Brimmed with the blood of men'.

167 **Would** See 3.2.29n.

---

156 SD1] *this edn; after* Woman. *1728a*   SD2] *this edn*   157 SD1, 2] *this edn*   163 SD] *this edn; after* me! *164 1728a*   eyes shake] *1767;* Eyesshake *1728a*   165 SD] *this edn*   167 SD1] *this edn; after* me! *1728a*   Would] (*'Would*)   SD2] *this edn*

MASTER

> Come, come, all this is not sufficient, child,
> To make a fool of me. This is a fine hand,
> A delicate fine hand. Never change colour –   170
> You understand me – and a woman's hand.

VIOLANTE

> You're strangely out. Yet if I were a woman,
> I know you are so honest and so good
> That, though I wore disguises for some ends,
> You would not wrong me –

MASTER   Come, you're made for love.   175

> Will you comply? I'm madder with this talk.
> There's nothing you can say can take my edge off.

VIOLANTE

> O, do but quench these foul affections in you
> That like base thieves have robb'd you of your reason,
> And I will be a woman and begin   180
> So sad a story that if there be aught
> Of human in you, or a soul that's gentle,
> You cannot choose but pity my lost youth.

MASTER

> No stories now –

VIOLANTE   Kill me directly, sir.

> As you have any goodness, take my life.   185

169–70 **This . . . hand** The 'elocutionary
afterthought' of 'fine . . . delicate
fine' is a device strongly associated
with Fletcher: see Kukowski, 87.
The adjective, *OED* delicate *adj.* 1d,
'delightful from its beauty; dainty to
behold; lovely, graceful, elegant', is
used in this meaning later than the
noun. See 139n.

172 **strangely out** oddly wide of the mark
177 **say** This could mean 'say' as in
'assay', attempt, try. The meaning is
clear enough: 'only action can satisfy

my sexual appetite'.
    take . . . off slake my desire; cf. *Ham*
    3.2.242–3, 'It would cost you a groan-
    ing to take off mine edge.'
178 **affections** passions
181 **sad a story** Cf. *TN* 2.4, where Viola
    tells such a story to Orsino.
182 **human** 1728a 'humane'. By 1727,
    the two spellings did not yet clearly
    differentiate the senses 'belonging to
    the human race' and 'exhibiting com-
    passionate human feelings'.
    gentle well born; kindly, merciful

182 human] *(humane)*

RODERICK (*within*)   Hoa! Shepherd, will you hear, sir?

MASTER

What bawling rogue is that, i'th' devil's name?

VIOLANTE

Blessings upon him, whatsoe'er he be!   *Runs out.*

Enter RODERICK.

RODERICK   Good even, my friend. I thought you all had
　　been asleep in this country.   190

MASTER   You had lied then, for you were waking when you
　　thought so.

RODERICK [*Takes off his hat.*]   I thank you, sir.

MASTER [*Indicates his hat.*]   I pray, be cover'd; 'tis not so
　　much worth, sir.   195

RODERICK   Was that thy boy ran crying?

MASTER   Yes; what then?

RODERICK   Why dost thou beat him so?

MASTER   To make him grow.

RODERICK   A pretty med'cine! Thou canst not tell me the   200
　　way to the next nunnery?

---

187 **bawling rogue** This unusual phrase
is recorded previously only in *WWM*
4.4.3.

194–5 **be . . . worth** put your hat back on,
because my rank is not so great as to
require your doffing it. In *AYL* 3.3.71,
Touchstone bids Jaques to 'pray be cov-
ered'. Hamlet and Osricke (thus spelt
in F) have a similar exchange about
the wearing of hats (F *Ham* 5.2.94–6).
Here, though Roderick is the socially
superior character, he takes off his hat
whereas the baser-born Master rudely
gives him permission to replace it.
'tis . . . worth Costard has this
exact phrase in *LLL* 5.2.554. A five-
word correspondence might suggest
forgery rather than coincidence, if
the phrase were not relatively com-

mon, even a commonplace, having
appeared in Christopher Marlowe's
Dr Faustus (1592) and in Fletcher and
Beaumont's *SL*, as well as in later
plays by (amongst others) Richard
Brome, Thomas Nabbes, and Cowley.

198–9 **beat . . . grow** possibly alludes to
a proverbial expression (not listed in
Tilley), or it is simply an impudent
non sequitur

200–1 **Thou . . . nunnery** This somewhat abrupt question reminds Frazier
(*Voices*, 137) that in *Ham* 3.1.120
Hamlet roughly advised Ophelia: 'Get
thee to a nunnery!'

201 **next** nearest

200–4 **Thou . . . not** The dramatic situation here of a churlish response to
a civil question is very closely rep-

MASTER   How do you know that? Yes, I can tell you, but
 the question is, whether I will or no. And, indeed, I will
 not. Fare you well.   *Exit.*

RODERICK

 What a brute fellow's this! Are they all thus?   205
 My brother Henriquez tells me by his letters,
 The mistress of his soul not far from hence
 Hath taken sanctuary; from which he prays
 My aid to bring her back. From what Camillo
 Hinted, I wear some doubts. Here 'tis appointed 210
 That we should meet. It must be here. 'Tis so.
 He comes.

Enter HENRIQUEZ.

 Now, brother, what's this post-haste business
 You hurry me about? Some wenching matter –

HENRIQUEZ

 My letter told you, sir.   215

RODERICK

 'Tis true it tells me that you've lost a mistress
 Whom your heart bleeds for, but the means to win her
 From her close life, I take it, is not mention'd.
 You're ever in these troubles.

---

licated in *WGC* 2.2.2–6, where the
gallant Pinac, in search of an intended
mistress, Lillia-Bianca, encounters a
servant. *Pinac:* 'Canst thou shew me
/ The way to her chamber? or where
I may conveniently / See her, or come
to talk to her? / *Servant:* That I can,
Sir; / But the question is whether I
will or no.'

206 **Henriquez** here with two syllables;
 or possibly 'broth'r'

210 **wear** entertain. *OED*'s closest definition is *v.*[1] 8a, 'To carry about with one
in one's heart, mind, or memory; to
have as a quality or attribute; to bear
(a name, title)', as in *MA* 1.1.70–2:
'He wears his faith but as the fashion
of his hat: it ever changes with the
next block.'

213 **post-haste** exceptionally urgent
 business three syllables

218 **close life** cloistered existence

204 SD] *(Exit* Master.*)*

HENRIQUEZ   Noble brother,
    I own, I have too freely giv'n a scope   220
    To youth's intemp'rate heat and rash desires.
    But think not that I would engage your virtues
    To any cause wherein my constant heart
    Attended not my eye. Till now my passions
    Reign'd in my blood, ne'er pierc'd into my mind;   225
    But I'm a convert grown to purest thoughts
    And must in anguish spend my days to come
    If I possess not her. So much I love.
RODERICK
    The means? She's in a cloister, is she not?
    Within whose walls to enter as we are   230
    Will never be. Few men but friars come there,
    Which we shall never make.
HENRIQUEZ   If that would do it,
    I would make anything.
RODERICK   Are you so hot?
    (*aside*) I'll serve him, be it but to save his honour.
    [*to Henriquez*] To feign a corpse – by th' mass, it shall
        be so!   235
    We must pretend we do transport a body
    As 'twere to's funeral; and coming late by,
    Crave a night's leave to rest the hearse i'th' convent.
    That be our course, for to such charity

---

224 **Attended not** was not in attendance
    on, i.e. not in control of
225 were the effects of lust rather than of
    rational choice
230 **as we are** i.e. as laymen
232 **make** achieve; i.e. we will never be holy
    enough to achieve that clerical position
235 **feign a corpse** For discussion of
    this piece of plotting, not in Shelton,
    see p. 45.
238, 241 *****hearse** 1728a has the spelling

'Herse' (and also at 5.1.13, 5.2.35).
The word exists in this spelling, but
with a different meaning; see *OED*
herse *n.*, where none of the recorded meanings resembles its meaning
here of coffin or bier (*OED* hearse
n. 5). 'Herse' was, however, a common variant, deployed many times by
Shakespeare, e.g. in *R2* and *Tem*; and
Fletcher, e.g. in *Bon*, *FP*, *LFL*, *Maid's*,
ML and elsewhere.

---

229 cloister] *(*Cloyster*)*   231 friars] *(*Fryars*)*   233 anything] *(*Any thing*)*   234 SD] *this edn; after*
Honour. *1728a*   235 SD] *this edn*   238, 241 hearse] *(*Herse*)*

Strict zeal and custom of the house give way.   240

HENRIQUEZ

And, opportune, a vacant hearse pass'd by
From rites but new perform'd. This for a price
We'll hire, to put our scheme in act. Ho! Gerald.

Enter GERALD, *whom Henriquez whispers; then
Gerald goes out.*

RODERICK

When we're once lodg'd, the means of her conveyance
By safe and secret force with ease we'll compass.   245
But, brother, know my terms. If that your mistress
Will to the world come back, and she appear
An object worthy in our father's eye,
Woo her and win her; but if his consent
Keep not pace with your purpose –

HENRIQUEZ   Doubt it not.   250

I've look'd not with a common eye, but chose
A noble virgin, who to make her so
Has all the gifts of heav'n and earth upon her.
If ever woman yet could be an angel,
She is the nearest.

RODERICK   Well, a lover's praise   255

---

240 **zeal** piety
   custom . . . house devotion to the
   rules of the order
241–3 **And . . . act** It is difficult to imagine
   that the plotting was so coincidence-
   dependent in earlier versions. This may
   be the result of extreme truncation in
   Theobald's revision.
243 **Gerald** Although giving the servant
   a name may be simply a device for
   introducing him, this may also provide
   some possible evidence for truncation.
   He has not previously appeared in
   the action and is not included in the
   Dramatis Personae at the beginning

of the published play. A schoolmaster
named Gerald appears in *TNK*.
245 **safe . . . force** It is not entirely clear
   what kind of *force* is meant here.
249 **Woo . . . ²her** Cf. *LLL* 4.3.345–6:
   'LONGAVILLE . . . Shall we resolve to
   woo these girls of France? / KING And
   win them too!'
252 **so** i.e. noble
255 SP The 1728a form *Rhod.* is anomalous and suggests a survival of a detail
   from the copy manuscript. Cf. the other
   anomalous SP form *Roder.* at 5.1.53.
255–6 **a . . . ear** Lovers' compliments
   are somewhat too exalted for ordinary

Feasts not a common ear. Now to our plot.
We shall bring night in with us.   *Exeunt.*

4.2   *Enter* JULIO *and two* Gentlemen.

1 GENTLEMAN
    Good sir, compose yourself.
JULIO   O Leonora,
    That heav'n had made thee stronger than a woman.
    How happy had I been!
1 GENTLEMAN [*to Second Gentleman*] He's calm again.
    I'll take this interval to work upon him.
    [*to Julio*] These wild and solitary places, sir,   5
    But feed your pain. Let better reason guide you,
    And quit this forlorn state that yields no comfort.
                                        Lute sounds within.

JULIO
    Ha! Hark, a sound from heav'n! Do you hear nothing?
1 GENTLEMAN
    Yes sir, the touch of some sweet instrument.
    Here's no inhabitant.
JULIO   No, no, the better.   10
1 GENTLEMAN
    This is a strange place to hear music in.

---

hearers; cf. Tilley, L570: 'Lovers' vows are not to be trusted.'
4.2 The scene is not indicated here. Presumably it has not changed from 4.1. Neither is it clear who exactly the two Gentlemen are who enter with Julio. Fabian and Lopez are still available from 2.1 – or at least the actors who represent them are. Neither their idiom nor their eavesdropping sug-

gests, however, that they are 'gentlemen'.
3 had I would I have
7 forlorn abandoned, forsaken, desolate. The stress here is on the first syllable.
10 Here's no inhabitant The First Gentleman presumably means no one to be making the music.
11 draws attention to the wildness of the scenery

4.2] *(SCENE II.)*   3 SD] *this edn*   5 SD] *this edn*

JULIO

    I'm often visited with these sweet airs.

    The spirit of some hapless man that died

    And left his love hid in a faithless woman

    Sure haunts these mountains.   15

VIOLANTE (*Sings within.*)

        Fond Echo, forego thy light strain,

           And heedfully hear a lost maid;

        Go tell the false ear of the swain

           How deeply his vows have betray'd.

        Go, tell him what sorrows I bear;   20

           See yet if his heart feel my woe;

        'Tis now he must heal my despair,

           Or death will make pity too slow.

1 GENTLEMAN

    See, how his soul strives in him! This sad strain

    Has search'd him to the heart.

JULIO   Excellent sorrow!   25

    You never lov'd?

1 GENTLEMAN   No.

---

12 **visited with** *OED* gives visited *ppl. a.* 1, 'afflicted with illness; attacked by plague or other epidemic'. Julio is not sure whether the music is a mental illness or actually exists.

sweet airs Cf. *Tem* 3.2.135–6, where Caliban pays unexpectedly lyrical tribute to the mysterious music on the island: 'The isle is full of noises, / Sounds and sweet airs that give delight and hurt not.' The phrase is used by Fletcher in collaborative plays, e.g. *FP*, 'The Triumph of Time', scene 1.60; *CC* 1.2.45; and *SV* 1.5.67.

16–23, 27–30 **Fond Echo** See pp. 29 and 57, and Appendix 5 on the play's music.

24 **sad strain** The phrase arises in a

relevant context in *Luc* 1128–34, supporting the view that the poem is an important source for Theobald as adapter. Lucrece compares her situation to that of Philomel and Tereus in Ovid's *Metamorphoses*, 6.424–676. She will join her song, as a maid ravished by Tarquin, to that of the earlier victim: 'Come, PHILOMEL, that sing'st of ravishment, / Make thy sad grove in my dishevelled hair. / As the dank earth weeps at thy languishment, / So I at each sad strain will strain a tear, / And with deep groans the diapason bear; / For burden-wise I'll hum on TARQUIN still, / While thou on TEREUS descants better skill.'

---

16 SP, SD] *this edn;* Violante *sings within. after* Mountains. *15 1728a*   25–6] *Kennedy; 1728a lines* Heart. / Sorrow! / lov'd? / then. /

JULIO   Peace; and learn to grieve then.

VIOLANTE *(Sings within.)*

>   Go, tell him what sorrows I bear,
>   See yet if his heart feel my woe;
>   'Tis now he must heal my despair,
>   Or death will make pity too slow.   30

JULIO

Is not this heav'nly?

1 GENTLEMAN   I never heard the like, sir.

JULIO

I'll tell you, my good friends – but pray, say nothing –
I'm strangely touch'd with this. The heav'nly sound
Diffuses a sweet peace through all my soul.
But yet I wonder what new, sad companion   35
Grief has brought hither to out-bid my sorrows.
Stand off, stand off, stand off – friends, it appears.

[Julio and Gentlemen withdraw.]

Enter VIOLANTE *[with her hair loose].*

VIOLANTE

How much more grateful are these craggy mountains
And these wild trees than things of nobler natures;
For these receive my plaints and mourn again   40
In many echoes to me. All good people

33–4 **The . . . soul** There is a close parallel here with the passage of action in which Pericles hears the music of the spheres, *Per* 5.1.212–22.

37.1 Violante's loose hair makes her true gender obvious to the onstage characters.

38–9 The lines call to mind the sentiments of Duke Senior in *AYL* 2.1.3–4: 'Are not these woods / More free from peril than the envious court?'

Taking fuller account of the dramatic situation, the moralizing speech of Belarius in *Cym* 3.3.21–6 may be closer. Leading the princes on their 'mountain sport', he comments, 'O, this life / Is nobler than attending for a check: / Richer than doing nothing for a robe, / Prouder than rustling in unpaid-for silk: / Such gain the cap of him that makes him fine, / Yet keeps his book uncross'd: no life to ours.'

27 SP, SD] *this edn;* Violante *sings within. after* then. 26 *1728a* 31] *Kennedy; prose 1728a* 31 SP2] *this edn* 37 SD] *this edn* 37.1 with . . . loose] *this edn*

Are fall'n asleep forever. None are left,
That have the sense and touch of tenderness
For virtue's sake – no, scarce their memory –
From whom I may expect counsel in fears,   45
Ease to complainings or redress of wrongs.

JULIO

This is a moving sorrow, but say nothing.

VIOLANTE

What dangers have I run and to what insults
Expos'd this ruin of myself? O, mischief
On that soul-spotted hind, my vicious master!   50
Who would have thought that such poor worms as
     they –
Whose best feed is coarse bread, whose bev'rage,
     water –
Should have so much rank blood? I shake all over
And blush to think what had become of me
If that good man had not reliev'd me from him.   55

JULIO

Since she is not Leonora, she is heav'nly.
When she speaks next, listen as seriously
As women do that have their loves at sea
What wind blows ev'ry morning.

---

50 **soul-spotted** Salerno (45) points out that such hyphenated compound adjectives are common in Shakespeare – though it should be observed that they may be compositorial. This particular collocation only occurs in *DF*.

51–3 **Who ... blood** Cf. *Mac* 5.1.40–1, where the sleepwalking Lady Macbeth says: 'who would have thought the old man to have had so much blood in him?' Lady Macbeth uses the word literally, whereas Violante's reference is probably to humoral medicine. The Master is of a 'sanguine' disposition: having excessive blood provokes his lust. 'Rank' is a common adjective in Shakespeare, as in Hamlet's 'things rank and gross in nature' (*Ham* 1.2.136), and also in Fletcher. *TNK* 5.1.63 has 'o'er-rank states'.

51 **worms** Cf. *Tem* 3.1.31, 'Poor worm, thou art infected!' Whereas Prospero uses the term in respect of his daughter as an endearment or expression of pity, Violante uses it as a contemptuous insult. Shakespeare also uses the contemptuous form, as in *MW* 5.5.84, Pistol's 'Vile worm, thou wast o'erlooked even in thy birth.'

54 **had** would have

56 **Leonora** three syllables

VIOLANTE

I cannot get this false man's memory 60
Out of my mind. You maidens that shall live
To hear my mournful tale when I am ashes,
Be wise; and to an oath no more give credit,
To tears, to vows – false both! – or anything
A man shall promise, than to clouds that now 65
Bear such a pleasing shape and now are nothing.
For they will cozen (if they may be cozen'd)
The very gods they worship. Valour, justice,
Discretion, honesty and all they covet
To make them seeming saints are but the wiles 70

61–71 You . . . destruction Muir
(*Shakespeare*, 153*)* comments that
this passage 'recalls, without actual
echoing, the laments of Aspatia in
The Maid's Tragedy'. It could, though,
refer back to an older tradition of
rhyming moralizing drama wherein
the audience is addressed directly, as
revived in, for example, Heywood's
A Woman Killed with Kindness (1607),
sig. G1ʳ: 'Oh women, women, you that
have yet kept / Your holy matrimo-
niall vows unstaind, / Make me your
instance when you tread awry, / Your
sins like mine will on your conscience
lye.' A further exemplar is the Jailer's
Daughter's speech reported by the
Wooer in *TNK* 4.1.70–93.
63 oath . . . credit Cf. *TNK* 3.6.223–4,
'it concerns your credit / And my
oath equally'. Parallels such as this are
compelling evidence for the hand of
Fletcher in the play – as distinctive as
it is unobtrusive.
65–6 clouds . . . nothing Several
instances occur in Shakespeare of
clouds assuming shapes, e.g. Hamlet's
leading on Polonius in *Ham* 3.2.367–
73; and *Tem* 4.1.151–6, where Prospero
exposes the insubstantial, airy nature
of the masque of nymphs and reapers.
67 they . . . they i.e. men

cozen deceive, cheat
if . . . cozened refers forward to *gods*
in 68
68 very gods The phrase occurs in *Cym*
4.2.346, 'Last night the very gods
show'd me a vision'.
68–71 Valour . . . destruction The list
of abstract nouns in this passage, combined with the occurrence of words
used elsewhere in Theobald's *oeuvre*,
suggests his hand.
70 seeming saints The collocation calls
Angelo in *MM* to mind. The term
'seeming' is applied to him both by
Isabella and by the Duke (2.4.149,
3.1.222); in 2.2.180–1, he refers to
himself and Isabella as 'saints': 'O
cunning enemy, that, to catch a saint,
/ With saints dost bait thy hook!'
seeming Theobald uses the adjective
on five occasions in *Fatal Secret* (Act 1,
pp. 1, 4, 7; Act 2, p. 13; Act 4, p. 39). It
occurs twice in *Happy Captive*, twice
in *Orestes* (1731) and twice in *Persian
Princess*, as well as singly in other dramatic works.
wiles commonly used by Theobald.
The word occurs no fewer than five
times in *Perfidious Brother* (Act 1,
p. 2; Act 3, pp. 24, 27, 29, 34). It occurs
twice in *Orestes* (Act 5, pp. 63, 71); and
in three other works by him.

64 anything] *(any Thing)*

By which these sirens lure us to destruction.

JULIO

Do not you weep now? I could drop myself
Into a fountain for her.

1 GENTLEMAN

She weeps extremely.

JULIO   Let her weep; 'tis well.

Her heart will break else. Great sorrows live in tears.   75

VIOLANTE

O false Henriquez!

JULIO   Ha!

VIOLANTE   And O, thou fool,

Forsaken Violante – whose belief
And childish love have made thee so – go, die!
For there is nothing left thee now to look for
That can bring comfort but a quiet grave.   80
There all the miseries I long have felt
And those to come shall sweetly sleep together.
Fortune may guide that false Henriquez hither
To weep repentance o'er my pale, dead corpse
And cheer my wand'ring spirit with those lov'd
    obsequies. *Going*   85

---

71 **sirens** dangerous bird-women who
lure sailors to their deaths in Greek
mythology, best known from Homer's
Odyssey, Book 12. In Theobald's
Orestes, Thoas refers to Circe's '*Siren*'s
Face' (5.1, p. 66). Unusually here,
Violante figures the sirens as male.

72 **drop myself** dissolve; cf. 3.2.30, and
see 30–1n.

74 **extremely** This usage is identical to
the typically Fletcherian use of the
adverb, as found in e.g. *Cox* 2.1.103–4,
'I love your wife extreamely', and in
Val 3.3.103, 'Do we not love extremely?' See further 4.1.81n.

75 **Great ... tears** Tears are the element
in which sorrow lives; weeping keeps

sorrow fresh.

78 **so** i.e. forsaken

79 **look for** expect, look forward to

80 **quiet grave** Fletcher uses the phrase
in two plays, *Val* 5.2.145, and, in
collaboration with Beaumont, *CR*
3.2.213.

85 This long line is an alexandrine (though
it requires elision to 'obs'quies', or
monosyllabic 'spir't'), placed at the
end of Violante's elegiac speech to give
it emphasis and closure.
  obsequies funeral rites or ceremonies.
In *RJ* 5.3.16–17, Paris weeps over Juliet's
grave in similar terms: 'The obsequies
that I for thee will keep / Nightly shall
be to strew thy grave and weep.'

84 corpse] *this edn;* Coarse *1728a;* Corse *1767*

JULIO [*Comes forward.*]

    Stay, lady, stay. Can it be possible

    That you are Violante?

VIOLANTE   That lost name

    Spoken by one that needs must know my fortunes

    Has taken much fear from me. Who are you, sir?

    For, sure, I am that hopeless Violante.   90

JULIO

    And I, as far from any earthly comfort

    That I know yet, the much-wrong'd Julio.

VIOLANTE   Julio!

JULIO

    I once was thought so. If the curst Henriquez

    Had pow'r to change you to a boy, why, lady,

    Should not that mischief make me anything,   95

    That have an equal share in all the miseries

    His crimes have flung upon us?

VIOLANTE   Well I know it.

    And pardon me I could not know your virtues

    Before your griefs. Methought when last we met

    The accent of your voice struck on my ear   100

---

93 **curst** In this spelling, the word occurs often in Fletcher. *OED ppl. a.* 4a records this spelling of 'cursed' under a separate meaning: 'Malignant; perversely disagreeable or cross; cantankerous, shrewish, virulent.' Cf. *MND* 3.2.300, where Helena says of herself 'I was never curst'. The word attaches to Beatrice in *MA* and to Katherine in *TS*. Beaumont and Fletcher use the word thus adjectivally in *Phil* 2.3.40, 'Hadst thou a curst master, when thou went'st to School?'; and Fletcher in *LS* 3.4.52.

97 **flung** Kukowski (85) points out how distinctive of Fletcher's lexis the word 'fling' and cognates are.

99 **when . . . met** Violante presumably

refers to the previous scene, 4.1, in which they met, both in disguise. This may be, however, more evidence of missing material in the early acts of a previous version, in which Julio and Violante were acquainted. In *DF* as the text now stands, no means is suggested by which Violante and Julio could have known one another prior to their meeting in 4.1. In the source, *Don Quixote*, Cardenio (Julio) is from the outset aware that Fernando (Henriquez) has had an intrigue with a peasant girl, whose name is Dorotea. This may, however, be another example of Aristotelian 'necessary improbability' or economy in exposition.

86 SD] *this edn*

Like something I had known, but floods of sorrow
Drown'd the remembrance. If you'll please to sit
(Since I have found a suff'ring true companion)
And give me hearing, I will tell you something
Of Leonora that may comfort you.   105

JULIO

Blessing upon thee! Henceforth, I protest
Never to leave thee, if heav'n say 'Amen'.
But soft, let's shift our ground, guide our sad steps
To some remoter gloom, where undisturb'd
We may compare our woes; dwell on the tale   110
Of mutual injuries till our eyes run o'er
And we infect each other with fresh sorrows.
Talk'd you of comfort? 'Tis the food of fools,
And we will none on't but indulge despair.
    So, worn with griefs, steal to the Cave of Death   115
    And in a sigh give up our latest breath.   *Exeunt.*

End of the fourth act

102 **Drown'd the remembrance** Cf. *TN* 2.1.28–9, where Sebastian recalls his seemingly drowned sister Viola: 'though I seem to drown her remembrance again with more [tears]'.

108–16 **let's ... breath** similar in cadence to Lear's melancholy picture of innocence invoked for Cordelia, beginning 'We two alone will sing like birds i'the cage' (*KL* 5.3.9–17). There is perhaps even more of the Restoration in the sentiments; cf. Nahum Tate's *The History of King Lear* (1681), which ends with Lear suggesting to Edgar that 'Thou, *Kent* and I, retir'd to some cool Cell / Will gently pass our short reserves of Time / In calm Reflections on our Fortunes past, / Cheer'd with relation of the prosperous Reign / Of this celestial Pair; Thus our Remains / Shall in an even Course of Thought be past, / Enjoy the present Hour, nor fear the Last' (Act 5, p. 67).

108 **sad steps** Cf. *KL* 5.3.287, and Sir Philip Sidney's famous sonnet 31 from *Astrophil and Stella* (1591): 'With how sad steps, ô Moone, thou climb'st the skies' (Sidney, *Astrophil*, 180).

109 **remoter gloom** The phrase is unique to *DF*.

113–14 Cf. *R2* 3.2.144–5, 'Of comfort no man speak! / Let's talk of graves, of worms and epitaphs'.

113 **food of fools** Fletcher describes flattery as the 'food of fooles' in *RDN* 5.2.15. Dryden later uses the expression in *King Arthur* (1691), Act 3, p. 23.

115 **Cave of Death** Julio might have a quasi-allegorical sense of a particular cave.

116.1 *End*] *(The End)*

5.1   *The prospect of the mountains continued*

Enter RODERICK, LEONORA *veil'd,* HENRIQUEZ, [*and*]
          Attendants as mourners.

RODERICK
  Rest certain, lady, nothing shall betide you
  But fair and noble usage. Pardon me
  That hitherto a course of violence
  Has snatch'd you from that seat of contemplation
  To which you gave your after-life.
LEONORA   Where am I?   5
RODERICK
  Not in the nunnery. Never blush, nor tremble;
  Your honour has as fair a guard as when
  Within a cloister. Know then, what is done
  (Which, I presume, you understand not truly)
  Has this use, to preserve the life of one   10
  Dying for love of you: my brother, and your friend.
  Under which colour we desir'd to rest
  Our hearse one night within your hallow'd walls,
  Where we surpris'd you.
LEONORA   Are you that Lord Roderick,
  So spoken of for virtue and fair life,   15

5.1
0 SD *The ... continued* suggests that
   the scene has remained the same
   throughout Act 4 and now into Act
   5. This might explain why there is no
   scene specified at the heading of 4.2.
4 **seat of contemplation** i.e. the convent. The phrase is used by Brome
   in *The Weeding of the Covent Garden*
   (1638), 5.3, p. 91; and by John
   Vanbrugh in *Aesop* (1697), 1.1, p. 8
   – in both cases to mean the mind or
   soul. The earliest non-dramatic use

of the phrase is 1631, in Richard
Brathwaite's conduct manual *The
English Gentlewoman*, p. 44.
5 **your after-life** the rest of your life
6 **blush** See 4.1.155n.
10 **use** aim, purpose
11 an alexandrine
12 **Under which colour** for which pur-
    pose (here, without the more usual
    suggestion of 'colour' as 'false col-
    our')
13 *hearse** See 4.1.238, 241n.
14 **surpris'd** captured

5.1] *(ACT V. SCENE I.)*   0 SD *The*] SCENE, *The 1728a*   5] *Kennedy; prose 1728a*   8 cloister]
(Cloyster)   13 hearse] *(Herse)*

279

And dare you lose these to be advocate
For such a brother, such a sinful brother,
Such an unfaithful, treacherous, brutal brother?

RODERICK (*Looks at Henriquez.*)

This is a fearful charge.

LEONORA   If you would have me
Think you still bear respect for virtue's name,   20
As you would wish your daughters, thus distress'd,
Might find a guard, protect me from Henriquez
And I am happy.

RODERICK   Come, sir, make your answer,
For as I have a soul, I am asham'd on't.

HENRIQUEZ

O Leonora, see, thus self-condemn'd   25
I throw me at your feet and sue for mercy.
If I have err'd, impute it to my love:
The tyrant god that bows us to his sway,
Rebellious to the laws of reas'ning men,

16–17 **advocate . . . brother** Salerno
(65) suggests *Tem* 1.2.477–8, 'What,
/ An advocate for an impostor?'
Here, Prospero is testing Miranda,
who is prepared to stand surety for
Ferdinand. This is a one-word link,
however, and repetitious phrasings of
this emphatic kind are found often in
Fletcher.

17 **sinful brother** In dramatic literature,
the phrase is unique to *DF*. It is found,
though not commonly, in religious
works such as Henry More's *Discourses
on Several Texts of the Scripture* (1692),
271, where the term appears to have
the quasi-technical meaning of a monk
or religious man who has gone to the
bad. There is a play here on *brother* in
the sense of blood relationship and in
the sense of monk.

18 **unfaithful, treacherous** Cf. Hamlet's
verdict on Claudius, 'Remorseless,
treacherous, lecherous, kindless villain!'

(*Ham* 2.2.516). It is typical of Fletcher
to pile up accumulating phrases of this
kind: e.g. *Maid's* 3.2.4–5, Calianax to
Melantius, 'Thou art a slave, a cut-throat
slave, a bloody treacherous slave.'

brutal brother another surprisingly
uncommon phrase. In 1567, it is found
in the plural form of 'brutal breth-
ren' in the second volume of William
Painter's *Palace of Pleasure* (192). It
may be significant that Painter is here
telling the story of the Duchess of
Malfi. Theobald produced a version
of Webster's play under the title *The
Fatal Secret*. Thomas Otway uses it
in his tragedy first published in 1719,
Heroic Friendship (1.1, p. 8). Its context in Otway is the wronging of one
brother by another in amatory affairs.
OED brutal *a.* and *n.* 4, giving the
meaning 'inhuman; coarsely cruel, sav-
age, fierce', considers the word to date
from around the mid-17th century.

19 SD] *this edn; after* Charge. *1728a*

That will not have his votaries' actions scann'd,   30
But calls it justice when we most obey him.
He but commanded what your eyes inspir'd,
Whose sacred beams, darted into my soul,
Have purg'd the mansion from impure desires
And kindled in my heart a vestal's flame.   35

LEONORA

Rise, rise, my lord, this well-dissembled passion
Has gain'd you nothing but a deeper hate.
Should I imagine he can truly love me
That, like a villain, murders my desires?
Or should I drink that wine, and think it cordial,   40
When I see poison in't?

RODERICK [*Leads Leonora aside.*] Draw this way, lady.

30 **scann'd** scrutinized; another possible reference to Hamlet's relationship with Claudius, where Hamlet, thinking about his intention to kill the King when he is at prayer, remarks 'That would be scanned' (*Ham* 3.3.75)

34 **mansion** See 2.2.35–7 and n. The metaphor of the heart as a mansion or dwelling-place is frequent in Shakespeare and in plays of his period.

35 **vestal's flame** Vestal virgins were the legendarily chaste priestesses who guarded the sacred fire of the goddess Vesta in Rome. Shakespeare uses the adjective in *Luc* 883 and in *VA* 752; and also in the collaborative later plays. In *Per* 3.4.8–10, Thaisa laments, 'My wedded lord, I ne'er shall see again, / A vestal livery will I take me to / And never more have joy.' In *TNK* 5.1.149–50 Emilia says, 'This is my last / Of vestal office.' The word would not usually be associated with a male. The phrase 'vestal's flame', popular in Caroline poetry and deployed by both Jonson and Shirley, achieves prominence in

the drama of the later 17th century, where it appears in plays by Joseph Addison, John Bancroft, Behn, Cibber, Davenant, Thomas Killigrew, Pix and Tate.

36 **well-dissembled** a phrase in common use from Shakespeare's period onwards, though not used by Shakespeare himself. It is very popular in drama of the Restoration period.

40 **cordial** 'A medicine, food, or beverage which invigorates the heart and stimulates the circulation; a comforting or exhilarating drink' (*OED a.* and *n.* B. 1a). This is a significant word in Shakespeare's later plays, where it occurs in *Cym* 1.6.64, 4.2.327 and 5.5.247; and in *WT* 1.2.318 and 5.3.77. Both plays associate cordial with poison. The word is equally important to Fletcher and his collaborators, occurring in at least 12 of his plays. It remains common throughout the Restoration and 18th century.

41 **Draw . . . lady** Roderick separates Leonora from Henriquez.

41 SD] *this edn*

I am not perfect in your story yet,
But see you've had some wrongs that want redress.
Only you must have patience to go with us
To yon small lodge, which meets the sight from hence,   45
Where your distress shall find the due respect.
Till when, your griefs shall govern me as much
As nearness and affection to my brother.
Call my attendants yours and use them freely,
For, as I am a gentleman, no pow'r   50
Above your own will shall come near your person.

As they are going out, VIOLANTE *enters [in boy's clothes],*
and plucks Roderick by the sleeve; the rest go out.

VIOLANTE
    Your ear a moment: scorn not my tender youth.
RODERICK [*Calls after them.*]
    Look to the lady there. I follow straight.
    – What ails this boy? Why dost thou single me?
VIOLANTE
    The due observance of your noble virtue   55
    Vow'd to this mourning virgin makes me bold
    To give it more employment.
RODERICK   Art not thou

---

42 **perfect in** fully conversant with
43 **want** lack, require
44 **Only** i.e. you need patience only for as long as it takes to reach yon small lodge
46 **due respect** attention it requires or deserves. The phrase is not used by Shakespeare or Fletcher, though it is very common in literature from Shakespeare's period through to Theobald's.
51 **Above** overriding
53 SP See 4.1.255n.
    Look . . . there an echo of *Mac*

2.3.125, 'Look to the Lady', but here in the routine sense of attend
54 **single me** separate me; single me out; draw me apart. Shakespeare's usages in these senses are mainly in earlier plays, *LLL, 3H6, Tit*; but it is not an echo of a familiar line that a plagiarist would recall. More generally, Roderick's reaction to Violante here recalls that of Posthumus to Imogen in *Cym* 5.5.228–9, though Roderick does not strike her.
55–6 **your . . . Vow'd** your noble and virtuous vow

51.1 *in boy's clothes*] *this edn*   53 SP] *(Roder.); Rod. 1767*   SD] *this edn*

The surly shepherd's boy that, when I call'd
To know the way, ran crying by me?
VIOLANTE   Yes, sir.
And I thank heav'n and you for helping me.   60
RODERICK
How did I help thee, boy?
VIOLANTE
I do but seem so, sir, and am indeed
A woman – one your brother once has lov'd,
Or, heav'n forgive him else, he lied extremely.
RODERICK
Weep not, good maid. O, this licentious brother!   65
But how came you a wand'rer on these mountains?
VIOLANTE
That as we pass, an't please you, I'll discover.
I will assure you, sir, these barren mountains
Hold many wonders of your brother's making.
Here wanders hapless Julio, worthy man!   70
Besides himself with wrongs.
RODERICK   That once again –
VIOLANTE
Sir, I said, Julio. Sleep weigh'd down his eyelids,
Oppress'd with watching, just as you approach'd us.
RODERICK
O brother, we shall sound the depths of falsehood.

62–3 **I ... woman** It is likely that Violante here adjusts her headgear so as to 'discover' her hair, as does Euphrasia, who is disguised as a male page, in *Phil* 5.5.112: '*Kneels to* Dion *and discovers her haire.*' Julia in *TGV* is involved in similar acts of covering and uncovering her hair: see 2.7.45–6 and 46n.; and 5.4.98 SD.

64 **extremely** See 4.1.81n., and cf. 4.2.74. This adverbial usage is found in Fletcher and Shakespeare.

65 **licentious brother** another in the series of negative adjectives after *sinful* (17) and *brutal* (18). The phrase appears to be unique to *DF*.

71 **That once again** Roderick's attention is arrested by mention of Julio's name, and he either wishes it to be repeated, or exclaims because the name is beginning to acquire significance in his mind.

73 **watching** wakefulness

59] *Kennedy; prose 1728a*

If this be true, no more but guide me to him,   75
I hope a fair end will succeed all yet.
If it be he, by your leave, gentle brother,
I'll see him serv'd first. Maid, you have o'erjoy'd me.
Thou shalt have right too. Make thy fair appeal
To the good Duke, and doubt not but thy tears   80
Shall be repaid with interest from his justice.
Lead me to Julio.   *Exeunt.*

5.2   *An apartment in the lodge*

Enter DUKE, DON BERNARD *and* CAMILLO.

CAMILLO Ay, then your grace had had a son more, he, a
daughter; and I, an heir. But let it be as 'tis; I cannot
mend it. One way or other, I shall rub it over with
rubbing to my grave, and there's an end on't.

---

76 **succeed** follow
78 **o'erjoy'd** an unusual word, especially in the verbal and transitive
construction used here, 'To fill with
extreme joy; to transport with joy
or gladness' (*OED* overjoy *v.* 2a).
OED provides examples dating from
1571, and the word occurs in *Cym*
5.5.402–3, 'All o'erjoy'd, / Save in
these bonds'.
78–80 **Maid ... tears** Roderick's shift
from *you* to *Thou/thy* is motivated by
personal concern for Violante.
79–81 **appeal ... justice** reminiscent of
the opening of the final act of *MM*,
where Isabella is exhorted by the Duke
to appeal for justice to Angelo
5.2
0 SD returns to an interior scene, but a
more rustic back shutter than has previously been represented, as indicated
by *lodge* as hunting-lodge
1 **had had** would have had
3–4 **rub ... rubbing** Two meanings of
the word 'rub' are involved: *OED* rub

v.[1] 3a, 'To affect painfully or disagree-
ably; to annoy, irritate', and 2b, '*fig*. To
revive, stir up, in respect of memory
or recollection'. In Shakespeare the
word will often signal a metaphor from
the game of bowls, sometimes with a
bawdy reference to masturbation, as in
Boyet's by-play with Costard in *LLL*
4.1.138, not present in Camillo's grave
speech. Salerno (67) suggests a parallel
with *Tem* 2.1.139–40, where Gonzalo
is rebuking Sebastian for making
matters worse for Alonso (who, like
Camillo, believes he has lost a son):
'You rub the sore / When you should
bring the plaster.'
4 **there's ... on't** an expression much
liked by Fletcher. It occurs in *MT*
5.1.64; *WGC* 2.1.127; and, as 'there's
an end', in *WP* 1.4.28. It is also a
very popular way of rounding off
a blunt remark in the Restoration,
used frequently by such as Behn,
Dryden, D'Urfey, Shadwell and
Southerne.

5.2] *(SCENE II.)*

DUKE

    Our sorrows cannot help us, gentlemen.   5

CAMILLO Hang me, sir, if I shed one tear more. By Jove,

    I've wept so long I'm as blind as justice. When I come

    to see my hawks (which I held a toy next to my son),

    if they be but house-high I must stand aiming at them

    like a gunner.   10

DUKE

    Why, he mourns like a man. Don Bernard, you

    Are still like April, full of show'rs and dews;

    And yet I blame you not, for I myself

    Feel the self-same affections. – Let them go.

    They're disobedient children.

DON BERNARD   Ay, my lord.   15

    Yet they may turn again.

CAMILLO Let them e'en have their swing. They're young

    and wanton; the next storm we shall have them gallop

    homeward, whining as pigs do in the wind.

DON BERNARD

    Would I had my daughter any way.   20

---

7 **blind as justice** Justice, like Fortune, is proverbially blind. See Tilley, F604.

7–10 **When . . . gunner** Camillo's eyes will be half-closed through excess weeping, so that he will resemble a gunner taking aim when he looks at his hawks in the air. Fletcher and Beaumont use the image of Cupid as a 'blinde gunner' in *CR* 1.1.128.

8 **held a toy** regarded as of slight value

9 **house-high** flying at the height of a house. In this compound form, the descriptor is unique to *DF*.

12 **like April** Showery April weather is proverbially connected with inconstant behaviour, e.g. Tilley, S410: 'He is like an April shower, that wets the stone nine times an hour.'

    show'rs In this elided form, the word is vastly popular in Restoration theatre, though it also occurs in plays of the 1590s. Theobald uses it in all of his major translations, adaptations and original plays.

14 **affections** passions

17 **swing** freedom of action; full scope; inclination: equivalent to the modern 'have their head'

19 **whining . . . wind** Cf. *Bon* 4.1.20–1, 'The other runs thee whining up and down / Like a pig in a storm'; and *TNK* 5.4.69–71: 'pig–like he whines / At the sharp rowell, which he frets at rather / Than any jot obeys'. Here the subject is Arcite's horse; but it is clear that pigs were supposed to make a whining noise under stormy conditions.

CAMILLO   Wouldst thou have her with bairn, man, tell me
   that?

DON BERNARD
   I care not, if an honest father got it.

CAMILLO
   You might have had her so in this good time,
   Had my son had her. Now you may go seek   25
   Your fool to stop a gap with.

DUKE
   You say that Rod'rick charg'd you here should wait him.
   He has o'erslipp'd the time at which his letters
   Of speed request that I should also meet him.
   I fear some bad event is usher'd in   30
   By this delay. How now?

Enter Gentleman.

GENTLEMAN   So please your grace,
   Lord Rod'rick makes approach.

DUKE   I thank thee, fellow,
   For thy so timely news. Comes he alone?

GENTLEMAN
   No sir, attended well, and in his train   34
   Follows a hearse with all due rites of mourning.   *Exit.*

---

21 **with bairn** perhaps characterizing
Camillo's idiom as rustic, since the
word is Scots dialect
25–6 **seek . . . with** Cf. *RJ* 2.4.91–2, where
Mercutio's expression is in the same
bawdy semantic field as here: 'this drivel-
ling love is like a great natural that runs
lolling up and down to hide his bauble in
a hole'. The fool's bauble was a stick with
an ornately carved or inflated end.
28 **o'erslipp'd** missed, i.e. is late
29 **Of speed** speedily; relating to *meet
him*, but the phrase might also refer

back to *letters* in the sense of urgent,
hastily written
30 **event** outcome
32 **makes approach** The phrase is not
in Shakespeare or Fletcher, though
it does appear in the period, e.g. in
Marston's *Antonio and Mellida* (1599).
Its popularity with Theobald himself
suggests that it might be his. He uses
it in *Fatal Secret* (5.1, p. 48) and in
Happy Captive (2.7.1), as well as in
Perseus, (p. 9) and *Orestes* (1.2, p. 5).
35 *****hearse** See 4.1.238, 241n.

21 bairn] *(Bearn)*   35 hearse] *(Herse)*   SD] *(Exit Gent.)*

DUKE

Heav'n send Henriquez live!

CAMILLO   'Tis my poor Julio.

Enter RODERICK *hastily.*

DUKE   O welcome, welcome, welcome, good Rod'rick! Say,
what news?

CAMILLO

Do you bring joy or grief, my lord? For me,
Come what can come, I'll live a month or two   40
If the gout please, curse my physician once more,
And then –
                    Under this stone
                    Lies sev'nty-one.

RODERICK

Signior, you do express a manly patience.   45
My noble father, something I have brought
To ease your sorrows: my endeavours have not
Been altogether barren in my journey.

DUKE

It comes at need, boy; but I hop'd it from thee.

Enter LEONORA *veiled,* HENRIQUEZ *behind, and Attendants.*

---

40 Come . . . come This phrase, found
twice in *TNK* (2.3.18, 3.6.127) and in
Fletcher's *Pilg*, is not found in drama
of the later period.

43–4 The somewhat lame rhyming of
stone / one might continue the suggestion of Camillo's rusticity – his recall
of simple graveyard epitaphs or other
folk material. On this, see AT 4 in
Duncan-Jones & Woudhuysen, 447,
and Kökeritz, 132.

45 manly patience a phrase with a
long dramatic pedigree, appearing in
Fletcher and Massinger's *EB* and in

other plays by Massinger, Heywood
and Brome. It also occurs in Theobald's
friend Philip Frowde's *The Fall of
Saguntum* (1727), Act 2, p. 19; and in
John Gay's *The Captives* (1724), 2.8,
p. 23, making it difficult to decide
whether the phrase predates Theobald.

49 comes at need comes when needed;
at the height of necessity. The phrase
does not occur before this use of it in
DF.

49.1 *veiled* similar staging to *MM* 5.1,
where Mariana enters under the protection of a veil, or *MA* 5.4, where

37] *this edn; 1728a lines* O welcome, welcome, / News? /

RODERICK

The company I bring will bear me witness   50
The busiest of my time has been employ'd
On this good task. Don Bernard finds beneath
This veil his daughter; you, my royal father,
Behind that lady find a wand'ring son.
How I met with them and how brought them hither   55
More leisure must unfold.

HENRIQUEZ [*aside*]   My father here!
And Julio's! O confusion! (*to the Duke*) Low as earth
I bow me for your pardon.

DON BERNARD   O my girl!
(*Embraces Leonora.*) Thou bringst new life.

DUKE (*to Roderick*)   And you, my son, restore me
One comfort here that has been missing long.   60
(*to Henriquez*) I hope thy follies thou hast left abroad.

CAMILLO   Ay, ay; you've all comforts but I. You have ruin'd
me, kill'd my poor boy – cheated and ruin'd him; and I
have no comfort.

RODERICK

Be patient, signior. Time may guide my hand   65
To work you comfort too.

CAMILLO   I thank your lordship.
Would grandsire Time had been so kind to've done it,

Hero returns masked, rather than
veiled. Here, the veil seems to be
lifted too soon for maximum theatrical effect.

59 **new life** The phrase is found in *Tit*
1.1.466 and, in the Fletcher canon, in
LCu 1.3.43 and *KM* 4.2.16. It is not a
distinctive expression, however.

59–61 The respectful *you* for Roderick, as
against the dismissive *thou* reserved for

Henriquez, is notable here.

67 *****Would** See 3.2.29n.

grandsire Time Camillo's personification here may recall Time as a chorus
prefacing Act 4 of *WT*, as well as
16th- and 17th-century iconographical
representations of the figure of Time,
equipped with scythe and hourglass.
The healing power of time is of course a
major theme of Shakespeare's last plays.

56 SD] *this edn*   57 SD] *this edn; after* Pardon. *58 1728a*   58] *Kennedy; prose 1728a*   59 SD1] *this
edn; after* Life. – *1728a*   SD2] *this edn; after* me *1728a*   61] *this edn; To* Henriq. *after* abroad.
1728a   66] *Kennedy; prose 1728a*   67 Would] (ˈWould)

We might have joy'd together like good fellows;
But he's so full of business, good old man,
'Tis wonder he could do the good he has done.   70

DON BERNARD

Nay, child, be comforted. These tears distract me.

DUKE

Hear your good father, lady.

LEONORA   Willingly.

DUKE

The voice of parents is the voice of gods:
For to their children they are heav'n's lieutenants;
Made fathers not for common uses merely   75
Of procreation (beasts and birds would be
As noble then as we are), but to steer
The wanton freight of youth through storms and dangers,
Which with full sails they bear upon, and straighten
The moral line of life they bend so often.   80
For these are we made fathers; and for these
May challenge duty on our children's part.
Obedience is the sacrifice of angels,
Whose form you carry.

73–84 Similar advice is given by Theseus to Hermia in *MND* 1.1.47: 'To you your father should be as a god'. The Duke's speech on the reciprocal duties of parents and children, however, with its heavy emphasis on parental authority, is not typical of the closing sentiments in late Shakespeare. It suggests the didactic strain that is found in Theobald's original plays and adaptations.

74 **heav'n's lieutenants** God's representatives. The phrase is not in Shakespeare or Fletcher. It is used in Middleton's poem *Father Hubburd's Tales, or the Ant and the Nightingale* (1604), l. 151 (*Works*, p. 167), and in Settle's play *The Female Prelate* (1680), 5.2, p. 71; but does not occur after the later Restoration period.

78 **wanton freight** wayward cargo. The phrase is unique to *DF*.

79 **bear upon** are headed towards

80 **line of life** The thread of human life spun by the Fates is the lifeline. The phrase is very common in Shakespeare's period and is used by him to refer to palmistry in *MV* 2.2.152–3, where Launcelot Gobbo says 'go to, here's a simple line of life'. *Son* 74.3 puns on lifeline/line of verse in 'My life hath in this line some interest'. The usage survives throughout the 18th century.

79 straighten] (streighten)

DON BERNARD   Hear the Duke, good wench.

LEONORA

    I do most heedfully. (*to the Duke*) My gracious lord,   85
    Let me be so unmanner'd to request
    He would not farther press me with persuasions
    O'th' instant hour, but have the gentle patience
    To bury this keen suit till I shake hands
    With my old sorrows –

CAMILLO   Why dost look at me?   90
    Alas! I cannot help thee.

LEONORA   And but weep
    A farewell to my murder'd Julio –

CAMILLO

    Blessing be with thy soul whene'er it leaves thee!

LEONORA

    For such sad rites must be perform'd, my lord,
    Ere I can love again. Maids that have lov'd,   95
    If they be worth that noble testimony,
    Wear their loves here, my lord – here, in their hearts –
    Deep, deep within; not in their eyes, or accents.
    Such may be slipp'd away, or with two tears
    Wash'd out of all remembrance: mine, no physic   100
    But time, or death, can cure.

HENRIQUEZ

    You make your own conditions, and I seal them

---

87 **He** Henriquez

88 **instant hour** Fletcher and Massinger specify immediacy using this phrase in *LPr* 1.1.203. It is found frequently in the plays of Theobald's time; he himself reuses it in *Happy Captive*, 3.9, p. 40.

89 **keen suit** eager request. The phrase is unique to *DF*.

89–90 **shake hands / With** part with, clear away

92 **Julio** requires the full three syllables

95 ***Ere** See 1.2.26n.

96 **noble testimony** i.e. the noble designation of being a maid and/or a lover

99 **slipp'd away** easily lost or overlooked; allowed to escape almost unnoticed

100 **physic** medicine

102–3 ***You . . . hand** 1728a has this speech by Henriquez marked as an aside, but it seems more likely that what Henriquez says has to be clearly heard by Camillo and the Duke, especially since the former completes his half-line. On the other hand, it meets with no response.

84] *Kennedy; prose 1728a*   85 SD] *this edn; after* Lord, *1728a*   95 Ere] *(E'er)*

Thus on your virtuous hand.

CAMILLO   Well, wench, thy equal
Shall not be found in haste, I give thee that.
Thou art a right one, ev'ry inch. Thy father   105
(For, without doubt, that snuff never begot thee)
Was some choice fellow, some true gentleman.
I give thy mother thanks for't – there's no harm done.
Would I were young again and had but thee,
A good horse under me and a good sword,   110
And thus much for inheritance. [*Snaps his fingers.*]
  [*In the course of this speech*] *Violante offers once or*
  twice to show herself, but goes back.

DUKE   What boy's that,
Has offer'd twice or thrice to break upon us?
I've noted him, and still he falls back fearful.

RODERICK

A little boy, sir, like a shepherd?

DUKE   Yes.

RODERICK

'Tis your page, brother – one that was so, late.   115

---

105 **right one** one who reasons well; or in women, a sincere heart. It is a favourite phrase of Fletcher's, especially as a compliment to a woman, occurring in at least nine of his plays, sometimes on more than one occasion.

106 **snuff** Camillo insults Don Bernard by calling him something like a smouldering end of a candle: an inconsequential thing, a 'has been'. In *KL* 4.6.39, Gloucester speaks of 'My snuff and loathed part of nature' – the end of what time of life remains to him.

111 SD2 *Violante . . . back* Violante's entrance in disguise begins a process of resolution that is typical of Shakespeare's later plays and roman-

tic tragicomedies. *MM* is resolved in similar fashion, as the veiled Mariana slowly reveals circumstances that lead to the unmasking of the villainous Angelo. In *AW*, Bertram is finally brought to accept Helena's status as his wife, through revelations made by Diana. The accusation of Henriquez by a disguised Violante of perfidy that he denies, Violante's leaving the stage to summon a witness, the reading of an incriminating letter, and the re-appearance of Violante as herself are all reminiscent of the situation involving Bertram, the King of France and Bertram's accusers.

112 **Has** who has
113 **still he falls** he keeps falling

103 hand] *this edn;* Hand. [*Aside. 1728a* Well . . . equal] *Kennedy; prose 1728a*   111 SD1] *this edn*   SD2 *In . . . speech*] *this edn*   show] *(shew)*   114] *Kennedy; prose 1728a*

HENRIQUEZ

    My page! What page?

RODERICK   E'en so he says, your page;

    And more, and worse, you stole him from his friends

    And promis'd him preferment.

HENRIQUEZ   I, preferment!

RODERICK

    And on some slight occasion let him slip

    Here on these mountains, where he had been starv'd,   120

    Had not my people found him as we travell'd.

    This was not handsome, brother.

HENRIQUEZ   You are merry.

RODERICK

    You'll find it sober truth.

DUKE   If so, 'tis ill.

HENRIQUEZ

    'Tis fiction all, sir. Brother, you must please

    To look some other fool to put these tricks on;   125

    They are too obvious. – Please your grace, give leave

    T'admit the boy. If he know me and say

    I stole him from his friends and cast him off,

    Know me no more. Brother, pray do not wrong me.

Enter VIOLANTE [*in boy's clothes*].

---

120 **had been starv'd** would have been
frozen, famished
121 **my people** presumably the servants
with whom Roderick is travelling.
Roderick appears to travel alone in
the play we see. Theobald possibly
cut down a more elaborate train in an
earlier version. It is equally possible to
argue that whereas he enters alone, he
may have a retinue nearby.

122 **You are merry** Henriquez suggests
that his brother is in jest, though
Roderick's response (*sober truth*) may
imply intoxication.
125 **look** search out; in this grammatical
construction, 'look some other fool', it
appears to be unique to *DF*.
129.1 It is unclear what motivates Violante
to enter at exactly the right moment.
(See the discussion on p. 30.)

116 E'en] *(Ev'n)*   118] *Kennedy; prose 1728a*   129.1 *in boy's clothes*] *this edn*

RODERICK

    Here is the boy. If he deny this to you,   130

    Then I have wrong'd you.

DUKE   Hear me: what's thy name, boy?

VIOLANTE

    Florio, an't like your grace.

DUKE   A pretty child.

    Where wast thou born?

VIOLANTE   On t'other side the mountains.

DUKE

    What are thy friends?

VIOLANTE   A father, sir; but poor.

DUKE

    How camest thou hither? How, to leave thy father?   135

VIOLANTE (*pointing to Henriquez*)

    That noble gentleman pleas'd once to like me

    And, not to lie, so much to dote upon me

    That with his promises he won my youth

    And duty from my father: him I follow'd.

RODERICK

    How say you now, brother?

CAMILLO   Ay, my lord, how say you?   140

HENRIQUEZ

    As I have life and soul, 'tis all a trick, sir.

    I never saw the boy before.

VIOLANTE   O sir,

    Call not your soul to witness in a wrong:

    And 'tis not noble in you to despise

---

132 **Florio** rarely used character name in Jacobean or Caroline plays, though one occurrence is in Ford's celebrated *'Tis Pity She's a Whore* (1632). It may be relevant that John Florio was the Italian tutor to Shakespeare's patron the Earl of Southampton and pos-sibly to Shakespeare himself (see Bate, 55–7). If Shakespeare had any first-hand knowledge of Spanish and could read *Don Quixote* in the original, it may have come from him.

134 **but poor** merely a poor man

136 SD] *this edn; after* me, *1728a*

What you have made thus. If I lie, let justice   145
Turn all her rods upon me.

DUKE   Fie, Henriquez;
There is no trace of cunning in this boy.

CAMILLO
A good boy! [*to Violante*] Be not fearful; speak thy
    mind, child.
Nature, sure, meant thou shouldst have been a wench –
And then't had been no marvel he had bobb'd thee.   150

DUKE
Why did he put thee from him?

VIOLANTE   That to me
Is yet unknown, sir. For my faith he could not;
I never did deceive him. For my service
He had no just cause; what my youth was able,
My will still put in act to please my master.   155
I cannot steal, therefore that can be nothing
To my undoing; no, nor lie. My breeding,
Though it be plain, is honest.

DUKE   Weep not, child.

CAMILLO   This lord has abused men, women and children
    already. What farther plot he has, the devil knows.   160

DUKE
If thou canst bring a witness of thy wrong
(Else it would be injustice to believe thee,
He having sworn against it), thou shalt have,
I bind it with my honour, satisfaction
To thine own wishes.

VIOLANTE   I desire no more, sir.   165
I have a witness, and a noble one,

---

150 **then't had** then it would have
   bobb'd fooled, deceived, cheated.
   The word may have carried a sexual
   innuendo, since 'dry bob' was an
expression meaning to copulate without emission.
156–7 **nothing ... undoing**   cannot
   contribute anything to my downfall

148 SD] *this edn*

For truth and honesty.

RODERICK   Go, bring him hither.   *Exit Violante.*

HENRIQUEZ

This lying boy will take him to his heels,
And leave me slander'd.

RODERICK   No; I'll be his voucher.

HENRIQUEZ

Nay then 'tis plain: this is confederacy.   170

RODERICK

That he has been an agent in your service
Appears from this. Here is a letter, brother
(Produc'd, perforce, to give him credit with me),
The writing, yours; the matter, love; for so,
He says, he can explain it.

CAMILLO   Then, belike,   175
A young he-bawd.

HENRIQUEZ

This forgery confounds me!

DUKE   Read it, Roderick.

RODERICK *(Reads.)   Our prudence should now teach us to
forget what our indiscretion has committed. I have already
made one step towards this wisdom –*   180

---

169 **voucher** 'One who vouches for
the truth or correctness of a fact or
statement or corroborates another
person in this respect; an author or
literary work serving this purpose'
(*OED n.*[2] 1a). One example is dated
1612; otherwise all other instances
in *OED* are post-Restoration. The
word does occur, however, in *Cym*,
where Iachimo, intent on deceiving
Posthumus and seeing the mole on
Imogen's left breast, says 'Here's a
voucher, / Stronger than ever law
could make' (2.2.39–40). Theobald has
this term in *Fatal Secret*, Act 5, p. 55.
170 **confederacy** The word occurs in
Shakespeare and Fletcher's *H8* 1.2.2–
3, where the King thanks Wolsey for

preserving him: 'I stood i'th' level / Of
a full-charged confederacy'. In *MND*
3.2.192, Helena speaks of Hermia as
being 'one of this confederacy'.
175–6 **Then . . . he-bawd** Camillo's role
here, preserving a low, bawdy idiom,
somewhat resembles that of Lucio at
the ending of *MM*.
176 **This forgery** presumably the story
being concocted by Roderick and
Violante, rather than the letter that
he has not yet read. Cf. 2.1.13 (see
n.): this is another line that would be
self-reflexive if Theobald had forged
the play.
178–80 The letter is read in Violante's
absence, perhaps for reasons of propriety.

177] *this edn; prose 1728a*

HENRIQUEZ

Hold, sir. (*aside*) My very words to Violante!

DUKE

Go on.

HENRIQUEZ   My gracious father, give me pardon;
I do confess I some such letter wrote
(The purport all too trivial for your ear),
But how it reach'd this young dissembler's hands   185
Is what I cannot solve. For, on my soul
And by the honours of my birth and house,
The minion's face till now I never saw.

RODERICK

Run not too far in debt on protestation.
Why should you do a child this wrong?

HENRIQUEZ   Go to.   190
Your friendships past warrant not this abuse.
If you provoke me thus, I shall forget
What you are to me. This is a mere practice
And villainy to draw me into scandal.

RODERICK

No more; you are a boy. Here comes a witness,   195
Shall prove you so. No more.

---

188 **minion** hanger-on, follower, under-
ling. *OED n.*[1] A.I 1a states that in
earlier uses the word had homosexual
connotations. In this scene, Camillo
makes such insinuations in 159–60,
possibly picked up by Henriquez in
the insulting word *minion*.

189 **Run . . . debt** don't overstretch your
credit

193 **practice** underhand, treacherous
scheme or plot; machination; conspir-
acy. In *MM* 5.1.110 and 126, the Duke
applies the term to Isabella's conduct,
and Angelo picks it up at 238. Here,
Roderick turns the term on Henriquez
at 199.

195 **you . . . boy** There are very many
Shakespearean analogues for this dismissive insult, Tullus Aufidius's sear-
ing dismissal of Coriolanus as 'thou
boy of tears' in *Cor* 5.6.101 being
amongst the most significant. Several
examples occur in *AW*: 2.3.152; 3.2.26;
4.3.211, 216, 294. As here, they usually relate to presumptuous young
men of the upper class. Fletcher and
Beaumont deploy it in *CR* 4.5.76.
It comes down to Restoration plays
such as Lee's *Theodosius* (1680) and
Otway's *The Soldier's Fortune* (1681),
but appears to be obsolete by the 18th
century.

181 SD] *this edn; after Violante! 1728a*

Enter JULIO, *disguised;* VIOLANTE *as a woman.*

HENRIQUEZ   Another rascal!

DUKE

Hold!

HENRIQUEZ (*seeing Violante*) Ha!

DUKE   What's here?

HENRIQUEZ (*aside*)

By all my sins, the injur'd Violante.

RODERICK

Now, sir, whose practice breaks?

CAMILLO (*to Henriquez*)   Is this a page?

RODERICK

One that has done him service,   200

And he has paid her for't, but broke his covenant.

VIOLANTE

My lord, I come not now to wound your spirit.

Your pure affection dead, which first betray'd me.

My claim die with it! Only let me not

Shrink to the grave with infamy upon me.   205

Protect my virtue, though it hurt your faith,

And my last breath shall speak Henriquez noble.

HENRIQUEZ [*aside*]

What a fierce conflict shame and wounded honour

Raise in my breast – but honour shall o'ercome.

She looks as beauteous and as innocent   210

As when I wrong'd her. [*to Violante*] Virtuous Violante –

Too good for me – dare you still love a man

200–1 **service . . . paid** with sexual undertones

203–4 **Your . . . it** Since your love (*affection*), by which I was first betrayed, is dead, let my claim to that love also die.

205 **Shrink . . . grave** Rowe gives the expression 'shrink to my grave' to

his character Altamont in the closing of Act 4 of *The Fair Penitent* (1714), p. 58.

207 **speak** in this transitive sense, meaning declare, proclaim

209 **shall** might have the Jacobean force of 'must'

197] *this edn; prose 1728a* SD] *this edn; after* Ha! *1728a* 198 SD] *this edn; after Violante. 1728a* 199 SD] *this edn; after* Page? *1728a* 208 SD] *this edn* 211 SD] *this edn*

So faithless as I am? I know you love me.
Thus, thus and thus [*kissing her*] I print my vow'd
    repentance:
Let all men read it here. My gracious father,   215
Forgive, and make me rich with your consent,
This is my wife; no other would I choose,
Were she a queen.

CAMILLO

Here's a new change. Bernard looks dull upon't.

HENRIQUEZ

And fair Leonora, from whose virgin arms   220
I forc'd my wrong'd friend Julio, O forgive me.
Take home your holy vows and let him have 'em
That has deserv'd them. O that he were here,
That I might own the baseness of my wrong
And purpos'd recompense. My Violante,   225
You must again be widow'd: for I vow
A ceaseless pilgrimage, ne'er to know joy,
Till I can give it to the injur'd Julio.

CAMILLO

This almost melts me. But my poor lost boy –

RODERICK

I'll stop that voyage, brother.
[*Presents Julio still in disguise.*] Gentle lady,   230
What think you of this honest man?

---

214 **vow'd repentance** The phrase appears only once before *DF*, in *The Spanish Gipsy* (1623), 1.3.77, now attributed to Middleton (Middleton, *Works*, p. 1730).

216–17 **Forgive . . . wife** i.e. if the Duke forgives, then Henriquez will marry Violante

219 **Bernard . . . upon't** Don Bernard appears still to entertain hopes that Henriquez will marry his daughter.

220 **Leonora** here has three syllables, and at 237, 248

222 **holy vows** The audience has not seen Leonora give any holy vows, though it can perhaps be inferred that she intends to join the convent. The phrase may simply be Henriquez's reference to a supposed betrothal.

224 **own** own up to

231 **What . . . man?** It is difficult to tell why Roderick asks Leonora this question. He is not party to the plot device through which the disguised Julio is brought onstage. Perhaps this is further evidence of textual lesions.

214 SD] *this edn*   230 SD] *this edn*   231] *this edn; prose 1728a*

LEONORA   Alas!
My thoughts, my lord, were all employ'd within!
He has a face makes me remember something
I have thought well of. How he looks upon me!
Poor man, he weeps. Ha! Stay, it cannot be –   235
He has his eye, his features, shape and gesture –
Would he would speak.

JULIO (*Throws off his disguise.*) Leonora!

LEONORA   Yes, 'tis he.
O ecstasy of joy!   (*They embrace.*)

CAMILLO   Now, what's the matter?

RODERICK
Let 'em alone; they're almost starv'd for kisses.

CAMILLO
Stand forty foot off; no man trouble 'em.   240
Much good may't do your hearts! What is he, lord,
What is he?

RODERICK
A certain son of yours.

CAMILLO   The devil he is!

RODERICK
If he be the devil, that devil must call you father.

CAMILLO
By your leave a little, ho. Are you my Julio?   245

JULIO [*Kneels.*]
My duty tells me so, sir,
Still on my knees. But love engross'd me all.
[*Rises and embraces Leonora.*] O Leonora, do I once
    more hold thee?

---

237 *Would See 3.2.29n.
238 Now . . . matter This is simply an
    interjection, or suggests that Camillo
    does not see well. Cf. 7–10.
240 forty foot off The reference here
    may be to the distance spectators keep

from the scaffold.
245 There may be a naive internal rhyme
    here (*ho/Julio*), further characterizing
    Camillo as a simple, possibly rural,
    character; cf. 43–4 (see n.). The dif-
    ficult scansion heightens the effect.

237 Would] ('Would) SD] *this edn; after* Leonora, – *1728a* 246 SD] *this edn* 249 SD] *this edn*

CAMILLO   Nay, to't again. I will not hinder you a kiss.
(*Leaps.*) 'Tis he –   250

LEONORA

The righteous pow'rs at length have crown'd our loves.
Think, Julio, from the storm that's now o'erblown,
Though sour affliction combat hope awhile,
When lovers swear true faith the list'ning angels
Stand on the golden battlements of heav'n   255
And waft their vows to the eternal throne.
Such were our vows, and so are they repaid.

DUKE

E'en as you are, we'll join your hands together.
A providence above our pow'r rules all.
(*to Henriquez*) Ask him forgiveness, boy.

JULIO   He has it, sir.   260
The fault was love's, not his.

251–7 Leonora's speech shows much evidence of Theobald's hand in its drafting. The Providential notes sounded in this speech and at 259 are shared with the endings of *Cym* and *TNK*. Reconciliation of friendship recalls *TGV*.

251 **righteous pow'rs** The phrase occurs in *Orestes*, Act 3, p. 38, where Iphigenia says, 'You righteous Pow'rs, that from your awful Thrones / Look down with Pity'. 'Righteous' is a favourite adjective of Theobald's, qualifying 'Powers' again in his adaptation of *Richard II* and in *Perseus*, and occurring some 15 times in his plays.

253 **sour affliction** The phrase occurs in *2H6* 3.2.301.
affliction The phrase 'stern Affliction' is found in *Fatal Secret* (4.1, p. 36); in *Perfidious Brother*, 'Affliction' is 'sharp' (4.1, p. 42). The word is used nine times in Theobald's dramatic writing.

255 **battlements** The phrase 'Castle's tatter'd Battlements' occurs in *Richard II*, Act 2, p. 16.

256 **waft** The verb is common in Theobald, occurring twice in *Orestes*, once collocated with 'throne': 'To waft the Hero to his native Throne?' (Act 2, p. 28); and on six other occasions in his dramatic writing.
eternal throne The phrase occurs in *The Rape of Proserpine* (1727), scene 2, p. 3.

259 Cf. *TNK* 5.4.113–15, 120–2, 131–6.

260–5 **forgiveness . . . brother** The ending here resembles that of *TNK*, where the dying Arcite blesses Palamon's union with Emilia, amidst a welter of mutual forgiveness, though brotherhood is not involved: 'PALAMON Arcite, if thy heart, / Thy worthy, manly heart, be yet unbroken, / Give me thy last words. I am Palamon, / One that yet loves thee dying. ARCITE Take Emilia / And, with her, all the world's joy. Reach thy hand; / Farewell. I have told my last hour. I was false / Yet never treacherous. Forgive me, cousin' (5.4.87–93).

250 SD] *this edn; after* he – *1728a*   260 SD] *this edn; after* Boy. *1728a*

HENRIQUEZ   Brave, gen'rous Julio!
   I knew thy nobleness of old, and priz'd it
   Till passion made me blind. Once more, my friend,
   Share in a heart that ne'er shall wrong thee more.
   And brother –
RODERICK   This embrace cuts off excuses.   265
DUKE

   I must, in part, repair my son's offence.
   At your best leisure, Julio, know our Court;
   And, Violante (for I know you now),
   I have a debt to pay. Your good old father
   Once when I chas'd the boar preserv'd my life.   270
   For that good deed, and for your virtue's sake,
   Though your descent be low, call me your father.
   A match drawn out of honesty and goodness
   Is pedigree enough. Are you all pleas'd?
     Gives her to Henriquez.

CAMILLO
   All.
HENRIQUEZ, DON BERNARD   All, sir.
JULIO   All.   275
DUKE

   And I not least. We'll now return to court;
   And that short travel, and your loves completed,
   Shall, as I trust, for life restrain these wand'rings.
   There, the solemnity and grace I'll do

268 This very late placing of Violante and (at 269–70) her family keeps her status usefully vague throughout the action. She now has social and moral credentials for her future with Henriquez.

272 **Though . . . low** The point about Violante's birth begins at 134 and 157–8, where she herself says 'My breeding, / Though it be plain, is hon-est.' Polixenes makes similar remarks about Perdita in *WT* 4.4.156–7: 'This is the prettiest low-born lass that ever / Ran on the green-sward' – though in her case they are not accurate.

278 **these wand'rings** Henriquez's moral *wand'rings* as well as an ostensible ban on future travel in remote places. The word is being set up for use in the final line.

275] *this edn; 1728a lines* All. / Sir, / All. /   SP2, 3] *Henr. and D.Bern. linked with brace*

Your sev'ral nuptials shall approve my joy,   280
   And make griev'd lovers that your story read
   Wish true love's wand'rings may like yours succeed.

Curtain falls.

FINIS

281–2 This final couplet is not indented in 1728a, most probably because the last line fills the measure and a turnover line would look inelegant. See 1.2.76–7n.

EPILOGUE

Written by a friend

Spoken by MRS OLDFIELD

Well, heaven defend us from these ancient plays,
These moral bards of good Queen Bess's days!
They write from virtue's laws and think no further,
But draw a rape as dreadful as a murder.
You modern wits, more deeply vers'd in nature,   5
Can tip the wink, to tell us you know better;
As who should say, ''Tis no such killing matter –

EPILOGUE The Epilogue was added, presumably, by Theobald himself. 18th-century epilogues are, to modern ears, remarkably irreverent. They do not make any attempt to preserve the mood of the play they conclude. Following tragedies, for example, they sometime comically 'resurrect' the corpses created by the play; and they do not scruple to make bawdy jokes even when closing tragedies. Here, the use of heroic couplets creates an immediate contrast with the play itself, setting up a sparkling, fashionable tone. As the comparison between Shakespeare's age and the contemporary period proceeds, however, it becomes clear that despite the rakish *attitudes* of modern life, Jacobean actions spoke louder than modern words.

0.2 MRS OLDFIELD Anne Oldfield (1683–1730) was supposedly discovered by George Farquhar reading a play behind the bar of the Mitre Tavern, St James's. She joined the Drury Lane company in 1699. From 1711 onwards, she was continuously employed there, even challenging for a management role, though that was denied to her on gender grounds.

Taking over the mantle of Susanna Verbruggen and seeing off the rivalry of Anne Bracegirdle, Oldfield was the unchallenged doyenne of the stage by the 1720s, enjoying massive success as Lady Betty Modish in Cibber's *The Careless Husband* (1704). Cibber says of her that: 'Had her Birth plac'd her in a higher Rank of Life, she had certainly appear'd, in reality, what in this Play she only, excellently, acted, an agreeably gay Woman of Quality, a little too conscious of her natural Attractions. I have often seen her, in private Societies, where Women of the best Rank might have borrow'd some part of her Behaviour, without the least Diminution of their . . . Dignity' (*Apology*, 1.177). She became exceptionally wealthy, and merited burial in Westminster Abbey (*ODNB*).

5–11 The rhymes in this section, in the triplet – *nature/better/matter* – and in the four lines that follow, call attention to their irregularity. Something could be made of this in delivery. Polysyllabic rhymes such as *intention/ comprehension* at 20–1 are included for their comic potential.

6 **tip the wink** slyly signal

Epilogue   5–7] *marked with brace as rhyming triplet 1728a*

We've heard old stories told, and yet ne'er wonder'd,
Of many a prude that has endur'd a hundred:
And Violante grieves, or we're mistaken,   10
Not because ravish'd, but because – forsaken.'
    Had this been written to the modern stage
Her manners had been copied from the age.
Then, though she had been once a little wrong,
She still had had the grace to've held her tongue,   15
And after all with downcast looks been led
Like any virgin to the bridal bed.
There, if the good man question'd her misdoing,
She'd stop him short: 'Pray, who made you so knowing?
What, doubt my virtue! What's your base intention?   20
Sir, that's a point above your comprehension.'
    Well, heav'n be prais'd, the virtue of our times
Secures us from our gothic grandsires' crimes.
Rapes, magic, new opinions, which before
Have fill'd our chronicles, are now no more: 25
And this reforming age may justly boast
That dreadful sin polygamy is lost.
So far from multiplying wives, 'tis known

---

9 **prude** 'A person (in early use esp. a
   woman) who has or affects an attitude
   of extreme propriety or modesty, esp.
   in sexual matters; an excessively prim
   person' (*OED* prude A. *n.*). The earliest entry in *OED* is 1676.

11 **forsaken** Violante points out that she
   objects not to losing her virtue but
   to being abandoned by her undoer.
   This is in the manner of 18th-century
   epilogues, which are frequently bawdy
   burlesques of the serious main action.

13 **had been** would have been

15 **still ... grace** would have had the
   good sense to continue to keep quiet

16 **been led** Perhaps the sense here of the
   Latin *in matrimoniam ducere* (to lead

   into matrimony)

20–1 See 5–11n.

23 **gothic** belonging to the 'dark ages',
   uncivilized

27–8 **polygamy ... multiplying**
   Contemporary audiences might pick
   up an allusion to the famous opening
   of Dryden's *Absalom and Achitophel*
   (1681): 'In pious times, ere priest-
   craft did begin, / Before polygamy
   was made a sin; / When man on
   many multiplied his kind, / Ere one
   to one was cursedly confined' (1–4).
   For those who did, the repositioning
   of monogamy as due to lack of energy
   in dealing with exhausting wives will
   strike home as a witty thrust.

18 misdoing] *(Mis-doing)*

Our husbands find they've work enough with one.
Then, as for rapes, those dangerous days are past: 30
Our dapper sparks are seldom in such haste.

   In Shakespeare's age the English youth inspir'd,
Lov'd as they fought by him and beauty fir'd.
'Tis yours to crown the Bard, whose magic strain
Could charm the heroes of that glorious reign   35
Which humbled to the dust the pride of Spain.

30 **dangerous** The metre seems to require 'dang'rous'.

31 **dapper sparks** neat, well-dressed young men of foppish character, with connotations of effeminacy

34 **Bard** The capital (retained from 1728a) reflects the process of Bardolatry that was entering its initial phase at this time.

36 **pride of Spain** Anti-Spanish sentiment, ascribed to Shakespeare's era, sorts oddly with a play set in Spain and based on the work of a Spanish author.

It reflects contemporary politics. In 1725, responding to the threat posed by the treaty of Vienna (1724) between Spain and the Habsburg emperor, Lord Townshend concluded the alliance of Hanover with France and Prussia. For the next three years Europe organized itself into two great armed camps, and a short war broke out between Britain and Spain in 1726–7, a war not entirely popular because many Whigs believed in the necessity of allying with Austria to resist French aggression.

34–6] *marked with brace as rhyming triplet 1728a*   35 Could] *(Cou'd)*

APPENDIX 1

LEWIS THEOBALD AND ALEXANDER POPE

The animosity that eventually developed between Lewis Theobald and Alexander Pope[1] had not always been evident in their lengthy relationship, which was mutually supportive after they first met in around 1713–14. In the years 1715 and 1717, capitalizing on the success of the *Spectator*, Theobald had produced a tri-weekly cultural magazine called *The Censor*. Number 33 for 5 January 1717 was fulsome in its praise for what had by then been published of Pope's *Iliad* translation – despite the fact that at one time Theobald was under contract to Pope's printer Bernard Lintot to translate the *Odyssey* himself (see Jones, 8). As Michael Suarez has shown, Pope contributed two poems to a miscellany edited by Theobald in 1721 entitled *The Grove*, and went on to subscribe for four royal paper copies of the collection (Suarez). When, in 1726, Theobald published his aggressively titled *Shakespeare Restored: or a specimen of the many errors, as well committed, as unamended, by Mr Pope in his late edition of this poet*, Pope must have been deeply shocked. Although the introduction expresses veneration for Pope, distinguishing between those editors who simply transmit and multiply earlier errors, and Pope's edition prepared for Jacob Tonson the Younger, which is based on the desire to *revise*,

---

1 For the benefit of readers, I have recapitulated in this appendix the introductory material supplied on pp. 66–70.

nevertheless Theobald's comments have a thinly veiled ironic tone that quietly subverts the achievement of Pope's edition and his premises as an editor. Theobald quotes Pope's 'religious Abhorrence of all Innovation' and comments:

> I cannot help thinking this Gentleman's *Modesty* in this Point too *nice* and *blameable*; and that what he is pleased to call a *religious Abhorrence* of *Innovation*, is downright *Superstition*: Neither can I be of Opinion, that the Writings of Shakespeare are so *venerable*, as that we should be excommunicated from good Sense, for daring to *innovate properly*; or that we ought to be as cautious of altering *their* Text, as we would That of the *sacred Writings*. And yet even They, we see, have admitted of some Thousands of *various Readings*; and would have a great many more, had not Dr. Bentley some particular Reasons for not prosecuting his Undertaking upon the *New Testament*, as he propos'd.
>
> (*Shakespeare Restored*, iv)

Throughout this work, Pope is sneered at and mocked as an inadequate editor who failed to collate his edition with the early quartos. Typical enough is the following on page 75:

> No Body shall persuade me that Mr. *Pope* could be awake, and with his Eyes open, and revising a Book which was to be publish'd under his Name, yet let an Error, like the following, escape his Observation and Correction.

Famously, the analysis of Pope's *Hamlet* edition that follows, and the smaller-fount Appendix giving a sample of what Theobald could do to the rest of Pope's edition – the whole running to close on 200 pages – left readers in no doubt that in him, Pope had met a powerful cultural adversary. Hard on the heels of *Shakespeare Restored*, *Double Falsehood* can clearly be seen as a bid for cultural ownership of the supremely valuable literary property that Shakespeare had become.

The second Preface to *Double Falsehood* is an unmistakeable self-puff, probably directed at Tonson, publisher of Pope's Shakespeare, and in whose gift it was to appoint his successor.

By 1727, Pope was actively involved in the Opposition cell organized by his friend Henry St John, Lord Bolingbroke, based in the latter's residence at Dawley Farm, Middlesex. From there issued the *Craftsman*, which, by late 1727, had established the satirical habit of referring to Robert Walpole as Harlequin and Horatio Walpole as Punch. A particularly fine *Craftsman* issue, number 74 for Saturday 2 December 1727, offers a pantomime scenario entitled 'The Mock Minister; or, Harlequin a Statesman' that goes through Robert Walpole's career as if it were one of Theobald's pantomimes. From 1723 onwards, John Rich mounted, in collaboration with Theobald, hugely successful pantomimes at Lincoln's Inn Fields theatre – entertainments that staged dance versions of mythological stories diversified by comic harlequinades and lavish special effects. The goings-on of Rich (who was, astonishingly, the dedicatee of *Shakespeare Restored*) and Theobald, who, the *Craftsman* implies, have succumbed to the lure of government gold and are actively promoting Walpole's bread and circuses policy, come under fierce scrutiny.[1] To Pope and his associates, *Double Falsehood* was an especially valuable target – its publication leaving Theobald and his government sponsors clearly vulnerable. His first direct attack on the play was published in *Peri Bathous, or The Art of Sinking in Poetry* in the third volume of *Miscellanies in Prose and Verse* by Pope and Jonathan Swift, on 8 March 1728, in the same month as John Watts published the second issue of the play itself. In chapter 7, he singled out and misquoted the line 'None but Itself can be its Parallel' from the play (3.1.17) as an unrivalled instance of bathos – Pope prints '*None but* himself *can be his* parallel' – and two further lines from a play that Pope wilfully

---

1   Caleb D'Anvers [Nicholas Amhurst] (ed.), *The Craftsman: Being a Critique on the Times. By Caleb D'Anvers, of Gray's Inn, Esq; Vol. II. For the year 1727* (1728), 324–36.

mistitled *Double Distress* are also mocked.[1] Also published in this third (1728) volume of the Pope/Swift *Miscellanies* was an early version of what would later become the famous Atticus portrait in the *Epistle to Dr Arbuthnot* (1735). This 'Fragment of a Satire' must have etched itself on Theobald's consciousness, relegating as it does all of his outstanding contributions to the new science of verbal criticism and scholarly editing to pedantic quibbling devoid of genuine taste or judgement. Here Pope first forms the contraction of his name down to 'Tibbald', so potent as a satirical weapon in its assonance with 'piddling':

> Should some more sober Criticks come abroad,
> If wrong, I smile; if right, I kiss the Rod.
> Pains, Reading, Study, are their just Pretence,
> And all they want is Spirit, Taste, and Sense.
> *Commas* and *Points* they set exactly right;
> And 'twere a Sin to rob them of their *Mite*.
> In future Ages how their Fame will spread,
> For routing *Triplets* and restoring *ed.*
> Yet ne'er one Sprig of Laurel graced those Ribbalds,
> From sanguine *Sew[ell]* down to piddling *T[ibbald]s.*
> Who thinks he *reads* when he but *scans* and *spells*,
> A Word-catcher, that lives on Syllables.
> Yet ev'n this Creature may some Notice claim,
> Wrapt round and sanctified with *Shakespear's* name;
> Pretty, in Amber to observe the forms
> Of Hairs, or Straws, or Dirt, or Grubs, or Worms:
> The *Thing*, we know, is neither rich nor rare,
> But wonder how the Devil it got there.
>
> (Pope, 'Satire', 129–30)

---

1 Pope, *Peri Bathous*, 3.31. Pope's other selections from *Double Falsehood* are, in chapter 11 under 'Hyperbole or the Impossible', these lines from 1.3: 'Th' obscureness of her birth / Cannot eclipse the lustre of her eyes, / Which make her all one light' (8–10); and in ch. 12 another line, from 2.2, is chosen to illustrate the 'Buskin, or *stately*' style: 'Wax! render up thy trust' (25). (pp. 52, 70).

Theobald replied to Pope in an article in *Mist's Weekly Journal* for 27 April 1728, in which he accused Pope of personal malice towards him brought about by his being 'right, in the Main, in my Corrections' of his Shakespeare. He considers each of the three instances adduced in *Peri Bathous* as examples of ridiculous rhetoric: in the case of 'Wax! Render up thy trust' (2.2.25), the apostrophe uttered by Violante before she opens the letter from Henriquez, Theobald is able to offer two parallel examples from Shakespeare – from *King Lear* and from *Cymbeline* (which I have cited in the commentary). Finally, Theobald takes on the line that Pope had misquoted as '*None but* himself *can be his* Parallel', misquotes it in his turn as '*Nought but* himself *can be his* Parallel', and goes on to defend it in a statement of importance for the question of authorship:

> If this were such *Nonsense*, as Mr. *Pope* would willingly
> have it, it would be a very bad Plea for me to alledge,
> as the Truth is, that the Line is in *Shakespeare*'s old
> Copy; for I might have suppress'd it.

('Reply to Pope', 46)

He goes on to defend the line 'None but Itself' by reference to what was doubtless intended to be an impressive series of parallel examples of similarly self-reflexive lines in the *Amphitryo* of Plautus and in *Romeo and Juliet*, *The Winter's Tale* and *Hamlet* (47).[1] Theobald's learning displayed here, however, simply made him more vulnerable to the stereotype of the pedantic trifler, whose obscure knowledge blinded him to genuine cultural values that Pope's mighty *Dunciad* would fix upon him later in the year. To some, misquoting the line that he simultaneously claimed to be 'in *Shakespeare*'s old Copy' might be a sinister sign: Freudian evidence, perhaps, of malfeasance. There may be nothing Freudian or otherwise remarkable in Theobald's reliance on imperfect memory, however: he was surely not the

---

1   See further Appendix 3.

first or the last writer guilty of unintentionally misquoting either his own or others' work. When Samuel Johnson quotes his own writing to illustrate his *Dictionary* definitions, they are usually inaccurate in similarly minor ways.

The Dunciad was published in May 1728 with Lewis Theobald as the hero of the mock-epic, the individual who instantiates its central values as the epic hero does of the classical epic. In Book 3, lines 223–72, Theobald's entire writing career is surveyed. The ghost of Elkanah Settle shows Theobald the creation of a new world of Dulness. This image of anti-Creation is the world of Rich's theatre at Lincoln's Inn Fields; its physics are the topsy-turvy laws of Theobald's theatrical effects as devised in *The Rape of Proserpine*, *Harlequin a Sorcerer* and other contemporary pantomimes and farces. Settle informs the astonished Theobald that he himself is the new Creator, borrowing for the purpose the line that Theobald's article in *Mist's Weekly Journal* had tried to defend:

> And are these wonders, Son, to thee unknown?
> Unknown to thee? These wonders are thy own.
> For works like these let deathless Journals tell,
> 'None but Thy self can be thy parallel.'
>
> (Pope, *Dunciad*, 3.269–72)

By April 1729, when *The Dunciad Variorum* appeared with its endless critical apparatus, this line had gained a lengthy explication which not only ridiculed Theobald's heavy-handedness as a textual editor, but also implied that the play was a forgery, an accusation particularly hurtful because he was due a benefit performance of *Double Falsehood* on 21 April. The first note in the 1729 *Dunciad* reads as follows:

> 272. *None but thy self can be thy parallel*] A marvellous line of *Theobald*; unless the Play call'd the *Double Falshood* be, (as he would have it believed) *Shakespear*'s: But whether this line be his or not, he proves *Shakespear*

to have written as bad, (which methinks in an author
for whom he has a Veneration almost *rising to idolatry*,
might have been concealed) as for example,
   Try what *Repentance* can: What can it not?
   But what can it, when one cannot *repent?*
         – For *Cogitation*
   Resides not in the Man who does not *think*. &c.
                        MIST'S JOURN.
It is granted they are all of a piece, and no man doubts
but herein he is able to imitate *Shakespear*.

This note refers to the phrase in Theobald's preface to *Double
Falsehood* that speaks of his veneration for Shakespeare, and then
goes on to call that in question because in the article in *Mist's
Weekly Journal* discussed above, he had presumed to relate lines
in his play to some of Shakespeare's weaker lines in *Hamlet* and
in *The Winter's Tale*.[1] Immediately after this annotation, there
is printed another even lengthier one attributed to Martinus
Scriblerus, the mock-learned pedant who is supposed to be
the general editor for the entire *Dunciad* project. This makes
more extensive reference to Theobald's arguments in favour of
Shakespeare's authorship, by reductively paraphrasing them;
and it goes on then to apply Theobald's cherished methods
of conjectural emendation to *Double Falsehood* itself. Overall,
the note is a parody of Theobald's own editorial methods, as is
clearest in the reference to the rhetorical figure of anadiplosis,
which had been cited by Theobald in *Shakespeare Restored*.

   272. The former Annotator seeming to be of opinion that
   the *Double Falshood* is not *Shakespear*'s; it is but justice

---

1 The quoted lines refer to Claudius's speech in *Ham* 3.3.65–6 and to Leontes' in *WT* 1.2.271–2.
   In later editions of the 1729 *Dunciad*, Pope clearly came to think that he had allowed too much to
   Theobald by insinuating that there actually were weak passages in Shakespeare. The 1736 edition
   of Pope's *Works* alters the last sentence of that annotation to: 'But this last line is no man's non-
   sense but *Tibbald*'s, as he might have found, had he read the Context – who does not think / My
   wife is slippery – *Cymbeline*.' Pope's authority is not enhanced by the fact that he misattributes the
   passage to *Cymbeline*. See Pope, *Works*, 4.213.

to give Mr. *Theobald*'s Arguments to the contrary: First that the MS. was above sixty years old; secondly, that once Mr. *Betterton* had it, or he hath heard so; thirdly, that some-body told him the author gave it to a bastard-daughter of his: But fourthly and above all, 'that he has a *great mind* every thing that is good in our tongue *should be* Shakespeare's.' I allow these reasons to be truly critical; but what I am infinitely concern'd at is, that so many Errors have escaped the learned Editor: a few whereof we shall here amend, out of a much greater number, as an instance of our regard to this *dear Relick*.

Act 1. Scene 1.

> I have his letters of a modern date,
> Wherein by *Julio*, *good Camillo*'s son
> (Who as he says shall follow hard upon,
> And whom I with the growing hour expect)
> He doth solicit the return of gold,
> To purchase certain horse that *like him well*. [33–8]

This place is corrupted: the epithet *good* is a meer insignificant expletive, but the alteration of that single word restores a clear light to the whole context, thus,

> I have his letters of a modern date,
> Wherein, by *July*, (by *Camillo*'s son,
> (Who as he *saith*, shall follow hard upon,
> And whom I with the growing hours expect)
> He doth solicit the return of gold.

Here you have not only the *Person* specify'd, by whose hands the return was to be made, but the most necessary part, the *Time*, by which it was required. *Camillo*'s son was to follow hard upon – What? Why upon *July*. – Horse that *like him well*, is very absurd: Read it, without contradiction,

> – Horse, that *he likes well*.

314

ACT 1. at the end.

– I must stoop to gain her,

Throw all my gay *Comparisons* aside,

And turn my proud additions out of service: [1.3.72–4]
saith *Henriquez* of a maiden of low condition, objecting
to his high quality: What have his *Comparisons* here to
do? Correct it boldly,

> Throw all my gay *Caparisons* aside,
> And turn my proud additions out of service

ACT 2. SCENE 1.

All the verse of this Scene is confounded with prose.

– O that a man

Could reason down this *Feaver* of the blood,

Or sooth with *words* the tumult of his heart!

Then *Julio*, I might be *indeed* thy friend. [52–5]

Read – this *fervor* of the blood,

Then *Julio* I might be in *deed* thy friend.
marking the just opposition of deeds and words.

ACT 4. SCENE 1.

How his eyes *shake* fire! – said by *Violante*, [163]
observing how the lustful shepherd looks at her. It
must be, as the sense plainly demands,

– How his eyes *take* fire!

And measure every piece of youth about me!
Ibid. That, tho' I *wore disguises* for some *ends*. [174]
She had but one disguise, and wore it but for one end.
Restore it, with the alteration but of two letters,

> That, tho' I *were disguised* for some *end*.

ACT 4. SCENE 2.

– To oaths no more give credit,

To tears, to vows; false *both!* – [63–4]

False Grammar I'm sure. *Both* can relate but to *two*
things: And see! How easy a change sets it right!
　To tears, to vows, false *troth* –
I could shew you that very word troth, in *Shakespear*
a hundred times.
　Ib. For there is nothing left thee now to look for,
　That can bring *comfort*, but a *quiet grave.* [79–80]
This I fear is of a piece with *None but itself can be its
parallel*: for the grave *puts an end* to all sorrow, it can
then need no *comfort*. Yet let us vindicate *Shakespear*
where we can: I make no doubt he wrote thus,
　For there is nothing left thee now to look for,
　Nothing that can bring *quiet*, but the grave.
Which reduplication of the word gives a much stronger
emphasis to *Violante*'s concern. This figure is called
Anadyplosis. I could shew you a hundred just such in
him, if I had nothing else to do. SCRIBLERUS.

The mock 'Testimonies of authors concerning our poet and
his works', with which the 1729 *Dunciad* begins, collects several
quotations actually or purportedly from Theobald, designed
to show how self-contradictory he is on the subject of Pope.
His praise for Pope's Homer in the *Censor* is cast up to him,
at the same time as he is credited with letters to *Mist's Weekly
Journal* for 30 March and 8 June 1728 in which the translations
are disparaged as well as the Shakespeare edition.[1] Certainly
Theobald was responsible for hastily putting together a pamphlet
called 'Of Mr Pope's taste of Shakespeare' dated 16 April 1729
and superscribed with his private address 'Wyan's-Court in
Great-Russell-Street', in which he rebuts various charges made
in *The Dunciad Variorum*, makes various complaints about Pope's
mealy-mouthed failures to render him any material assistance in
pursuing his career, and concludes:

1　Pope, *Dunciad 4* (1743), 50–69 *passim.*

> The *Publick* should not have been troubled with this State of the Case, had not these Insinuations been industriously propagated at this Crisis, both to hurt my Interest in my *Subscription* for my *Remarks on* SHAKESPEARE ... and in that *Play*, which is designed for my *Benefit* on Monday next in the Theatre at *Drury Lane.*
>
> ('Pope's taste', 41)

Theobald had his defenders in the pamphlet war that followed the publication of *The Dunciad*, but despite his attempts to prevent it Pope's insinuation that he had forged a play and passed it off as Shakespeare caught on. The *Grub Street Journal*, which some considered to be an organ of Pope's, published on 11 November 1731, in parody of Theobald's royal licence, a Bill

> for the ... preventing ... of books ... written, or pretended to be written by any person convicted of death ... Provided, nothing herein contained, shall be construed to prejudice L.T-, Esq; or the heirs of his body, lawfully begotten, in any right or title, which he, or they, may have, or pretend to have, of affixing the name of WILLIAM SHAKESPEARE, alias Shakespear, to any book, pamphlet, play, or poem, hereafter to be by him, or them, or any other person for him, or them, written, made, or devised.

A week later, the *Journal* published anonymously an eight-line squib called 'The Modern Poets' that accuses Theobald directly of forgery:

> See! T . . . leaves the Lawyer's gainful train,
> To wrack with poetry his tortur'd brain:
> Fir'd or not fir'd, to write resolves with rage,
> And constant pores o'er SHAKESPEAR's sacred page;
> – Then starting cries, I something will be thought:
> I'll write – then – boldly swears 'twas SHAKESPEAR wrote.

> Strange! he in Poetry no forgery fears,
> That knows so well in Law he'd lose his ears.

Two years later, David Mallet in his poem *Of Verbal Criticism: An Epistle to Mr Pope*, recalls those lines in making the same accusation against Theobald:

> See him on *Shakespear* pore, intent to steal
> Poor farce, by fragments, for a third-day meal.
> Such that grave *Bird* in northern seas is found,
> Whose name a *Dutchman* only knows to sound:
> Where-e'er the King of fish moves on before,
> This humble friend attends from shore to shore;
> His eyes still earnest, and his Bill declin'd,
> He picks up what his patron drops behind,
> With those choice cates his palate to regale,
> And is the careful *Tibbald* of a whale.
>
> (Mallet, *Epistle*, ll. 65–74)[1]

Years after the controversy over 'None but Itself' had died away, it continued to bother Theobald and he could not let the matter rest. Editing *The First Part of King Henry VI* for his 1733 edition of Shakespeare, he provides extensive annotation for Regnier's line 'I could be well content / To be mine own Attorney in this case' (5.2.186–7). Glossing it as 'I could like to act in my own Behalf in this Affair, to negotiate for myself', he goes on to admit that 'this kind of Expression, in strictness of Sense, or Language, may not be so justifiable'. Similar expressions, however, are documented by him in *The Two Gentlemen of Verona*, *Hamlet*, and three Beaumont and Fletcher plays. These 'Authorities' are produced, he explains, in response to Pope being 'pleas'd to be very smart upon me, as he thought, for a Line, in a *posthumous* Play of our Author's which I brought upon the Stage' (*Shakespeare*, 4.187–8). This is the first time

---

1   It is interesting that Mallet should refer , via the 'northern' bird, to the uncertainty in the pronunciation of Theobald's name, which was presumably a problem for his contemporaries as well as for us.

that Theobald has referred to the play as 'posthumous' rather than late-career. As in the *Mist's Weekly Journal* article referred to above, he again misquotes the line, though differently, as '*Nought, but* itself, *can be its* Parallel'. He goes on to justify it, this time by means of a long list of quotations taken from classical authors.

It is ironic that Pope's own final words on the subject should be to deny that he ever accused Theobald of forgery. Aaron Hill's letter to Pope of 11 May 1738 reproaches the poet for the sharpness of his censure in *Peri Bathous*, particularly regarding the examples culled from *Double Falsehood*. Pope's reply of 9 June is another of his masterly evasions:

> What you have observed in your Letter I think just; only I would acquit myself in one Point: I could not have the least *Pique* to Mr. *Th.* in what is cited in the Treatise of the *Bathos* from the play which I never supposed to be his: He gave it as *Shakespear*'s, and I take it to be of that Age.
>
> (Pope, *Correspondence*, 4.102)

APPENDIX 2

'PIDDLING TIBBALD' AND THEOBALD'S NAME

In Alexander Pope's *The Dunciad Variorum* of 1729 (the annotated version of the 1728 first edition), which has Lewis Theobald as hero and dunce-in-chief, he provided a note to the phrase 'in Tibbald's monster-breeding breast' (1.106) that begins: *'Lewis Tibbald* (as pronounced) or *Theobald* (as written) was bred an Attorney . . .'. Pope was therefore initially responsible for the promulgation of the pronunciation 'Tibbald'. Was Pope registering, or inventing, this contracted pronunciation? Was he capturing the actual pronunciation of the name, or did he do it so that he could set up such satisfying alliterations as 'piddling Tibbald'? David Mallet's *Of Verbal Criticism: An Epistle to Mr Pope. Occasioned by Theobald's Shakespear, and Bentley's Milton*, published in Edinburgh in 1733, in attacking Theobald alludes to the ambiguity in pronunciation of his name that was clearly registered by Theobald's contemporaries (ll. 67–8). The ambiguous pronunciation of Theobald's surname was exploited in satirical sideswipes at him: Jonathan Swift, for example, posing as 'Simon Wagstaff' introducing *A Complete Collection of Genteel and Ingenious Conversation* (1738), writes: 'In the like Manner, the divine Mr. *Tibbalds*, or *Theobalds*, in one of his Birth-day Poems . . .' (Swift, *Works*, 4.121). Neil Pattison writes in his doctoral thesis:

> Iain Sinclair, in his psychogeographical novel *London Orbital*, researches the phonology of London's Theobald Park, which had been variously represented in the sixteenth and seventeenth centuries, Sinclair

writes, as 'Thebaudes' and 'Tibbolds'. This is not
evidence, however, for the factual truth of Pope's note
in the instance of Theobald's name, and suggests
only that his assertion is plausible. Given the crucial
insight that eighteenth-century phonology had a
strong socially coercive and corrective tendency, I
believe it is more fruitful to explore accordingly the
literary contexts and poetic effects of Pope's renaming
of Theobald as 'Tibbald' than to conjecture on either
side of this ultimately intractable question.

(Pattison, 'King Tibbald', 40–1)

Pattison goes on to explore, very fruitfully, how the name works
in *The Dunciad*. Even if we add the suggestive fact that the manor
upon which the famous palace of Theobalds was built was called
Thebaudes, Tibbolds or Theobalds from 1440 onwards, I am
inclined to agree that this is an intractable question, considered
historically. In the headnote to her edition of the 1728 *Dunciad*,
Valerie Rumbold points to an article by Barbara Everett in which
she argues that Pope's spelling is close to a name proverbially
given to cats and concludes that

it is unclear whether ['Tibbald'] represented the then
prevalent pronunciation, but the spelling would have
been quite effective enough in diminishing Theobald
as a presence in the world of print even if it had
functioned only as a visual reminder that his name
was effectively the same as one proverbially given to
cats.[1]

---

1   Pope, *Dunciad Variorum*, 2, citing Barbara Everett, 'Tibbles: A new life of Pope', in *Poets in Their Time: Essays on English Poetry from Donne to Larkin* (1986), 120–39.

APPENDIX 3

'NONE BUT ITSELF CAN BE ITS PARALLEL'

Appendix 1 discusses the context within which this ill-fated line (3.1.17) became an object of ridicule to Alexander Pope. The terms in which Theobald tried to defend the line are also set out there. Supplementary to that defence, it might be pointed out that the line shares its self-reflexiveness with a similarly mocked phrase in *TNK* 1.2.58–60: 'Either I am / The forehorse in the team or I am none / That draw i'th' sequent trace.' Equally involuted in its comparison of something with itself is *E3* 1.2.99–101: 'fair is she not at all, / If that herself were by to stain herself, / As I have seen her when she was herself'. Theobald is not known to have worked on *Edward III*, however, so this passage was presumably not available to him. John Fletcher was himself very fond of involutedly self-reflexive expressions. In *Philaster*, Philaster says of Arathusa: 'Is she not parrallesse? Is not her breath / Sweet as *Arabian* winds, when fruits are ripe?' (3.1.201–2). Could Fletcher have written 'None but itself can be its parallel'?; or perhaps this line suggested it to Theobald? The lines go on: 'Are not her breasts two liquid Ivory balls? / Is she not all, a lasting Mine of joy?' (203–4), as if to prove that Fletcher can be as tasteless as Theobald was supposed by his detractors to be.

Perhaps the most convincing evidence that this line was not Theobald's original is brought forward by Edmond Malone in the annotations he made to a copy of the play's second issue (see pp. 5, 94). Malone notes that there is an inscription on a print of Colonel Giles Strangeways 'by Loggan – He died in 1675', that includes the lines: 'The artist in this draught doth art excell, / None but him self himself can parallel' (Malone, *DF*, 24). Strangeways was MP for Dorset and a staunch Royalist in the Civil War. The artist David Loggan (1634–92) did indeed engrave a portrait of Strangeways, and the inscription does contain the tribute recalled by Malone. As Malone indicates, Strangeways died in 1675, long after any possible Shakespeare play containing the lines would have been written. Malone, in turn, might have recalled the Strangeways inscription from the Rev. James Granger's *A Biographical History of England from Egbert the Great to the Revolution*. Granger notes:

> Theobald seems to have adopted this line, with very little variation, in his 'Double Falshood,'
> None but himself can be his parallel.
> The thought is so very singular, that it is extremely improbable, that two persons should have hit upon it, and varied so little in the expression. Sir William Temple has varied more; where speaking of Caesar, he says, that he was 'equal only to himself'.
>
> (Granger, 3.378)

Demonstrating that the line was not by Theobald was not, in Malone's eyes, tantamount to thinking it might have been by Shakespeare. His hypothesis was in any event that Theobald was trying to pass off a play, possibly by Philip Massinger, as Shakespeare's. As part of his claim that the original possessed by Theobald was a play by Massinger, Malone's notes cite, slightly inaccurately, a passage from 'Massinger's Duke of Millaine 1623'. The passage is from 4.3 of Massinger's play, and reads: 'Her goodnesse does disdaine comparison, / And but her selfe admits no paralell.' There is, though, a further twist here. In 2007, a portrait of John Fletcher appeared in the National Portrait Gallery's *Searching for Shakespeare* exhibition. Katherine Duncan-Jones wrote in the *Times Literary Supplement*, 17 March 2007: 'This is a privately owned portrait of a handsome, well dressed, fair-haired John Fletcher resting his right hand near some verses which conclude that, despite the painter's skill, "Non but thy owne penn could / Thy witt express'" (see Fig. 18) The original line may be Fletcher's, imitated by whoever painted the portrait (now in the National Portrait Gallery) and further imitated by Loggan on the Strangeways engraving.

18 Portrait of John Fletcher (anonymous). The verses by his right hand include the words 'Non but thy owne penn could / Thy witt express'

APPENDIX 4

SCENE PLAN FOR *DOUBLE FALSEHOOD*

Stage directions as supplied in the text

1.1 A royal palace
1.2 Prospect of a village at a distance
1.3 Unspecified – presumed balcony scene, played above stage left proscenium door
2.1 Prospect of a village
2.2 An apartment
2.3 Prospect of a village, before Don Bernard's house
2.4 Another prospect of Don Bernard's house
3.1 Prospect of a village
3.2 Don Bernard's house
    Opens to a large hall. An altar prepared with tapers
3.3 Prospect of a village at a distance
4.1 A wide plain, with a prospect of mountains at a distance
4.2 Unspecified – same as 4.1
5.1 The prospect of the mountains continued
5.2 An apartment in the lodge

Possible shutter plan

In the theatre of the early eighteenth century, scenery was created by means of pairs of shutters that ran in grooves, meeting in the middle and forming an entire picture, with co-ordinating wing flats and top borders (see Milhous & Hume, 52–66). There may have been two grooves at each shutter and wing position, to enable more elaborate staging. Milhous and Hume assume that the Drury Lane theatre, opened in 1673, provided no more than six different sets of shutters for an average production. If those were divided into two distinct groups of three, a discovery space would be available between the two sets.

The stage directions in *Double Falsehood* appear to call for eight locations indicated by differing scenery, in addition to the balcony scene 1.3. If we assume that '*Prospect of a village at a distance*' can be adapted for the close-up of Don Bernard's house required in 2.3, and that Violante's apartment in 2.2, presumably already rusticated, might be reused for the rustic hunting lodge in which the final scene takes place, differentiated by some simple props, the locations can be reduced to six. A possible shutter plan might be as follows (where 2a–c are the rear shutter positions and 1a–c are the front shutter positions):

2c   Wide plain with mountain prospect (4.1, 4.2, 5.1)
2b   Exterior of Don Bernard's house (2.4)
2a   Violante's apartment/lodge apartment (2.2, 5.2)

1c   Interior of Don Bernard's house (3.2, incorporating discovery scene opening to a large hall)
1b   Village at distance/close-up of Don Bernard's house (1.2, 2.1, 2.3, 3.1, 3.3)
1a   Royal palace (1.1)

Fig. 19 gives a pictorial representation of this plan.

There are of course other possibilities for staging the play. It might have been considered wasteful to deploy a set for only one scene (1.1, 2.4), and ways may have been found to avoid that. On the other hand, royal palaces were stock scenes that appear on contemporary theatre inventories and the opening scene would need to make an impact.

It seems likely that scene changes would take place in full view of the audience, without any attempt being made to conceal them behind drop curtains or any other kind of concealment device (painted rollers are sometimes conjectured: see p. 112). Wing-and-shutter scenery, while it was a move in the direction of illusion, was some distance away from unqualified illusionism. In the early eighteenth-century, the creation of illusion through scenery was still a limited ambition; preserving that illusion did not assume the importance it would have when naturalism gained ground in the following century.

19   Suggested scene plan at opening of *Double Falsehood*

APPENDIX 5

MUSIC IN *DOUBLE FALSEHOOD*

Music is a prominent feature of *Double Falsehood* as we have it, as it doubtless was in the original *Cardenio* play and in any possible Restoration intermediary. Henriquez organizes musicians to serenade Violante as a seduction aid in 1.3. Offstage music is extremely important for creating the atmosphere in 3.2, when the marriage of Leonora and Henriquez is intended to take place. In Act 4, it becomes crucial rather than merely important, and it is here that the closest resemblance to the use of music in Shakespeare's later romantic tragicomedies is found. We learn in 4.1 from the First Shepherd that the Master's 'boy' (Violante) has sung a 'love ditty' (22) that has captured the attention of the wild and violent man (Julio) who leads a skulking existence in the remote mountains. When Julio and Violante meet a little later in the scene, the former infers from the fact that Violante's is a love song a parallel between their two situations as forsaken lovers, and this becomes a bonding agent. In 4.2, Julio and the Gentleman hear the sound of a lute, provoking from Julio a sentiment very similar to the unexpected lyricism of Caliban in *The Tempest*:

> I'm often visited with these sweet airs.
> The spirit of some hapless man that died
> And left his love hid in a faithless woman
> Sure haunts these mountains.

> (12–15)

From offstage is heard the haunting sound of Violante's 'Fond Echo, forego thy light strain' (see Fig. 3, p. 14). There is a reprise of the second half of the song, and Julio gives testimony to its spellbinding power over him: 'I'm strangely touch'd with this. The heav'nly sound / Diffuses a sweet peace through all my soul' (33–4). No further music is called for explicitly, but it is likely that in production, music was heard towards the play's finale.

An account of the music in *Double Falsehood* has to begin speculatively, with research undertaken by the historian and television documentarist Michael Wood when he was working on a series of films for BBC television in 2001, *In Search of Shakespeare*. The existence of four songs set by the King's lutenist Robert Johnson (*c.* 1583–1633),[1] in the British Library manuscript BL Add. 11608, has long been known.[2] One of them, 'Myn Ost's song', is certainly from Fletcher's *The Lover's Progress* (*c.* 1623), but the others have no certain provenance in plays of the period. Two of the songs – 'Woods, Rocks, & Mountaynes' (fols 15^v–16^r, the first page of which is reproduced in Fig. 20) and 'With endles teares' (fol. 15) – are of interest to us. Wood has pointed out that at the equivalent point in the source text (Thomas Shelton's translation of *Don Quixote*) to the music's intervention in *Double Falsehood*, there is a call for music:

> the sound of a voyce, which without being accompanied by any instrument, did resound so sweet and melodiously, as they remained greatly admired, because they esteemed not that to be a place wherein any so good a Musitian might make his abode. For although it is vsually said, that in the woods and

---

1   The relevant paragraph of Matthew Spring's *ODNB* entry on Johnson makes clear the significant connection that Johnson maintained with the King's Men: 'The lord chamberlain, Sir George Carey, was both Johnson's patron and patron of the King's Men, who performed masques and plays at the Globe and Blackfriars theatres. Probably through this connection Johnson began to be associated with the theatre from 1607 onwards. The compositions for which he is best known are the many songs he wrote for theatre productions, including Shakespeare's *Cymbeline* (*c.*1609), *The Winter's Tale* (*c.*1611), and *The Tempest* (1611), Middleton's *The Witch* (1609), Webster's *The Duchess of Malfi* (*c.*1613), Jonson's *The Gypsies Metamorphosed* (1621), and five plays by Beaumont and Fletcher, *The Captain* (*c.*1612), *Valentinian* (*c.*1614), *The Mad Lover* (*c.*1616), *The Chances* (*c.*1617), and *The Lover's Progress* (1623).'

2   See John P. Cutts, 'Robert Johnson: King's musician in His Majesty's public entertainment', *Music and Letters*, vol. 36, no. 2 (1955), 110–25.

20 First page of Robert Johnson's song 'Woods, Rocks, & Mountaynes' (British Library Add. 11608, fol. 15ᵛ)

fields are found Shepheards of excellent voyces, yet is this rather a Poetical indeerement, than an approved truth; and most of al when they perceiued that the verses they heard him singing were not of rusticke composition, but rather of delicate and Courtly inuention . . .

The song was concluded with a profound sigh; and both the others lent attentiue eare to heare if hee would sing any more; but perceiuing that the musicke was conuerted into throbs and dolefull plaints, they resolued to goe and learne who was the wretch, as excellent for his voyce, as dolorous in his sighes.

(Shelton, 3.13.262–4)

Wood suggests, plausibly, that the passage in Shelton would have prompted a song at this point in the original Shakespeare–Fletcher play, and that Theobald is likely to have taken the same opportunity at a similar point in his adaptation to call for a song. On the basis of verbal parallels between Shelton and the lyrics of Johnson's 'Woods, Rocks, & Mountaynes', Wood infers that this was the song in *The History of Cardenio* (see Fig. 21), and that the lyrics of Theobald's 'Fond Echo' are (even if we might add 'distantly') related to it:

Woods rocks & Mountaines & you desert places
where nought but bitter cold & hunger dwells
heare a poore maids last words killd wth disgraces
slide softly while I sing you silver fountaines
& lett yo[r] hollow waters like sad bells
ring ring to my woes while miserable I
cursing my fortunes dropp dropp dropp a teare & dye

(quoted in Wood, 6)[1]

---

1   The lyrics cited by Wood are at variance with those illustrated in Fig. 20 because, as he indicates in the next quoted passage, two differing manuscript settings of the song are extant: BL Add. 11608 (illustrated) and Bodleian MS Don. c. 57. On this, see John P. Cutts, 'A Bodleian Song-Book: Don. C.57', *Music and Letters*, 34 (1953), 192–211 (193, 197).

21 Cardenio (Rob Whitelock) and a Gentleman (Jo Stone Fewings) listen to Robert Johnson's song 'Woods, Rocks, & Mountaynes' in Act 4 of the lost *Cardenio* (reconstruction made by Michael Wood and the Royal Shakespeare Company, directed by Gregory Doran for the BBC's *In Search of Shakespeare* series, 2003)

Wood is on more speculative territory when he goes on to argue that another of the Johnson songs in the manuscript, 'With endles teares', may have been the first song sung in The History of Cardenio, and alluded to rather than included in Theobald's adaptation:

> Shelton describes a song 'sweet and melodious' which ended with 'a profound sigh . . . throbs, and dolefull playnts . . . dolorous sighes', and it is reasonable to expect that the composer and lyricist in 1613 took those hints as their guide. If so, there is another Johnson song which looks like a companion piece to 'Woods rocks and mountaynes,' and which precedes it in both the manuscripts in which these songs are preserved:
>
> > With endles teares that never cease
> > I saw a hart lye bleeding
> > Whose greifes did more and more increase,
> > Her paynes were so exceedinge.
> > When dying sighes could not prevaile
> > She then would weepe a maine
> > When flowinge teares began to faile,
> > She then would sighe againe.
> >
> > Her sighes like raging winds did blow,
> > Some grievous storm foretelling,
> > & Tydes of tears did overflowe,
> > Her cheeks that Rose excellinge.
> > Confounding thoughts so fyl'd her brest,
> > She could no more contayne,
> > But Cryes alowd, hath love noe rest,
> > No Joyes but Endless payne.
>
> (Wood, 8)

Wood speculates that this is the second song heard originally in *The History of Cardenio* but dropped by Theobald except in allusion. It is a speculation that deserves to be heard. The songs are available on the CD *Away Delights* (2004), performed by Matthew Wadsworth on lute, with soprano Carolyn Sampson and Mark Levy on bass viol.[1] Not everyone, however, is entirely convinced that their provenance is the lost *Cardenio*. Christopher Goodwin writes in *Early Music* for February 2008 that 'on closer examination the imagery and diction of this song is suspiciously close to that of *Away delights* (words by Beaumont and Fletcher) and *Care-charming sleep* (by Fletcher), so perhaps one should avoid over-excitement on this score' (141). Goodwin's argument appears to presume that Wood (or anyone else) thinks *Cardenio* was a single-authored play by Shakespeare. Given its collaborative authorship in which Fletcher had a hand, the similarities to other songs in which he also had a hand would surely strengthen, not weaken, the case.

We are on firmer ground in asserting that the song setting which the audience in 1727 actually heard ('Fond Echo, forego thy light strain', 4.2.16–23) was eighteenth century, with lyrics by Theobald himself. A musical setting for the song first appeared in *The Merry Musician*, vol. 2 (1728), in a setting by Gouge. About the same time, it was anonymously published as 'The Forsaken Maid. A new song in the tragedy called "Double Falsehood" by Shakespeare'. In 1729 it was reprinted in *The Musical Miscellany*, vol. 2, where it was described as 'sung in The Distrest Lovers, The words by Mr. Theobald'. In *Calliope or English Harmony*, vol. 1 (1746), the words are again ascribed to Shakespeare. A recent recording has been made of the song by the contralto Emma Curtis and The Frolick.[2] A very similar song to this one is sung by Zorayda under similar dramatic conditions in Theobald's later Cervantic play *The Happy Captive* (1741) (1.9.22–8); and it seems likely that both songs are his. That 'Fond Echo' was a very popular feature

---

1   *Away Delights: Lute Songs by Robert Johnson* (2004), Avie AV 2053.
2   *Calliope: Beautiful Voice* (2006), Avie AV 2102.

of the play is suggested by the fact that when it was revived towards the end of the eighteenth century, first in 1770 at Drury Lane and then in 1791 at Covent Garden, the song was singled out for resetting by popular composers of the day, respectively James Hook and William Shield. To date I have been unable to find those settings and I must presume that they have not survived.[1]

1   Hook wrote extensively for the theatre and for entertainments given in Vauxhall Gardens, while Shield was appointed house composer at Covent Garden after the enormous success of his opera *Rosina* in 1782. This gained lasting fame because the overture ended with a tune reminiscent of the bagpipes that was later deployed by Robert Burns for 'Auld Lang Syne'.

APPENDIX 6

DON QUIXOTE:
EXCERPTS FROM
THOMAS SHELTON'S
TRANSLATION

The following four extracts are taken from Thomas Shelton, *The history of the valorous and wittie knight-errant, Don-Quixote of the Mancha. Translated out of the Spanish. The first parte* (London: Printed by William Stansby, for Ed. Blount and W. Barret, 1612). The extracts are reproduced in facsimile courtesy of the Durning-Lawrence Library, Senate House Library, University of London.

The facsimiles exclude the part number and page number printed at the top of each page, with the running title '*The delightfull Historie of the*' (verso pages) '*wittie Knight Don-Quixote.*' (recto pages). The part, chapter and page numbers are instead printed above each facsimile page, in the form used in the text of this edition (e.g. 3.5.155). Extracts 2, 3 and 4 are preceded by a summary of the intervening action. Superfluous text on the page where an extract begins or ends is omitted.

EXTRACT 1

From Part 3 chapter 5, '*Of the discreet discourses passed betweene Sancho and his Lord: with the aduenture succeeding of a dead body: and other notable occurrences.*'

Being in these and other such discourses, the night ouertooke them in the way, before they could discouer any lodging, and that which was worst of all, they were almost famisht with hunger, for by the losse of their wallets, they lost at once both their prouision and warderhouse. And to accomplish wholly this disgrace, there succeeded a certaine aduenture, which certainly hapned as wee lay it downe without any addition in the world, and was this: the night did shut vppe with some darkenesse, yet notwithstanding they trauailed on still, Sancho beleeuing that since that was the high way, there must be within a league or two in all reason some Inne. Trauailing therefore as I haue said, in a darke night, the Squire being hungry, and the Master hauing a good stomacke, they saw comming towards them in the very way they trauailed, a great multitude of lights, resembling nothing so well as wandering starres. Sancho beholding them was strucke into a wonderfull amazement, and his Lord was not much better. The one drew his Asse halter, the other held his horse, and both of them stoode still, beholding attentiuely what that might be, and they perceiued that the lights drew still nearer vnto them; and the more they approched, they appeared the greater, at the sight Sancho did tremble like one infected by the sauour of Quicksiluer, and Don-Quixotes haire did stand vp like bristles, who animating himselfe a little, said, Sancho this must be questionlesse a great and most dangerous aduenture, wherein it is requisite that I shew all my valour and strength. Vnfortunate I, quoth Sancho, if by chance this aduenture were of Ghosts, as it seemeth to me that it is, where will there bee ribbes to suffer it? bee they neuer so great Ghosts, said Don-Quixote, I will not consent that they touch one haire of thy garment: For if they iested with thee the other time, it was because I could not leape

over

ouer the walles of the yard, but now wee are in plaine
field where I may brandifh my fword as I pleafe. And if
they inchant and bennmme you as they did the other time
quoth *Sancho*, what will it then auaile vs to bee in open
field or no? For all that replyed *Don-Quixote*, I pray thee
Sancho bee of good courage, for experience fhall fhew
thee how great my valour is; I will, and pleafe God,
quoth *Sancho*, and fo departing fomewhat out of the
way, they beganne againe to view earneftly what that of
the trauailing lights might bee; and after a very little
fpace they efpied many white things, whofe dreadfull vifions did in that very inftant conclude *Sancho Pança* his
courage, and now beganne to chatter with his teeth, like
one that had the cold of a *Quartane*, and when they did
diftinctly perceiue what it was, then did his beating and
chattering of teeth increafe, for they difcouered about
fome twenty all couered with white a horfe-backe, with
Tapers lighting in their hands, after which followed a litter couered ouer with blacke, and then infued other fixe
a horfe-backe, attired in mourning, and likewife their
Mules, euen to the very ground; for they perceiued that
they were not horfes, by the quietneffe of their pace. The
white folke rode murmuring fomewhat among themfelues with a low and compaffiue voice. Which ftrange
vifion, at fuch an houre, and in places not inhabited, was
very fufficient to ftrike feare into *Sanchos* heart, and euen
in his Mafters. If it had beene any other then *Don-Quixote*, but *Sancho* tumbled here and there, being quite o-
uerthrowne with terrour. The contrary hapned to his
Lord, to whom in that fame houre his imagination reprefented vnto him moft liuely, the aduenture wherein
hee was to bee fuch a one, as hee oftimes had read in his
bookes of Chiualry. For it is figured vnto him, that the
litter was a beere, wherein was carryed fome grieuoufly
wounded or dead Knight, whofe reuenge was only referued for him. And without making any other difcourfe
                                                                    he

hee set his Launce in the rest, seated himselfe surely in his
saddle, and put himselfe in the middest of the way by
which the white folke must forcibly passe, with great spirit and courage. And when he saw them draw neare,he
said with a lowde voice: stand Sir Knight, whosoeuer you
be, and render me account what you are ? from whence
you come ? where you goe ? and what that is which you
carry in that beere ? for according as you shew,either you
haue done to others, or others to you some iniury. And it
is conuenient and needfull that I know it, either to cha-
stice you for the ill you haue comitted, or else to reuenge
you of the wrong which you haue suffered, we are in hast
quoth one of the white men, and the Inne is farre off,and
therefore cannot expect to giue so full relation as you request, and with that spurring his Mule, passed forward.
Don-Quixote, highly disdayning at the answere,tooke by
the bridle and held him, saying, stay prowde Knight, and
bee better mannerd another time, and giue mee account
of that which I demanded, if not, I defie you all to mortall battaile. The Mule whereon the white man rode was
somewhat fearefull and skittish, and being taken thus
rudely by the bridle, shee tooke such a fright, that rising
vp on her hinder legges, shee vnhorsed her Rider ; one of
the Lackeyes that came with them seeing him fallen, beganne to reuile *Don-Quixote*, who being by this throughly enraged, without any more adoe, putting his Launce
in the rest, runne vpon one of the mourners, and threw
him to the ground very sore wounded : and turning vpon
the rest, it was a thing worthy the noting with what dexterity he did assault, breake vpon them, and put them all
to flight, and it seemed none other, but that *Rozinante*
had gotten then wings, hee bestirred himselfe so nimbly
and couragiously.

All those white men were fearefull people, and vnar-
med, and therefore fled away from the skirmish in a trice,
and beganne to trauerse that field with their Tapers lighting,

339

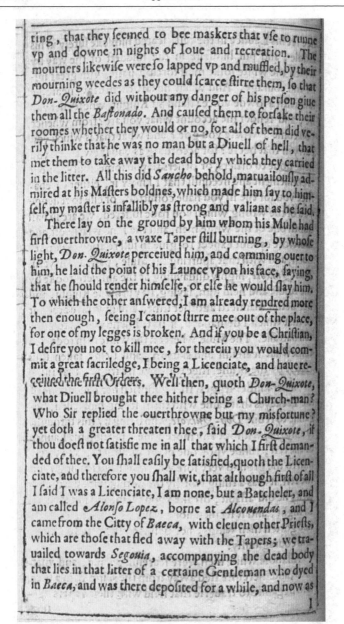

ting, that they seemed to bee maskers that vſe to runne
vp and downe in nights of Ioue and recreation. The
mourners likewiſe were ſo lapped vp and muffled, by their
mourning weedes as they could ſcarce ſtirre them, ſo that
Don-Quixote did without any danger of his perſon giue
them all the *Baſtonado*. And cauſed them to forſake their
roomes whether they would or no, for all of them did verily thinke that he was no man but a Diuell of hell, that
met them to take away the dead body which they carried
in the litter. All this did *Sancho* behold, matuaiſouſly admired at his Maſters boldnes, which made him ſay to him-
ſelf, my maſter is infallibly as ſtrong and valiant as he ſaid.

There lay on the ground by him whom his Mule had
firſt ouerthrowne, a waxe Taper ſtill burning, by whoſe
light, *Don-Quixote* perceiued him, and comming ouer to
him, he laid the point of his Launce vpon his face, ſaying,
that he ſhould render himſelfe, or elſe he would ſlay him.
To which the other anſwered, I am already rendred more
then enough, ſeeing I cannot ſtirre mee out of the place,
for one of my legges is broken. And if you be a Chriſtian,
I deſire you not to kill mee, for therein you would commit a great ſacriledge, I being a Licenciate, and haue receiued the firſt Orders. Well then, quoth *Don-Quixote*,
what Diuell brought thee hither being a Church-man?
Who Sir replied the ouerthrowne but my misfortune?
yet doth a greater threaten thee, ſaid *Don-Quixote*, if
thou doeſt not ſatisfie me in all that which I firſt demanded of thee. You ſhall eaſily be ſatisfied, quoth the Licenciate, and therefore you ſhall wit, that although firſt of all
I ſaid I was a Licenciate, I am none, but a Batcheler, and
am called *Alonſo Lopez*, borne at *Alconendas*, and I
came from the Citty of *Baeca*, with eleuen other Prieſts,
which are thoſe that fled away with the Tapers; we trauailed towards *Segouia*, accompanying the dead body
that lies in that litter of a certaine Gentleman who dyed
in *Baeca*, and was there depoſited for a while, and now as

I say, we carry his bones to his place of buriall, which is in *Segonia*, the place of his birth. And who killed him, quoth *Don-Quixote*? God, quoth the Batcheler, with certaine pestilentiall feauers that he tooke. In that manner, quoth *Don-Quixote*, our Lord hath deliuered mee from the paines I would haue taken to reuenge his death, if any other had slaine him. But hauing kild him, he that did it, there is no other remedy but silence, and to lift vp the shoulders, for the same I must my selfe haue done, if hee were likewise pleased to flea me. And I would haue your reuerence to vnderstand, that I am a Knight of the *Mancha*, called *Don Quixote*, and mine office and exercise is to goe throughout the world righting of wrongs, and vndoing of iniuries. I cannot vnderstand how that can be of righting wrongs, quoth the Batcheler, seeing you haue made me who was right before, now very crooked by breaking of my legge, which can neuer be righted a-gaine, as long as I liue, and the iniury which you haue vn-done in me, is none other but to leaue me so iniuried, as I shall remaine iniuried for euer. And it was very great disuenture to haue encountred with you, that goe about to see aduentures. All things, quoth *Don-Quixote*, suc-ceede not of one fashion: the hurt was Master Batcheler *Alonso Lopez*, that you trauailed thus by night couered with those Surplices, with burning Tapers, and couered with weedes of dole, so that you appeared most properly some badde thing, and of the other world, and so I could not omit to fulfill my duty, by assaulting you, which I would haue done although I verily knew you to bee the *Sathans* themselues of hell. For, for such I iudged and accounted you euer till now.

Then since my badde fortune hath so disposed it, quoth the Batcheler, I desire you good Sir Knight errant (who hath giuen me so euill an errant) that you will helpe me to get vp from vnder this Mule, who holds still my legge betwixt the stirrop and saddle. I would haue staid talking
vntill

vntill to morrow morning, quoth *Don-Quixote*, and why did you expect so long to declare your griefe to me ? he presently called to *Sancho Panca* to come ouer : but hee had little minde to doe , for hee was otherwise imployed, ranfacking of a fumpture Mule, which thofe good folke brought with them, well furnifhed with belly ware. *Sancho* made a bagge of his Cafacke, and catching all that he might, or could containe, he laid it on his beaft, and then prefently after repaired to his Mafter , and holpe to deliuer the good Batcheler from the oppreffion of his Mule. And mounting him againe on it , he gaue him his Taper, and *Don-Quixote* bade him to follow his fellowes, of whom he fhould defire pardon in his name,for the wrong hee had done them.   For it lay not in his hands to haue done the contrary. *Sancho* faid to him alfo, if thofe Gentlemen would by chance know, who the valorous Knight is, that hath vfed them thus , you may fay vnto them that hee is the famous *Don-Quixote of Mancha* , otherwile called the Knight of the *Ilfauourd face.*

EXTRACT 2

From Part 3 chapter 9, '*Of that which befell the famous* Don-Quixote *in* Siera Morena, *which was one of the most rare aduentures, which in this or any other so authenticall a History is recounted.*', and chapter 10

After Don Quixote chivalrously releases a number of criminals bound for the galleys from their captors, his squire Sancho Panza persuades him to flee from the authorities in the mountains of the Sierra Morena. Here they find an abandoned saddlebag containing money and a notebook.

Then he opened it, and the first thing that he found written in it, as it were a first draught, but done with a very faire Character, was a Sonnet which he read aloude, that *Sancho* might also heare it, and was this which ensues.

OR loue of vnderstanding quite is voyde:
    Or he abounds in cruelty, or my paine
Th'occasion equals not ; for which I bide
The torments dyre, he maketh me sustaine.
But if loue be a God, I dare maintaine
    He nought ignores : and reason aye decides
    Gods should not cruell be : then who ordaines
This paine I worship, which my heart diuides?
Filis ! I erre, if thou I say it is :
    For so great ill and good cannot consist.
    Nor doth this wracke from heau'n befall but yet.
That shortly I must die, can no way misse :
    For th'euill whose cause is hardly well exprest
    By miracle alone, true cure may get.

Nothing can be learned by that verse, quoth *Sancho*, if

if by that * *Hilo* or threed which is said there, you gather not where lies the rest of the clue, what *Hilo* is heere, quoth *Don-Quixote*? Me thought, quoth *Sancho*, that you read *Hilo* there. I did not but *Fili*, said *Don-Quixote*, which is without doubt the name of the Lady, on whom the Authour of this Sonnet complaines, who in good truth seemes to be a reasonable good Poet, or els I know but little of that arte. Why then, quoth *Sancho*, belike you doe also vnderstand *Poetry*? That I doe, and more then thou thinkest, quoth *Don-Quixote*; as thou shalt see when thou shalt carry a letter from me to my Lady *Dulcinea del Toboso*, written in verse from the one end to the other: For I would thou shouldest know *Sancho*, that all or the greater number of Knights errant in times past were great Versifiers and Musitians, for these two qualities, or graces as I may better terme them, are annext to amourous Knights aduentures. True it is that the verses of the auncient Knights are not so adorned with words, as they are rich in conceits. I pray you reade more, quoth *Sancho*, for perhaps you may finde somewhat that may satisfie. Then *Don-Quixote* turned the leafe, and said, This is prose, and it seemes to be a letter. What Sir, a missiue letter, quoth *Sancho*? No but rather of loue, according to the beginning, quoth *Don-Quixote*. I pray you therefore, quoth *Sancho*, reade it loude enough, for I take great delight in these things of loue. I am content, quoth *Don-Quixote*, and reading it loudly as *Sancho* had requested, it said as ensueth.

Thy false promise and my certaine misfortune, do carry me to such a place, as from thence thou shalt sooner receiue newes of my death, then reasons of my iust complaints. Thou hast disdained me (*O ingrate*) for one that hath more, but not for one that is worth more then I am: but if vertue were a treasure of estimation, I would not emulate other mens fortunes, nor weep thus for mine own misfortunes. That which thy beauty erected, thy works

P   haue

haue ouerthrowne : by it I deemed thee to be an Angell, and by thefe I certainely know thee to be but a woman. Reft in peace (*O caufer of my warre*) and let heauen worke fo that thy fpoufes deceipts remaine ftill concealed, to the end thou maift not repent what thou didft, and I bee conftrained to take reuenge of that I defire not.

Hauing read the letter, *Don-Quixote* faid, we can collect leffe by this then by the letter. What the Authour is, other then that he is fome difdayned louer, and fo paffing ouer all the booke, he found other Verfes and Letters, of which hee could read fome, others not at all. But the fumme of them all were, accufations, plaints, and miftrufts, pleafures, griefes, fauours, and difdaines, fome folemnized, others deplored. And whileft *Don-Quixote* paft ouer the booke, *Sancho* paft ouer the mallet, without leauing a corner of it, or the cuſhion vnfearched, or a feame vnript, nor a locke of wooll vncarded, to the end nothing might remaine behinde for want of diligence, or carelefleneffe, they found gold which paft a hundred crowns, had ftird in him fuch a greedineffe to haue more. And though he got no more then that which he found at the firft, yet did he account his flights in the couerlet, his vomiting of the drench, the benedictions of the packe flaues, the blowes of the Carrier, the loffe of his wallet, the robbing of his Caffocke, and all the hunger, thirft, and wearineffe that he had paft in the feruice of his good Lord and Mafter, for well imployed; accounting himfelfe to be more then well paied, by the gifts receiued of the money they found. The Knight of the *Il fauoured face* was the while poffeffed with a maruailous defire to know who was the owner of the mallet, coniecturing by the Sonnet, and letter, the gold, and linnen, that the enamoured was fome man of worth, whom the difdaine and rigour of his Lady had conducted to fome defperate termes. But by reafon that no body appeared, through that

that inhabitable and defart place, by whom he might be informed; he thought on it no more, but only roade on, without choofing any other way, then that which pleafed *Rozinante* to trauaile, who tooke the plaineft and eafieft to paffe through : hauing ftill an imagination that there could not want fome ftrange aduenture, amidft that Forreft.

And as he roade on, with this conceipt he faw a man on the toppe of a little mountaine that ftood iuft before his face, leape from rocke to rocke, and tuffe to tuffe with wonderfull dexterity. And as he thought he was naked, had a blacke and thicke beard, the haires many and confufedly mingled, his feete and legges bare, his thighes were couered with a paire of hofe, which feemed to bee of Murry veluet, but were fo torne that they difcouered his flefh in many places : his head was likewife bare, and although he paft by with the haft we haue recounted, yet did *the Knight of the Il fauoured face*, note all thefe particularities, and although he indeuoured, yet could not hee follow him, for it was not in *Rozinantes* power, in that weake ftate wherein he was to trauaile fo fwiftly among thofe rocks, chiefly being naturally very flow and flegmatike. *Don-Quixote* after efpying him did inftantly imagine him to be owner of the cufhion and mallet; and therefore refolued to goe on in his fearch, although hee fhould fpend a whole yeare therein among thofe mountaines : and commanded *Sancho* to goe about the one fide of the mountaine, and he would goe the other, and quoth hee, it may befall that by vfing this diligence wee may incounter with that man, which vanifhed fo fuddainely out of our fight. I cannot doe fo, quoth *Sancho*, for that in parting one ftep from you, feare prefently fo affaults mee with a thoufand vifions and affrightments. And let this ferue you hereafter for a warning, to the end you may not from henceforth part me the blacke of a naile from your prefence. It fhall bee fo, anfwereth

the *Knight of the ill-fauoured face.* And I am very glad
that thou dost thus build vpon my valour, the which shall
neuer faile thee, although thou didst want thy very soule:
and therefore follow me by little and little, or as thou
maist, and make of thine eyes two Lant-hornes, for wee
giue a turne to this little rocke, and perhaps wee may
meete with this man whom we saw euen now, who
doubtlesly can be none other then the owner of our boo-
tie. To which *Sancho* replyed, it were much better not to
finde him: for if we should meet him, and were by chance
the owner of this money, it is most euident that I must restore it to him, and therefore it is better without vsing
this vnprofitable diligence to let me possesse it *bona fide,*
vntill the true Lord shall appeare by some way lesse curious and diligent : which perhaps may fall at such a time
as it shall be all spent; and in that case I am freed from all
processes by priuiledge of the King. Thou deceiuest thy
selfe *Sancho* therein, quoth *Don. Quixote,* for seeing wee
are falne already into suspition of the owner, wee are
bound to search and restore it to him : and when wee
would not seeke him out, yet the vehement presumption
that we haue of it hath made vs possessors *mala fide,* and
renders vs as culpable, as if he whom we surmise, were verily the true Lord. So that friend *Sancho,* be not grieued
to seeke him, in respect of the griefe whereof thou shalt
free me if he be found. And saying so, spurd *Rozinante,*
and *Sancho* followed after a foote, animated by the hope
of the young Asses his Master had promised vnto him:
& hauing compassed a part of the mountain, they found a
little streame, wherin lay dead, and halfe deuoured by dogs
and crows, a Mule sadled and bridled, al which confirmed
more in them the suspition that hee which fledde away,
was owner of the Mule and cushion. And as they looked
on it, they heard a whistle, much like vnto that which
Sheepheards vse, as they keepe their flockes, and presently appeared at their left hand a great number of Goates,
after

after whom the Goatheard that kept them, who was an aged man, followed on the toppe of the mountaine; and *Don-Quixote* cried to him, requesting him to come down to them, who answered them againe as loudly, demaunding of them who had brought them to those desarts, rarely troden by any other then Goats, Wolues, or other sauage beastes which frequented those mountaines? *Sancho* answered him, that if hee would descend where they were, they would giue him account thereof. With that the Sheepheard came downe, and arriuing to the place where *Don-Quixote* was, he said, I dare wager that you looke on the hyred Mule which lies dead there in that bottom; well, in good faith he lies in that very place these sixe moneths. Say, I pray you, haue not you met in the way with the master thereof? We haue encountred no body but a cushion and a little Mallet which wee found not very farre off from hence. I did likewise finde the same, replyed the Goatheard, but I would neuer take it vp nor approach to it, fearefull of some misdemeanor, or that I should be hereafter demaunded for it as for a stealth. For the Diuell is crafty, and now and then something riseth, euen from vnder a mans feete, whereat hee stumbles and falles, without knowing how, or how not. That is the very same I say, quoth *Sancho*, for I likewise found it, but would not approach it the cast of a stone. There I haue left it, and there it remaines as it was; for I *would not haue a dogge with a bell.* Tell me good fellow, quoth *Don-Quixote*, dost thou know who is the owner of all these things?

That which I can say, answered the Goatheard, is that about some sixe moneths past, little more or lesse; there arriued at a certaine sheepe-fold some three leagues off, a young Gentleman of comely personage, and presence, mounted on that very *Mule* which lies dead there, and with the same Cushion and Mallet which you say you met, but touched not. He demaunded of vs which was

P 3

the

the moſt hidden and inacceſſable part of the mountaine,
and we told him that this wherein we are now : and it is
true ; for if you did enter but halfe a league farther, perhaps you would not finde the way out againe ſo readily:
and I doe greatly maruell how you could finde the way
hither it ſelfe; for there is neyther high way nor path that
may addreſſe any to this place. I ſay then, that the young
man as ſoone as he heard our anſwere, hee turned the
bridle, and trauelled towards the place wee ſhewed to
him, leauing vs all with very great liking of his comelines
and maruell, at his demaund and ſpeed wherewith he departed and made towards the mountaine : and after that
time we did not ſee him a good many of daies, vntill by
chance one of our ſheepheards came by with our proui-
ſion of victuals, to whom he drew neere, without ſpeak-
ing a word, and ſpurned and beate him welfauourdly, and
after went to the Aſſe which carried our victuals, and taking away all the bread and cheeſe that was there, hee
fled into the mountaine with wonderfull ſpeede. When
we heard of this, ſome of vs Goatheards, wee went to
ſearch for him, and ſpent therein almoſt two dayes in the
moſt ſolitary places of this mountaine, and in the end
found him lurking in the hollow part of a very tall and
great Corke tree ; who as ſoone as he perceiued vs, came
forth to meete vs, with great ſtayednes: his apparrell was
all torne, his viſage disfigured, and toſted with the Sunne
in ſuch manner, as we could ſcarce know him, if it were
not that his attire, although rent, by the notice we had of
it did giue vs to vnderſtand, that hee was the man for
whom we ſought. He ſaluted vs courteoully, and in briefe
and very good reaſons he ſaid, that we ought not to maruell, ſeeing him goe in that manner : for that it behoued
to doe ſo, that hee might accompliſh a certaine penance
inioyned to him, for the many ſinnes he had committed.
We prayed him to tell vs what he was, but we could neuer perſwade him to it. We requeſted him likewiſe that
                                                      when

whenſoeuer he had any neede of meat(without which he could not liue) he ſhould tell vs where wee might finde him and we would bring it to him with great loue and diligence ; and that if he alſo did not like of this motion, that he would at leaſtwiſe come and aske it, & not take it violently as he had done before from our Sheepheards. He thanked vs very much for our offer, and intreated pardon of the aſſaults paſſed, and promiſed to aske it from thence forward for Gods ſake, without giuing annoyance to any one. And touching his dwelling or place of abode, he ſaid that he had none other then that where the night ouertooke him, and ended his diſcourſe with ſo feeling laments, that we might well be accounted ſtones which heard him, if therein we had not kept him company, conſidering the ſtate wherein we had ſeene him firſt; and that wherein now he was. For as I ſaid he was a very comely and gracious young man, and ſhewed by his courteous and orderly ſpeech, that he was well borne, and a courtlike perſon. For though wee were all Clownes, ſuch as did heare him, his Gentility was ſuch, as could make it ſelfe knowne, euen to rudeneſſe it ſelfe : and being in the beſt of his Diſcourſe, he ſtopt and grew ſilent, fixing his eyes on the ground a good while, wherein wee likewiſe ſtood ſtill ſuſpended, expecting in what that diſtraction would end, with no little compaſſion to behold it; for we eaſily perceiued that ſome accident of madnes had ſurpriſed him, by his ſtaring and beholding the earth ſo fixedly, without once mouing the eye-lidde, and other times by the ſhutting of them, the biting of his lips, and bending of his browes. But very ſpeedily after he made vs certaine thereof himſelfe : for riſing from the ground (whereon he had throwne himſelfe a little before) with great furie, he ſet vpon him that ſate next vnto him, with ſuch courage and rage, that if wee had not taken him away, he would haue ſlaine him with blows and bites, and he did all this, ſaying, O treacherous *Fernando* here, heere

P 4   thou

thou shalt pay me the iniurie that thou didst me : these
handes shall rent out the heart, in which do harbour and
are heaped all euils together, but principally fraude and
deceit : and to these he added other wordes, all addrest
to the dispraise of that *Fernando*, and to attach him of
treason and vntruth. Wee tooke from him at last, not
without difficulty our fellow, and hee without saying a
word departed from vs, embushing himselfe presently a-
mong the bushes & brambles, leauing vs wholly disabled
to follow him in those rough and vnhaunted places. By
this we gathered that his madnes comes to him at times,
and that some one called *Fernando*, some ill worke of
such waight, as the terms shew, to which it hath brought
him. All which hath after beene yet confirmed as often,
(which were many times) as he came out to the fieldes,
sometimes to demaund meat of the Sheepheards, and o-
ther times to take it of them perforce : for when hee is
taken with this fit of madnesse, although the Sheepheards
doe offer him meat willingly, yet will not he receiue, vn-
lesse he take it with buffets : and when hee is in his right
sense he askes it for Gods sake, with courtesie and huma-
nity, and renders many thankes, and that not without
teares. And in very truth Sirs, I say vnto you, quoth the
Goatheard, that I and foure others, whereof two are my
men, other two my friends, resolued Yesterday to search
vntill we found him ; and being found, eyther by force or
faire meanes, we will carry him to the towne of *Almo-
dauar*, which is but eight leagues from hence ; and there
will we haue him cured, if his disease may be holpen, or
at least we shall learne what he is, when he turnes to his
wits; and whether he hath any friends to whom notice of
his misfortune may be giuen. This is Sirs, all that I can
say concerning that which you demaunded of me; and
you shall vnderstand that the owner of those things
which you saw in the way is the very same, whome you
saw passe by you so naked & nimble. For *Don-Quixote*
had

and told him by this, that hee had feene that man goe by leaping among the Rockes.

Don-Quixote refted maruelloufly admired at the Goat-heards tale, & with greater defire to know who that vnfortunate mad-man was, purpofed with himfelfe , as hee had already refolued to fearch him throughout the mountaines, without leauing a corner or Caue of it vnfought, vntill he had gotten him. But fortune difpofed the matter better then he expected , for he appeared in that very inftant in a clift of a Rocke , that anfwered to the place where they flood fpeaking , who came towards them murmuring fomewhat to himfelfe which they could not bee vnderflood neere at hand, and much leffe a farre off. His apparell was fuch as we haue deliuered, onely differing in this as *Don Quixote* perceiued when he drew neerer,that he wore on him,although torne, a leather Ierkin of *Ambar*. By which he throughly collected , that the perfon which wore fuch attire, was not of the leaft qualitie. When the young man came to the place where they difcourfed,he faluted them with a hoarfe voyce,but with great courtefie: and *Don-Quixote* returned him his greetings with no leffe complement ; and allighting from *Rozinante*,he aduanced to embrace him with very good carriage and countenance , and held him a good while flraightly betweene his armes , as if he had knowne him of long time ; the other whom we may call the vnfortunate Knight of the Rocke , as well as *Don-Quixote* the Knight of the ill fauoured face, after hee had permitted himfelfe to be embraced a while; did flep a little off from our Knight ; and laying his hand on his fhoulders,began to behold him earneftly , as one defirous to call to minde whether he had euer feene him before : being perhaps no leffe admired to fee *Don-Quixotes* figure,proportion and armes;then *Don-Quixote* was to view him. In refolution the firft that fpoke after the embracing was the ragged Knight,and faid what we will prefently recount.

CHAP.

Chap. X.

Wherein is prosecuted the aduenture of Sierra Morena.

 He History affirmes that great was the a-
tention , wherewithall *Don-Quixote*
listened to the vnfortunate *Knight of the
Rock* , who began his speech in this manner : Truely good Sir, whatsoeuer you be
(for I know you not) I doe with all my
heart gratifie the signes of affection and courtesie which
you haue vsed towards me, & wish heartily that I were in
termes to serue with more then my will , the good
will you beare towards me as your courteous entertainment denotes: but my fate is so niggardly , as it affoords
me no other meanes to repay good workes done to me,
then only to lend me a good desire sometime to satisfie
them. So great is mine affection , replied *Don-Quixote*,
to serue you,as I was fully resolued neuer to depart out
of these mountaines vntill I had found you,and known of
your selfe whether there might be any kind of remedie
found for the griefe, that this your so vnusuall a kinde of
life argues, doth possesse your soule. And if it were requisite to search it out with all possible diligence : and when
your disaster were known of those which clap their doors
in the face of comfort , I intended in that case to beare a
part in your lamentations,& plaine it with the dolefullest
note; for it is a consolation in afflictions to haue one that
condoles in them.And if this my good intention may merite any acceptance,or be gratified by anycourtesie,let me
intreat you Sir by the excesse therof, which I see accumu-
lated in your bosom,& iointly I coniure you by that thing
which you haue,or do presently most affect that you will
please to disclose vnto me who you are,& what the cause
hath bin that perswaded you to come , to liue and die into these desarts, like a bruit beast, seeing you liue among
such,so alienated from your selfe, as both your attire and

coun-

countenance demonstrate. And I doe vow (quoth *Don-Quixote*) by the high order of Chiualry, which I (although vnworthy & a sinner) haue receiued, and by the profession of Knights errant, that if you do pleasure me herein, to assist you with as good earnest as my profession doth binde me, either by remedying your disaster, if it can be holpen; or els by assisting you to lament it, if it be so desperate.

The *Knight of the Rocke*, who heard him of *the ill fauoured face* speake in that maner, did nothing else for a great while, but behold him again & again, and rebehold him from top to toe. And after viewing him wel he said; if you haue any thing to eate, I pray you giue it me for Gods sake, & after I haue eaten I will satisfie your demand thorowly, to gratifie the many courtesies & vndeserued proffers you haue made vnto me. *Sancho* and the Goatheard presents the one out of his Wallet, the other out of his Scrip, tooke some meat and gaue it to the Knight of the Rocke to allay his hunger, and he did eate so fast, like a distracted man, as he left no intermission between bit & bit, but clapt them vp so swiftly, as he rather seemed to swallow then to chew them; & whilst he did eate, neither he or any of the rest spoke a word: & hauing ended his dinner, he made them signes to follow him, as at last they did, vnto a little meadow seated hard by that place, at the folde of a mountain; where being arriued, he stretched himselfe on the grasse, which the rest did likewise in his imitation, without speaking a word, vntill that he after setling himselfe in his place, began in this manner: if Sirs, you please to heare the immanity of my disasters briefly rehearsed, you must promise me, that you will not interrupt the file of my dolefull narration, with either demaund or other thing; for in the very instant that you shall do it, there also must remain that which I say depending. These words of our ragged Knights, called to *Don-Quixotes* remembrance the tale which his Squire had told vnto him when he erred in the account of his Goats, which had passed the riuer,

riuer,for which that History remained suspended. But returning to our ragged man; hee said , this preuention which now I giue , is to the end that I may compendiously passe ouer the discourse of my mishaps, for the reuoking of them to remembrance only,serues me to none other steed,then to increase the olde by adding of new misfortunes; and by how much the fewer your questions are,by so much the more speedily shal I haue finished my pittifull Discourse; and yet I meane not to omit my essentiall point of my woes vntoucht,that your desires may be herein sufficiently satisfied. *Don-Quixote* in his own, and his other companions name , promised to performe his request; whereupon hee began his relation in this manner :

My name is *Cardenio*,the place of my birth, one of the best Cities in *Andaluzia* , my linage noble , my parents rich,and my misfortunes so great,as I thinke my parents haue e're this deplored , & my kinsfolke condoled them; being very little able with their wealth to redresse them; for the goods of fortune are but of smal vertue to remedy the disasters of heauen. There dwelt in the same Citie a heauen,wherin loue had placed all the glory that I could desire; so great as the beauty of *Luscinda* , a damzell as noble and rich as I : but more fortunate and lesse constant then my honourable desires expected. I loued , honoured and adored this *Luscinda* , almost from my very infancy; and she affected me likewise , with all the integrity and good will,which with her so young yeares did accord. Our parents knew our mutuall amity; for which they were nothing aggrieued, perceiuing very well, that although we continued it , yet could it haue none other end but that of Matrimony; a thing which the equality of our blood and substance did of it selfe almost inuite vs to. Our age and affection increased in such sort , as it seemed fit to *Luscindas* father,for certaine good respects to denie me the entrance of his house any longer ; imita-

ting

ting in a manner therein *Tisbi*, so much solemnized by
the Poets, her parents; which hinderance serued onely to
adde flame to flame, and desire to desire: for although
it set silence to our tongues, yet could they not impose it
to our pens, which are wont to expresse to whom it pleased, the most hidden secrecies of our soules with more liberty then the tong; for the presence of the beloued doth
often distract, trouble, & strike dumbe the boldest tongue
and firmest resolution. O heauens, how many letters haue
I written vnto her? What cheerefull and honest answers
haue I receiued? How many ditties and amorous verses
haue I composed, wherein my soule declared and published her passions, declined her enflamed desires, entertained her remembrance, and recreated her will? In effect
perceiuing my selfe to be forced, and that my soule consu-
med with a perpetuall desire to behold her, I resolued to
put my desires in execution, and finish in an instant that
which I deemed most expedient for the better atchieuing
of my desired and deserued reward; which was (as I did
indeede) to demaund her of her father for my lawfull
Spouse. To which he made answere, that he did gratifie
the good will which I shewed by honouring him, and
desire to honour my selfe with pawnes that were his: but
yet seeing my father yet liued, the motion of that matter
properly most conecrned him. For if it were not done
with his good liking and pleasure, *Luscinda* was not a
woman to be taken or giuen by stealth. I rendred him
thankes for his good will, his wordes seeming vnto mee
very reasonable, at that my father would agree vnto
them, as soone as I should explane the matter; and therefore departed presently to acquaint him with my desires;
who at the time which I entred into a chamber, wherein
he was, stood with a letter open in his hand; and espying
me, e're I could breake my minde vnto him, gaue it me,
saying: by that letter *Cardenio*, you may gather the de
sire that Duke *Ricardo* beares, to doe you any pleasure or
fauour.

fauour. This Duke *Ricardo*, as I thinke you know *Sirs* already, is a *Grande* of *Spaine*, whose Dukedome is seated in the best part of all *Andaluzia*. I tooke the letter and read it; which appeared so vrgent; as I my selfe accounted it would be ill done, if my father did not accomplish the contents thereof, which were indeed, that he should presently addresse me to his Court, to the end I might be companion (and not seruant) to his eldest sonne; and that he would incharge himselfe with the aduancing of me to such preferments as might be answerable vnto the value and estimation he made of my person. I past ouer the whole letter, & was strucken dumbe at the reading thereof, but chiefly hearing my father to say *Cardenio*, thou must depart within two dayes, to accomplish the Dukes desire; and omit not to render Almighty God thankes, which doth thus open the way, by which thou mayest attaine in fine to that which I know thou doest merite; and to these words added certaine others of fatherly counsaile and direction. The terme of my departure arriued, and I spoke to my *Luscinda* on a certaine night, and recounted vnto her all that passed, and likewise to her father, intreating him to ouerslip a few daies, & deferre the bestowing of his daughter else-where, vntill I went to vnderstand Duke *Ricardo* his will: which he promised me, and shee confirmed it with a thousand oathes and promises. Finally, I came to Duke *Ricardoes* Court, as was so friendly receiued and entertained by him, as euen very then enuie began to exercise her accustomed function, being forthwith emulated by the auncient Seruiters; perswading themselues, that the tokens the Duke shewed to doe me fauours, could not but turne to their preiudice. But hee that reioyced most at mine arriuall, was a second sonne of the Dukes called *Fernando*, who was young, gallant, very comely, liberall, and amorous; who within a while after my comming held me so deerely, as euery one wondred thereat: and though the elder loued me well, and did me fauour,

fauour, yet was it in no respect comparable to that wherewithall *Don Fernando* loued and treated me. It therefore befell, that as there is no secresie amongst friends so great, but they will communicate it the one to the other, and the familiarity which I had with *Don Fernando*, was now past the limits of fauour, and turned into decrest amity, be reuealed vnto me all his thoughts, but chi fly one of his loue, which did not a little molest him. For he was enamoured on a Farmers daughter that was his fathers vassall, whose parents were maruellous rich, and she her selfe so beautifull, wary, discreete, and honest, as neuer a one that knew her could absolutely determine wherein in which of all her perfections she did most excell or was most accomplished, And those good parts of the beautifull countrey-maide reduced *Don Fernando* his desires to such an exigent, as he resolued that he might the better gaine her good will, and conquere her integrity, to passe her a promise of marriage, for otherwise he should labour to effect that which was impossible, and but striue against the streame. I, as one bound thereunto by our friendship, did thwart and disswade him from his purpose with the best reasons, & most efficacious words I might : and seeing all could not preuaile, I determined to acquaint the Duke *Ricardo* his father therewithall. But *Don Fernando* being very crafty and discreete, suspected and feared as much, because he considered that in the law of a faithfull seruant, I was bound not to conceale a thing that would turne so much to the preiudice of the Duke my Lord: and therefore both to diuert and deceiue me at once, that he could finde no meanes so good, to deface the remembrance of that beauty out of his minde, which held his hart in such subiection, then to absent himself for certaine moneths: and he would likewise haue that absence to be this, that both of vs should depart together, and come to my fathers house, vnder pretence (as hee would informe the Duke) that he went to see and chea-
                                                              pen

pen certaine great horfes that were in the Citie wherein
I was borne ; a place of breeding the beft horfes in the
world. Scarce had I heard him fay this (when borne a-
way by the naturall propenfion each one hath to his
countrey, and my loue ioynde) although his defignment
had not beene fo good , yet would I haue ratified it , as
one of the moft expedient that could be imagined, becaufe I faw occafion and oportunity fo fairely offred, to
returne and fee againe my *Lufcinda*. And thereof fet on
by this thought and defire, I approued his opinion , and
did quicken his purpofe, perfwading him to profecute it
with all poffible fpeede, for abfence would in the end
work her effect in defpite of the moft forcible and vrgent
thoughts; and when he faid this to me , hee had already
vnder the title of a husband (as it was afterward knowne)
reaped the fruits of his longing defires , from his beautifull countrey maide, and did onely await an oportunity
to reueale it without his owne detriment ; fearefull of
the Duke his fathers indignation, when he fhould vnderftand his errour.

It afterward hapned that as loue in young men is not
for the moft part loue but luft, the which (as it euer pro-
pofeth to it felfe as his laft end and period is delight) fo
as foone as it obtaineth the fame, it likewife decaieth and
maketh forcibly to retire that which was termed loue;
for it cannot tranfgreffe the limits which Nature hath
affigned it, which boundings or meares nature hath in
no wife allotted to true and fincere affection. I would
fay that as foone as *Don Ferdinando* had inioyed his
Country laffe, his defires weakned, and his importunities
waxed colde; and if at the firft he fained an excufe to ab-
fent himfelfe, that he might with more facility compaffe
them, he did now in very good earneft procure to depart
to the end he might not put them in execution. The
Duke gaue him licenfe to depart , and commaunded me
to accompany him. We came to my Citie, where my father

ther entertayned him according to his calling. I saw *Lu-scinda*, and then againe were reuiu'd (although indeede they were neither dead nor mortified)my desires, and acquainted *Don Fernando* (alas to my totall ruine) with them, because I thought it was not lawfull by the law of amity to keepe any thing concealed from him. There I dilated to him, on the beauty, wit, and discretion of *Lu-scinda* in so ample manner, as my prayses stirred in him a desire to view a damzell so greatly adorned, and inriched with so rare endowments : and this his desire I through my misfortune satisfied, shewing her vnto him by the light of a candle, at a window where we two were wont to parle together; where he beheld her to be such, as was sufficient to blot out of his memory al the beauties which euer he had viewed before. He stood mute, beside him-selfe and rauished : and moreouer rested so greatly ena-moured, as you may perceiue in the Discourse of this my dolefull narration. And to inflame his desires the more, (a thing which I fearefully auoyded, and onely discoue-red to heauen)fortune so disposed that he found after me one of her letters, wherein she requested that I would demand her of her father for wife; which was so discreet, honest and amorously penned, as he said after reading it, that in *Luscinda* alone were included all the graces of beauty and vnderstanding ioyntly, which were diuided and separate in all the other women of the world. Yet in good sooth I wil here confesse the truth, that although I saw cleerely how deseruedly *Luscinda* was thus extolde by *Don Ferdinando*, yet did not her praises please me so much pronounced by him; and therefore began to feare and suspect him, because he let no moment ouerslip vs without making some mention of *Luscinda*, and would still himselfe begin the discourse, were the occasion euer so far-fetched : a thing which rowsed in me I cannot tell what iealousie ; not that I did feare any trauerse in *Lu-scindas* loyalty, but yet for all my fates made me the very

Q   thing

thing which they most assured me : and *Don Ferdinando* procured to read all the papers I sent to *Luscinda*, or she to me, vnder pretext that he tooke extraordinary delight to note the witty conceits of vs both. It therefore fell out, that *Luscinda* hauing demaunded of me a booke of Chiualry to reade, wherein she tooke maruellous delight, and was that of *Amadis du Gaule*.

Scarce had *Don-Quixote* well heard him make mention of bookes of Knighthood, when he replied to him; if you had good Sir but once tolde me at the beginning of your Historicall narration, that your Lady *Luscinda* was affected to the reading of Knightly aduentures, you needed not to haue vsed any amplification to indeere or make plaine vnto me the eminencie of her wit ; which certainly could not in any wise be so excellent and perspicuous as you haue figured it , if she wanted the propension and feeling you haue rehearsed , to the perusing of so pleasing discourses: so that henceforth with me, you need not spend any more words to explane and manifest the height of her beauty, worthes and vnderstanding; for by this onely notice I haue receiued of her deuotion two books of Knighthood, I doconfirm her for the most faire and accomplished woman for all perfections in the world: and I would to God good Sir , that you had also sent her together with *Amadis* the Histories of the good *Don Rugel of Grecia*; for I am certaine the Lady *Luscinda* would haue taken great delight in *Darayda* and *Garaya*, and in the wittie conceits of the Sheepheard *Darinel*, and in these admirable verses of his Bucolickes , sung and rehearsed by him with such grace, discretion and liberty. But a time may come, wherein this fault may be recompenced, if it shall please you to come with me to my village ; for there I may giue you three hundred bookes, which are my soules greatest contentment , and the intertainment of my life; although I doe now verily beleeue that none of them are left, thankes be to the malice

lice of euill and enuious inchanters. And I befeech you to pardon me this tranfgreffion of our agreement at the firft, promifed not to interrupt your Difcourfes: for when I heare any motion made of Chiualry or Knights errant, it is no more in my power to omit to fpeake of them, then in the Sunne-beames to leaue off warming, or in the Moones to render things humid. And therefore I intreat pardon, and that you will profecute your Hiftory, which is that which moft imports vs.

Whileft *Don-Quixote* fpoke thofe wordes *Cardenio* hanged his head on his breft, giuing manifeft tokens that he was exceeding fad. And although *Don-Quixote* requefted him twice to follow on with his Difcourfe, yet neither did he lift vp his head, or anfwer a word, till at laft after he had ftood a good while mufing, hee held vp his head and faid; it cannot be taken out of my minde, nor is there any one in the world can depriue me of the conceit, or make me beleeue the contrary : and hee were a bottle-head that would thinke or beleeue otherwife then that the great villaine, Mafter *Elifabat* the Barber kept Queene *Madafima* as his Lemman. That is not fo I vow by fuch and fuch, quoth *Don-Quixote* in great choler (and as he was wont, rapt out three or foure round oathes) and it is great malice, or rather villany to fay fuch a thing. For Queene *Madafima* was a very noble Lady, and it ought not to be prefumed that fo high a Princeffe would fall in loue with a Quack-faluer : and whofoeuer thinkes the contrary, lies like an arrant villaine; as I will make him vnderftand a horfebacke or a foote, armed or difarmed, by night or by day, or as he beft liketh. *Cardenio* ftood beholding him very earneftly as he fpoke thefe wordes, whom the accident of his madneffe had by this poffeffed, and was not in plight to profecute his Hiftory : nor would *Don-Quixote* giue eare to it, he was fo mightily difgufted to heare Queene *Madafima* detracted. A maruellous accident, for he tooke her defence as earneft-

Q 2 ly,

ly,as if fhe were verily his true and naturall Princeffe; his wicked bookes had fo much diftracted him. And *Cardenio* being by this furioufly madde,hearing himfelfe anfwered with the lie, and the denomination of a villaine, with other the like outrages,he tooke the reft in ill part, and lifting vp a ftone that was neere vnto him,gaue *Don Quixote* fuch a blow therewithall, as he ouerthrew him to the ground on his backe. *Sancho Panca* feeing his Mafter fo roughly handled, fet vpon the foole with his fift fhut ; and the ragged man receiued his affault in fuch manner,as he likewife ouerthrew him to his feete with one fift,and mounting afterward vpon him, did worke him with his feete like a piece of dough : and the Goatheard who thought to fuccour him, was like to incurre the fame danger. And after hee had ouerthrowne and beaten them all very well,he departed from them and entred into the wood very quietly. *Sancho* arofe, and with rage to fee himfelfe fo belaboured without defert, he ran vpon the Goatheard to be reuenged on him, faying that he was in the fault, who had not premonifhed them,how that mans rauing fits, did take himfo at times; for had they beene aduertifed thereof, they might haue ftood all the while on their guard. The Goatheard anfwered, that he had already aduifed them thereof; and if hee had not beene attentiue thereunto, yet he was therefore nothing the more culpable. *Sancho Panca* replied, and the Goatheard made a reioyndrie thereunto, but their difputation ended at laft,in the catching hold of one anothers beards,and befifting themfelues fo vncompaffionately,as if *Don Quixote* had not pacified them, they would haue torne one another to pieces. *Sancho* holding ftill the Goatheard faft, faid vnto his Lord, Let mee alone Sir *Knight of the ill fauoured face*, for on this man who is a Clowne as I am my felfe,and dubbed Knight,I may fafely fatisfie my felfe of the wrong he hath done me, by fighting with him hand to hand like an honourable man. It is

true,

true, quoth *Don-Quixote*, but I know well, that he is no wise culpable of that which hath hapned. And saying so appeased them; and turned againe to demaund of the Goatheard, whether it were possible to meet again with *Cardenio*; for he remained possessed with an exceeding desire to know the end of his History. The Goatheard turned againe to repeat what he had said at the first, to wit, that he knew not any certaine place of his abode: but if he baunted that Commarke any whife, he would sometime meete with him, eyther in his madde or modest humour.

EXTRACT 3

From Part 3 chapter 13, Part 4 chapters 1 and 2

Don Quixote decides to run mad for love in the manner of Cardenio, Amadis de Gaul or Orlando, sending Sancho Panza away with a love-message to his beloved Lady Dulcinea del Toboso. Sancho, returning to their native village, meets Don Quixote's friends the curate and the barber, who hope to lure him home – in order to cure him of his obsession with chivalric romances – by posing as a damsel in distress and her squire.

Pages 3.13.267 and 4.1.286 contain the following marginal notes, not included in the facsimiles reproduced here:

3.13.267 line 14, *Iulian*: '*One who for the rape of his daughter, committed by* Rodericke *King of Spaine, brought in the Moores and destroyed all the Countrey.*'

4.1.286 line 6, *Vellido*: '*One that murdered* Sancho *King of Castile, as he was easing himselfe at the siege of Camora.*'

Sancho liftened to all the talke and inftructions, and bore them away well in memory, and gaue them great thankes for the intention they had to counfellhis Lord to become an Emperour, and not an Archbifhop : for as he faid , hee imagined in his fimple iudgement that an Emperours were of more ability to reward their Squires then an Archbifhops errant. Hee likewife added that he thought it were neceffary he went fomewhat before them to fearch him , and deliuer his Ladies anfwere : for perhaps it alone would be fufficient to fetch him out of that place , without putting them to any further paines. They liked of *Sancho Pancas* deuice, and therefore determined to expect him, vntil his returne with the newes of finding his Mafter. With that *Sancho* entred in by the clifts of the rockes (leauing them both behinde together) by which ran a little fmooth ftreame ,

S 3 to

to which other Rockes and some trees that grew neere vnto it, made a fresh and pleasing shaddow. The heates, and the day wherein they arriued there, was one of those of the moneth of August, when in those places the heate is intollerable: the houre, about three in the afternoone. All which did render the place more grateful, and inuited them to remaine therein vntill *Sanchoes* returne. Both therefore arresting there quietly vnder the shadow, there arriued to their hearing the sound of a voyce, which without being accompanied by any instrument, did resound so sweet and melodiously, as they remained greatly admired, because they esteemed not that to be a place wherein any so good a Musitian might make his abode. For although it is vsually said that in the woods and fields are found Shepheards of excellent voyces, yet is this rather a Poetical indeerement, then an approued truth; and most of al when they perceiued that the verses they heard him singing were not of rusticke composition, but rather of delicate and Courtly inuention. The truth whereof is confirmed by the verses, which were these:

WHo doth my weale diminish thus and staine?
            Disdaine.
And say by whom, my woes augmented be?
            by Iealousie.
And who my patience doth by triall wrong?
            an absence long.
If that be so, then for my grieuous wrong
  No remedie at all, I may obtaine,
  Since my best hopes I cruelly finde slaine
  By Disdaine, Iealousie, and Absence long.
Who in my minde, those dolors still doth mone?
            Dire Loue.
And who my glories ebbe, doth most importune?
            Fortune.
And to my plaints, by whom increase is giuen?
            By heauen.   *If*

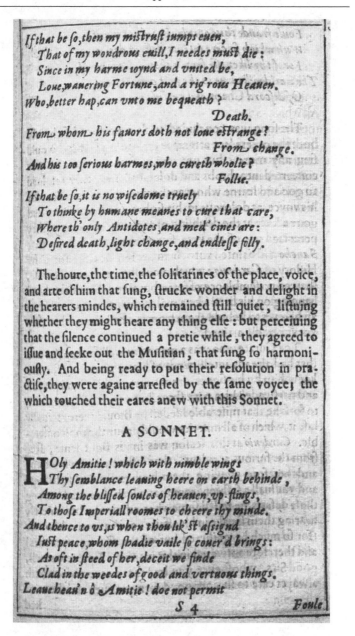

If that be so, then my mistrust iumps euen,
  That of my wondrous euill, I needes must die:
  Since in my harme ioynd and vnited be,
  Loue, wauering Fortune, and a rig'rous Heauen.
Who, better hap, can vnto me bequeath?
                        Death.
From whom his fauors doth not loue estrange?
                       From change.
And his too serious harmes, who cureth wholie?
                         Follie.
If that be so, it is no wisedome truely
  To thinke by humane meanes to cure that care,
  Where th' only Antidotes, and med'cines are:
  Desired death, light change, and endlesse folly.

The houre, the time, the solitarines of the place, voice, and arte of him that sung, strucke wonder and delight in the hearers mindes, which remained still quiet, listning whether they might heare any thing else : but perceiuing that the silence continued a pretie while, they agreed to issue and seeke out the Musitian, that sung so harmoniously. And being ready to put their resolution in practise, they were againe arrested by the same voyce; the which touched their eares anew with this Sonnet.

A SONNET.

*H*Oly Amitie! which with nimble wings
    Thy semblance leaning heere on earth behinde,
  Among the blissed soules of heauen, vp-flings,
  To those Imperiall roomes to cheere thy minde.
And thence to vs, is when thou lik'st assignd
  Iust peace, whom shadie vaile so couer'd brings:
  As oft in steed of her, deceit we finde
  Clad in the weedes of good and vertuous things.
Leaue heau'n ô Amitie! doe not permit

               S 4   *Foule*

Foule fraude thus openly thy robes t'inuest ;
With which sincere intents, destroy does it.
For if thy likenesse from't thou dost not wrest,
The world will turne, to the first conflict soone,
Of discord Chaos and confusion.

The song was concluded with a profound sigh; and both the others lent attentiue eare to heare if hee would sing any more; but perceiuing that the musicke was conuerted into throbs and dolefull plaints, they resolued to goe and learne who was the wretch, as excellent for his voyce, as dolorous in his sighes : and after they had gone a little at the doubling of the point of a cragge, they perceiued one of the very same forme and fashion that *Sancho* had painted vnto them, when he tolde them the History of *Cardenio* : which man espying them likewise, shewed no semblance of feare, but stood stil with his head hanging on his brest like a malecontent, not once lifting vp his eyes to behold them from the first time, when they vnexpectedly arriued.

The Curate who was a man very well spoken (as one that had already intelligence of his misfortune, for hee knew him by his signes) drew neerer to him, and prayed and perswaded him with short, but very forcible reasons, to forsake that miserable life, lest he should there eternally lose it, which of all miseries would proue the most miserable. *Cardenio* at this season was in his right sense, free from the furious accident, that distracted him so often; and therefore viewing them both attired in so strange and vnusuall a fashion from that which was vsed among those desarts, he rested somewhat admired ; but chiefely hearing them speake in his affaire, as in a matter knowne (for so much he gathered out of the Curates speeches) and therefore answered in this manner : I perceiue well, good Sirs (whosoeuer you be) that heauen which hath alwayes care to succour good men, yea euen and the wic-

ked

ked many times, hath without any defert addreft vnto me
by thefe defarts and places fo remote from vulgar haunt,
perfons, which laying before mine eyes with quicke and
pregnant reafons the little I haue to leade this kinde of
life, doe labour to remoue me from this place to a better :
and by reafon they know not as much as I doe, and that
after efcaping this harme, I fhall fall into a farre greater,
they account me perhaps for a man of weake difcourfe,
and what is worfe for one wholly deuoide of iudgement.
And were it fo, yet is it no maruell ; for it feemes to me
that the force of the imagination of my difafters is fo
bent and powerfull in my deftruction, that I without being able to make it any refiftance, do become like a ftone,
voyde of all good feeling and knowledge : and I come to
know the certainty of this truth, when fome men doe recount and fhew vnto me tokens of the things I haue
done, whileft this terrible accident ouer-rules me : and
after I can doe no more, then be grieued though in vaine,
and curfe without benefite my too froward fortune ; and
render as an excufe of my madneffe, the relation of the
caufe thereof, to as many as pleafe to heare it : for wife-
men perceiuing the caufe, will not wonder at the effects.
And though they hiue me no remedie, yet at leaft wil not
condemne me, for it will conuert the anger they conceiue
at my mifrules, into compaffion of my difgraces. And Sirs
if by chance it be fo, that you come with the fame intention that others did, I requeft you ere you inlarge farther
your difcreet perfwafions, that you will giue eare a while
to the relation of my mifhaps : for perhaps when you
haue vnderftood it, you may faue the labour that you
would take, conforting an euill wholly incapable of con-
folation.

Both of them which defired nothing fo much then to
vnderftand from his owne mouth, the occafion of his
harmes, did intreate him to relate it, promifing to do nothing elfe in his remedie or comfort, but what himfelfe
pleafed.

pleaſed. And with this the ſorrowfull Gentleman began
his doleſull Hiſtorie, with the very ſame wordes almoſt
that he had rehearſed it to *Don-Quixote* and the Goatheard a few dayes paſt, when by occaſion of Maſter *Eliſa-
bat* and *Don. Quixotes* curioſitie in obſeruing the *Decorum* of Chiualry, the tale remained imperfect, as our Hi-
ſtory left it aboue. But now good fortune ſo diſpoſed
things, that his fooliſh fit came not vpon him, but gaue
him leiſure to continue his ſtorie to the end; and ſo arriuing to the paſſage that ſpoke of the Letter *Don Ferdinando* found in the booke of *Amadis du Gaule*, *Cardenio*
ſaid that he had it very well in memory; and the ſenſe
was this.

Lvscinda to Cardenio.

*I Diſcouer daily in thee worthes, that oblige & inforce me
to holde thee deere: and therefore if thou deſireſt to haue
me diſcharge this debt, without ſeruing a writ on my honour,
thou mayeſt eaſily doe it. I haue a father that knowes thee,
and loues me likewiſe well; who without forcing my will, will
accompliſh that which iuſtly thou oughteſt to haue : if it be
ſo, that thou eſteemeſt me as much as thou ſayeſt, and I doe
beleeue.*

This Letter moued me to demand *Luſcinda* of her father for my wife, as I haue already recounted ; and by it
alſo *Luſcinda* remained in *Don Ferdinandos* opinion
crowned, for one of the moſt diſcreete women of her
time. And this billet Letter was that which firſt put him
in minde to deſtroy me, e're I could effect my deſires. I
tolde to *Don Ferdinando* wherein conſiſted all the diffi-
cultie of her fathers protracting of the marriage, to wit,
in that my father ſhould firſt demaund her ; the which I
dared not to mention vnto him, fearing leſt hee would
not willingly conſent therunto; not for that the qualitie,
bountie, vertue, and beautie of *Luſcinda*, were to him
vn-

vnknowne, or that she had not partes in her able to en-
noblish and adorne any other linage of Spaine whatsoeuer: but because I vnderstood by him that he desired not
to marrie me vntill hee had seene what Duke *Ricardo*
would doe for me. Finally, I tolde him that I dared not
reueale it to my father, as well for that inconuenience, as
for many others that made me so affraid, without knowing what they were, as me thought my desires would neuer take effect. To all this *Don Ferdinando* made me answere that he would take vpon him to speake to my father, and perswade him to treate of that affaire also with
Luscindas. O ambitious *Marius*. O cruell *Cataline*. O
facinorous *Quila*. O treacherous *Galalon*. O trayterous
Vellido. O reuengefull *Iulian*. O couetous *Iudas*. Traytor, cruell, reuengefull, and cousening, what indeserts did
this wench commit, who with such plaines discouered to
thee the secrets and delights of his heart? What offence
committed I against thee? What words did I speake, or
counsel did I giue, that were not all addrest to the increasing of thine honour and profite? But on what doe I of
all wretches the worst complaine, seeing that when the
current of the starres do bring with it mishaps, by reason
they come downe precipitarely from aboue, there is no
earthly force can with-hold, or humane industry preuent
or euacuat them? Who would haue imagined that *Don
Fernando* a noble Gentleman, discreete, obliged by my
deserts, and powerfull to obtaine whatsoeuer the amorous desire would exact of him, where and whensoeuer
it seazed on his heart (would as they say) become so corrupt as to depriue me of one onely sheepe, which yet I did
not possesse? But let these considerations be laide apart
as vnprofitable, that we may knit vp againe the broken
threede of my vnfortunate History. And therefore I say,
that *Don Ferdinando* beleeuing that my presence was a
hinderance to put his treacherous and wicked designe in
execution, he resolued to send me to his eldest brother,
vnder

vnder pretext to get some money of him, for to buy sixe
great horses, that he had of purpose, and onely to the end
I might absent my selfe, bought the very same day that he
offered to speake himselfe to my father, and would haue
me goe for the money (because he might bring his treacherous intent the better to passe) could I preuent this
treason? Or could I perhaps but once imagin it? No truly; but rather glad for the good merchandize hee had
made, did make proffer of my selfe to depart for the money very willingly. I spoke that night to *Luscinda*, and
acquainted her with the agreement past betweene mee
and *Don Ferdinando*, bidding her to hope firmely that
our good iust desires would sort a wished and happie end.
She answered me againe (as little suspecting *Don Ferdinandos* treason as my selfe) bidding me to returne with all
speede, because she beleeued that the conclusion of our
affections should be no longer deferred, then my father
deferred to speake vnto hers. And what was the cause I
know not, but as soone as she had said this vnto me, her
eyes were filled with teares, and somewhat thwarting her
throate, hindered her from saying many other things,
which me thought she striued to speake.

I rested admired at this new accident vntill that time
neuer seene in her; for alwaies as many times as my good
fortune and diligence graunted it, we conuersed with all
sport and delight, without euer intermedling in our discourses, any teares, sighes, complaints, suspitions, or fears.
All my speech was to aduance my fortune; for hauing receiued her from heauen as my Ladie and Mistresse, then
would I amplifie her beautie, admire her worth, & praise
her discretion. She on the other side would returne mee
the exchange, extolling in me, what she as one enamoured accounted worthy of laude and commendation. After this we would recount a hundred thousand toyes and
chaunces befalne our neighbours and acquaintance, and
that to which my presumption dared farthest to extend it
selfe,

selfe, was sometimes to take her beautifull and Iuorie hands perforce, and kisse them as well as I might through the rigorous strictnesse of a niggardly Iron grate which deuided vs. But the precedent night to the day of my sad departure, she wept, sobd, and sighed, and departed, leauing me full of confusion and inward assaults, amazed to beholde such new and dolefull tokens of sorrow and feeling in *Luscinda*. But because I would not murder my hopes, I did attribute all these things to the force of her affection towards me, and to the griefe which absence is wont to stirre in those that loue one another deerely. To be briefe, I departed from thence sorrowfull and pensiue, my soule being ful of imaginations and suspitions, and yet know not what I suspected or imagined. Cleere tokens, foretelling the sadde successe and misfortune which attended me. I arriued to the place where I was sent, and deliuered my letters to *Don Ferdinandos* brother, & was well intertained, but not wel dispatched; for he commanded me to expect (a thing to me most displeasing) eight dayes; and that out of the Duke his fathers presence; because his brother had written vnto him to send him certaine moneyes vnknowne to his father. And all this was but false *Don Ferdinandos* inuention, for his brother wanted not money wherewithall to haue dispatched me presently, had not he written the contrary.

This was so displeasing a commandement & order, as almost it brought me to termes of disobeying it, because it seemed to me a thing most impossible to sustaine my life so many daies in the absence of my *Luscinda*. And specially hauing left her so sorrowfull as I haue recounted; yet notwithstanding I did obey like a good seruant, although I knew it would be with the cost of my health. But on the fourth day after I had arriued, there came a man in my search with a letter, which he deliuered vnto me, and by the indorsement I knew it to be *Luscindas*; for the hand was like hers. I opened it not without feare and

and assailement of my senses, knowing that it must haue
beene some serious occasion, which could moue her to
write vnto me, being absent, seeing she did it so rarely, e-
uen when I was present. I demaunded of the bearer before I read, who had deliuered it to him, and what time
he had spent in the way. He answered me that passing by
chaunce at mid-day through a streete of the Citie, a very
beautifull Ladie did call him from a certaine window:
Her eyes were all beblubbered with teares; and said vnto
him very hastily: Brother, if thou beest a Christian, as thou
appearest to be one, I pray thee for Gods sake, that thou
doe forthwith addresse this letter to the place and person
that the superscription assigneth, (for they be well knowen)and therein thou shalt doe our Lord great seruice.
And because thou mayest not want meanes to doe it, take
what thou shalt finde wrapped in that Handkerchife:
and saying so, she threw out of the window a handkerchife, wherein were lapped vp a hundred Rials, this ring
of golde which I carie here, and that letter which I deliuered vnto you; and presently without expecting mine
answere she departed, but first saw me take vp the handkerchife and letter; and then I made her signes that I
would accomplish herein her command: and after perceiuing the paines I might take in bringing you it so well
considered, and seeing by the indorsement, that you were
the man to whom it was addrest. For Sir I know you verie well; and also obliged to doe it by the teares of that
beautiful Ladie, I determined not to trust any other with
it, but to come and bring it you my selfe in person: and in
sixteene houres since it was giuen vnto me, I haue trauelled the iourney you know, which is at least eighteene
leagues long. Whilest the thankefull new messenger
spake thus vnto me, I remained in a manner hanging on
his words, and my thighes did tremble in such manner, as
I could very hardly sustaine my selfe on foote: yet taking
courage, at last I opened the letter; whereof these were
the Contents.   *The*

The word that Don Ferdinando hath past vnto you to speake to your father, that he might speake to mine, he hath accomplished more to his owne pleasure then to your profite. For Sir you shall vnderstand, that he hath demaunded mee for his wife; and my father, borne away by the aduantage of worthes which he supposes to be in Don Ferdinando more then in you, hath agreed to his demaund in so good earnest, as the espousals shall bee celebrated within these two daies, and that so secretly and alone, as onely the heauens and some folke of the house shall be witnesses. How I remaine, imagine, and whether it be conuenient you should returne you may consider: and the successe of this affaire shall let you to perceiue, whether I loue you well or no. I beseech Almighty God that this may arriue vnto your hands, before mine shall see it selfe in danger to ioyne it selfe with his, which keepeth his promised faith so ill.

These were in summe, the contents of the letter, and the motiues that perswaded me presently to depart, without attending any other answere, or other monies: for then I conceiued clearly, that it was not the buyall of the horses, but that of his delights, which had moued *Don Ferdinando* to send me to his brother. The rage which I corceiued against him ioyned with the feare to lose the iewell which I had gained by so many yeares seruice, and desires, did set wings on mee, for I arriued as if I had flien the next day at mine owne Citie, in the houre and moment fit to goe speake to *Luscinda.* I entred secretly, and left my Mule whereon I rode in the honest mans house, that had brought mee the letter: and my fortune purposing then to be fauourable to me, disposed so mine affaires that I found *Luscinda* sitting at that yron grate, which was the sole witnesse of our loues. *Luscinda* knew me straight and I her, but not as we ought to knew one another. But who is hee in the world which may truly vaunt, that he hath penetrated, and throughly exhausted the confused thoughts, and mutable nature of women?

women? truly none. I say then to proceede with my tale,
that as soone as *Luscinda* perceiued me she said *Cardenio*
I am attired with my wedding garments, and in the Hall
doe waite for mee, the traitor *Don Ferdinando*, and my
couetous father with other witnesses, which shall rather
be such of my death, then of mine espousals; bee not
troubled deare friend, but procure to be present at this
sacrifice, the which if I cannot hinder, by my perswasions
and reasons, I carry hidden about me a poynard secretly
which may hinder more resolute forces, by giuing end to
my life, and a beginning to thee, to know certaine the affection which I haue euer borne, and doe beare vnto
thee. I answered her troubled and hastily, fearing I should
not haue the leasure to reply vnto her, saying sweete Ladie, let thy works verifie thy words, for if thou carriest a
poynard to defend thy credit, I doe heere likewise beare
a sword wherewithall, I will defend thee, or kill my selfe if
fortune proue aduerse and contrary. I beleaue that she
could not heare all my words by reason she was called
hastily away as I perceiued, for that the bridegroome expected her comming. By this the night of my sorrowes did
throughly fall, and the Sunne of my gladnesse was set:
and I remained without light in mine eyes, or discourse
in my vnderstanding. I could not finde the way into her
house, nor could I moue my selfe to any part: yet considering at last how important my presence was, for that
which might befall in that aduenture, I animated my selfe
the best I could, and entred into the house; and as one
that knew very well all the entries and passages thereof, and specially by reason of the trouble and bu-
sinesse that was then in hand, I went in vnperceiued of
any. And thus without being seene, I had the oportuni-
tie to place my selfe in the hollow roome of a window
of the same Hall, which was couered by the endes of
two incountring peeces of tapestry, from whence I could
see all that was done in the Hall, remaining my selfe
vnuiewed

vnuiewed of any. VVho could now deſcribe the aſſiults and ſurpriſals of my heart whilſt I there abode : The thoughts which incountred my mind, the conſiderations which I had, which were ſo many and ſuch, as they can neither be ſaid, nor is it reaſon they ſhould. Let it ſuffice you to know, that the bridegroome entred into the Hall without any ornament, wearing the ordinary array hee was wont, and was accompanied by a couſen Germaine of *Luſcindas*, and in all the Hall there was no ſtranger preſent, nor any other then the houſehold ſeruants, within a while after *Luſcinda* came out of the Parlour accompanied by her mother and two waiting maides of her owne, as richly attired and deckt, as her calling and beautie deſerued, and the perfection of courtly pompe and brauery could affoord my diſtraction and trouble of mind lent me no time to note particularly the apparrell ſhee wore, and therefore did onely marke the colours which were carnation and white; and the ſplendour which the precious ſtones and Iewels of her tires, and all the reſt of her garments yeelded : yet did the ſingular beauty of her faire and golden treſſes ſurpaſſe them ſo much, as being in competencie with the precious ſtones, and flame of foure linkes that lighted in the Hall, yet did the ſplendour thereof ſeeme farre more bright and glorious to mine eies. O memory the mortall enemie of mine eaſe, to what end ſerues it now to repreſent vnto me the vncomparable beautie of that my adored enemy. Were it not better cruel memory to remember & repreſent that which ſhe did then, that being moued by ſo manifeſt a wrong, I may at leaſt endeuour to loſe my life, ſince I cannot procure a reuenge? Tire not good ſirs to heare the digreſſions I make, for my griefe is not of that kinde that may be rehearſed ſuccinctly and ſpeedily; ſeeing that in mine opinion euery paſſage of it is worthy of a large diſcourſe.

To this the Curate anſwered; that not onely they were

T   not

not tyred or wearied, hearing of him, but rather the receaued maruellous delight to heare him recount each minutie and circumstance, because they were such, as deserued not to be past ouer in silence, but rather merited as much attention as the principall parts of the History: you shall then wit (quoth *Cardenio*) that as they thus stood in the Hall, the Curate of the Parish entred, and taking them both by the hand, to doe that which in such an act is required at the saying of, *Will you Ladie* Luscinda *take the Lord* Don Ferdinando *who is heere present for your lawfull spouse, according as our holy mother the Church commands?* I thrust out all my head and neck out of the tapistry, and with most attentiue eares and a troubled mind, setled my selfe to heare what *Luscinda* answered; expecting by it the sentence of my death, or the confirmation of my life. O if one had dared to sally out at that time, and cried with a loud voice : O *Luscinda, Luscinda,* see well what thou doest, consider withall what thou owest me. Behold how thou art mine, and that thou canst not be any others, note that thy saying of yea, and the end of my life shall be both in one instant. O traytor *Don Ferdinando* robber of my glory, death of my life, what is this thou pretendest? what wilt thou doe ? Consider that thou canst not Christianlike atchieue thine intention, seeing *Luscinda* is my spouse, and I am her husband. O foolish man now that I am absent, and farre from the danger, I say what I should haue done, and not what I did. Now after that I haue permitted my deere Iewel to be robbed, I exclaime on the theefe, on whom I might haue reuenged my selfe, had I had as much heart to doe it as I haue to complaine. In fine since I was then a coward and a foole, it is no matter though I now die ashamed, sory, and franticke. The Curate stood expecting *Luscindaes* answere a good while erre she gaue it, and in the end, when I hoped that she would take out the Poynard to stab her selfe, or would vnloose her tongue to say some truth, or vse

vse some reason or perswasion that might redound to
my benefit, I heard heere in stead thereof answere with a
dismaied and languishing voice the word: *I will* : and
then *Don Fernando* said the same, and giuing her the
ring, they remained tyed with an indissoluble knot. Then
the bridegroome comming to kisse his spouse, she set her
hand vpon her heart, and fell in a trance betweene
her mothers armes.

Now onely remaines vntold the case wherein I was,
seeing in that, yea, which I had heard my hopes deluded,
Luscindaes words and promises fallified ; and my selfe
wholy disabled to recouer in any time the good which
I lost in that instant, I rested void of counsell, abandoned
(in mine opinion) by heauen, proclaimed an enemy to
the earth which vpheld me, the ayre denying breath e-
nough for my sighes, and the water, humour sufficient to
mine eyes: only the fire increased in such maner, as I burned throughly with rage and iealousie. All the house was
in a tumult for this sodaine amazement of *Luscinda*, and
as her mother vnclasped her bosome to giue her the ayre,
there appeared in it a paper foulded vp, which *Don Fernando* presently seazed on, and went aside to reade it by
the light of a torch, and after he had read it, he sate down
in a chayre, laying his hands on his cheeke, with manifest
signes of melancholy discontent, without bethinking
himselfe of the remedies that were applied to his spouse,
to bring her againe to her selfe. I seeing all the folke of
the house thus in an vprore, did aduenture my selfe to
issue, not waighing much whether I were seene or no;
bearing withall a resolution (if I were perceiued) to play
such a rash part as all the world should vnderstand the
iust indignation of my breast, by the reuenge I would
take on false *Don Fernando*, and the mutable and dismaied traytresse: But my destinie which hath reserued
me for greater euils, if possibly there may be any greater
then mine owne, ordained that instant my wit should

abound, whereof euer since I haue so great want : and therefore without will to take reuenge of my greatest e-nemies (of whom I might haue taken it with all facilitie, by reason they suspected so little my being there) I de-termined to take it on my selfe, and execute in my selfe the paine which they deserued; and that perhaps with more rigour then I would haue vsed towards them, if I had slaine them at that time, seeing that the sodaine death finisheth presently the pain, but that which doth lingringly torment, kils alwaies without ending the life. To be short, I went out of the house, and came to the other where I had left my Mule, which I caused to bee sadled, and without bidding mine hoast adieu, I mounted on her, and rode out of the Citie, without daring like ano-ther *Lot* to turne back and behold it: and then seeing my selfe alone in the fields, and that the darkenesse of the night did couer me, and the silence thereof inuite me to complain, without respect or feare to be heard or known, I did let slip my voyce and vntied my tongue with so ma-ny curses of *Luscinda* and *Don Ferdinando*, as if thereby I might satisfie the wrong they had done me. I gaue her the title, of cruell, vngratefull, false, and scornefull, but specially of couetous, seeing the riches of mine enemie, had shut vp the eyes of her affection, to depriue me ther-of, and render it to him, with whom fortune had dealt more frankly and liberally : and in the midst of this tune of maledictions and scornes, I did excuse her saying: that it was no maruaile that a Mayden kept close in her pa-rents house, made and accustomed alwaies to obey them, should at last condiscend to their will specially, seeing they bestowed vpon her for husband so noble, so rich and proper a Gentleman as to refuse him, would be reputed in her to proceed either from want of iudge-ment, or from hauing bestowed her affections elsewhere, which things must of force greatly preiudice her good opinion and renowne. Presently would I turne againe to say

say, that though she had told them that I was her spouse, they might easily perceiue that in chusing me she had not made so ill an election, that she might not be excused, seeing that before *Don Fernando* offred himselfe, they themselues could not happen to desire, if their wishes were guided by reason, so fit a match for their daughter as my selfe: and she might easily haue said, before shee put her selfe in that last and forcible passe, of giuing her hand, that I had already giuen her mine, which I would come out to confesse and confirme all that she could any way faine in this case: and concluded in the end, that little loue, lesse iudgement, much ambition and desire of greatnesse caused her to forget the wordes, wherewithall she had deceiued, intertained, and sustained me in my firme hopes and honest desires.

Vsing these wordes, and feeling this vnquietnesse in my brest, I trauelled all the rest of the night, and strucke about dawning into one of the entries of these mountaines, through which I trauelled three dayes at random, without following or finding any path or way, vntill I arriued at last to certaine meddowes and fieldes, that lie I know not in which part of these mountaines: and finding there certaine heards, I demaunded of them which way lay the most craggy and inaccessible places of these rocks, and they directed me hither; and presently I trauelled towards it, with purpose here to end my life: and entring in among those desarts, my Mule through wearinesse and hunger fell dead vnder me, or rather as I may better suppose, to disburden himselfe of so vile and vnprofitable a burden as he carried in me. I remained a foote, ouercome by nature, and pierced thorow and thorow by hunger, without hauing any helpe, or knowing who might succour me; and remained after that manner I know not how long prostrate on the ground; and then I arose againe without any hunger, and I found neere vnto mee certaine Goatheards, who were those doubtlesly that

T 3   fedde

fedde me in my hunger. For they tolde me in what manner they found me, and how I spake so many foolish and madde wordes, as gaue certaine argument that I was deuoide of iudgement. And I haue felt in my selfe since that time that I enioy not my wits perfectly, but rather perceiue them to be so weakened and impaired, as I commit a hundred follies, tearing mine apparrell, crying loudly thorow these desarts, cursing my fates, and idely repeating the beloued name of mine enemie, without hauing any other intent or discourse at that time, then to endeauour to finish my life ere long: and when I turne to my selfe, I am so broken and tyred, as I am scarce able to stirre me. My most ordinary Mansion place is in the hollownes of a Corke tree, sufficiently able to couer this wretched carkasse. The Cowheards and the Goatheards that feede their cattell here in these mountaines, moued by charity, gaue me sustenance, leauing meate for me by the wayes, and on the rockes which they suppose I frequent, and where they thinke I may finde it: and so although I doe then want the vse of reason, yet doth naturall necessity induce me to know my meate, and stirreth my appetite to couet, and my will to take it. They tell me when they meete me in my wits, that I doe other times come out to the high wayes, and take it from them violently, euen when they themselues doe offer it vnto mee willingly. After this manner doe I passe my miserable life, vntill heauen shall be pleased to conduct it to the last period, or so change my memorie, as I may no more remember on the beauty and treacherie of *Luscinda*, or the iniurie done by *Don Ferdinando*; for if it doe me this fauour without depriuing my life, then will I conuert my thoughts to better discourses: if not, there is no other remedie but to pray God to receiue my soule into his mercie; for I neyther finde valour nor strength in my selfe to ridde my bodie out of the straites, wherein for my pleasure I did at first willingly intrude it.

This

This is Sirs the bitter relation of my difasters : wherefore iudge if it be such as may be celebrated with lesse feeling and compassion then that, which you may by this time haue perceiued in my selfe ? And doe not in vaine labour to perswade or counsel me that which reason shal affoord you may bee good for my remedie : for it will worke no other effect in me then a medicine prescribed by a skilfull Physitian, to a Patient that will in no sort receiue it. I will haue no health without *Luscinda*, and since she pleaseth to be alienate her selfe , being or seeing she ought to be mine : so doe I also take delight to be of the retinue of mishap , although I might be a retainer to good fortune. She hath ordained that her changing shall establish my perdition. And I will labour by procuring mine owne losse, to please and satisfie her wil : and it shal be an example to ensuing ages, that I alone wanted that, wherewithall all other wretches abounded, to whom the impossibility of receiuing comfort , proued sometimes a cure ; but in me it is an occasion of greater feeling and harme, because I am perswaded that my harmes cannot end euen with very death it selfe. Here *Cardenio* finished his large discourse, and vnfortunate and amorous Hiftory; and iust about the time that the Curate was bethinking himselfe of some comfortable reasons to answer and perswade him : he was suspended by a voyce which arriued to his hearing, which with pittifull accents said what shall be recounted in the fourth part of this Narration. For in this very point the wise and most absolute Historiographer *Cid Hamete Benengeli* finished
the third Part of this
HISTORY.

T 4   THE

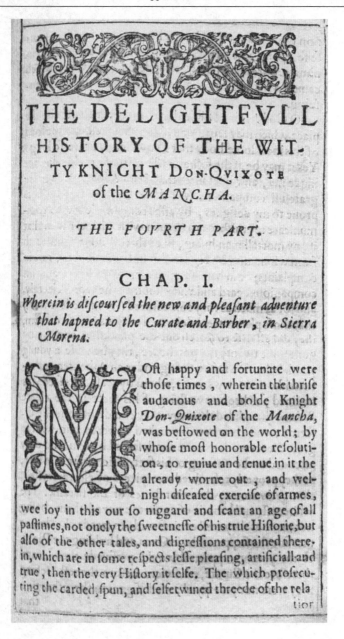

THE DELIGHTFVLL
HISTORY OF THE WIT-
TY KNIGHT Don-Qvixote
of the *MANCHA*.

THE FOVRTH PART.

CHAP. I.

Wherein is discoursed the new and pleasant aduenture that hapned to the Curate and Barber, in Sierra Morena.

Ost happy and fortunate were those times, wherein the thrise audacious and bolde Knight *Don-Quixote* of the *Mancha*, was bestowed on the world; by whose most honorable resoluti-on, to reuiue and renue in it the already worne out, and wel-nigh diseased exercise of armes, wee ioy in this our so niggard and scant an age of all pastimes, not onely the sweetnesse of his true Historie, but also of the other tales, and digressions contained there-in, which are in some respects lesse pleasing, artificiall and true, then the very History it selfe. The which prosecu-ting the carded, spun, and selfetwined threede of the rela

tion

tion fayes,that as the Curate beganne to bethinke himfelfe vpon fome anfwere that might both confort and a-
nimate *Cardenio* , hee was hindered by a voyce which
came to his hearing , faid very dolefully the words en-
fuing.

O God ! is it pofsible that I haue yet found out the
place which may ferue for a hidden Sepulchre,to the load
of this loathfome body that I vnwillingly beare fo long ?
Yes it may be,if the folitarineffe of thefe rockes doe not
illude me , ah vnfortunate that I am ! How much more
gratefull companions will thefe cragges and thickets
proue to my defignes , by affoording me leifure to communicate my mifhaps to heauen with plaints ; then that
if any mortall man liuing , fince there is none vpon earth
from whom may be expected counfell in doubts , eafe in
complaints, or in harmes remedie. The Curate and his
companions heard and vnderftood all the words cleerely,
and for as much as they coniectured (as indeede it was)
that thofe plaints were deliuered very neere vnto them,
they did all arife to fearch out the plaintiffe; and hauing
gone fome twenty fteppes thence , they behelde a young
youth behinde a rocke,fitting vnder an Afhe tree,and attired like a country Swaine,whom by reafon his face was
inclined , as hee fate wafhing of his feete in the cleere
ftreame that glided that way, they could not perfectly difcerne ; and therefore approched towards him with fo
great filence,as they were not defcryed by him who only
attended to the wafhing of his feet,which were fo white,
as they properly refembled two pieces of cleere cryftall,
that grew among the other ftones of the ftreame. The
whiteneffe and beautie of the feete amazed them , being
not made as they well coniectured , to treade cloddes, or
meafure the fteppes of lazie Oxen,and holding the Plow,
as the youthes apparrell would perfwade them ; and
therefore the Curate, who went before the reft , feeing
they were not yet efpyed , made fignes to the other two
that

that they fhould diuert a little out of the way, or hide themfelues behinde fome broken cliffes that were neere the place, which they did all of them, noting what the youth did with very great attention. Hee wore a little browne Capouch, gyrt very neere to his body with a white Towell; alfo a paire of Breeches and Gamafheos of the fame coloured cloth, and on his head a clay coloured Cap. His Gamafheos were lifted vp halfe the legge, which verily feemed to be white *Alablafter*. Finally, hauing wafhed his feete, taking out a linnen Kerchife from vnder his Cappe, he dried them therewithall, and at the taking out of the Kerchife, he held vp his face, and then thofe which ftood gazing on him had leifure to difcerne an vnmatchable beautie, fo furpafsing great, as *Cardenio* rounding the Curate in the eare, faid, this bodie fince it is not *Lufcinda* can be no humane creature, but a diuine. The youth tooke off his Cappe at laft, and fhaking his head to the one and other part, did difheauell and difcouer fuch beautifull haires, as thofe of *Phœbus* might iuftly emulate them : and thereby they knew the fuppofed Swaine to be a delicate woman, yea and the faireft that euer the firft two had feene in their liues, or *Cardenio* himfelfe, the louely *Lufcinda* excepted; for as he after affirmed, no feature faue *Lufcindas* could contend with hers. The long and golden haires did not onely couer her fhoulders, but did alfo hide her round about, in fuch fort, as (her feete excepted) no other part of her body appeared, they were fo neere and long. At this time her hands ferued her for a Combe, which as her feete feemed pieces of cryftall in the water, fo did they appeare among her haires like pieces of driuen Snow. All which circumftances did poffeffe the three which ftood gazing at her with great admiration, and defire to know what fhe was; and therefore refolued to fhew themfelues; and with the noyfe which they made when they arofe, the beautifull mayden held vp her head, and remouing her haires from

before

before her eyes with both handes, she espyed those that had made it, and presently arising full of feare and trouble, she laid hand on a packet that was by her, which seemed to be of apparrell, and thought to flie away, without staying to pull on her shooes, or to gather vp her haire: But scarce had she gone sixe paces when her delicate and tender feete, vnable to abide the rough encounter of the stones made her to fall to the earth. Which the three perceiuing, they came out to her, and the Curate arriuing first of all, said to her: Ladie, whatsoeuer you be, stay and feare nothing; for we which you beholde here, come only with intention to doe you seruice, and therefore you neede not pretend so impertinent a flight, which neyther your feete can endure nor would we permit. The poore Gyrle remained so amazed and confounded, as shee answered not a word: wherefore the Curate and the rest drawing neerer, he tooke her by the hand, and then hee prosecuted his speech, saying, What your habite concealed from vs Ladie, your haires haue bewrayed, being manifest arguments that the causes were of no small moment which haue thus bemasked your singular beauty, vnder so vnworthy array; and conducted you to this all-abandoned desart; wherein it was a wonderfull chaunce to haue met you, if not to remedie your harmes, yet at least to giue you some comfort, seeing no euill can afflict and vexe one so much, and plunge him in so deepe extreames, (whilest it depriues not the life) that will wholly abhorre from listening to the aduice that is offered, with a good and sincere intention; so that faire Ladie, or Lord, or what else you shall please to be termed, shake off your affrightment, and rehearse vnto vs your good or ill fortune, for you shall finde in vs ioyntly, or in euery one apart, companions to helpe you to deplore your disasters.

Whilest the Curate made this speech, the disguised woman stood as one halfe asleepe, now beholding the one, now the other, without once mouing her lippe or
saying

laying a word; much like vnto a rusticke Clowne, when
rare and vnseene things to him before, are vnexpectedly
presented to his view. But the Curate insisting and vsing
other perswasiue reasons addrest to that effect, won her
at last to make a breach on her tedious silence, and with
a profound sigh blow open her currall gates, saying som-
what to this effect : Since the solitarinesse of these rockes
hath not beene potent to conceale me, nor the disheaue-
ling of my disordered haires, licensed my tongue to belie
my sexe, it were in vaine for me to faine that anew, which
if you beleeued it, would be more for courtesies sake then
any other respect. Which presupposed, I say good Sirs,
that I doe gratifie you highly for the liberall offers you
haue made me; which are such, as haue bound me to satisfie your demaund as neere as I may; although I feare
the relation which I must make to you of my mishappes,
will breede sorrow at once with compassion in you, by
reason you shal not be able to find any salue that may cure,
comfort, or beguile them : yet notwithstanding to the
end my reputation may not houer longer suspended in
your opinions, seeing you know me to be a woman, and
view me, young, alone and thus attyred, being things all
of them able eyther ioyned or parted, to ouerthrow the
best credite, I must be enforced to vnfolde, what I could
otherwise most willingly conceale. All this she that appeared so comely spoke without stoppe, or staggering,
with so ready deliuerie and so sweete a voice, as her discretion admired them no lesse then her beautie. And re-
newing againe their complements and intreaties to her,
to accomplish speedily her promise, she setting all coynesse
apart, drawing on her shooes very modestly, and winding
vp her haire, sate her downe on a stone, and the other
three about her, where she vsed no little violence to smo-
ther certaine rebellious teares that stroue to breake forth
without her permission : and then with a reposed and
cleere voyce she began the Historie of her life in this
manner.   In

In this Prouince of *Andaluzia* there is a certaine Towne, from whence a Duke deriues his denomination, which makes him one of those in Spain are call'd *Grandes*: He hath two sonnes, the elder is heire of his States, and likewise as may be presumed of his vertues; the younger is heire I know not of what, if it be not of *Velleda* his treacheries, or *Galalons* fraudes. My parents are this No blemans vassals, of humble and low calling; but so rich, as if the goods of nature had equalled those of their fortunes, then should they haue had nothing else to desire, nor I feared to see my selfe in the misfortunes, wherein I now am plunged. For perhaps my mishaps proceed from that of theirs in not being nobly descended. True it is that they are not so base, as they should therefore shame their calling, nor so high as may check my conceit, which perswades me, that my disasters proceede from their lownesse. In conclusion, they are but Farmours, and plaine people, but without any touch or spot of badde bloud, and as we vsually say, Olde rustie Christians, yet so rustie and auncient, as it, their riches, and magnificent porte, gaines them by little and little the title of Gentilitie; yea, and of worship also; although the treasure and Nobility, whereof they made most price and account, was to haue had me for their daughter: and therefore as well by reason that they had none other heire then my selfe, as also because as affectionate parents, they held me most deere: I was one of the most made of and cherished daughters that euer father brought vp: I was the mirrour wherein they beheld themselues, the staffe of their olde age, and the subiect to which they addrest all their desires. From which, because they were most vertuous, mine did not stray an inch: and euen in the same manner that I was Ladie of their mindes, so was I also of their goods. By me were seruants admitted or dismissed: the notice and account of what was sowed or reaped, past through my handes, of the Oyle-mils, the Wine-presses, the number of
great

great and little cattell, the Bee-hiues; in fine , of all that which so rich a Farmour as my father was, had or could haue; I kept the account , and was the Steward thereof and Mistresse, with such care of my side and pleasure of theirs, as I cannot possible endure it enough. The times of leisure that I had in the day , after I had giuen what was necessary to the head seruants , and others, labourers I did intertaine in those exercises, which were both commendable and requisite for maydens , to wit , in sowing, making of bone-lace , and many times handling the Distaffe: and if sometimes I left those exercises to recreate my minde a little, I would then take some godly booke in hand, or play at the Harpe; for experience had taught me, that musicke ordereth disordered mindes, and doth lighten the passions that afflict the spirit. This was the life which I ledde in my fathers house: the recounting wherof so particularly , hath not beene done for ostentation, nor to giue you to vnderstand that I am rich , but to the end you may note how much , without mine owne fault haue I falne from that happy state I haue said, vnto the vnhappie plight into which I am now reduced. The Historie therefore is this, that passing my life in so many occupations, and that with such recollection as might bee compared to a religious life, vnseene as I thought by any other person then those of our house: for when I went to Masse it was commonly so earely, and so accompanied by my mother and other maid-seruants.; and I my selfe so couerd and watchfull , as mine eyes did scarce see the earth whereon I treade: and yet notwithstanding those of loue , or as I may better terme them, of idlenesse , to which *Linces* eyes may not be compared, did represent me to *Don Ferdinandos* affection and care ; for this is the name of the Dukes younger sonne , of whom I spake before. Scarce had she named *Don Ferdinando* when *Cardenio* changed colour, and began to sweate with such alteration of bodie and countenance, as the Curate and

Barber

Barber which beheld it, feared that the accident of fren-
zie did affault him which was wont as they had heard to
poffeffe him at times. But *Cardenio* did nothing elfe then
fweat, and ftood ftill beholding now and then the countrey gyrle imagining ftraight what fhe was, who without taking notice of his alteration, followed on her difcourfe in this manner. And fcarce had he feene me when
(as he himfelfe after confeft) he abode greatly furpri-
zed by my loue, as his actions did after giue euident
demonftration.

But to conclude, foone the relation of thofe misfortunes which haue no conclufion, I will ouerflip in filence
the diligences and practifes of *Don Ferdinando* vfed to
declare vnto me his affection:he fuborned all the folke of
the houfe. He beftowed gifts and fauours on my parents:
euery day was a holy day,and a day of fports in the ftreets
where I dwelled : at night no man could fleepe for mu-
ficke ; the letters were innumerable that came to my
hands without knowing who brought them; farfed too
full of amorous conceits and offers; and containing more
promifes and proteftations then they had characters. All
which,not onely could not mollifie my mind, but rather
hardened it as much as if he were my mortal enemie,and
therefore did conftrue all the indeuours he vfed to gaine
my good will to be practifed to a contrary end : which
I did not,as according *Don Fernando* vngentle, or that I
efteemed him too importunat,for I took a kind of delight
to fee my felfe fo highly efteemed and beloued of fo noble a Gentleman : nor was I any thing offended to fee
his papers written in my praife;for if I be not deceiued in
this point, be we women euer fo foule, we loue to heare
men call vs beautifull.But mine honefty was that which
oppofed it felfe vnto all thefe things , and the continuall
admonitions of my parents, which had by this plainely
perceiued *Don Fernandos* pretence as one that cared not,
all the world fhould know it. They would often fay vnto

to me, that they had depofited their honours and reputation in my vertue alone and difcretion, and bad me
confider the inequality that was betweene *Don Fernando*
and me, and that I might collect by it how his thoughts
(did he euer fo much affirme the contrary) were more
addreft to compaffe his pleafures then my profit. And that
if I feared any inconuenience might befail, to the end
they might croffe it, & caufe him to abandon his fo vniuft
a purfuite they would match me where I moft liked, eyther to the beft of that towne, or any other towne adioyning, faying they might eafily compaffe it, both by
reafon of their great wealth and my good report. I fortified my refolution and integrity with thefe certaine promifes, and the knowne truth which they told me, and
therefore would neuer anfwere to *Don Fernando* any
word, that might euer fo farre of argue the leaft hope of
condifcending to his defires. All which cautions of mine
which I think he deemed to be difdains, did inflame more
his lafciuious appetite (for this is the name wherewithal
I intitle his affection towards me) which had it beene
fuch as it ought, you had not knowne it now, for then
the caufe of reuealing it had not befalne me. Finally *Don
Fernando* vnderftand how my parents meant to marrie
mee: to the end they might illude his hope of euer pof-
feffing me, or at leaft fet more gards to preferue mine honour, and this newes or furmife was an occafion that hee
did, what you fhall prefently heare.

For one night as I fate in my chamber only attended by
a young Mayden that ferued me, I hauing fhut the doores
very fafe, for feare leaft through any negligence my hone-
ftie might incur any danger without knowing or imagining how it might happe: notwithftanding all my dilige-
ces vfed and preuentions, & amidft the folitude of this filence and recollection, he ftood before me in my chamber. At his prefence I was fo troubled as I loft both fight
and fpeech, and by reafon thereof could not crie, nor I
V   thinke

thinke he would not though I had attempted it, permit me. For he prefently ranne ouer to me, and taking me betweene his armes (for as I haue faid I was fo amazed, as I had no power to defend my felfe) he faid fuch things to me as I knew not how it is poffible that vntruth fhould haue the ability to faine things refembling in fhew fo much the truth: and the traytor caufed teares, to giue credit to his words, and fighes to giue countenance to his intention. I poore foule being alone amidft my friends, & weakly practifed in fuch affairs began I know not how to account his leefings for verities, but not in fuch fort, as his teares or fighes might any wife moue me to any compaffion that were not commendable. And fo the firft trouble & amazement of mind being paft, I began again to recouer my defectiue fpirits, and then faid to him with more courage then I thought I fhould haue had, if as I am my Lord betweene your armes, I were betweene the pawes of a fierce *Lyon*, and that I were made certaine of my liberty on condition to doe or fay any thing preiudiciall to mine honour: it would proue as impoffible for me to accept it, as for that which once hath beene, to leaue off his effence and being. Wherefore euen as you haue ingyrt my middle with your armes, fo likewife haue I tied faft my minde with vertuous and forcible defires, that are wholy difcrepant from yours, as you fhall perceiue, if feeking to force me, you prefume to paffe further with your inordinate defigne, I am your vaffall, but not your flaue, nor hath the nobility of your bloud power nor ought it to harden, to difhonour, ftaine or hold in little account the humility of mine; and I doe efteeme my felfe though a countrey wench and farmers daughter, as much as you can your felfe, though a Nobleman and a Lord: With me your violence fhall not preuaile, your riches gaine any grace, your words haue power to deceiue, or your fighes and teares be able to moue: yet if I fhall finde any of thefe properties mentioned in him when

when my parents fhall pleafe to beftow on me for my
fpoufe, I will prefently fubiect my will to his, nor fhall
it euer varie from his minde a iot: So that if I might remaine with honor,although I refted void of delights,yet
would I willingly beftow on you,that which you prefently labour fo much to obtaine: all which I do fay to diuert
your ftraying thought from euer thinking that any one
may obtaine of me ought who is not my lawfull fpoufe:
If the let onely confiftes therein moft beautifull *Dorotea*
(for fo I am called) anfwered the difloyall Lord: behold I
giue thee here my hand to be thine alone:and let the hea-
uens from which nothing is concealed; and this Image of
our Lady which thou haft heere prefent, be witneffes of
this truth.When *Cardenio* heard her fay that fhe was called *Dorotea*, he fell again into his former fufpicion,and in
the end confirmed his firft opinion to be true:but would
not interrupt her fpeech,being defirous to know the fucceffe, which he knew wholy almoft before,and therefore
faid onely. Lady is it poffible that you are named *Doro-*
tea. I haue heard fpeake of another of that name, which
perhaps hath runne the like courfe of your misfortunes:
but I requeft you to continue your relatiõ,for a time may
come wherein I may recount vnto you things of the fame
kinde, which will breed no fmall admiration. *Dorotea*
noted *Cardenios* words,and his vncouth, and difaftrous
attire, and then intreated him very inftantly if he knew
any thing of her affaires, he would acquaint her therewithall. For if fortune had left her any good, it was onely the courage which fhe had to beare patiently and difa-
fter that might befall her, being certaine in her opinion
that no new one could arriue which might increafe a whit
thofe fhe had alreadie. Ladie I would not let flip the occafion (quoth *Cardenio*) to tell you what I thinke, if that
which I imagine were true: and yet there is no commo-
ditie left to doe it: nor can it auaile you much to know
it. Let it be what it lift faid *Dorotea*: but that which af-

V 2   ter

ter befell, of my relation was this : That *Don Fernando*
tooke an Image that was in my chamber for witnesse of
our contract, and added withall most forcible words and
vnusuall oathes, promising vnto me to become my husband. Although I warned him, before he had ended his
speech, to see well what he did, and to weigh the wrath
of his father, when he should see him married to one so
base, and his vassall, and that therefore he should take
heede that my beautie such as it was should not blinde
him. Seeing he should not finde therein a sufficient excuse for his errour: and that if he meant to doe me any
good, I coniured him by the loue that he bore vnto me,
to licenfe my fortunes to roule in their owne spheare, according as my quality reached : For such vnequall mat-
ches doe neuer please long, nor perseuer with that delight
wherewithall they begunne.

All the reasons heere rehearsed, I said vnto him, and
many moe ; which now are falne out of minde, but
yet proued of no efficacy to weane him from his obstinate
purpose, euen like vnto one that goeth to buy; which
intention neuer to pay for what he takes : and therefore
neuer considers the price, worthinesse, or faultlesse of the
stuffe he takes to credit. I at this season made a briefe dif-
course, and said thus to my selfe : I may doe this, for I
am not the first which by matrimonie hath ascended from
a low degree to a high estate : nor shall *Don Fernando*
be the first whom beautie or blind affection (for that is
the most certaine) hath induced to make choyce of a consort vnequall to his greatnesse. Then since herein I create no new world, nor custome, what error can be committed by embracing the honour wherewithall fortune
crownes me : Although it so befell that his affection to
to me endured no longer then till he accomplish his will,
for before God, I certes shall still remaine his wife. And if
I should disdainfully giue him the repulse, I see him now
in such termes, as perhaps forgetting the dutie of a Noble
man,

man, hee may vſe violence, and then ſhall I remaine
for euer diſhonoured,and alſo without excuſe of the im-
putations of the ignorant which knew not how much
without any fault I haue falne into this ineuitable danger. For, what reaſons may be ſufficiently forcible to
perſwade my father and other that this Noble man did
enter into my chamber without my conſent? All theſe
demaunds and anſwers did I in an inſtant reuolue in
mine imagination, and found my ſelfe chiefly forced
(how I cannot tell) to aſſent to his petition, by the
witneſſes hee inuoked,the teares hee ſhed, and finally
by his ſweete diſpoſition and comely feature, which accompanied with ſo many arguments of vnfained affection, were able to conquere and enthrall any other
heart, though it were as free and wary as mine owne.
Then called I for my waiting Maide that ſhe might on
earth accompany the celeſtiall witneſſes. And then
Don Fernando turned againe to reiterate and confirme
his oathes, and added to his former, other new
Saints as witneſſes, and wiſhed a thouſand ſucceeding
maledictions to light on him, if he did not accompliſh
his promiſe to me. His eyes againe waxed moyſt, his
ſighes increaſed, and himſelfe inwreathed mee more
ſtraightly betweene his armes, from which he had neuer once looſed mee : and with this, and my Maydens
departure, I left to be a Mayden, and hee beganne to be
a traytor, and diſloyall man. The day that ſucceeded to
the night of my miſhaps came not I thinke ſo ſoone as
Don Fernando deſired it : for after a man hath ſatisfied
that which the appetite couets, the greateſt delight it
can take after is to appart it ſelfe from the place where
the deſire was accompliſhed. I ſay this, becauſe *Don
Fernando* did haſten his departure from me, by my Maids
induſtrie, who was the very ſame that had brought him
into my chamber, hee was got in the ſtreete before
dawning. And at his departure from mee he ſaid (although

though not with so great shew of affection and vehe-
mencie, as hee had vsed at his comming) that I might
be secure of his faith, and that his oathes were firme
most true: and for a more confirmation of his word hee
tooke a rich ring off his finger, and put it on mine. In
fine he departed and I remained behinde I cannot well
say, whether ioyfull or sad; but this much I know that
I rested confused and pensiue, and almost beside my selfe
for the late mischance; yet eyther I had not the heart,
or else I forgot to chide my Maide for her treacherie
committed by shutting vp *Don Fernando* in my chamber: for as yet I could not determine, whether that which
hadbefalne mee, was a good or an euill. I said to *Don*
Ferdinando at his departure that he might see mee other
nights when he pleased by the same meanes hee had
come that night seeing I was his owne, and would rest
so, vntill it pleased him to let the world know that I
was his wife. But hee neuer returned againe, but the
next night following; could I see him after for the
space of a moneth eyther in the streete or Church, so as
I did but spend time in vaine to expect him: although I
vnderstoode that hee was still in towne, and rode euerie
other day a hunting an exercise to which hee was much
addicted.

Those dayes were I know, vnfortunate and accursed to
me, and those houres sorrowfull; for in them I began to
doubt, nay rather wholly to discredite *Don Fernando* his
faith: and my maide did then heare loudly the checkes I
gaue vnto her for her presumption, euer vntill then dis-
sembled. And I was moreouer constrained to watch and
keepe guard on my teares and countenance, lest I should
giue occasion to my parents to demaund of me the cause
of my discontents, and therby ingage me to vse ambages
or vntruthes to couer them. But all this ended in an instant, one moment arriuing whereon all these respects
tumbled, all honourable discourses ended, patience was
lost,

loſt, and my moſt hidden ſecrets iſſued in publicke: which was when there was ſpread a certaine rumour through-out the towne within a few dayes after, that *Don Fernando* had married in a Citie neere adioyning, a damzell of ſurpaſſing beautie, and of very noble birth, although not ſo rich, as could deſerue by her preferment or dowrie ſo worthy a husband. It was alſo ſaid, that ſhe was named *Luſcinda*, with many other things that hapned at their Spouſals, worthy of admiration. *Cardenio* hearing *Luſcinda* hamed, did nothing elſe but lift vp his ſhoulders, bite his lippe, bend his browes, and after a little while ſhedde from his eyes two floods of teares. But yet for all that *Dorotea* did not interrupt the file of her Hiſtorie, ſaying, This dolefull newes came to my hearing, and my heart in ſteede of freezing thereat, was ſo inflamed with choler and rage, as I had welnigh runne out to the ſtreets, and with outcries publiſhed the deceit and treaſon that was done to me : but my furie was preſently aſſwaged by the reſolution which I made, to doe what I put in execution the very ſame night, and then I put on this habite which you ſee, being giuen vnto me by one of thoſe that among vs Countrey-folke are called Swaines, who was my fathers ſeruant; to whom I diſcloſed all my misfor-tunes, and requeſted him to accompany me to the Citie, where I vnderſtood maine enemie ſoiourned. He, after he had reprehended my boldneſſe, perceiuing me to haue an inflexible reſolution, made offer to attend on me as hee ſaid, vnto the end of the world: and preſently after I truſ-ſed vp in a pillowbeare, a womans attire, ſome mony and jewels, to preuent neceſſities that might befall ; and in the ſilence of night, without acquainting my treacherous maide with my purpoſe, I iſſued out of my houſe, accom-panied by my ſeruant, and many imaginations : and in that manner ſet on towards the Citie, and though I went on foote, was yet borne away flying, by my deſires, to come if not time enough to hinder that which was paſt,

V 4 yet

yet at least to demaund of *Don Fernando* that he would tell me with what conscience or soule he had done it. I arriued where I wished within two dayes and a halfe; and at the entry of the Citie I demaunded where *Luscinda* her father dwelled? and he of whom I first demaunded the question answered me more then I desired to heare: he shewed me the house, and recounted to me all that befell at the daughters marriage, being a thing so publique and knowne in the Citie, as men made meetings of purpose to discourse thereof. Hee said to me that the very night wherein *Don Fernando* was espoused to *Luscinda*, after that she had giuen her consent to be his wife, shee was instantly assayled by a terrible accident, that strucke her into a traunce, and her spouse approching to vnclaspe her bosome, that she might take the ayre, found a paper foulded in it, written with *Luscindas* owne hand, wherein she said and declared, that she could not be *Don Fernandoes* wife, because she was already *Cardenioes*, who was, as the man tolde me, a very principall Gentleman of the same Citie; and that if she had giuen her consent to *Don Fernando*, it was onely done because she would not disobey her parents: in conclusion he tolde me, that the Billet made also mention, how shee had a resolution to kill her selfe presently after the marriage, and did also lay downe therein the motiues she had to doe it. All which as they say, was confirmed by a poynard that was found hidden about her in her apparrell. Which *Don Fernando* perceiuing, presuming that *Luscinda* did flout him, and holde him in little account, hee set vpon her ere she had turned to her selfe, and attempted to kill her with the very same poynard; and had done it if her father and other friends which were present had not opposed themselues, and hindered his determination. Moreouer they reported that presently after *Don Fernando* absented himselfe from the Citie, and that *Luscinda* turned not out of her agony vntill the next day, and then recounted to her parents

how

how fhe was verily Spoufe to that *Cardenio* of whom we
fpake euen now. I learned befides that *Cardenio* as it is
rumourd,was prefent at the marriage, and that as foone
as he faw her married,being a thing he would neuer haue
credited,departed out of the Citie in a defperate moode,
but firft left behinde him a letter, wherein he fhewed at
large the wrong *Lufcinda* had done to him, and that hee
himfelfe meant to go to fome place where people fhould
neuer after heare of him. All this was notorious, and
publiquely bruited throughout the Citie,and euery one
fpoke thereof,but moft of all hauing very foone after vnderftood that *Lufcinda* was miffing from her parents
houfe and the Citie ; for fhee could not be found in neyther of both : for which her parents were almoft befide
themfelues, not knowing what meanes to vfe to finde
her.

These newes reduced my hopes again to their rancks,
and I efteemed it better to find *Don Fernando* vnmarried
then married,prefuming that yet the gates of my remedy
were not wholly fhut, I giuing my felfe to vnderftand
that heauen had peraduenture fet that impediment on
the fecond marriage, to make him vnderftand what hee
ought to the firft ; and to remember, how he was a *Chriftian*,and that he was more obliged to his foule then to
humane refpects. I reuolued all thefe things in my mind,
and comfortleffe did yet comfort my felfe, by faining
large yet languifhing hopes to fuftaine that life which
I now do fo much abhor. And whileft I ftaide thus in the
Citie,ignorant what I might doe,feeing I found not *Don
Fernando*,I heard a cryer goe about publikely,promifing
great rewards to any one that could finde me out,giuing
fignes of the very age & apparrell I wore. And I likewife
heard it was bruited abroad,that the youth which came
with me had carried me away from my fathers houfe. A
thing that touched my foule very neerely, to view my
credite fo greatly wrackt, feeing that it was not fufficient
                                                        to

to haue loſt it by my comming away, without the addition of him with whom I departed, being a ſubiect ſo baſe
and vnworthy of my loftier thoughts. Hauing heard this
crie, I departed out of the Citie with my ſeruant : whoe
uen then began to giue tokens that he faultred in the fi-
delitie he had promiſed to me : and both of vs together
entred the very ſame night into the moſt hidden parts of
this mountaine, fearing leſt we might be found. But as it
is commonly ſaid, that one euill cals on another, and that
the end of one diſaſter is the beginning of a greater, ſo
proued it with me; for my good ſeruant, vntill then faithfull and truſtie, rather incited by his owne villany then
my beautie, thought to haue taken the benefite of the o-
portunity which theſe inhabitable places offered; and ſol-
licited me of loue, with little ſhame and leſſe feare of
G O D or reſpect of my ſelfe : and now ſeeing that I
anſwered his impudencies with ſeuere and reprehen-
ſiue wordes, leauing the intreaties aſide, wherwithall
he thought firſt to haue compaſt his will, he began to vſe
his force. But iuſt heauen which ſeldome or neuer neg-
lects the iuſt mans aſſiſtance, did ſo fauour my procee-
dings, as with my weake forces, and very little labour, I
threw him downe a ſteepe rocke, and there I left him, I
know not whether aliue or dead. And preſently I entred
in among theſe mountaines, with more ſwiftneſſe then
my feare and wearineſſe required; hauing therein no o-
ther proiect or deſigne, then to hide my ſelfe in them, and
ſhunne my father and others, which by his intreaty and
meanes ſought for me euery where. Some moneths are
paſt ſince my firſt comming here, where I found a Heard-
man, who carried me to a village ſeated in the midſt of
theſe rockes, wherein he dwelled and intertained me,
whom I haue ſerued as a Sheepheard euer ſince, procuring
as much as lay in me to abide ſtill in the fielde, to couer
theſe haires, which haue now ſo vnexpectedly betraide
me. Yet all my care and induſtry was not very beneficiall,
seeing

seeing my Master came at last to the notice that I was no man but a woman, which was an occasion that the like euill thought sprung in him, as before in my seruant. And as fortune giues not alwayes remedie for the difficulties which occurre, I found neyther rocke nor downefall to coole and cure my Masters infirmitie, as I had done for my man: and therefore I accounted it a lesse inconuenience to depart thence and hide my selfe againe among these desarts, then to aduenture the triall of my strength or reason with him. Therefore, as I say, I turned to imboske my selfe, and search out some place, where without any encumbrance I might intreat heauen with my sighes and teares, to haue compassion on my mishap; and lend me industry and fauour, eyther to issue fortunately out of it, or else to die amidst these solitudes, not leauing any memory of a wretch, who hath ministred matter, although not through her owne default, that men may speake and murmure of her, both in her owne and in other countries.

Chap. II.

Which treates of the discretion of the beautifull Doro-
tea, and the artificiall manner vsed to disswade the
amorous Knight from continuing his penance: and
how he was gotten away; with many other delight-
full and pleasant occurrences.

 His is Sirs the true relation of my Trage-die, see therfore now and iudge, whether the sighes you heard, the words to which you listened, and the teares that gushed out at mine eyes haue not had sufficient occasion to appeare in greater abun-dance: and hauing considered the quality of my disgrace;
you

you shall perceiue all comfort to be vaine, seeing the remedie thereof is impossible. Only I will request at your handes one fauor which you ought and may easily grant, and is that you will addresse me vnto some place, where I may liue secure from the feare and suspition I haue to be found by those which I know doe daily trauell in my pursuit: for although I am sure that my parents great affection towards me, doth warrant me to be kindely receiued and intertained by them: yet the shame is so great that possesseth me onely to thinke that I shall not returne to their presence in that state which they expect, as I account it farre better to banish my selfe from their sight for euer, then once to beholde their face, with the least suspition that they againe would beholde mine diuorced from that honestie which whilome my modest behauiour promised. Here she ended, and her face suddenly ouer-run by a louely scarlet, perspicuously deuoted the feeling and bashfulnes of her soule.

The audients of her sad storie, felt great motions both of pitie and admiration for her misfortunes: and although the Curate thought to comfort and counsell her forthwith, yet was he preuented by *Cardenio*, who taking her first by the hand, said at last; Ladie, thou art the beautifull *Dorotea*, daughter vnto rich *Cleonardo*. *Dorotea* rested admired when she heard her fathers name, and saw of how little value he seemed, who had named him, For we haue already recounted how raggedly *Cardenio* was clothed; and therefore she said vnto him, and who art thou friend that knowest so well my fathers name; for vntill this houre (if I haue not forgotten my selfe) I did not once name him throughout the whole Discourse of my vnfortunate tale? I am (answered *Cardenio*) the vnluckie Knight whom *Luscinda* (as thou saidst) affirmed to be her husband. I am the disastrous *Cardenio*, whom the wicked proceeding of him that hath also brought thee to those termes wherein thou art, hath conducted me to the
state

ftate in which I am, and thou mayeft beholde ragged, naked, abandoned by all humane comfort, & what is worfe,
voyde of fenfe ; feeing I onely enioy it but at fome few
fhort times, and that, when heauen pleafeth to lend it me.
I am hee *Dorotea* that was prefent at *Don Fernandoes*
vnreafonable wedding, and that heard the confent which
Lufcinda gaue him to be his wife. I was hee that had
not the courage to ftay and fee the end of her traunce, or
what became of the paper found in her bofome. For my
foule had not power or fufferance, to beholde fo many
difuentures at once, and therefore abandoned the place
and my patience together, and onely left a Letter with
mine Hofte, whom I intreated to deliuer it into *Lufcinda*
her owne handes, and then came into thefe defarts, with
refolution to end in them my miferable life, which fince
that houre I haue hated as my moft mortall enemie. But
fortune hath not pleafed to depriue me of it, thinking it
fufficient to haue impaired my wit, perhaps referuing me
for the good fucceffe befalne me now in finding of your
felfe : for that being true (as I beleeue it is) which you
haue here difcourfed, peraduenture it may haue referued
yet better hap for vs both in our difafters then we doe expect. For prefuppofing that *Lufcinda* cannot marry with
Don Fernando becaufe fhe is mine, nor *Don Fernando*
with her becaufe yours : and that fhe hath declared fo
manifeftly the fame : we may well hope that heauen hath
meanes to reftore to euery one that which is his owne,
feeing it yet confifts in being not made away, or anihila-
ted. And feeing this comfort remaines, not fprung from
any very remote hope, nor founded on idle furmifes, I requeft thee faire Ladie to take another refolution in thine
honourable thought, feeing I meane to do it in mine, and
let vs accommodate our felues to expect better fucceffe.
For I doe vow vnto thee by the faith of a Gentleman and
Chriftian, not to forfake thee vntill I fee thee in *Don Fer-*
nandoes poffeffion, and when I fhall not by reafons be a-
ble

ble to induce him to acknowledge how farre he refts indebted to thee, then will I vfe the liberty graunted to me
as a Gentleman, and with iuft title challenge him to the
fielde, in refpect of the wrong he hath done vnto thee;
forgetting wholly mine owne iniuries, whofe reuenge I
will leaue to heauen, that I may be able to right yours
on earth.

Dorotea refted wonderfully admired hauing knowne
and heard *Cardenio*, and ignoring what competent thanks
fhe might returne him in fatisfaction of his large offers,
fhe caft her felfe downe at his feete to haue kift them,
which *Cardenio* would not permit : and the Licenciat
anfwered for both prayfing greatly *Cardenios* difcourfe:
and chiefly intreated, prayed, and counfelled them, that
they would go with him to his village, where they might
fitte hemfelues with fuch things as they wanted, and
alfo take order how to fearch out *Don Fernando*, or car-
rie *Dorotea* to her fathers houfe, or doe elfe what they
deemed moft conuenient. *Cardenio* and *Dorotea* gratified his courtefies, and accepted the fauour hee proffered.
The Barber alfo who had ftood all the while filent and
fufpended, made them a prettie Difcourfe, with as friendly an offer of himfelfe, and his feruice as Mafter Curate;
and likewife did briefly relate the occafion of their comming thither, with the extrauagant kinde of madneffe
which *Don Quixote* had, and how they expected now his
Squires returne, whom they had fent to fearch for him.
Cardenio hauing heard him named, remembred prefently
as in a dreame the conflict paft betweene them both, and
recounted it vnto them, but could not in any wife call to
minde the occafion thereof.

EXTRACT 4

From Part 4 chapters 9 and 10

Dorotea agrees to replace the barber as a simulated damsel in distress so as to help the barber and the curate bring Don Quixote home, and poses as the Princess Micomicona, telling Don Quixote that she needs him to come and rescue her parents from the giant who is oppressing the Kingdom of Micomicon. Cardenio, sane and shaved, joins the party. Herself well read in romances, Dorotea expertly humours Don Quixote as they journey to an inn at which he has already experienced various misadventures. At the inn, while Don Quixote sleeps, the curate entertains the company by telling the long inset story of the Curious Impertinent. While this tale progresses, Don Quixote destroys a great number of wine bags stored in the room where he is staying, thinking them giants.

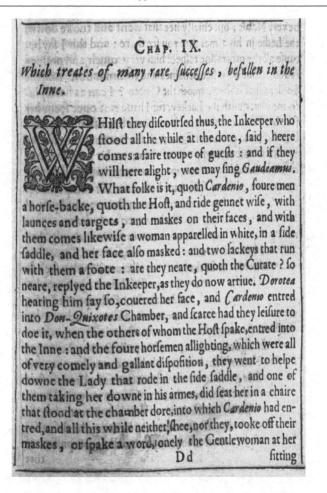

Chap. IX.

Which treates of many rare successes, befallen in the Inne.

Hilst they discoursed thus, the Inkeeper who stood all the while at the dore, said, heere comes a faire troupe of guests : and if they will here alight, wee may sing *Gaudeamus*. What folke is it, quoth *Cardenio*, foure men a horse-backe, quoth the Host, and ride gennet wise, with launces and targets, and maskes on their faces, and with them comes likewise a woman apparelled in white, in a side saddle, and her face also masked : and two lackeys that run with them a foote : are they neare, quoth the Curate ? so neare, replyed the Inkeeper, as they do now arriue. *Dorotea* hearing him say so, couered her face, and *Cardenio* entred into *Don-Quixotes* Chamber, and scarce had they leisure to doe it, when the others of whom the Host spake, entred into the Inne : and the foure horsemen allighting, which were all of very comely and gallant disposition, they went to helpe downe the Lady that rode in the side saddle, and one of them taking her downe in his armes, did seat her in a chaire that stood at the chamber dore, into which *Cardenio* had entred, and all this while neither, shee, nor they, tooke off their maskes, or spake a word, onely the Gentlewoman at her

D d   fitting

sitting downe in the chaire breathed forth a very deep sigh,
and let fall her armes like a sicke and dismayed person. The
Lackeyes carried away their horses to the stable. Master Curate seeing and noting all this, and curious to know what
they were that came to the Inne in so vnwonted an attyre,
and kept such profound silence therein, went to the Lackeies
and demaunded of one of them that which hee desired to
know. Who answered him, In good faith Sir I cannot tell
you what folke this is, only this I know, that they seeme to
be very Noble, but chiefly hee that went and tooke downe
the Ladie in his armes that you see there: and this I say because all the others doe respect him very much, and nothing
is done, but what hee ordaines and commaunds. And the
Ladie, what is shee, quoth the Curate? I can as hardly informe you, quoth the Lackey, for I haue not once seene her
face in all this iourney, yet I haue heard her often grone and
breathe out so profound sighes, as it seemes shee would giue
vp the Ghost at euery one of them; and it is no maruaile
that wee should know no more, then wee haue said, for my
companion and my selfe haue beene in their companie but
two dayes: for they incountred vs on the way and prayed
and perswaded vs to goe with them vnto *Andaluzia*, promising that they would recompence our paines largely. And
hast thou heard them name one another, said the Curate? no
truly answered the Lackey, for they all trauaile with such silence, as it is a wonder, for you shall heare not a word a-
mong them, but the sighes and throbs of the poore Ladie,
which doe moue in vs very great compassion, and wee doe
questionlesse perswade our selues that shee is forced, where-
soeuer shee goes, and as it may bee collected by her attyre
shee is a Nunne, or as is most probable goes to be one, and
perhaps shee goeth so sorrowfull as it seemes, because shee
hath no desire to become religious. It may very well be so,
quoth the Curate; and so leauing them hee returned to the
place where he had left *Dorotea*, who hearing the disguised
Ladie to sigh so often mooued by the natiue compassion of
that

that fexe, drew neare her and faid, what ailes you good Madame? I pray you thinke if it be any of thofe inconueniences to which women bee fubiect, and whereof they may haue vfe and experience to cure them, I doe offer vnto you my feruice, affiftance, and good will, to helpe you as much as lies in my power. To all thofe complements the dolefull Ladie anfwered nothing, and although *Dorotea* made her againe larger offers of her feruice, yet ftood fhee euer filent vntill the bemasked Gentleman (whom the Lackey faid the reft did obay) came ouer and faid to *Dorotea*: Ladie doe not trouble your felfe, to offer any thing to that woman, for fhee is of a moft ingratefull nature, and is neuer wont to gratifie any curtefie, nor doe you feeke her to anfwere vnto your demaunds, if you would not heare fome lie from her mouth. I neuer faid any (quoth the filent Lady) but rather becaufe I am fo true & fincere without guiles, I am now drowned here in thofe misfortunes, & of this I would haue thy felfe beare witnes, feeing my pure truth makes thee to be fo falfe & difloyal.

Cardenio ouerheard thefe words very cleere and diftinctly, as one that ftood fo neere vnto her that faid them, as onely *Don-Quixotes* chamber doore ftood betweene them, and inftantly when he heard them, he faid with a very loud voice, good God, what is this that I heare? what voyce is this that hath touched mine eare? The Ladie moued with a fodaine paffion turned her head at thofe outcries, and feeing fhee could not perceiue him that gaue them, fhe got vp, and would haue entred into the roome, which the Gentleman efpying, withheld her, and would not let her ftirre out of the place: and with the alteration and fodaine motion the maske fell off her face, and fhe difcouered an incomparable beautie, and an angelicall countenance, although it was fomewhat wanne and pale, and turned heere and there with her eies to euery place fo earneftly as fhe feemed to be diftracted; which motions without knowing the reafon why they were made, ftrucke *Dorotea* and the reft that beheld her into very great compaffion. The Gentleman held her very ftrongly faft by

Dd 2   the

the shoulders , that hee more on his owne face that
was falling , and was so busied therein , as hee could not
hold vp the maske , as it did in the end wholy: *Dorotea*
who had likewise embraced the Ladie, lifting vp her eyes by
chance, saw that he which did also embrace the Ladie was
her spouse *Don Fernando* : and scarce had she knowne him
when breathing out along and most pitifull *Alas* from the
bottome of her heart she fell backward in a trance. And if
the Barber had not bin by good hap at hand, she would haue
falne on the ground with all the waight of her bodie : the
Curate presently repaired to take off the vaile of her face,
and cast water thereon,& as soone as he did discouer it, *Don
Fernando*,who was he indeed that held fast the other , knew
her,& looked like a dead man as soone as he viewed her,but
did not all this let go *Luscinda*,who was the other whom he
held so fast, and that laboured so much to escape out of his
hands. *Cardenio* likewise heard the *Alas* that *Dorotea* said,
when she fell into a trance, and beleeuing that it was his *Luscinda*,issued out of the chamber greatly altered, and the first
he espied was *Don Fernando*,which held *Luscinda* fast ; who
forthwith knew him : and all the three , *Luscinda, Cardenio,*
and *Dorotea* stood dumbe and amazed, as folke that knew
not what had befalne vnto them. All of them held their
peace,and beheld one another. *Dorotea* looked on *Don Fernando. Don Fernando* on *Cardenio, Cardenio* on *Luscinda*,and
Luscinda againe on *Cardenio* : but *Luscinda* was the first that
broke silence, speaking to *Don Fernando* in this manner.
Leaue me off Lord *Fernando*, I coniure thee, by that thou
shouldest bee, for that which thou art ; if thou wilt not doe
it for any other respect : let me cleaue to the wall, whose Iuie
I am,to the supporter from whom neither thy importunities
nor threats,promises or gifts could once deflect mee. Note
how heauen by vnusuall, vnfrequented, and from vs concealed waies , hath set my true spouse before mine eyes : and
thou doest know well by a thousand costly experiences,that
onely death is potent to blot forth his remembrance out of
my memorie : let then so manifest truthes be of power (if

thou muſt doe none other) to conuert thine affliction into
rage, and thy good will into deſpight, and there withall end
my life, for if I may render vp the ghoſt in the preſence of my
deere ſpouſe, I ſhall account it fortunately loſt. Perhaps by
my death he will remaine ſatisfied of the faith, which I euer
kept ſincere towards him, vntill the laſt period of my life. By
this time *Dorotea* was come to her ſelfe, and liſtned to moſt
of *Luſcindas* reaſons, and by them came to the knowledge
of her ſelfe: but ſeeing that *Don Fernando* did not yet let her
depart from betweene his armes, nor anſwere any thing to
her words: encouraging her ſelfe the beſt that ſhe might, ſhe
aroſe, and kneeling at his feete, and ſhedding a number of
Criſtall and penetrating teares ſhe ſpoke to him thus.

If it be not ſo my Lord, that the beames of that Sunne
which thou holdeſt ecclipſed betwene thine armes, doe darken and depriue thoſe of thine eyes, thou mighteſt haue by
this perceiued how ſhe that is proſtrated at thy feet is the vnfortunate (vntill thou ſhalt pleaſe) and the diſtaſtrous *Do-*
rotea. I am that poore humble countriwoman, whom thou
eyther through thy bountie, or for thy pleaſure didſt deigne
to raiſe to that height that ſhe might call thee her owne. I
am ſhe which ſometime immured within the limits of hone-
ſtie did lead a moſt contented life, vntil it opened the gates of
her recollection and wearineſſe, to thine importunitie, and
ſeeming iuſt, and amorous requeſts, and rendred vp to thee
the keyes of her liberty, a greefe by thee ſo ill recompenſed,
as the finding my ſelfe in ſo remote a place as this: wherein you haue met with mee, and I ſeene you, may cleerely te-
ſtifie, but yet for all this, I would not haue you to imagine
that I come heere guided by diſhonourable ſteps being onely
hither conducted by the tracts of dolour, and feeling to ſee
my ſelfe thus forgotten by thee. It was thy will, that I ſhould
be thine owne, and thou didſt deſire it in ſuch a manner, as
although now thou wouldſt not haue it ſo, yet canſt not thou
poſſibly leaue off to be mine. Know my deare Lord that the
matchleſſe affection that I doe beare towards thee, may re-

Dd 3 com-

compense and be equiualent to her beautie and nobilitie, for whom thou doeſt abandon mee. Thou canſt not be the beautifull *Luſcindas*, becauſe thou art mine : nor ſhe thine, for as much as ſhe belongs to *Cardenio*, and it will be more eaſier, if you will note it well, to reduce thy will to loue her that adores thee , then to addreſſe hers that hates thee, to beare thee affection: Thou diddeſt ſollicite my wretchleſneſſe ; thou prayedſt to mine integrtie, and waſt not ignorant of my qualitie: thou knoweſt alſo very well vpon what termes I ſubiected my ſelfe to thy will, ſo as there remaines no place , nor colour to terme it a fraud or deceit. And all this being ſo, as in veritie it is, and that thou beeſt as Chriſtian as thou art noble, why doeſt thou with theſe ſo many vntoward wreathings dilate the making of mine ende happy, whoſe commencement thou diddeſt illuſtrate ſo much ? and if thou wilt not haue me for what I am, who am thy true and lawfull ſpouſe ; yet at leaſt take and admit mee for thy ſlaue, for ſo that I may be in thy poſſeſſion, I will account my ſelfe happy and fortunate. Doe not permit that by leauing and abandoning mee, meetings may be made to diſcourſe of my diſhonour.Doe not vexe thus the declining yeares of my parents, ſeeing that the loyall ſeruices which they euer haue done as vaſſailes to thine , deſerue not ſo honeſt a recompence. And if thou eſteemeſt that thy bloud by medling with mine ſhall be ſtayned or embaſed : conſider how ſewe Noble howſes or rather none at all are there in the world, which haue not runne the ſame way: and that the womans ſide is not eſſentially requiſite for the illuſtrating of noble deſcents, how much more, ſeeing that true nobilitie conſiſts in vertue , which if it ſhall want in thee by refuſing that which thou oweſt mee ſo iuſtly, I ſhall remaine with many more degrees of nobilitie then thou ſhalt. And in concluſion that which I will laſtly ſay is, that whether thou wilt or no I am thy wife , the witneſſes are thine owne words, which neither ſhould nor ought to lie, if thou doeſt prize thy ſelfe of that for whoſe want thou deſpiſeſt mee.Witneſſe ſhall

alſo

also be thine own hand writing. Witneſſe heauen which thou
didſt inuoke to beare witneſſe of that which thou didſt promiſe vnto mee: and when all this ſhall faile, thy very conſci-
ence ſhall neuer fayle from vſing clamours being ſilent in
thy mirth and turning for this truth, which I haue ſaid to
thee now, ſhall trouble thy greateſt pleaſure and delight.

Theſe and many other like reaſons did the ſweetely grieued *Dorothea* vſe with ſuch feeling and abundance of teares,
as all thoſe that were preſent, as well ſuch as accompanied
Don Fernando, as alſo the others that did accompany her.
Don Fernando liſtened to her without replying a word, vntill
ſhe had ended her ſpeech, and giuen beginning to ſo many
ſighes and ſobs, as the heart that could indure to beholde
them without mouing, were harder then braſſe. *Luſcinda*
did alſo regard her, no leſſe compaſsionate of her ſorrow
then admired at her diſcretion and beautie : and although
ſhe would haue approched to her, and vſed ſome conſolato-
rie wordes, yet was ſhe hindred by *Don Fernandoes* armes,
which held her ſtill embraced ; who full of confuſion and
maruell, after ſhe had ſtood very attentiuely beholding *Do-*
rotea a good while, opening his armes, and leauing *Luſcinda*
free, ſaid, Thou haſt vanquiſhed ; O beautifull *Dorotea*, thou
haſt vanquiſhed me. For it is not poſſible to reſiſt or denie
ſo many vnited truthes. *Luſcinda* through her former
traunce and weakeneſſe, as *Don Fernando* left her was like
to fall, if *Cardenio* who ſtood behinde *Don Fernando* all the
while, leſt he ſhould be knowne, ſhaking off all feare and in-
dangering his perſon, had not ſtarted forward to ſtay her
from falling, and claſping her ſweetly betweene his armes,
he ſaid, if pittifull heauen be pleaſed, and would haue thee
now at laſt take ſome eaſe my loyall, conſtant and beautifull
ladie, I preſume that thou canſt not poſſeſſe it more ſecurely,
then betweene theſe armes which doe now receiue thee, as
whilome they did when fortune was pleaſed, that I might
call thee mine own: and then *Luſcinda* firſt ſeuering her eyelids, beheld *Cardenio*, and hauing firſt taken notice of him by

Dd 4   his

* The line reads: 'maruell, after she had stood very attentively, beholding *Do*–'

his voyce, & confirmed it againe by her sight, like one quite distracted, without farther regarding modest respects, shecast both her arms about his neck, & ioyning her face to his, said; yea, thou indeed art my Lord : thou, the true owner of this poore captiue, howsoeuer aduerse fortune shall thwart it, or this life, which is only sustained and liues by thine, be euer so much thretned. This was a maruellous spectacle to *Don Fernando*, & all the rest of the beholders, which did vniuersally admire at this so vnexpected an euent: and *Dorotea* perceiuing *Don Fernando* to change color, as one resoluing to take reuenge on *Cardenio*, for he had set hand to his sword; which she coniecturing, did with maruellous expedition kneele, and catching holde on his legges, kissing them, she strained them with so louing embracements as he could not stirre out of the place, and then with her eyes ouerflowen with teares, said vnto him: what meanest thou to doe my onely refuge in this vnexpected traunce ? Thou hast heere thine owne spouse at thy feete, and her whom thou wouldest faine possesse, is betweene her owne husbands armes : iudge then whether it become thee, or is a thing possible to dissolue that which heauen hath knit, or whether it be any wise laudable to indeauour to raise and equall to thy selfe her, who contemning all dangers and inconueniences, and confirmed in faith and constancy, doth in thy presence bathe her eyes with amorous liquor of her true loues face and bosom. I desire thee for Gods sake, and by thine owne worths, I request thee that this so notorious a verity may not onely asswage thy choler, but also diminish it in such sort, as thou mayest quietly & peaceably permit those two louers to enioy their desires without any encumbrance, all the time that heauen shall graunt it to them : and herein thou shalt shew the generositie of thy magnanimous and noble breast, and giue the world to vnderstand how reason preuaileth in thee, and domineereth ouer passion. All the time that *Dorotea* spoke thus to *Don Fernando*, although *Cardenio* held *Luscinda* betweene his armes yet did he neuer take his eye of *Don*
Fernando

Fernando, with refolution, that if he did fee him once ftir in his preiudice, he would labour both to defend himfelfe, & offend his aduerfary, & all thofe that fhould ioine with him to do him any harme as much as he could, although it were with the reft of his life: but *Don Fernandos* friends, the Curate and Barber who were prefent and faw all that was paft repayred in the meane feafon, without omitting the good *Sancho Panca*, and all of them together compaffed *Don Fernando*, intreating him to haue regard of the beautifull *Doroteas* teares, and it being true (as they belecued it was) which fhe had faid he fhould not permit her to remain defrauded of her fo iuft & lawful hopes. And that he fhould ponder how it was not by chance, but ra-ther by the particular prouidence and difpofition of the hea-uens, that they had al met together fo vnexpectedly. And that he fhould remember as Mafter Curate faid very wel, that on-ly death could feuer *Lufcinda* from her *Cardenio*. And that although the edge of a fword might deuide and part them a funder, yet in that cafe they would account their death moft happie, and that in irremedileffe euents, it was higheft pru-dence, by ftraining and ouercomming himfelfe to fhew a ge-nerous minde, permitting that he might conquer his owne will they two fhould ioy that good, which heauen had alrea-die granted to them, and that he fhould conuert his eyes to behold the beautie of *Dorotea*, and he fhould fee that few or none could for feature paragon with her; and much leffe excell her, and that he fhould confer her humilitie and ex-treme loue which fhe bore to him, with her other indow-ments; and principally that if he gloried in the titles of No-bilitie or Chriftianitie, hee could not doe any other then ac-complifh the promife that he had paft to her : and that by fulfilling it, hee fhould pleafe God, and fatisfie difcreet per-fons, which know very well, how it is a fpeciall prerogatiue of beautie, though it be in an humble and meane fubiect, if it bee conforted with modeftie and vertue, to exalt and e-quall it felfe to any dignitie, without difparagement of him which doth helpe to raife, or vnite it to himfelfe. And when
                                                                    the

the strong lawes of delight are accomplished (so that there intercurre no sinne in the acting thereof) hee is not to bee condemned which doth follow them. Finally, they added to these reasons, others so many and forcible, that the valerous breast of *Don Fernando* (as commonly all those that are warmed and nourished by Noble bloud are wont) was mollified, and permitted it selfe to bee vanquished by that truth which he could not denie though hee would: and the token that hee gaue of his being ouercome, was to stoupe downe and imbrace *Dorotea*, saying vnto her, arise Ladie, for it is not iust that shee bee prostrated at my feete; whose Image I haue erected in my minde, and if I haue not hitherto giuen demonstrations of what I nowe auerre, it hath perhaps befallen through the disposition of heauen, to the end that I might by noting the constancie and faith wherewithall thou dost affect me, know after how to valewe and esteeme thee according vnto thy merits: and that which in recompence thereof I doe intreate of thee is, that thou wilt excuse in me mine ill maner of proceeding, and exceeding carelesnesse in repaying thy good will. For the very occasion and violent passions that made me to accept thee as mine, the very same did also impell me againe not to be thine: and for the more verifying of mine assertion, doe but once behold the eyes of the now contented *Luscinda*, and thou mayest reade in them a thousand excuses for mine errour: and seeing she hath found and obtained her hearts desire; and I haue in thee also gotten what is most conuenient; for I wish she may liue securely and ioyfully, many and happy yeares with her *Cardenio*, for I will pray the same, that it will license me to enioy my beloued *Dorotea*: and saying so, he embraced her againe, and ioyned his face to hers with so louely motion, as it constrayned him to holde watch ouer his teares, least violently bursting forth, they should giue doubtlesse arguments of his feruent loue, and remorse.

   Cardenio, Luscinda, and almost all the rest could not doe
so,

so, for the greater number of them shed so many teares, some for their priuate contentment, and others for their friends, as it seemed, that some grieuous and heauy misfortune had betided them all: euen very *Sancho Panca* wept, although he excused it afterward, saying, that he wept onely because that he saw that *Dorotea* was not the Queene *Micomicona* as he had imagined, of whom he hoped to haue received so great gifts and fauours. The admiration and teares ioyned, indured in them all for a pretty space, and presently after *Cardenio* and *Luscinda* went and kneeled to *Don Fernando*, yeelding him thankes for the fauour that hee had done to them, with so courteous complements, as he knew not what to answere; and therfore lifted them vp, and embraced them with very great affection and kindenesse; and presently after he demaunded of *Dorotea* how she came to that place, so farre from her owne dwelling? And she recounted vnto him all that she had tolde to *Cardenio*: whereat *Don Fernando* and those which came with him tooke so great delight as they could haue wished that her story had continued a longer time in the telling then it did, so great was *Doroteas* grace in setting out of her misfortunes. And as soone as she had ended, *Don Fernando* tolde all that had befalne him in the Citie, after that he had found the scroule in *Luscindas* bosome, wherein she declared *Cardenio* to be her husband; and that he therefore could not marry her, and also how he attempted to kill her, and would haue done it, were it not that her parents hindred him, and that he therefore departed out of the house full of shame and despite, with resolution to reuenge himselfe more commodiously; and how he vnderstood the next day following, how *Luscinda* was secretly departed from her fathers house, and gone no body knew where; but that he finally learned within a few moneths after that she had entred into a certain Monastery, with intention to remain there all the daies of her life, if she could not passe them with *Cardenio*: and that as soone as he had learned that, choosing those three Gentlemen for his associates, hee

came

came to the place where she was, but would not speake to her, fearing left that as soone as they knew of his being there they would increase the guardes of the Monastery, and therefore expected vntill he found on a day the gates of the Monastery open; and leauing two of his fellowes to keepe the doore, he with the other entred into the Abbey in *Luscindas* search, whom they found talking with a Nunne in the Cloyster, and snatching her away er'e she could retire her selfe, they brought her to a certaine village, where they disguised themselues in that sort they were; for so it was requisite for to bring her away. All which they did with the more facility, that the Monastery was seated abroad in the fields, a good way from any village. He likewise told, that as soone as *Luscinda* saw her selfe in his power, she fell into a sound, and that after she had returned to her selfe, she neuer did any other thing but weepe and sigh, without speaking a word; and that in that manner, accompanied with silence and teares, they had arriued to that Inne, which was to him as gratefull as an arriuall to heauen, wherein all earthly mishaps are concluded and finished.

CHAP. X.

Wherein is prosecuted the Historie of the famous Princesse Micomicona, *with other delightfull aduentures.*

Ancho gaue eare to all this with no small griefe of minde, seeing that all the hopes of his Lordship vanished away like smoake, and that the faire Princesse *Micomicona* was turned into *Dorotea*, and the Giant into *Don Fernando*, and that his Master slept so soundly and carelesse of all that had hapned. *Dorotea* could not yet assure her selfe whether the happinesse that she possest was a dreame, or no. *Cardenio* was in the very same taking, and

and also *Luscindas* thought, runne the same race. *Don Fer nando* yeel ted many thankes vnto heauen for hauing dealt with him so propitiously, and vnwinded him out of the in tricate *Labyrinth*, wherein straying, he was at the point to haue lost at once his soule and credite, and finally, as many as were in the Inne were very glad and ioyfull of the successe of so thwart, intricate, and desperate affaires. The Curate compounded and ordered all things through his discretion, and congratulated euery one of the good he obtained: but she that kept greatest *Iubilee* and ioy, was the Hostesse for the promise that *Cardenio* and the Curate had made to pay her the damages and harmes committed by *Don. Quixote*;

ABBREVIATIONS AND REFERENCES

In all references, place of publication is London unless otherwise stated.

ABBREVIATIONS

ABBREVIATIONS USED IN NOTES

*	precedes commentary notes involving readings that are not found in early printings
BL	British Library
esp.	especially
F	First Folio (1623)
fol.	folio
MS	manuscript
n.p.	no page number
n.s.	new series
opp.	opposite
SD	stage direction
sig.	signature
SP	speech prefix
subst.	substantially
t.n.	textual note
this edn	a reading adopted for the first time in this edition

WORKS BY AND PARTLY BY SHAKESPEARE

Quotations from and references to plays in the Shakespeare canon other than *Double Falsehood* are to the Arden Shakespeare Third Series where they exist; other references are to *The Arden Shakespeare Complete Works*, ed. Richard Proudfoot, Ann Thompson and David Scott Kastan, rev. edn (2001), and to *The Reign of King Edward the Third*, in *The Riverside Shakespeare*, gen. ed. G. Blakemore Evans with J.J. Tobin, 2nd edn (Boston, Mass., and New York, 1997).

AC	*Antony and Cleopatra*
AW	*All's Well That Ends Well*
AYL	*As You Like It*
CE	*The Comedy of Errors*
Cor	*Coriolanus*
Cym	*Cymbeline*

DF	*Double Falsehood*
E3	*Edward III*
Ham	*Hamlet*
1H4	*King Henry IV Part 1*
2H4	*King Henry IV Part 2*
H5	*King Henry V*
1H6	*King Henry VI Part 1*
2H6	*King Henry VI Part 2*
3H6	*King Henry VI Part 3*
H8	*King Henry VIII*
JC	*Julius Caesar*
KJ	*King John*
KL	*King Lear*
LC	*A Lover's Complaint*
LLL	*Love's Labour's Lost*
Luc	*The Rape of Lucrece*
MA	*Much Ado About Nothing*
Mac	*Macbeth*
MM	*Measure for Measure*
MND	*A Midsummer Night's Dream*
MV	*The Merchant of Venice*
MW	*The Merry Wives of Windsor*
Oth	*Othello*
Per	*Pericles*
PP	*The Passionate Pilgrim*
PT	*The Phoenix and Turtle*
R2	*King Richard II*
R3	*King Richard III*
RJ	*Romeo and Juliet*
Son	*Sonnets*
STM	*Sir Thomas More*
TC	*Troilus and Cressida*
Tem	*The Tempest*
TGV	*The Two Gentlemen of Verona*
Tim	*Timon of Athens*
Tit	*Titus Andronicus*
TN	*Twelfth Night*
TNK	*The Two Noble Kinsmen*
TS	*The Taming of the Shrew*
VA	*Venus and Adonis*
WT	*The Winter's Tale*

WORKS IN THE FLETCHER CANON

The dates are those given in Thomas L. Berger, William C. Bradford and Sidney L. Sondergard, *An Index of Characters in Early Modern English Drama Printed Plays, 1500–1660* (Cambridge, 1998), as 'Annals date', i.e. the first performance date as recorded in the various revisions of Alfred Harbage's *Annals of English Drama, 975–1700* (see the *Index*, p. 105, for bibliographical information). Unless otherwise indicated, quotations from and references to plays in the Fletcher canon are to Fredson Bowers (gen. ed.), *The Dramatic Works in the Beaumont and Fletcher Canon*, 10 vols (Cambridge, 1966–96).

BB	Fletcher ?and Massinger, *Beggar's Bush* (1622)
Bon	Fletcher, *Bonduca* (1613)
Capt	Fletcher, with ?Beaumont, *The Captain* (1612)
CC	Fletcher and Massinger, *The Custom of the Country* (1620)
Cha	Fletcher, *The Chances* (1617)
Cox	Fletcher, with Beaumont, *The Coxcomb* (1609)
CR	Fletcher, with Beaumont, *Cupid's Revenge* (1608)
DM	Fletcher and Massinger, *The Double Marriage* (1620)
EB	Fletcher and Massinger, *The Elder Brother* (1625)
FMI	Fletcher and others, *The Fair Maid of the Inn* (1626)
FP	Field and Fletcher, *Four Plays in One* (1613)
FSh	Fletcher, *The Faithful Shepherdess* (1608)
KM	Fletcher, Field and Massinger, *The Knight of Malta* (1618)
Knight	Beaumont (?Fletcher), *The Knight of the Burning Pestle* (1607)
KNK	Beaumont and Fletcher, *A King and No King* (1611)
LCu	Beaumont and Fletcher, rev. Massinger, *Love's Cure* (1606)
LFL	Fletcher and Massinger, *The Little French Lawyer* (1619)
LPi	Fletcher, with Beaumont, *Love's Pilgrimage* (1616)
LPr	Fletcher and Massinger, *The Lover's Progress* (1623)
LS	Fletcher, *The Loyal Subject* (1618)
Maid	Fletcher and Rowley, *The Maid in the Mill* (1623)
Maid's	Beaumont and Fletcher, *The Maid's Tragedy* (1610)
ML	Fletcher, *The Mad Lover* (1617)
MT	Fletcher, *Monsieur Thomas* (1615)
Phil	Beaumont and Fletcher, *Philaster* (1609)
Pilg	Fletcher, *The Pilgrim* (1621)
RDN	Fletcher, rev. Massinger, *Rollo, Duke of Normandy* (1617)
Rule	Fletcher, *Rule a Wife and Have a Wife* (1624)
SC	Fletcher and Massinger, *The Spanish Curate* (1622)
SL	Fletcher and Beaumont, *The Scornful Lady* (1613)
SV	Fletcher and Massinger, *The Sea Voyage* (1622)
Val	Fletcher, *Valentinian* (1614)

WGC	Fletcher, *The Wild Goose Chase* (1621)
WM	Fletcher, *A Wife for a Month* (1624)
WP	Fletcher, *The Woman's Prize* (1611)
WPl	Fletcher, *Women Pleased* (1620)
WWM	Fletcher, *Wit Without Money* (1614)

REFERENCES

EDITIONS OF *DOUBLE FALSEHOOD* COLLATED

1728a	*Double falshood; or, the Distrest Lovers. A play, as it is acted at the Theatre-Royal in Drury-Lane. Written originally by W. Shakespeare; and now revised and adapted to the stage by Mr. Theobald* (1728)
1728b	*Double falshood; or, the Distrest Lovers. A play, as it is acted at the Theatre-Royal in Drury-Lane. Written originally by W. Shakespeare; and now revised and adapted to the stage by Mr. Theobald. The second edition* (1728)
1728c	*Double falshood; or, the Distrest Lovers. A play, as it is acted at the Theatre-Royal in Drury-Lane. Written originally by W. Shakespeare; and now revised and adapted to the stage by Mr. Theobald* (Dublin, 1728)
1767	*Double Falsehood; or, the Distrest Lovers. A play, as it is acted at the Theatre-Royal in Drury-Lane. Written originally by William Shakespeare; and now revised and adapted to the stage by Mr. Theobald, etc. The third edition* (1767)
Graham 1920	*Double Falsehood*, ed. Walter Graham, Western Reserve University Bulletin (Cleveland, OH), vol. 23, no. 3 (1920)
Kahan 2004	*The Double Falsehood*, ed. Jeffrey Kahan, in *Shakespeare Imitations, Parodies and Forgeries: 1710–1820*, vol. 1 (2004), 159–242
Kennedy	*Double Falshood; or, The Distrest Lovers*, ed. John W. Kennedy, http://pws.prserv.net/jwkennedy/Double%20 Falshood/Double%20Falshood.html (2002–4)
Muir 1970	*Double Falsehood*, facsimile edition, intro. Kenneth Muir (1970)

WORKS BY THEOBALD CITED

Cato	*The Life and Character of Marcus Portius Cato Uticensis . . . Design'd for the Readers of Cato, a Tragedy* (1713)
Cave	*The Cave of Poverty* (1715)
Clouds	Translation of Aristophanes' *The Clouds* (1715)
Electra	Translation of Sophocles' *Electra* (1714)
Fatal Secret	*The Fatal Secret* (1735)
Happy Captive	*The Happy Captive* (1741)
Harlequin	*Harlequin a Sorcerer, with the Loves of Pluto and Proserpine* (1725)
Merlin	*Merlin* (1734)
Odyssey	*The Odyssey of Homer. Book 1. Translated from the Greek, with notes. By Mr. Theobald* (1717)
Oedipus	*Oedipus King of Thebes* (1715)
Orestes	*Orestes* (1731)
Perfidious Brother	*The Perfidious Brother* (1715)
Perseus	*Perseus and Andromeda* (1730)
Persian Princess	*The Persian Princess* (1715)
Plato	*Plato's Dialogue of the Immortality of the Soul. Translated from the Greek, By Mr. Theobald, Author of the Life of Cato Uticensis* (1713)
Plutus	Translation of Aristophanes' *Plutus* (1715)
'Pope's taste'	'Of Mr Pope's taste of Shakespeare', pamphlet reprinted in *A Miscellany on Taste by Mr. Pope, &c* (1732), p. 41 (BL T.1056(15))
Proserpine	*The Rape of Proserpine, as it is acted at the Theatre Royal in Lincoln's Inn Fields. Written by Mr. Theobald. And set to music by Mr. Galliard* (1727)
'Reply to Pope'	Letter to Pope in *Mist's Weekly Journal*, 27 April 1728, reprinted in *A Compleat Collection of all the Verses, Essays, Letters and Advertisements . . . Occasioned by the Publication of Three Volumes of Miscellanies by Pope and Company* (1728)
Raleigh	*Memoirs of Sir Walter Raleigh: his life, his military and naval exploits, his preferments and death* (1719)
Richard II	*The Tragedy of King Richard the II . . . Altered from Shakespear, by Mr Theobald* (1720)
Shakespeare	*The Works of Shakespeare*, 7 vols (1733)

Shakespeare Restored *Shakespeare Restored: or a specimen of the many errors, as well committed, as unamended, by Mr Pope in his late edition of this poet. Designed not only to correct the said edition, but to restore the true reading of Shakespeare in all the editions ever yet published* (1726)

OTHER WORKS CITED

Act, scene and line references to plays listed below are usually to first editions digitally reproduced on *Early English Books Online* (*EEBO*) at http://eebo.chadwyck.com/home, *Eighteenth-Century Collections Online* (*ECCO*) at http://www.gale.cengage.co.uk/ecco/ and the Chadwyck-Healey *Literature Online* database (*LION*) at http://lion.chadwyck.co.uk/. Where first editions have been used and lineations are not available, act/scene and page references are given. Dates of first editions may differ from dates of first performance given in the text. Editions other than first editions are specified below.

Ardila	J.A.G. Ardila (ed.), *The Cervantean Heritage: Reception and Influence of Cervantes in Britain* (2009)
Baker	David Erskine Baker, *Biographia Dramatica, or a Companion to the Playhouse*, 2 vols (1764; rev. edn Dublin, 1782)
Bate	Jonathan Bate, *The Genius of Shakespeare* (1997)
Baxter, *Cardenio*	Jean Rae Baxter, *Looking for Cardenio* (Hamilton, OH, 2008)
BCP	*Book of Common Prayer* (1662)
BDA	Philip H. Highfill, Jr, Kalman A. Burnim and Edward A. Langhans, *A Biographical Dictionary of Actors, Actresses, Musicians, Dancers, Managers and Other Stage Personnel in London, 1660–1800*, 15 vols (Carbondale and Edwardsville, Ill., 1973–93)
Behn, *King*	Aphra Behn, *The Young King, or The Mistake* (1683)
Bertram	Paul Bertram, *Shakespeare and* The Two Noble Kinsmen (New Brunswick, NJ, 1965)
Betterton, *Widow*	Thomas Betterton, *The Amorous Widow* (1706)
Bodleian MS A.239	Bodleian Library MS Rawl. A.239
Bowers	*The Dramatic Works in the Beaumont and Fletcher Canon*, ed. Fredson Bowers et al., 10 vols (Cambridge, 1966–96)
Bradford	Gamaliel Bradford, Jr, 'The History of Cardenio by Mr Fletcher and Shakespeare', *MLN*, 25 (February 1910), 51–6

Brathwaite	Richard Brathwaite, *The English Gentlewoman* (1631)
Briggs, *Lady's Tragedy*	Julia Briggs, introduction to her edition of *The Lady's Tragedy* in Middleton, *Works*, 835–6
Briggs, 'Tears'	Julia Briggs, 'Tears at the wedding: Shakespeare's last phase', in Richards & Knowles, 210–27
Brome, *Covent Garden*	Richard Brome, *The Weeding of the Covent Garden* (1638), in *Five New Plays* (1659)
Cadwalader	John Cadwalader, 'Theobald's alleged Shakespeare manuscript', *MLN*, 55 (1940), 108–9
Carew, *Poems*	Thomas Carew, *Poems by Thomas Carew, Esq.* (1640)
Carrell, *Secret*	J.L. Carrell, *The Shakespeare Secret* (2007, repr. 2008)
Carroll	William C. Carroll, *The Two Gentlemen of Verona*, Arden Shakespeare Third Series (2004)
Castle	Eduard Castle, 'Theobalds *Double Falshood* und *The History of Cardenio* von Fletcher und Shakespeare', *Archiv für das Studium der neueren Sprachen*, 169 (1936), 182–99
Centlivre, *Wonder*	Susanna Centlivre, *The Wonder! A Woman Keeps a Secret* (1714)
Cervantes	See *Don Quixote*
Chambers, 'Plays'	E.K. Chambers, 'Plays of the King's Men in 1641', *Malone Society Collections*, 1, parts IV and V, ed. W.W. Greg (Oxford, 1911), 364–7
Chambers, *Shakespeare*	E.K. Chambers, *William Shakespeare: A Study of Facts and Problems*, 2 vols (Oxford, 1930)
Chapman, *Iliad*	George Chapman, translation of Homer's *Iliad* (*c.* 1611)
Chapman, *May Day*	George Chapman, *May Day* (1602)
Chapman, *Usher*	George Chapman, *The Gentleman Usher* (1602), ed. Robert Ornstein, in *The Plays of George Chapman: The Comedies*, ed. Allan Holladay (Urbana and Chicago, Ill., and London, 1970)
Cibber, *Apology*	Colley Cibber, *An Apology for the Life of Mr. Colley Cibber, comedian, and late patentee of the Theatre Royal*, 2nd edn, 2 vols (1740)
Cibber, *Refusal*	Colley Cibber, *The Refusal, or The Ladies Philosophy* (1721)
Congreve, *Bachelor*	William Congreve, *The Old Bachelor* (1693)
Corbett	Charles Corbett, *A Catalogue of the Library of Lewis Theobald, Esq. deceased which will be sold by auction, on October 23rd, 1744, and the three following evenings at St Paul's Coffee House* (1744)

Cowley, *Riddle*   Abraham Cowley, *Love's Riddle* (1638)

Crowne, *Sir Courtly*   John Crowne, *Sir Courtly Nice* (1685)

Darby   Trudi Darby, 'William Rowley: a case study in influence', in Ardila, 249–58

Darby & Samson   Trudy L. Darby and Alexander Samson, 'Cervantes on the Jacobean Stage', in Ardila, 209–14

Davenant, *Distresses*   Sir William Davenant, *The Distresses* (1673)

Davenant, *Master*   Sir William Davenant, *The Man's the Master* (1669)

Davenant, *Rivals*   Sir William Davenant, *The Rivals* (1668), ed. Kenneth Muir (1970)

de Commynes   Philippe de Commynes, *The History of Philip de Commines* (1596)

Dekker, *Match Me*   Thomas Dekker, *Match Me in London* (1611)

Dessen & Thomson   Alan C. Dessen and Leslie Thomson, *A Dictionary of Stage Directions in English Drama, 1580–1642* (Cambridge, 1999)

Dillon   Janette Dillon, *The Cambridge Introduction to Early English Theatre* (Cambridge, 2006)

Dobson   Michael Dobson, *The Making of the National Poet: Shakespeare, Adaptation and Authorship 1660–1769* (Oxford, 1992)

Dodd   William Dodd, *The Beauties of Shakespear: regularly selected from each play. with a general index, digesting them under proper heads. illustrated with explanatory notes, and similar passages from ancient and modern authors*, 2 vols (1752)

Don Quixote   Miguel de Cervantes, *El ingenioso hidalgo Don Quijote de la Mancha*, Part 1 (Madrid, 1605). See also Shelton

Dryden, *Absalom*   *Absalom and Achitophel* (1681)

Dryden, *Don Sebastian*   John Dryden, *Don Sebastian* (1690)

Dryden, *Emperor*   John Dryden, *The Indian Emperor* (1667)

Dryden, *Friar*   John Dryden, *The Spanish Friar* (1681)

Dryden, *Granada*   John Dryden, *The Conquest of Granada, Part II* (1672)

Dryden, *King Arthur*   John Dryden, *King Arthur* (1691)

Dryden, *Ladies*   John Dryden, *The Rival Ladies* (1664)

Dryden, *Sigismonda*   John Dryden, *Sigismonda and Guiscardo*, in *Fables Ancient and Modern* (1700)

Dryden, *Sir Martin*   John Dryden, *Sir Martin Mar-All* (1691)

Dugas — Don-John Dugas, *Marketing the Bard: Shakespeare in Performance and Print, 1660–1740* (Columbia, Miss., 2006)

Duncan-Jones & Woudhuysen — *Shakespeare's Poems*, ed. Katherine Duncan-Jones and H.R. Woudhuysen, Arden Shakespeare Third Series (2007)

D'Urfey, *Don Quixote* — Thomas D'Urfey, *The Comical History of Don Quixote Part One* (1694)

D'Urfey, *Money* — Thomas D'Urfey, *Love for Money* (1691)

Edmond — Mary Edmond, entry on Sir William Davenant in *ODNB*

EEBO — *Early English Books Online*

ESTC — *English Short Title Catalogue*

Etherege, *Revenge* — Sir George Etherege, *The Comical Revenge* (1664)

Farmer — Richard Farmer, *An Essay on the Learning of Shakespeare* (2nd edn, Cambridge, 1767)

Fforde, *Lost* — Jasper Fforde, *Lost in a Good Book* (2002)

Fleissner — Robert F. Fleissner, 'The likely misascription of *Cardenio* (and thereby *Double Falsehood*) in part to Shakespeare', *Neuphilologische Mitteilungen*, vol. 97, no. 2 (1996), 217–30

Ford, *Fancies* — John Ford, *The Fancies* (1635)

Ford, *Heart* — John Ford, *The Broken Heart* (1633)

Ford, *Whore* — John Ford, *'Tis Pity She's a Whore* (1633)

Foster — Donald W. Foster, '*A Funeral Elegy*: W[illiam] S[hakespeare]'s "best-speaking witnesses"', *PMLA*, 111 (1996), 1080–1105

Frazier, 'Forger' — Harriet C. Frazier, 'Speculation on the motives of a forger', *Neuphilologische Mitteilungen*, 72 (1971), 285–96

Frazier, 'Revision' — Harriet C. Frazier, 'Theobald's *The Double Falsehood*: A Revision of Shakespeare's *Cardenio*?', *Comparative Drama*, 1 (1967), 219–33

Frazier, *Voices* — Harriet C. Frazier, *A Babble of Ancestral Voices: Shakespeare, Cervantes, Theobald* (The Hague, 1974)

Freehafer — John Freehafer, '*Cardenio*, by Shakespeare and Fletcher', *PMLA*, vol. 84, no. 3 (1969), 501–13

Frey — Charles Frey, '"O sacred, shadowy, cold, and constant queen": Shakespeare's imperilled and chastening daughters of romance', in Carolyn Lenz, Gayle Greene and Carol Thomas Neely (eds), *The Woman's Part* (Urbana, Ill., 1980), 295–313

Frost — David L. Frost, *The School of Shakespeare* (Cambridge, 1968)

Frowde, *Saguntum*   Philip Frowde, *The Fall of Saguntum* (Dublin, 1727)

Gay, *Captives*   John Gay, *The Captives* (1724)

Gentleman   Francis Gentleman, *The Dramatic Censor*, 2 vols (1770)

Gerrard   Christine Gerrard, *The Patriot Opposition to Walpole* (Oxford, 1994)

Gildon   Charles Gildon, *The Postman Robbed of His Mail* (1719)

Goodwin   'Lutes and voices', *Early Music*, 36 (2008), 140–2

Graham, 'Problem'   Walter Graham, 'The "Cardenio–Double Falsehood" problem', *Modern Philology*, vol. 14, no. 5 (September 1916), 269–80

Granger   Rev. James Granger, *A Biographical History of England from Egbert the Great to the Revolution*, 3 vols (1769–74; 2nd edn, 4 vols, 1775)

Greenblatt & Mee,   Stephen Greenblatt and Charles Mee, *Cardenio*,
Cardenio   rehearsal copy, 2008

Greg   Walter W. Greg, *A Bibliography of the English Printed Drama to the Restoration*, 4 vols (1939–59)

Gurr, *Playing*   Andrew Gurr, *The Shakespearian Playing Companies*
Companies   (Oxford, 1996, repr. 2003)

Gurr, *Shakespeare*   Andrew Gurr, *The Shakespeare Company, 1594–1642*
Company   (Cambridge, 2004)

Hamilton   Charles Hamilton (ed.), *Cardenio, or The Second Maiden's Tragedy* (Lakewood, Col., 1994)

Hammond, 'Cheat'   Brean S. Hammond, 'Theobald's *Double Falsehood*: an "Agreeable Cheat"?', *Notes and Queries*, n.s. 31, no. 1 (1984), 2–3

Hammond,   Brean S. Hammond, 'The performance history of a
'Performance'   pseudo-Shakespearean play: Theobald's *Double Falshood*', *British Journal for Eighteenth-Century Studies*, vol. 7, no. 1 (1984), 49–60

Hanham   A.A. Hanham, entry on George Dodington in *ODNB*

Harbage   Alfred Harbage, 'Elizabethan-Restoration palimpsest', *Modern Language Review*, 35 (1940), 287–319

Hattaway   Francis Beaumont, *The Knight of the Burning Pestle*, ed. Michael Hattaway, New Mermaid 2nd edn (London and New York, 2002)

Heminges & Condell   John Heminges and Henry Condell, dedicatory epistle to William Shakespeare, *Comedies, Histories, and Tragedies*, The First Folio (1623)

Heywood, *Four*   Thomas Heywood, *The Four Prentices of London* (1615)
Prentices

Heywood, *Woman*	Thomas Heywood, *A Woman Killed with Kindness* (1607)
Hill, *Elfrid*	Aaron Hill, *Elfrid, or The Fair Inconstant* (1710), in *The Dramatic Works of Aaron Hill*, 2 vols (1760)
Hill & Mitchell, *Extravagance*	Aaron Hill and Joseph Mitchell, *The Fatal Extravagance* (1726)
Hope	Jonathan Hope, *The Authorship of Shakespeare's Plays* (Cambridge, 1994)
Hoy	Cyrus Hoy, 'The shares of Fletcher and his collaborators in the Beaumont and Fletcher canon', *Studies in Bibliography*. Part I: 8 (1956), 129–46; Part II: 9 (1957), 143–62; Part III: 11 (1958), 85–106
Hume, *Drama*	Robert D. Hume, *The Development of English Drama in the Late Seventeenth Century* (Oxford, 1976)
Hume, *Fielding*	Robert D. Hume, *Henry Fielding and the London Theatre 1728–1737* (Oxford, 1988)
Index	Thomas L. Berger, William C. Bradford and Sidney L. Sondergard, *An Index of Characters in Early Modern English Drama Printed Plays, 1500–1660* (Cambridge, 1998)
Johnson	*The Works of Samuel Johnson, LL.D. With an Essay on His Life and Genius, by Arthur Murphy, Esq.*, 12 vols (1792)
Jones	Richard Foster Jones, *Lewis Theobald: His Contribution to English Scholarship with Some Unpublished Letters* (New York, 1919, repr. 1966)
Jonson, *Alchemist*	Ben Jonson, *The Alchemist* (1610), in *The Alchemist and Other Plays*, ed. Gordon Campbell (Oxford, 1995)
Jonson, *Case*	Ben Jonson, *The Case Is Altered* (1597)
Jonson, *Devil*	Ben Jonson, *The Devil Is an Ass* (1616)
Jonson, *Epicene*	Ben Jonson, *Epicene* (1609), in *The Alchemist and Other Plays*, ed. Gordon Campbell (Oxford, 1995)
Kahan, '*Spanish Curate*'	Jeffrey Kahan, '*The Double Falsehood* and *The Spanish Curate*: a further Fletcher connection', *ANQ*, 20 (2007), 33
Kastan	David Scott Kastan, *Shakespeare and the Book* (Cambridge, 2001)
Keach	Benjamin Keach, *The Display of Glorious Grace, or The Covenant of Peace Opened in Fourteen Sermons Lately Preached* (1698)
Kewes	Paulina Kewes, entry on John Downes in *ODNB*

King, 'Shakespeare'   Edmund G.C. King, 'In the character of Shakespeare: canon, authorship, and attribution in eighteenth-century England', PhD thesis, University of Auckland, 2008, especially ch. 6, 132–57

King, 'Theobald'   Edmund G.C. King, 'Cardenio and the eighteenth-century Shakespeare canon', in *The Quest for Cardenio*, ed. David Carnegie and Gary Taylor (Cambridge, forthcoming)

Kökeritz   Helge Kökeritz, *Shakespeare's Pronunciation* (New Haven, Conn., 1953)

Kukowski   Stephan Kukowski, 'The hand of John Fletcher in *Double Falsehood*', *SS 43* (1991), 81–9

Kyd, *Spanish Tragedy*   Thomas Kyd, *The Spanish Tragedy* (1592)

Lee, *Massacre*   Nathaniel Lee, *The Massacre of Paris* (1690)

Lee, *Theodosius*   Nathaniel Lee, *Theodosius* (1680)

Leigh, *Kensington Gardens*   John Leigh, *Kensington Gardens, or The Pretenders* (1720)

Lives   Robert Shiells, *The Lives of the Poets of Great Britain and Ireland, by Mr Cibber, and other hands*, 2nd edn, 5 vols (1753)

McMullan, *Fletcher*   Gordon McMullan, *The Politics of Unease in the Plays of John Fletcher* (Amherst, Mass., 1994)

McMullan, *Henry VIII*   *King Henry VIII*, ed. Gordon McMullan, Arden Shakespeare Third Series (2000, repr. 2002)

Mallet, *Epistle*   David Mallet, *Of Verbal Criticism: An Epistle to Mr Pope. Occasioned by Theobald's Shakespear and Bentley's Milton* ([Edinburgh], 1733)

Malone, '*Cardenio*'   Edmond Malone, entries on *Cardenio*, in Baker, 2.429, 155

Malone, *DF*   Edmond Malone's copy of the second issue of *Double Falshood*, Bodleian Library (Oxford) Mal. 171 (8)

Malone, *Order*   *Attempt to Ascertain the Order in which the Plays Attributed to Shakspeare Were Written* (1778)

Marchitello   Howard Marchitello, 'Finding *Cardenio*', *English Literary History*, 74 (2007) 957–87

Marlowe, *Faustus*   Christopher Marlowe, *Dr Faustus* (1592)

Mar-Martine   ?Thomas Nashe, *Mar-Martine*, 2nd edn (1589)

Marston, *Antonio*   John Marston, *Antonio and Mellida* (1599)

Marston, *Revenge*   John Marston, *Antonio's Revenge* (1600)

431

Marston, *Wonder*	John Marston, *The Wonder of Women* (1606)
Martin	Peter Martin, *Edmond Malone, Shakespearean Scholar: A Literary Biography* (Cambridge, 1995)
Massinger, *Duke*	Philip Massinger, *The Great Duke of Florence* (1627)
Massinger, *Guardian*	Philip Massinger, *The Guardian* (1633), in *The Plays and Poems of Philip Massinger*, ed. Philip Edwards and Colin Gibson, 5 vols (Oxford, 1976), vol. 4
Massinger, *Woman*	Philip Massinger, *A Very Woman* (1634)
Matthews & Merriam	Robert A.J. Matthews and Thomas V.N. Merriam, 'Neural computation in stylometry 1: an application to the works of Shakespeare and Fletcher', *Literary and Linguistic Computing*, vol. 8, no. 4 (1993), 203–9
Mesteyer, *Perfidious Brother*	Henry Mesteyer, *The Perfidious Brother*, 2nd edn (1720)
Metz, *Four Plays*	G. Harold Metz, *Four Plays Ascribed to Shakespeare: An Annotated Bibliography* (New York, 1982)
Metz, *Sources*	*Sources of Four Plays Ascribed to Shakespeare*, ed. and intro. G. Harold Metz (Columbia, Mo., 1989)
Middleton, *Works*	Gary Taylor and John Lavagnino (eds), *Thomas Middleton: The Complete Works* (Oxford, 2007)
Milhous & Hume	Judith Milhous and Robert D. Hume, *Producible Interpretation: Eight English Plays 1675–1707* (Carbondale and Edwardsville, Ill., 1985)
Milton	*The Poems of John Milton*, ed. John Carey and Alastair Fowler (London and Harlow, 1968)
MLN	*Modern Language Notes*
More	Henry More, *Discourses on Several Texts of the Scripture* (1692)
Mucedorus	Anon., *Mucedorus* (version published 1610)
Muir, *Shakespeare*	Kenneth Muir, *Shakespeare as Collaborator* (1960)
Nokes, *Papers*	David Nokes, *The Nightingale Papers* (2005)
ODNB	*Oxford Dictionary of National Biography* (Oxford, 2004)
OED	*Oxford English Dictionary* (*OED Online*) (http://dictionary.oed.com)
Oldmixon, *Amores*	John Oldmixon, *Amores Britannici* (1703)
Oliphant, *Beaumont and Fletcher*	E.H.C. Oliphant, *The Plays of Beaumont and Fletcher* (New Haven, Conn., 1927)

Oliphant, 'Double Falsehood'	E.H.C. Oliphant, '"Double Falsehood": Shakespeare, Fletcher, and Theobald', *Notes and Queries*, 12th series, 5 (February, March and April 1919), 30–2, 60–2, 86–8
Orlando Furioso	Ludovico Ariosto, *Orlando Furioso* (1532), trans. Sir John Harington (1591)
Orrell	John Orrell, 'The Agent of Savoy at the Somerset Masque', *Review of English Studies*, n.s. 28 (1977), 301–4
Otway, *Friendship*	Thomas Otway, *Heroic Friendship* (1719)
Otway, *Soldier's Fortune*	Thomas Otway, *The Soldier's Fortune* (1681)
Painter	William Painter, *The Palace of Pleasure*, 2 vols (1567)
Palmer	*Troilus and Cressida*, ed. Kenneth Palmer, Arden Shakespeare Second Series (1982)
Pattison, 'Brother'	Neil Pattison, '"O Brother! We shall sound the Depths of Falshood"', paper presented at the Queens' Arts Seminar, Queens' College, Cambridge, May 2009
Pattison, 'King Tibbald'	Neil Pattison, '"King Tibbald": The writing of Lewis Theobald in Alexander Pope's *The Dunciad Variorum*', PhD dissertation, University of Cambridge, 2007
Pettit	*Miscellanies in Prose and Verse by Pope, Swift and Gay*, ed. and intro. Alexander Pettit, 4 vols (2002)
Philips, *Pompey*	Katherine Philips, *Pompey* (1663), in *Poems by the Most Deservedly Admired Mrs. Katherine Philips, The Matchless Orinda; to which is added Monsieur Corneille's Pompey & Horace, Tragedies* (1664)
Pix, *Distress*	Mary Pix, *The Double Distress* (1701)
Pix, *Widows*	Mary Pix, *The Different Widows* (1703)
PMLA	*Publications of the Modern Language Association of America*
Pope, *Correspondence*	*The Correspondence of Alexander Pope*, ed. George Sherburn, 5 vols (Oxford, 1956)
Pope, *Dunciad*	Alexander Pope, *The Dunciad* (1728–9)
Pope, *Dunciad 4*	Alexander Pope, *The Dunciad in Four Books* (1743), ed. Valerie Rumbold (Harlow, England, 1999)
Pope, *Dunciad Variorum*	Alexander Pope, *The Dunciad Variorum* (1729), in *The Poems of Alexander Pope*, vol. 3, ed. Valerie Rumbold (Harlow, England, 2007)
Pope, *Iliad*	Alexander Pope, Translation of Homer's *Iliad* (1715)

Pope, *Peri Bathous*   Alexander Pope, *Peri Bathous, or The Art of Sinking in Poetry* (1728), in Pettit, vol. 3

Pope, *Poems*   *The Twickenham Edition of the Poems of Alexander Pope*, ed. J. Butt et al., 11 vols (1938–68)

Pope, *Rape*   Alexander Pope, *The Rape of the Lock* (1714)

Pope, 'Satire'   'Fragment of a Satire' (1728), in Pettit, vol. 3

Pope, *Works*   Alexander Pope, *The Works*, 4 vols (1736)

Proudfoot, 'Dramatists'   G.R. Proudfoot, 'Shakespeare and the new dramatists of the King's Men, 1606–1613', in *Later Shakespeare*, ed. J.R. Brown and Bernard Harris (1966), 235–61

Proudfoot, *Shakespeare*   Richard Proudfoot, *Shakespeare: Text, Stage and Canon* (2001)

Pujante   A. Luis Pujante, '*Double Falsehood* and the verbal parallels with Shelton's *Don Quixote*', *SS 51* (1998), 95–105

Richards   William Shakespeare and John Fletcher, *Cardenio*, reworked by Bernard Richards (Oxford, 2009)

Richards & Knowles   Jennifer Richards and James Knowles (eds), *Shakespeare's Late Plays: New Readings* (Edinburgh, 1999)

Rogers   Shef Rogers, 'The use of royal licences for printing in England, 1695–1760: a bibliography', *Library*, 7th series, 1 (2000), 133–92

Rowe, *Jane Shore*   Nicholas Rowe, *The Tragedy of Jane Shore* (1714)

Rowe, *Penitent*   Nicholas Rowe, *The Fair Penitent* (1714)

Rowe, *Shakespeare*   Nicholas Rowe (ed.), *The Works of Mr William Shakespear, in six volumes. Adorned with Cuts. Revised and Corrected, with an Account of the Life and Writings of the Author. By N. Rowe* (1709)

Rowe, *Stepmother*   Nicholas Rowe, *The Ambitious Stepmother* (1781)

Salerno   Henry Salerno, *Double Falshood and Shakespeare's Cardenio: A Study of a 'Lost' Play* (Philadelphia, Pa., 2000)

Sambrook   James Sambrook, entry on Philip Frowde in *ODNB*

Samson   Alexander Samson, '"Last thought upon a windmill"?: Cervantes and Fletcher', in Ardila, 223–33

Saxe Wyndham   Henry Saxe Wyndham, *The Annals of Covent Garden Theatre*, 2 vols (1906)

Seary, *ODNB*   Peter Seary, entry on Lewis Theobald in *ODNB*

Seary, *Theobald*   Peter Seary, *Lewis Theobald and the Editing of Shakespeare* (Oxford, 1990)

Settle, *Prelate*   Elkanah Settle, *The Female Prelate* (1680)

Shadwell, *Bury Fair*	Thomas Shadwell, *Bury Fair* (1689)
Shadwell, *Scowrers*	Thomas Shadwell, *The Scowrers* (1691)
SS	*Shakespeare Survey*
Shelton	Thomas Shelton, *The History of the Valorous and Witty Knight Errant, Don Quixote of the Mancha. Translated out of the Spanish. The first part* (1612). References in the text are to part, chapter and page
Shirley, *Gamester*	James Shirley, *The Gamester* (1633)
Shirley, *Venice*	James Shirley, *The Gentleman of Venice* (1639)
Sidney, *Astrophil*	Sir Philip Sidney, *Astrophil and Stella* (1591), in *The Poems of Sir Philip Sidney*, ed. William A. Ringler, Jr (Oxford, 1962; repr. 1989)
Smith	John Smith, *Christian Religion's Appeal from the Groundless Prejudices of the Sceptic to the Bar of Common Reason* (1675)
Southerne, *Marriage*	Thomas Southerne, *The Fatal Marriage* (1732)
Southerne, *Oroonoko*	Thomas Southerne, *Oroonoko* (1696)
Suarez	Michael F. Suarez, S.J., 'Uncertain proofs: Alexander Pope, Lewis Theobald, and questions of patronage', *Papers of the Bibliographical Society of America*, vol. 96, no. 3 (September 2002), 405–34
Swift	*The Prose Works of Jonathan* Swift, ed. H. Davis et al., 14 vols (Oxford, 1939–68)
Tate, *Lear*	Nahum Tate, *The History of King Lear* (1681)
Tilley	Morris Palmer Tilley, *A Dictionary of the Proverbs in England in the Sixteenth and Seventeenth Centuries: A Collection of the Proverbs Found in English Literature and the Dictionaries of the Period* (Ann Arbor, Mich., 1950)
Tuke, *Five Hours*	Sir Samuel Tuke and the Earl of Bristol, *The Adventures of Five Hours* (1663), ed. B. Van Thal (1927)
Vanbrugh, *Aesop*	John Vanbrugh, *Aesop* (1697)
Vickers	Brian Vickers, *Shakespeare, Co-Author* (Oxford, 2002)
Warning	Anon., *A Warning for Fair Women* (1599)
Webster, *Duchess*	John Webster, *The Duchess of Malfi* (1614)
Webster, *Law Case*	John Webster, *The Devil's Law Case* (1619)
Webster, *White Devil*	John Webster, *The White Devil* (1612)

Wilkins, *Miseries*   George Wilkins, *The Miseries of Enforced Marriage* (1607)

Williams   Gordon Williams, *A Glossary of Shakespeare's Sexual Language* (London, 1997)

Wilmot, *Poems*   John Wilmot, Earl of Rochester, *Poems, &c. on Several Occasions with* Valentinian, *a Tragedy* (1691)

Wilson, '*Cardenio*'   Richard Wilson, 'Unseasonable laughter: the context of *Cardenio*', in Richards & Knowles, 193–209

Wilson,   Richard Wilson, *Secret Shakespeare: Studies in Theatre,*
  Shakespeare   *Religion and Resistance* (Manchester, 2004)

Wilson,   Richard Wilson, '"To great St. Jacques bound": *All's*
  'Shakespeare's   *Well That Ends Well* in Shakespeare's Spain', in *Entre*
  Spain'   *Cervantes y Shakespeare / Between Shakespeare and Cervantes: Trails along the Renaissance*, ed. Zenon Luis-Martinez and Luis Gómez Canseco (Newark, NJ, 2006), 15–37

Wood   Michael Wood, '"A sound from heaven": new light on Shakespeare's *Cardenio*', unpublished essay, 2001

INDEX

Index